Bloom's Modern Critical Views

African American
Poets: Wheatley-
Tolson
Edward Albee
American and
Canadian Women
Poets, 1930–present
American Women
Poets, 1650–1950
Maya Angelou
Asian-American
Writers
Margaret Atwood
Jane Austen
James Baldwin
Honoré de Balzac
Samuel Beckett
Saul Bellow
The Bible
William Blake
Jorge Luis Borges
Ray Bradbury
The Brontës
Gwendolyn Brooks
Elizabeth Barrett
Browning
Robert Browning
Italo Calvino
Albert Camus
Lewis Carroll
Willa Cather
Cervantes
Geoffrey Chaucer
Anton Chekhov
Kate Chopin
Agatha Christie
Samuel Taylor
Coleridge
Joseph Conrad
Contemporary Poets
Stephen Crane
Dante
Daniel Defoe

Don DeLillo
Charles Dickens
Emily Dickinson
John Donne and the
17th-Century Poets
Fyodor Dostoevsky
W.E.B. DuBois
George Eliot
T. S. Eliot
Ralph Ellison
Ralph Waldo Emerson
William Faulkner
F. Scott Fitzgerald
Sigmund Freud
Robert Frost
Johann Wolfgang
von Goethe
George Gordon, Lord
Byron
Graham Greene
Thomas Hardy
Nathaniel Hawthorne
Ernest Hemingway
Hispanic-American
Writers
Homer
Langston Hughes
Zora Neale Hurston
Aldous Huxley
Henrik Ibsen
John Irving
Henry James
James Joyce
Franz Kafka
John Keats
Jamaica Kincaid
Stephen King
Rudyard Kipling
Milan Kundera
D. H. Lawrence
Ursula K. Le Guin
Sinclair Lewis
Bernard Malamud

Christopher Marlowe
Gabriel García
Márquez
Cormac McCarthy
Carson McCullers
Herman Melville
Arthur Miller
John Milton
Molière
Toni Morrison
Native-American
Writers
Joyce Carol Oates
Flannery O'Connor
Eugene O'Neill
George Orwell
Octavio Paz
Sylvia Plath
Edgar Allan Poe
Katherine Anne
Porter
J. D. Salinger
Jean-Paul Sartre
William Shakespeare:
Histories and
Poems
William Shakespeare:
Romances
William Shakespeare:
The Comedies
William Shakespeare:
The Tragedies
George Bernard Shaw
Mary Wollstonecraft
Shelley
Percy Bysshe Shelley
Alexander
Solzhenitsyn
Sophocles
John Steinbeck
Tom Stoppard
Jonathan Swift
Amy Tan

Bloom's Modern Critical Views

Modern Critical Views

ELIZABETH BARRETT BROWNING

Edited and with an introduction by
Harold Bloom
Sterling Professor of the Humanities
Yale University

CHELSEA HOUSE PUBLISHERS
Philadelphia

10 9 8 7 6 5 4 3 2

Library of Congress Cataloging-in-Publication Data

Elizabeth Barrett Browning / edited and with an introduction by
Harold Bloom.
       p. cm. – (Modern critical views)
    Includes bibliographical references and index.
    ISBN 0-7910-6450-6 (alk. paper)
    1. Browning, Elizabeth Barrett, 1806-1861--Criticism and
    interpretation. 2. Women and literature--England--History--
    19th century. I. Bloom, Harold. II. Series.

    PR4194 .E45 2001
    821'.8--dc21   2001047214

Chelsea House Publishers
1974 Sproul Road, Suite 400
Broomall, PA 19008-0914

http://www.chelseahouse.com

Contributing Editor: Pamela Loos

Contents

Editor's Note

My Introduction compares Barrett Browning's "A Musical Instrument" to Shelley's "Hymn of Pan."

Sarah Annes Brown explores the antithetical influence of Milton's *Paradise Lost* upon *Aurora Leigh*, after which Helen Cooper investigates Barrett Browning's ballads of 1844, finding in them presages of rebellion.

Deirdre David vividly portrays Barrett Browning's shocked vision of how "Hogarthian bodies invade the streets of Belgravia" in *Aurora Leigh*, while Susanna Egan shrewdly observes, of the same work, that "Marian's motherhood [is] related very closely to the creativity of the poet." The question of the aesthetic achievement of *Aurora Leigh*, which to me remains disputable, is not truly raised by any of the essays here, admirable as they are.

Whether Barrett Browning's poetic reputation was undermined (until now), by biographers and critics, is the question taken up by Tricia Lootens, after which Jerome Mazzaro defends the aesthetic sublimity of *Sonnets from the Portuguese*.

Dorothy Mermin argues that *Aurora Leigh* does more justice than the *Sonnets* to the poet's "distinctive, distinctively female voice," while Linda H. Peterson shrewdly uncovers in the Romantic poet, Letitia Elizabeth Landon, an authentic precursor of Barrett Browning.

The *Sonnets* are reconsidered by Margaret Reynolds, who movingly reminds us how central to our desperate idealizings of married love the story of the Brownings remains, and how crucially Barrett Browning's poems continue to inform our thoughts about passion.

Love is again the matrix in Glennis Stephenson's animated reading of "Lady Geraldine's Courtship," after which Marjorie Stone learnedly considers Barrett Browning's place in the ballad tradition, from Bishop Percy to Bob Dylan.

Aurora Leigh, which John Ruskin loved but I, alas, do not, is illuminated by Maureen Thum's study of its foreign-born heroine, whose narrative provides an alternative perspective to that of Barrett Browning's readers, while Anne D. Wallace examines gender differences in several of the poem's prevalent images.

Finally, Frederick Wegener intervenes on the poet's behalf against a famous stricture by Henry James.

Introduction

Like the bright hair uplifted from the head
Of some fierce Maenad...
—Shelley

1.

In the universities, colleges, and schools of the English-speaking world, the canon wars in one sense are pragmatically over, since the academies, joined by the media, have replaced virtually all aesthetic and cognitive standards by considerations of gender, race, ethnicity, sexual orientation, social class, and other irreducible resentments. There is, however, no necessary finality in this replacement. A considerable resistance still exists, even in the ruined academies, and an aesthetic underground has formed in many of those who staff the media. Much more important, as I have discovered throughout the last decade, there are hundreds of thousands of common readers, outside of the academies and the media, who are not contaminated by what has become fashionable "cultural criticism." I have given up all guest lecturing at academic institutions, and speak only on book tours, which are not intended as aesthetic revival meetings, but which hearten me nevertheless. One particularly mindless English Marxist cheerleader, waving his pom-poms, nastily compared me to Jimmy Swaggart, but as an aesthetic evangelist I happily acknowledge the influence of the divine Oscar Wilde, who would be rather startled to discover that Elizabeth Barrett Browning has eclipsed her husband, the creator of the strongest dramatic monologues in the English language.

I who have limped off too many canonical battlefields, acknowledge defeat in the academies, and am content to carry on the war elsewhere, and not in this Introduction. The partisans of Barrett Browning have much to say in her behalf, and many of those reprinted here say it eloquently. My Editor's Note hints at my reservations, but I will not expand upon them. I have always loved Barrett Browning's "A Musical Instrument" best among her poems, so I will confine myself to an appreciation of its beauty, and a comparison of it to Shelley's "Hymn of Pan," a lyric at least equal in splendor.

2.

Homer and Plato say that Pan, god of the woodlands, was the son of Hermes the messenger. As "panic" intimates, Pan has the effect of a sudden fear, like the night-terror he caused at Marathon, inducing the Persians to flee, and yet he was named "Pan" because, at his birth, he delighted all hearts, but particularly that of Dionysus, who recognized in the babe a kindred spirit of ecstasy. Attended by nymphs, Pan roams the wild places, and yet the other likely origin of his name means the "feeder" or herdsman, presumably of goats in Arcadia. Though sexually human, Pan has goats' ears and horns, and carries remarkably little mythology with him. His love affairs with Syrinx, Echo, and Pitys (nymph of the fir-tree) express his notorious amorousness, as does the music of his reed-pipe. Though Pan acquired no transcendental overtones, in the *Phaedrus* he is among the gods to whom Socrates appeals for an inward beauty.

Here is Barrett Bronwing's "A Musical Instrument," one of the best and most vitalizing lyrical poems in the language:

> What was he doing, the great god Pan,
>   Down in the reeds by the river?
> Spreading ruin and scattering ban,
> Splashing and paddling with hoofs of a goat,
> And breaking the golden lilies afloat
>   With the dragon-fly on the river.
>
> He tore out a reed, the great god Pan,
>   From the deep cool bed of the river;
> The limpid water turbidly ran,
> And the broken lilies a dying-lay,
> And the dragon-fly had fled away,
>   Ere he brought it out of the river.
>
> High on the shore sat the great god Pan
>   While turbidly flowed the river;

And hacked and hewed as a great god can,
With his hard bleak steel at the patient reed,
Till there was not a sign of the leaf indeed
    To prove it fresh from the river.

He cut it short, did the great god Pan
    (How tall it stood in the river!)
Then drew the pith, like the heart of a man.
Steadily from the outside ring,
And notched the poor dry empty thing
    In holes, as he sat by the river.

'This is the way,' laughed the great god Pan
    (Laughed while he sat by the river),
The only way, since gods began
To make a sweet music, they could succeed.'
Then, dropping his mouth to a hole in the reed,
    He blew in power by the river.

Sweet, sweet, sweet, O Pan!
    Piercing sweet by the river!
Blinding sweet, O great god Pan!
The sun on the hill forgot to die,
And the lilies revived, and the dragon-fly
    Came back to dream on the river.

Yet half a beast is the great god Pan
    To laugh as he sits by the river,
Making a poet out of a man;
The true gods sigh for the cost and pain
For the reed which grows nevermore again
    As a reed with the reeds in the river.

Had she written often thus, she would be beyond praise, and I am
puzzled that she did not cultivate her lyric powers. "A Musical Instrument"
was published in 1860, a year before her death in Florence, and in it Barrett
Browning rejoins the High Romantic vitalism of Shelley, Keats, the young
Tennyson, and the young Browning. She knew Shelley's "Hymn of Pan," and
I suspect she deftly writes an affectionate critique of it in her darker hymn of
Pan:

I.

From the forests and highlands
  We come, we come;
From the river-girt islands,
  Where loud waves are dumb
    Listening to my sweet pipings.
The wind in the reeds and the rushes,
  The bees on the bells of thyme,
The birds on the myrtle bushes,
  The cicale above in the lime,
And the lizards below in the grass,
Were as silent as ever old Tmolus was,
    Listening to my sweet pipings.

II.

Liquid Peneus was flowing,
  And all dark Tempe lay
In Pelion's shadow, outgrowing
  The light of the dying day,
    Speeded by my sweet pipings.
The Sileni, and Sylvans, and Fauns,
  And the Nymphs of the woods and the waves,
To the edge of the moist river-lawns,
  And the brink of the dewy caves,
And all that did then attend and follow,
Were silent with love, as you now, Apollo,
  With envy of my sweet pipings.

III.

I sang of the dancing stars,
I sang of the daedal Earth,
And of Heaven—and the giant wars,
  And Love, and Death, and Birth—
    And then I change my pipings—
Singing how down the vale of Maenalus
  I pursued a maiden and clasped a reed.

Gods and men, we are all deluded thus!
   It breaks in our bosom and then we bleed:
All wept, as I think both ye now would,
If envy or age had not frozen your blood,
   At the sorrow of my sweet pipings.

I love both hymns, and appreciate their differences and originalities. Shelley's Pan chants in the first person, but sings also for the nymphs who accompany him, and addresses two auditors, Apollo and the reader. Pan's tone is sublimely exuberant and self-confident, content as he is to have subdued (aesthetically) all nature with his sweet pipings, which are the envy of Apollo, god of Poetry. A music of earth challenges and overgoes the Olympian art. There is both a high Shelleyan irony and a universal male lament in the exquisite:

I pursued a maiden and clasped a reed.
Gods and men, we are all deluded thus!

This omits the perspective of the maiden Syrinx, whose metamorphosis saved her from Pan's lust, and thus provided him with a reed he transformed into his musical instrument. Barrett Browning, with her own superb irony, shows us Pan turning a male into a reed-pipe, and at the close reveals that her exquisite lyric is a parable of the incarnation of the poetic character itself:

Yet half a beast is the great god Pan
   To laugh as he sits by the river,
Making a poet out of a man;
The true gods sigh for the cost and pain
For the reed which grows nevermore again
   As a reed with the reeds by the river.

I read this as a profound fable of the denaturalization of the male poet, as opposed to the female, with the "true" or Olympian gods showing a very uncharacteristic sorrow, as if they too had been feminized. That Barrett Browning had the gifts that would have made her into a great lyric poet, I do not doubt. What diverted them, into narrative and sonnet sequence, is a complex matter, not to be discussed in this brief context, but she does seem to me most herself in ballads and dramatic lyrics. Yet the matter of her canonical eminence, or lack of it, remains to be resolved, perhaps when our age of ideology passes into another time.

SARAH ANNES BROWN

Paradise Lost and Aurora Leigh

Lord Illingworth. *The Book of Life begins with a man and a woman in a garden.*
Mrs. Allonby. *It ends with Revelations.*

The same is almost true of *Aurora Leigh*; although the crucial meeting
between Aurora and her cousin Romney in the garden does not take place
until book 2, the very last lines of the poem clearly allude to John's vision of
the New Jerusalem.

> He stood a moment with erected brows
>   In silence, as a creature might who gazed—
>   Stood calm, and fed his blind, majestic eyes
>   Upon the thought of perfect noon: and when
>   I saw his soul saw—"Jasper first." I said,
>   "And second, sapphire; third, chalcedony;
>   The rest in order—last, an amethyst.

The framing of the poem with recollections of Genesis and
Revelation, fall and redemption, can be seen to find an echo in the deeper
pattern of *Aurora Leigh*, in which Aurora and Romney begin by
misunderstanding each other and parting, but by the end of the poem have

From *Studies in English Literature 1500-1900*, 37, no. 4. © 1997, by William Marsh, Rice
University .

reached mutual comprehension and love. However, additional tensions and complexities may be identified if we place *Aurora Leigh* not simply within a biblical, but within a specifically Miltonic, context. For although in many ways *Aurora Leigh* most obviously recalls the poetry of Wordsworth, and particularly *The Prelude*, it can also be read as a palinode to *Paradise Lost*. The tensions within *Aurora Leigh*, the way the poem's ostensibly measured plea on behalf of women seems to conceal hints of a more inflammatory view lurking beneath its surface, are mirrored in the poem's slippery relationship with *Paradise Lost*.

The first line of *Aurora Leigh*, "Of writing many books there is no end" is an unmistakable echo of Ecclesiastes 12:12 KJV, "And further, by these my son, be admonished: of making many books there is no end; and much study is a weariness of the flesh." But within the context of reinvented epic, the text most strongly invoked, by means of difference, is not the Bible, but Milton's *Paradise Lost*. We are prepared for a statement of epic content by the very first word—whether it be man's first disobedience, arms and the man, or the wrath of Achilles—but are cheated when we are instead presented with a rather oblique assertion. The apparently epic opening was but a feint. In direct contrast with the public, grandiose, all-encompassing importance of the subject matter of Homer, Virgil, and particularly Milton, Elizabeth Barrett Browning's poem seems to be folded inward:

> And I who have written much in prose and verse
> For others' uses, will write now for mine—
> Will write my story for my better self
> As when you paint your portrait for a friend,
> Who keeps it in a drawer and looks at it
> Long after he has ceased to love you, just
> To hold together what he was and is.

The immediate retreat into subjectivity, concealment, even sentiment, adumbrates the peculiar problems of writing as a female poet, problems which dominate the entire poem, and which fulfill the hint contained in the first line, that this will be a poem about writing poetry, rather than about the conventional matter of epic.

Instead of Milton's Muse we are taken into the presence of Aurora's dead parents; the influence of her father is particularly felt. Whereas Milton seeks to be uplifted, Aurora appears to court literal depression:

> What in me is dark,
> Illumine, what is low, raise and support;
> That to the highth of this great argument

I may assert eternal providence,
And justify the ways of God to men.

                    O my father's hand,
Stroke heavily, heavily the poor head down,
Draw, press the child's head closer to thy knee!
I'm still too young, too young, to sit alone.

Aurora Leigh's dependence upon her natural father may be aligned with her creator's reliance upon her masculine poetic ancestry, particularly when we remember her oft quoted lament, "I look everywhere for grandmothers and see none." The importance of Milton as a poet against whom later female writers, such as Charlotte Brontë and Mary Shelley, reacted, subverting his supposed misrepresentation of woman through the character of Eve, has been widely discussed. But although *Aurora Leigh* can be seen as a paradigmatic female riposte to *Paradise Lost*, this aspect of the poem has been strangely neglected by Barrett Browning's critics.

Her conversation with Milton began some time before the writing of *Aurora Leigh*. The work which bears the most obvious debt to *Paradise Lost* is her lyric drama set immediately after the Fall, *A Drama of Exile*. In her preface to this piece, Barrett Browning expresses her sense of unfitness to follow in Milton's footsteps: "I had promised my own prudence to shut close the gates of Eden between Milton and myself, so that none might say I dared to walk in his footsteps. He should be within, I thought, with his Adam and Eve unfallen or falling,—and I, without, with my EXILES,—I also an exile!" Yet even as she voices her doubts, we are offered a hint of self-assertion, of self-justification:

> For the rest, Milton is too high, and I am too low, to render it necessary for me to disavow any rash emulation of his divine faculty on his own ground; while enough individuality will be granted, I hope, to my poem, to rescue me from that imputation of plagiarism which should be too servile a thing for every sincere thinker. After all, and at the worst, I have only attempted, in respect to Milton, what the Greek dramatists achieved lawfully in respect to Homer . . . For the analogy of the stronger may apply to the weaker, and the reader may have patience with the weakest while she suggests the application.

Clearly *A Drama of Exile* is the most obvious starting point for a discussion of Barrett Browning's engagement with Milton, focusing as it does on the role of Eve which the poet claims has been "imperfectly apprehended hitherto." Yet an apparently innocuous reference to Milton in *Casa Guidi Windows* could be said to strike an even more important first blow in a battle which is continued in *Aurora Leigh*. In the passage quoted above, Barrett Browning talks of Milton within the context of a literary heritage embracing Homer and the Greek tragedians. Bloom's *Map of Misreading* offers an analysis of one particular aspect of this imitative process, Milton's allusion to the leaves of Vallombrosa, used to express the impotence of the fallen angels. "His legions, angel forms, who lay entranced / Thick as autumnal leaves that strew the brooks / In Vallombrosa." Bloom traces the relationship between these lines and a whole array of previous comparisons between men and leaves in the *Iliad*, the *Aeneid*, and the *Inferno*. Here, and in other densely allusive passages, Milton is seen to be engaging in a dialectical relationship with his illustrious forebears, eluding anxiety of influence by "troping upon his forerunners' tropes."

By the nineteenth century, references to the leaves of Vallombrosa often specifically alluded to the image's Miltonic provenance. The following quotation from *Casa Guidi Windows* establishes that Barrett Browning shared this consciousness that Vallombrosa was particularly associated with *Paradise Lost*:

> The Vallombrosan brooks were strewn as thick
> That June day, knee-deep, with dead beechen leaves,
> As Milton saw them ere his heart grew sick,
> And his eyes blind.

So when Vallombrosa is mentioned in *Aurora Leigh* it seems reasonable to assume that Milton was at the back of Barrett Browning's mind: "Not a grand nature. Not my chestnut woods / Of Vallombrosa, cleaving by the spurs / To the precipices." Whereas Milton uses the simile to belittle the fallen angels, for Aurora the woods of Vallombrosa represent an Italian ideal, beside which the countryside of England appears tame and subdued. Immediately prior to these lines comes a description of English sheep who run "Along the fine clear outline, small as mice / That run along a witch's scarlet thread."

An anxiety of influence slippage seems to be at work here—the puny leaves of Milton's simile have been magnified, transformed into an unattainable object of Aurora's imaginings. If Milton's leaves may perhaps be seen as a sign of the male poet, the lines preceding them invoke a specifically feminine discourse, with their little mice, transgressive witches, and suggestion of some feminine art in the mention of the scarlet thread—weaving or embroidery.

There is a second flurry of Italian leaves in book 2 of *Aurora Leigh*, when the heroine spurns her cousin's offer of financial assistance by tearing up his deed of gift. It is significant that her refusal of masculine support is accompanied by this return to the image of falling leaves—just as Aurora rebuffs Romney, so Barrett Browning explicitly checks herself from emulating Milton:

> As I spoke, I tore
> The paper up and down, and down and up
> And crosswise, till it fluttered from my hands,
> As forest-leaves, stripped suddenly and rapt
> By a whirlwind on Valdarno, drop again,
> Drop slow, and strew the melancholy ground
> Before the amazed hills . . . why, so, indeed,
> I'm writing like a poet, somewhat large
> In the type of the image, and exaggerate
> A small thing with a great thing, topping it.

Again, she is going against the grain of Milton's use of the leaf simile, claiming that it is too large for what she has to describe and not, as in Milton, suggestive of something tiny and derisory. Part of the reason why she thinks it is too large is that it has become part of the male epic tradition. The reappearance of the leaves in the context of a written document highlights their potential to represent leaves in a book such as those in *Paradise Lost* itself.

Another faint echo of Milton's leaves comes in book 5. Aurora has been describing the shortcomings of the poem "The Hills." Yet again, the leaves are associated with the difficulty of living up to a poetic tradition, although perhaps Aurora's gradual growth in confidence is signaled by the fact that they have returned to their proper Miltonic place as an indicator of weakness:

> For us, we are called to mark
> A still more intimate humanity
> In this inferior nature, or ourselves
> Must fall like dead leaves trodden underfoot
> By veritable artists.

A final invocation of leaves which, as they are of the chestnut, are associated with Vallombrosa, comes in book 6:

> Through the grate
> Within the gardens, what a heap of babes,
> Swept up like leaves beneath the chestnut-trees

> From every street and alley of the town,
> By ghosts perhaps that blow too bleak this way
> A-looking for their heads!

Perhaps this is the final stage in the battle for poetic control: finally the leaves are no longer a symptom of poetic anxiety, but merely a descriptive tool as they were for Milton. The fact that she uses them to evoke babies might be an indication of Barrett Browning's apparent interest in carving out a feminine niche for herself, a less spectacular but perhaps just as telling detail as the extraordinary passage in book 5, where artistic creation is explicitly associated with the female body:

>   Never flinch,
> But still, unscrupulously epic, catch
> Upon the burning lava of a song
> The full-veined, heaving, double-breasted Age:
> That, when the next shall come, the men of that
> May touch the impress with reverent hand, and say
> "Behold—behold the paps we all have sucked!
> This bosom seems to beat still, or at least
> It sets ours beating: this is living art,
> Which thus presents and thus records true life."

But it is not only in the imagery of *Aurora Leigh* that we can trace a struggle between Barrett Browning and her poetic ancestor. A parallel conflict is played out between their two heroines, Eve and Aurora.

    Returning to the first allusion to Vallombrosa in book 1, Aurora goes on further to characterize England, in feminine terms. It is tame and enclosed, it discourages aspiration, it is conciliatory but stifling—it is also explicitly compared to the prelapsarian Eden. "On English ground / You understand the letter—ere the fall / How Adam lived in a garden." But although Edenic, the landscape also offers echoes of the temptations faced by Eve. At the beginning of book 5 Eve recounts a troubling dreams to Adam:

>   methought
> Close at mine ear one called me forth to walk
> With gentle voice, I though it thine; it said,
> Why sleep'st thou, Eve? . . .
> . . . .
>   in vain,
> If none regard, heaven wakes with all his eyes,

> Whom to behold but thee, Nature's desire,
> In whose sight all things joy, with ravishment
> Attracted by the beauty still to gaze.

Aurora is also summoned by an external agency—the sun—to wake and rise:

> The sun came, saying, "shall I lift this light
> Against the lime tree, and you will not look?
> I make the birds sing—listen! but, for you."

As with Eve, the invitation is made more tempting by the suggestion that Nature's works are in some way there for her special benefit. Aurora goes on to describe her nighttime escapade in terms of temptation and transgression:

> Capacity for joy
> Admits temptation. It seemed, next, worth while
> To dodge the sharp sword set against my life;
> To slip downstairs through all the sleepy house,
> As mute as any dream there, and escape
> As a soul from the body, out of doors,
> Glide through the shrubberies, drop into the lane.

The reference to the sword in particular might recall Adam and Eve's eventual exile from Eden, whose gate will henceforth be guarded by "the brandished sword of God".

Within the chronology of *Paradise Lost* Eve's disturbing dream is *The Prelude* to her decision to work apart from Adam, and thus to her fall itself. In *Aurora Leigh* too, the heroine's nighttime vision is followed by a disputation in the garden, in this case concerning the viability of Aurora's poetic vocation, and Romney's desire to marry her. Both Eve and Aurora assert their wish for independence and for separation, whereas both Romney and Adam counsel caution and invoke feminine weakness to back up their case. In both works the argument is tossed back and forth, and in each case the woman has the final word and secures her desired independence. But whereas in the case of Eve the parting with Adam leads to her ruin, for Aurora it is the beginning of a successful career as a poet. This very broad structural affinity would not of course in itself suggest a link with *Paradise Lost*, but there is a complex network of allusions to the earlier poem which, taken together, place *Aurora Leigh* in opposition to Milton. One of the most telling connections with *Paradise Lost* is the simple fact that the heroine's name, Aurora, is of course the Latin name for Eos, goddess of the dawn, and she is thus by implication the opposite of Eve. Aurora is thus a second Eve—and yet that is a role which, in Christian tradition, had already been triumphantly fulfilled by Mary. Perhaps there is a further significance in the fact that the name of the poem's secondary heroine is the adjectival form of Mary, Marian.

Garlands have an important function in both poems. Aurora has gone outside to crown herself with ivy leaves:

> Ah—there's my choice—that ivy on the wall,
> That headlong ivy! Not a leaf will grow
> But thinking of a wreath. Large leaves, smooth leaves,
> Serrated like my vines, and half as green.
> I like such ivy, bold to leap a height
> 'Twas strong to climb.

Her choice of plant is interesting; the ivy is explicitly connected with feminine subjection by Milton—Eve mentions the need to "direct / The clasping ivy where to climb." The suggestion that Aurora is reinventing the ivy as a bold and aspiring plant, fitting in with her desire to find a new feminine poetic idiom, is upheld by the apparently gratuitous comparison between the ivy and the vine, for the latter plant is also a type of woman's dependence upon the male in Milton.

In *Paradise Lost* Adam weaves a garland for Eve while he awaits her return, only to let it fall in dismay when he realizes she has eaten the apple. This incident is echoed when Aurora, made a little petulant by Romney's caution against writing poetry, drops the wreath she has made as a prelude to speaking to her cousin with defiance:

> "You'll see—you'll see! I'll soon take flight,
> You shall not hinder." He, as shaking out
> His hand and answering, "Fly then," did not speak,
> Except by such a gesture . . .
> . . . .
>   he abruptly caught
> At one end of the swinging wreath, and said
> "Aurora!"

A little later he explicitly invokes Eve:

>   You, you are young
> As Eve with nature's daybreak on her face,

> But this same world you are come to, dearest coz,
> Has done with keeping birthdays, saves her wreaths
> To hang upon her ruins.

But the difference between the two women is signaled when, at the end of the argument, Aurora bends to retrieve her garland; she, unlike Eve, is capable of crowning her own merit if no one else will do it for her.

The wreath is only one sign of Milton's presence in this section of the poem. One striking passage recalls Eve's dream as well as her debate with Adam:

> "Now," I said, "may God
> Be witness 'twixt us two!" and with the word,
> Meseemed I floated into a sudden light
> Above his stature.

Aurora's mysterious assertion that she seemed to float might recall Eve's words to Adam in book 5. She explains that she was tempted to eat the forbidden fruit:

> the pleasant savoury smell
> So quickened appetite, that I, methought,
> Could not but taste. Forthwith up to the clouds
> With him I flew, and underneath beheld
> The earth outstretched immense, a prospect wide
> And various: wondering at my flight and change
> To this high exaltation; suddenly
> My guide was gone, and I, me thought, sunk down,
> And fell asleep.

Aurora contrasts her ambition with Romney's wish that she should turn to a more "worthy work" Her own side of the debate is imaged forth in language which again invokes her as an overreaching Eve, yet without conceding that her position is evil or flawed. She speaks of Romney:

> finding me
> Precisely where the devil of my youth
> Had set me, on those mountain-peaks of hope,
> All glittering with the dawn-dew, all erect
> And famished for the noon—exclaiming, while
> I looked for empire and much tribute.

Clearly the story of the temptation of Christ is on the surface more firmly suggested than Eve's fall. But within the context of an established connection between Aurora and Eve, it is the latter tale which resonates most strongly. The phrase "famished for the noon" might recall the following lines in particular: "Mean while the hour of noon drew on, and waked / An eager appetite." A further proof that Barrett Browning had Eve rather than Christ at the back of her mind is the strong similarity with a passage from her earlier *Drama of Exile*, describing the moment at which the Fall took place:

> On a mountain-peak
> Half-sheathed in primal woods and glittering
> In spasms of awful sunshine at that hour,
> A lion couched, part raised upon his paws.

Perhaps the strongest Miltonic resonance in book 2 may be found in its lines:

> But so,
> Even so, we let go hands, my cousin and I,
> And in between us rushed the torrent-world
> To blanch our faces like divided rocks,
> And bar for ever mutual sight and touch
> Except through swirl of spray and all that roar.

We might recall that lovely, but foreboding, moment when Eve lets fall Adam's hand: "Thus saying, from her husband's hand her hand / Soft she withdrew" or else the poem's famous final lines: "They hand in hand with wandering steps and slow, / Through Eden took their solitary way." The reference to their letting go of hands at the end of book 2 is made more prominent by Romney's earlier plea to Aurora: "Ah my sweet, come down, / And hand in hand we'll go where yours shall touch / These victims, one by one!".

Barrett Browning's reformulation of the traditional relationship between the sexes is twice described in a way which offers a ghostly echo of some of the most famous lines in *Paradise Lost*:

> Not equal, as their sex not equal seemed;
> For contemplation he and valour formed,
> For softness she and sweet attractive grace,
> He for God only, she for God in him.

> Always Romney Leigh
> Was looking for the worms, I for the gods.
> A godlike nature his; the gods look down,
> Incurious of themselves.

Barrett Browning simultaneously accepts Milton's division between the sexes and slyly questions its validity. If the gods look down on worms they are making scant use of their lofty stature. We might also compare: "he, overfull / Of what is, and I, haply overbold / For what might be". Here too present male superiority is presented as having the potential for reversal, for diminution, within itself.

The strength of Barrett Browning's oppositional voice is most evident toward the end of the poem, when Romney reminisces back to that meeting in the garden of ten years ago in terms which vividly recall *Paradise Lost*, yet which also acknowledge that his own second Eve was right in leaving him:

> you, who keep
> The same Aurora of the bright June day
> That withered up the flowers before my face,
> And turned me from the garden evermore
> Because I was not worthy.

He recalls her garland very clearly, saying that he

> came here to abase myself,
> And fasten, kneeling, on her regent brows
> A garland which I startled thence one day
> Of her beauitful June youth.

Their reconciliation is marked by the joining of their hands, which Romney associates with the idea of a "fall":

> Ah, you've left your height,
> And here upon my level we take hands,
> And here I reach you to forgive you, sweet,
> And that's a fall, Aurora.

Indeed their reunion has in a sense less to do with the final note on which the poem ends—Revelation—than with Milton's description of the Fall. It is as though Eve, after leaving Adam in order to court temptation, had returned to him, not to be blamed and wept over, but to be feted, not to have her garland cast down, but to be crowned in triumph with it. This reversal may be compared with Shelley's subversive reconfiguration of Miltonic material in *Prometheus Unbound*. Perhaps it is no coincidence that there are only nine books in *Aurora Leigh*. Barrett Browning gives her heroine the traits which in Eve led to the Fall, and shows them to be the precise qualities which enable Aurora to achieve fulfillment as both poet and woman, binding her and Romney together rather than driving them further apart.

So far there would appear to be a strong degree of congruity between the Miltonic echoes in *Aurora Leigh* and the poem's brave, yet essentially conservative, feminism. The reworking of *Paradise Lost* suggests Barrett Browning's own view of the relationship between the sexes; she desires greater autonomy for women than did Milton, yet still envisages men and women working together in partnership. Whereas Mary Shelley's *Frankenstein* may be viewed as a radical rejection of Milton, *Aurora Leigh* seems to represent a far more measured reinvention of *Paradise Lost*, particularly as there is no overt questioning of divine authority as there is in *Prometheus Unbound*. On the surface at least, *Aurora Leigh* rejects any truly radical attack on patriarchal society, and the poem ends in a comfortingly traditional way, with a marriage and a happy ending. However, the conclusion of the poem is not of course entirely unproblematic. The strong resemblance between the fates of Romney Leigh and Mr. Rochester was apparent to the poem's earliest readers, and the interpretation of *Jane Eyre* as a novel whose hero must be punished, even symbolically castrated, before he is rewarded with the heroine is equally applicable to *Aurora Leigh*.

One of the strangest links with *Paradise Lost* may be found in book 4, in the description of the abortive wedding of Romney and Marian. It is not unlikely that Barrett Browning was in at least partial control of the Miltonic echoes in book 2, in which explicit references to Eve and to Eden are included. According to the pattern of connections already described, Romney must be seen as a type of Adam, who may need to have some of his views modified, but who is essentially a positive force. But in book 4 he seems to have been metamorphosed into a Satanic figure. How far, if at all, this was a deliberate strategy on Barrett Browning's part is difficult to ascertain. In book 10 of *Paradise Lost* Satan returns to Hell to celebrate his supposed triumph against God and Man. But even as he awaits the applause, he finds that he and all his fellow fallen angels are being transformed into snakes. A vision of the tree of life springs up, but when the snakes attempt to eat the apples they taste of ashes.

Many poor people come to the wedding of Romney and Marian. The description of their entrance provides an extraordinary comparison with Milton's account of the fallen angels:

> They clogged the streets, they oozed into the church
> In a dark slow stream like blood . . .
> . . . .
> While all the aisles, alive and black with heads,
> Crawled slowly toward the altar from the street,
> As bruised snakes crawl and hiss out of a hole
> With shuddering involution.
>
>   dreadful was the din
> Of hissing through the hall, thick swarming now
> With complicated monsters head and tail,
> Scorpion, and asp, and amphisbaena dire,
> Cerastes horned, hydrus, and ellops drear,
> And dipsas (not so thick swarmed once the soil
> Bedropped with blood of Gorgon, or the isle
> Ophiusa).

The comparison between the congregation and a bruised snake strengthens the potential biblical and Miltonic resonance, and the shared association of snakes and blood provides a further link between the two passages. A little later in *Aurora Leigh* we are explicitly invited to think of hell: "'twas as if you had stirred up hell / To heave its lowest dreg-fiends uppermost / In fiery swirls of slime." Satan's audience had been "now expecting / Each hour their great adventurer from the search / Of foreign worlds." Romney's audience is also expectant, although they pass the time while they await Marian by indulging in spiteful gossip, until it is revealed that Romney has been jilted. The horrific transformation which Aurora witnesses, making it difficult for her to believe it is really him, and his inability to speak both stem from natural causes yet recall the similar effects of Satan's metamorphosis:

> A murmur and a movement drew around,
> A naked whisper touched us. Something wrong.
> What's wrong. The black crowd, as an overstrained
> Cord, quivered in vibration, and I saw . . .
> Was that *his* face I saw? . . . his . . . Romney Leigh's . . .
> Which tossed a sudden horror like a sponge
> Into all eyes—while himself stood white upon
> The topmost altar-stair and tried to speak,
> And failed, and lifted higher above his head
> A letter . . . as a man who drowns and gapes.

> from the door
> Of that Plutonian hall, invisible
> Ascended his high throne . . .
> . . . .
> Forth rushed in haste the great consulting peers,
> Raised from their dark divan, and with like joy
> Congratulant approached him, who with hand
> Silence, and with these words attention won . . .
> . . . .
> 　　So having said, a while he stood, expecting
> Their universal shout and high applause,
> To fill his ear, when contrary he hears
> On all sides, from innumerable tongues
> A dismal universal hiss, the sound
> Of public scorn . . .
> . . . .
> 　　　　　　　　　　　　he would have spoke,
> But hiss for hiss returned with forked tongue
> To forked tongue.

Ostensibly, within the narrative of the poem, Romney and the congregation are opposed; however, the Miltonic context serves to draw them together, implicating Romney in the disturbing hideousness of his audience. The crowd of poor people, thinking Romney has cast off Marian, erupts in fury, treating Romney's conciliatory words in the same way Satan's cohorts do the fruit:

> 　　　　　　　Through the rage and roar
> I heard the broken words which Romney flung
> Among the turbulent masses, from the ground
> He held still with his masterful pale face—
> As huntsmen throw the ration to the pack,
> Who falling on it headlong, dog on dog
> In heaps of fury, rend it, swallow it up
> With yelling hound-jaws—his indignant words,
> Whereof I caught the meaning here and there
> By his gesture . . . torn in morsels, yelled across,
> And so devoured.
>
> But on they rolled in heaps, and up the trees
> Climbing, sat thicker than the snaky locks

> That curled Megaera: greedily they plucked
> The fruitage fair to sight, like that which grew
> Near that bituminous lake where Sodom flamed;
> This more delusive, not the touch, but taste
> Deceived; they fondly thinking to allay
> Their appetite with gust, instead of fruit
> Chewed bitter ashes, which the offended taste
> With spattering noise rejected.

The context of Satan's metamorphosis sheds some light on these curious echoes. Within the chronology of *Paradise Lost* he has just brought about the fall of Eve. In *Aurora Leigh* the departure of Marian, instigated by the jealous Lady Waldemar, has ensured her own fall in the eyes of society. By aligning him with Satan at the very moment when we learn of her disappearance, Romney is, by analogy, implicated in the brutal treatment of Marian. A literal reading of the poem completely clears him of any such charge, yet Barrett Browning may be unconsciously projecting her own awareness that she lives in a society where a wealthy man is far more likely to seduce and abandon a penniless girl than be jilted by her.

The significance of this link between Romney and Satan is strengthened by a further association between Romney and a snake in book 8, when he apologizes to Aurora for doubting the wisdom of her earlier choice.

>   Set down this
> For condemnation—I was guilty here;
> I stood upon my deed and fought my doubt,
> As men will—for I doubted—till at last
> My deed gave way beneath me suddenly
> And left me what I am:—the curtain dropped,
> My part quite ended, all the footlights quenched,
> My own soul hissing at me through the dark.

The idea of his real self being revealed and shown to be wanting, the reference to a triumphant spectacle being undercut, and particularly the image of his soul hissing at him in darkness, all contribute to reinforce the Satanic link. These suggestions of a submerged hostility to Romney are consistent with his eventual "punishment."

Helen Cooper believes that the analogy which Barrett Browning draws between Milton and Romney through their shared blindness, a similarity explicitly referred to in one of the poet's letters, suggests that she has "finally made peace with her precursor". But if Romney may also be aligned with Satan, such "peace" seems more problematic, and Deirdre David's assertion that the poem represents a "ratification of a deep-rooted foundation of Victorian patriarchy—women serve men, and men and women together serve God" is called into question.

HELEN COOPER

Rebellion: Eve's Songs of Innocence

The "system" of man.
—The Letters of Robert Browning
and Elizabeth Barrett Barrett, 1845–1846

The 1844 ballads were enormously popular. According to reviewers of the *Poems of 1844*, they contained "some of the best ballad-writing we have met with for many a day": in the ballads Barrett "has struck out many new tones in the rhythmical scale; rich and recondite harmonies, full of originality"; "Lady Geraldine's Courtship" was the "best performance of the whole, because the most real, the most closely allied to the work-day world around us all"; "Rhyme of the Duchess May" as "a ballad and for merit of various kinds, may rank with the highest of the class." The *Athenaeum* favored the ballads, recognizing the contrast between Barrett's poetic voice and the poetesses' work: "Between her poems and the slighter lyrics of most of the sisterhood, there is all the difference which exists between the putting on of 'singing-robes' for altar-service, and the taking up lute or harp to enchant an indulgent circle of friends and kindred."

Like her Romantic precursors and her immediate contemporary, Tennyson, Barrett represented the present in the costumes of the past. Her

From *Elizabeth Barrett Browning, Woman and Artist.* © 1988 by University of North Carolina Press.

ballads, reminiscent of "The Eve of St. Agnes," "La Belle Dame Sans Merci," "Christabel," and "The Lady of Shalott," portray gender relations in a medieval setting. The male poets locate a mystery in the nature of sexual experience itself, whereas Barrett dramatizes woman's challenge to "the 'system' of man."

Barrett's most intimate observation of marriage was of her father's "thunder" and her mother's submission, which caused the latter a "mark, a plait, within, . . . a sign of suffering." She saw too often marriages of convenience without happiness, and consequently had never sought the state herself. She believed that "women generally *lose* by marriage" and therefore had a "loathing dread of marriage as a loveless state." She "always did certainly believe in love" defined as mutual passion and intellectual equality, but found that "a fulness of sympathy, a sharing of life, one with another, . . . is scarcely ever looked for except in a narrow conventional sense. Men like to come home and find a blazing fire and a smiling face and an hour of relaxation. Their serious thoughts, and earnest aims in life, they like to keep on one side. And this is the carrying out of love and marriage almost everywhere in the world—and this, the degrading of women by both." Barrett, cognizant of the double standard applied to marital infidelities—" the crushing into dust for the woman—and the 'oh you naughty man'ism for the betrayer"—protested this "injustice which cries upwards from the earth." When Browning criticized women's calculating behavior, she upbraided him, describing contemporary marriages as "worse than solitudes and more desolate":

> The falseness and the calculations!—why how can you, who are *just, blame women* . . . when you must know what the "system" of man is towards them,—& of men not ungenerous otherwise? Why are women to be blamed if they act as if they had to do with swindlers?—is it not the mere instinct of preservation which makes them do it? These make women what they are. . . . Why there are, to be sure, cold & heartless, light & changeable, ungenerous & calculating women in the world!—that is sure. But for the most part, they are only what they are made . . . & far better than the nature of the making.

Her early observation of "the 'system' of man" and of marriage convinced her that it too seldom provided happiness for women.

Barrett's examination of the sexual economy of courtship and marriage in poems with medieval settings locates her within a tradition that favored the ballad form and "the lyrical narrative of dramatic confrontation."

My discussion here will focus on six poems. "Bertha in the Lane," akin to the work of the poetesses, represents woman enacting "love's divine self-abnegation." "The Romaunt of the Page," "The Lay of the Brown Rosary," and "Rhyme of the Duchess May" reject the conventions both of courtly love and of female self-abnegation. In each poem Barrett narrates an Eve who transgresses—by refusing her role of subservient, silent woman—and is punished by death. "Lady Geraldine's Courtship" both presents and questions courtly rhetoric and ideology, but its heroine lives. Finally, "The Romance of the Swan's Nest" prefigures Barrett's rejection of the ballad form as too confining.

Barrett's early ballads, "The Romaunt of the Ganges" (1838), "The Romaunt of the Page" (1839), and "The Lady of the Brown Rosary" (1840), were published in *Findens' Tableaux*. This annual of verse, edited by Mary Russell Mitford, published a few sentimental poems by minor male poets, but the majority of its contributors were women. The *Findens' Tableaux* in which "The Romaunt of the Page" appeared carried the full title *Findens' Tableaux of the Affections: A Series of Picturesque Illustrations of the Womanly Virtues* (1839). The "affections" and "womanly virtues" establish the ideology to which the annual subscribed. Inclusion apparently located Barrett's work in a female genre whose allegiances were to such womanly virtues; however, the 1844 ballads suggest a redefinition of what constitutes the virtuous woman.

That such a redefinition involved a rejection of the poetess's as much as of the male poet's voice is manifest in "Bertha in the Lane," a poem that admirably demonstrates woman's self-abnegation. It resonates to the work of the poetesses, acting, therefore, as a touchstone from which to judge Barrett's subversion of that female genre in the other ballads. The speaker, Bertha's older sister, is the only female protagonist in the 1844 poems who narrates her own tale. Her rebellious sisters in the other ballads are under the control of a narrator. This narrative represents woman at her most self-sacrificially virtuous. The speaker overhears that her fiancé, Robert, loves Bertha (who is seven years younger) but will dutifully marry his betrothed whom he "esteems." Apparently making her own wedding dress, the speaker surprises Bertha by offering her the dress and Robert. Asking Bertha to help her to bed, she complains, "Though the clock stands at the noon / I am weary." The speaker's virtue is not, however, self-willed but learned from her mother, now dead:

> Mother, mother, up in heaven,
>   Stand up on the jasper sea,
> And be witness I have given

All the gifts required of me,—
Hope that blessed me, bliss that crowned,
Love that left me with a wound,
Life itself that turneth round!

The price she is "required" by her mother to pay—hope, bliss, love and
life—is steep; and she cannot always sustain the façade of easy compliance.
Initially she welcomes her mother's spiritual presence in the room:

Mother, mother thou art kind,
     Thou art standing in the room,
In a molten glory shrined
     That rays off into the gloom!

But the word "gloom" ushers in a more realistic vision—a fear of the death
the mother demands from her daughter:

But thy smile is bright and bleak
Like cold waves—I cannot speak,
I sob in it, and grow weak.

Ghostly mother, keep aloof
     One hour longer from my soul,
For I still am thinking of
     Earth's warm-beating joy and dole!

The striking image of her mother's "smile bright and bleak / Like cold
waves" transforms the dutiful daughter into one who fears death and resents
self-sacrifice.

     In a flashback the speaker tells Bertha how she learned of the love
between her and Robert, then gives instructions for her burial—evoking the
ghastly image of the living death she imagines:

On that grave drop not a tear!
     Else, though fathom-deep the place,
Through the woollen shroud I wear
     I shall feel it on my face.

She will not die easily, requesting Bertha to kiss her eyes, so that as she dies
the light will go

> Sweetly, as it used to rise
> When I watched the morning-grey
> Strike, betwixt the hills, the way
> He was sure to come that day.

She remembers the love she longs for but succumbs to her fate, "no more vain words be said!" She asks her mother to "smile now on thy Dead, / I am death-strong in my sou.l." Under her mother's bright, bleak smile she connects her own female suffering with that of Jesus:

> Jesus, Victim, comprehending
> Love's divine self-abnegation,
> Cleanse my love in its self-spending,
> And absorb the poor libation!

The emotional impact of the poem enforces the notion that women's self-sacrifice is learned from mothers, the subtle, successful agents of patriarchy. Yet the poem's last line, "I aspire while I expire," in which the speaker imagines her ascension into Heaven, is so bad, its verbal play so inappropriate, that the poem's seriousness is undercut and we question how virtuous is the speaker's self-sacrifice.

None of Barrett's other heroines die so meekly, but the rebellion against such a destiny is voiced far from the "Sidmouth town" of "Bertha in the Lane." Barrett's defiant heroines wear medieval costume, props so popularized by the early nineteenth-century revival of interest in the Middle Ages that they disguised the subversive nature of the poems' propositions. Barrett's early steps onto her own poetic ground enticed but did not incite her readers. Three poems that challenge the patriarchal assumptions of courtly literature and the "womanly virtues" extolled by the poetesses are "The Romaunt of the Page," "The Lay of the Brown Rosary," and the "Rhyme of the Duchess May." Each dramatizes an Eve who refuses Milton's dictum "He for God only, she for God in him," and each, because of her defiance, dies.

"The Romaunt of the Page" was written in 1838 (just before Barrett's eight years of chronic invalidism) in response to an engraving sent to her by Mitford, the editor of *Findens' Tableaux*. Mitford often sent engravings to poets as subject matter for poems. The underlying assumption that women can produce verses to order determined that the poetry was unrepresentative of the writers' concerns—except when such pictures were in the hands of a poet like Barrett who refused the role of poetess even as she relinquished the assumed role of male poet. The engraving about which

Barrett wrote "The Romaunt of the Page" "represents a girl dressed as a squire or page but . . . obviously feminine in appearance. . . . She is kneeling at the foot of a tree and looking with a wistful expression toward the back of a fully armed knight on a horse that is pawing the air and is about to charge away. On the ground in front of the page are a casque and a murderous-looking instrument, which seems to be a combination of cross-bow and battle-axe." It is the stuff of which the young adolescent Barrett dreamed when she acknowledged, "Through the whole course of my childhood, I had a steady indignation against Nature who made me a woman, and a determinate resolution to dress up in men's clothes . . . & go into the world 'to seek my fortune.' '*How*,' was not decided; but I rather leant towards being poor Lord Byron's PAGE." Reminiscent of Shakespeare's romantic comedies, the poem employs disguise to enable the woman to test her lover before committing herself to him. Although the protagonist, dressed as a page, is married to the knight she serves, the rushed midnight wedding before the knight's departure to the crusades results in an unconsummated marriage in which husband and wife are ignorant even of each other's appearance. The woman-as-page is strong and brave, one who " 'fearest not to steep in blood / The curls upon [his] brow,' " and who " 'once in the tent, and twice in the fight,' " saved her master, Sir Hubert, from a " 'mortal blow.' " The page talks of the " 'bloody battle-game,' " and when the knight imagines introducing his page to his wife, he tells her " 'her bower may suit thee ill' " for " 'fitter thy hand for my knightly spear / Than thy tongue for my lady's will.' " The page is thus established as capable in the violence of battle and more suited to the male "battle-game" than the female "bower."

Only in retrospect do we understand the mention of "his" curls and why "no lady in her bower . . . / Could blush more sudden red" than "he." The page "slowly and thankfully" accepts the knight's praise not because "he" imagines his valiant future as a knight, but because *she* assumes that the knight's pleasure in her suitability for the battlefield rather than lady's rooms confirms his acceptance of her unorthodox actions. The page's blushing assertion, " 'thy lady's bower to me / Is suited well' ", indicates not the titillation of a page in training as a warrior and courtly lover, but reveals the woman's relief that her mystery husband has passed her test and will welcome his valiant, assertive wife. In this ironic moment, the knight—and initially the reader—understands one meaning, and the page—and eventually the reader—quite another.

At this ambiguous moment a dirge is heard from the "convent on the sea, / One mile off" where nuns mourn the death of their Lady Abbess, "*Beati, beati, mortui!*" ("Blessed be the dead.") The nuns' long laments function as a Greek chorus. Although the relevance of their grief is inexplicable here, its ominous note that "wheeleth on the wind around" eerily undermines the page's confidence in "his" suitability to the "lady's bower." The protagonist's unconventional actions seem jeopardized when her blushing self-absorption in her own future well-being tunes out the nuns' chanting. They mourn a woman's death: "And the knight heard all, and the page heard none," but instead talks on confidently.

The woman provokes the knight into revealing his feelings about his wife and her beauty. Her ruse works, but the story she hears about herself is a bitter one; it is rife with slander, duels, murders, and vengeance, which necessitated the knight's upholding his honor by marrying the daughter of a man who avenged his father's murder while he was away riding "the lists at court." The speedy marriage before he left for the crusades—" 'the steed thrice neighed, and the priest fast prayed' "—occurred in the dead of a moonless night. He has, therefore, no idea of his wife's appearance. The knight is a victim of the gender economy he perpetuates; without parents the daughter had no honorable place. The knight to be honorable had to marry her.

When the page discusses how "her sister" disguised herself as a page to fight by her knight/husband, the pleasant intimacy between knight and page abruptly ceases. Deaths must be avenged, marriages arranged, and knights leave their wives for the battle-field; a lady must not leave her castle to join her husband in battle. In this "system of man," the wife whom the knight resents must act according to the "womanly virtues": " 'My love, so please you, shall requite / No woman, whether dark or bright, / Unwomaned if she be.' " From the safety of her male disguise, the page/wife challenges such hypocrisy:

> The page stopped weeping and smiled cold—
>   "Your wisdom may declare
> That womanhood is proved the best
> By golden brooch and glossy vest
>   The mincing ladies wear;
> Yet it is proved, and was of old,
> Anear as well, I dare to hold,
>   By truth, or by despair."
>
> He smiled no more, he wept no more,
>   But passionate he spake—
> "Oh, womanly she prayed in tent,
>   When none beside did wake!
> Oh, womanly she paled in fight,
>   For one belovèd's sake! —

And her little hand, defiled with blood,
Her tender tears of womanhood
   Most woman-pure did make!"

—"Well done it were for thy sistèr,
   Thou tellest well her tale!
But for my lady, she shall pray
   I 'the kirk of Nydesdale.
Not dread for me but love for me
   Shall make my lady pale;
No casque shall hide her woman's tear—
It shall have room to trickle clear
   Behind her woman's veil."

—"But what if she mistook thy mind
   And followed thee to strife,
Then kneeling did entreat thy love
   As Paynims ask for life?"
—"I would forgive, and evermore
Would love her as my servitor,
   But little as my wife.

"Look up—there is a small bright cloud
   Alone amid the skies!
So high, so pure, and so apart,
   A woman's honour lies."
The page looked up—the cloud was sheen—
A sadder cloud did rush, I ween,
   Betwixt it and his eyes.

Then dimly dropped his eyes away
   From welkin unto hill—
Ha! who rides there?—the page is 'ware,
   Though the cry at his heart is still:
And the page seeth all and the knight seeth none,
Though banner and spear do fleck the sun,
   And the Saracens ride at will.

Challenging a "wisdom" that reveres the superficial "golden brooch," "glossy vest," and "mincing ladies," the page extols a womanhood not limited to costumes and postures, but manifest in enduring qualities, "By truth, or by despair." In her system the "sister's" active loyalty to her husband in the field, rather than her passive waiting in the domestic interiors of the castle, is what makes her truly "woman-pure." Whatever we may feel about the morality of advocating war as superior to domestic life, there is an integrity in the page's assertion that a virtuous woman is one who takes creative initiative, involves herself in the public sphere, is physically strong and courageous, and expresses her love by cooperation not by dependency. The knight refuses such a woman: his response to a wife who mistook his mind by following him into battle would be to forgive her and "love her as [his] servitor, / But little as [his] wife." Though he bridles at marriage he proves a textbook knight and courtly lover with exalted notions of woman: "Look up—there is a small bright cloud / Alone amid the skies! / So high, so pure, and so apart, / A woman's honour lies." A woman whose hair is "steep[ed] in blood" and whose "hand, defiled with blood" can "ward [him] a mortal blow" is abhorrent to a man who idealizes and trivializes woman as "so high, so pure, and so apart."

The page failed to hear the nuns' ominous funeral lament because she was so confident in her bright future as the knight's trusted wife. Likewise the knight, idealizing his wife's(distant) place in the future, proves inadequate as a soldier. He is so absorbed in his sentimental rhetoric, so bound in by his fictional world, that he fails to hear the approach of the very Saracens he has come to fight; "the page seeth all and the knight seeth none." She, seeing the Saracens, sends the knight to safety, excusing her own lingering,

> "For I must loose on saddle-bow
>   My battle casque that galls, I trow,
> The shoulder of my steed."

The knight smiles "free at the fantasy," destined to be enacted, that the page will join him later " 'as parted spirits cleave / To mortals too beloved to leave,' " and fails to notice her distress. "Had the knight looked up to the page's face," he might have averted the tragic outcome. He exhibits no such sensitivity leaving the page "alone, alone," where she bitterly reveals her true identity: " 'Have I renounced my womanhood, / For wifehood unto *thee?*' " Although she asks " 'God save thee,' " she wishes the knight a wife " 'more woman-proud and half as true' " as herself who is " 'false page, but truthful woman.' " Her authority succumbs to the knight's system, "How bright the little cloud appears."

Yet her final act is defiant: she bloodies herself saving the knight's life instead of staying "so apart" from earthly turmoil. The ending is violent indeed with its "tramp of hoof," and "flash of steel," with the Paynims who "smote her low" and "cleft her golden ringlets through." The gruesome final vision reveals how she "felt the scimitar gleam down, / And met it from beneath." Yet accompanying all this violence is her smile, "bright in victory."

We may ask, what is her "victory"? She has succeeded, through self-sacrifice, in saving her husband; the poem, therefore, appears to dramatize the extreme of womanly self-abnegation. And yet, she has also usurped the male role by dying in battle to protect her family. The knight seems incapable of protecting himself without his page to notice the enemy's approach and ward off "moral blows." Her victory is her indictment of the knight's system: far from being "so high, so pure, and so apart," the woman proves her competence outside the home. And yet, within patriarchy, the woman, whatever her strength, is sacrificed by the knight: to irrelevancy at home, to death outside of it. The poem dramatizes a macabre counterpoint to "The Lady of Shalott." The page is slaughtered and the poem ends with the nuns' lament:

> Dirge for abbess laid in shroud
> Sweepeth o'er the shroudless dead,
> Page or lady, as we said,
> With the dews upon her head,
> All as sad if not as loud.
>   *Ingemisco, ingemisco*!
> Is ever a lament begun
> By any mourner under sun,
> Which, ere it endeth, suits but *one*?

The dirge of the "weary nuns" binds their cloistered existence to their sister's cultural imprisonment.

Although the ending of "The Romaunt of the Page" is punitive, the poem indicts courtly worship of woman and its misogynistic heart. It thereby subverts the acquiescent female tradition to which its publication in *Findens' Tableaux* suggests that it belongs.

"The Lay of the Brown Rosary" also first appeared (as "The Legend of the Brown Rosarie") in *Findens' Tableaux* (entitled that year *The Iris of Prose, Poetry, and Art for 1840*). The poem was republished in 1844 in the New York *Ladies' Companion and Literary Expositor*, emphasizing the poem's identification with a female literary tradition. The picture for this poem had "in the margins around the central picture of two women and a little boy in a chapel . . . faint representations of a 'brown rosarie,' an 'old convent ruin,' a nun, angels, an 'evil spirit,' the 'bridegroom' and 'Leonora' both on horseback, and 'the priest at the altar' with his 'grave young sacristans.' "

Barrett described writing this poem to her sister, Arabel: "When you once begin a story you can't bring it to an end all in a moment—and what with nuns and devils and angels and marriages and death and little boys, I couldn't get out of the mud without a great deal of splashing." The "splashing" reveals a superficially Christian framework for the poem, the struggle between God and the Devil for Onora's soul, concealing an alignment of men with God and women with the Devil. The Eve who repudiates Lucifer in "*A Drama of Exile*" understands her allegiance with the feminized Devil who rebels against male authority. The male figures, however,—God, father, brother, angels, priest, and bridegroom—outnumber and outweigh the female ones, Onora, nun, and mother.

The poem centers on the appearance of Onora's dead father to his daughter in her dreams. God has ordained that Onora should also die, although God and her father become indistinguishable as the originator of the summons: "God decreed my death and I shrank back afraid. / Have patience, O dead father mine!" Onora wishes to live because "Love feareth death," and she longs for her "lover [who] to battle is gone"; she has "barter[ed] love'; / God's love for man's." She is aided in refusing God's order by an Evil Spirit represented as a nun, cruelly interred alive in the convent wall for her refusal to confess to the Priest. The choice between submission to male authority and rebellion that brings the punishment of death-in-life is, it is implied, a choice that unites women.

The poem is structurally fascinating. Parts 1 and 3 have stanzas of five lines of amphibrachs. Part 2 contains Onora's dream, first of the angels, and then of her dialogue with the Evil Spirit dressed as the nun. The angels, God's messengers, speak in brisk octosyllabics, whereas the extended dream dialogue between Onora and the nun/Evil Spirit, to whom Onora repeats her vows to the Devil, is in rhyming fourteener couplets. This latter form is repeated in Part 4 in which Onora dies. This repetition is crucial: although Onora submits to the rule of God and her father, her death is represented rhythmically by a structure that ties her not to God's angels but still to the nun, to her female tradition of rebellion. Structurally Barrett implies that men may appropriate women but cannot finally change their form/body/being. Women, for her, remain different from men and resistant even in apparent submission. This poem would have been very different had she written Part 4 in the octosyllabics the angels use to represent God's will.

Parts 1 and 3 represent conventional ballad lore, such that without Parts 2 and 4 they would make a complete poem. A knight is away at battle. He survives the world of male heroics only to return to the destructive powers of woman. These two sections, although told by a narrator, reveal

Onora's young brother's perspective. He, in Part 1, warns their mother that Onora sits with the nun of the brown rosary in a ruined convent:

> "The old convent ruin the ivy rots off,
> Where the owl hoots by day and the toad is sun-proof,
> Where no singing-birds build and the trees gaunt and grey
> As in stormy sea-coasts appear breasted one way—
>   But is *this* the wind's doing?
>
> "A nun in the east wall was buried alive
> Who mocked at the priest when he called her to shrive,
> And shrieked such a curse, as the stone took her breath,
> The old abbess fell backwards and swooned unto death
>   With an Ave half-spoken."

Our sympathies are divided between the boy's horror at female disobedience enacted initally by the nun and now by his sister, and the nun, victim of this gruesome punishment. Onora, making no mention of the nun, quells her mother's alarm at the boy's tale and anticipates her lover's return from battle. Part 1 ends with mother and daughter planning the marriage, and with the boy "half-ashamed and half-softened."

Part 3 opens with a "morn for a bridal":

> While down through the wood rides that fair company,
> The youths with the courtship, the maids with the glee,
> Till the chapel-cross opens to sight, and at once
> All the maids sigh demurely and think for the nonce,
>   "And so endeth a wooing!"
>
> And the bride and the bridegroom are leading the way,
> With his hand on her rein, and a word yet to say;
> Her dropt eyelids suggest the soft answers beneath,
> And the little quick smiles come and go with her breath
>   When she sigheth or speaketh.

This conventional portrait presents the bridegroom reining in Onora's horse while she prepares for her role as demure wife. At the chapel her young brother tries to prevent the marriage because Onora wears the nun's brown rosary. But the wedding guests just laugh and the priest retorts, "Thou art wild, pretty boy! Blessed she / Who prefers at her bridal a brown rosary / To a worldly arraying." The happy wedding scene is interrupted by a laugh heard at the altar; the bride looks "as if no bride she were, / Gazing cold at the priest without gesture of prayer"; the priest "whenever the Great Name [is] there to be read, / His voice [sinks] to silence"; and the bridegroom gives his bride the kiss fatal to himself. The boy's accusations are finally justified. Onora rips the brown rosary from her neck:

> She dashed it in scorn to the marble-paved ground
> Where it fell mute as snow, and a weird music-sound
> Crept up, like a chill, up the aisles long and dim.

With no reason to live, she throws herself on her dead husband: "I am ready for dying".

As such the poem would be emotionally and structurally conventional, even if a little mysterious. The boy would be exonerated and woman proven still to be destructive. The drama in Part 3 represents an exaggerated version of "La Belle Dame Sans Merci": instead of being Keats's wretched wight, / Alone and palely loitering" after he had "shut her wild sad eyes— / So kiss'd to sleep," the knight in "The Lay of the Brown Rosary" "kisseth the bride" and "fell stark at her foot." It is arguable that sudden death is preferable to the "death-pale" life of which Keats's knight dreams in which "starv'd lips in the gloom / With horrid warning gaped wide": either way sexual involvement with a woman is dramatized as destructive.

However, quite a different tale emerges when Part 2 intrudes into this ballad narrative. Onora's dream explains both her commitment to the nun and also the strange events of her wedding day; the destructive woman is transformed into one who enacts strategies for survival against the destructive power of *male* authority. In her dream two angels appear. One, hearing Onora is a sinner, is eager to save her:

> She so young, that I who bring
> Good dreams for saintly children, might
> Mistake that small soft face tonight,
> And fetch her such a blessed thing.

The other sternly rebukes him—"It is not WILLED"—and they depart. The angels, although often associated with women in nineteenth-century rhetoric, are here manifestations of male will and authority, whereas the Devil, whose incarnation as Lucifer was masculine, inhabits the rebellious, sexual spirit of the female in this poem. With the departure of the angels, the nun, who dressed as an Evil Spirit embodies the cultural view of unorthodox womanhood, appears in the dream where Onora walks, "among the fields, beneath the autumn-sun, / With [her] dead father, hand in hand, as [she had] often done." She longs to stay with her father, whose feet are "tied . . . beneath the kirkyard stone" but who in dreams calls, " 'Come forth, my daughter, my beloved, and walk the fields with me!' " Barrett's strategy for revealing Onora's story lies in the nun's insistence that Onora repeat it aloud for when her thoughts wander "too near heaven":

> "Stand up where thou dost stand
> Among the fields of Dreamland with thy father hand in
>   hand,
> And clear and slow repeat the vow, declare its cause
>   and kind,
> Which not to break, in sleep or wake thou bearest on
>   thy mind."

Step by step Onora tells her story until she finally rehearses her vow to the nun. She sold her soul to the Devil, "because that God decreed [her] death"; she could not suffer on the day she was engaged; "to lie content and still beneath a stone, / And feel [her] own betrothed go by." She vows to the nun, "upon thy rosary brown," she will never repeat God's name, thereby allying herself with the woman who also refused patriarchal authority. She chooses life and love, not death and God. She describes her final dream image: " 'my love! I felt him near again! / I saw his steed on mountain-head, I heard it on the plain!' " On waking she is uneasy, but "her hands tremble fast as their pulses and, free / From the death-clasp, close over—the BROWN ROSARY."

Onora's pact with the Devil infects the wedding day with tension. The boy's anxiety is revealed to have a basis in truth, and the strange altar behavior of the priest is clarified. Because Onora has resisted to some degree, she wins a limited victory. The bridegroom dies, not Onora herself. The victory is limited because although she lives, she does not have love on earth, and hence her despair, " 'I am ready for dying.' " Instead, she must linger on, dead in life, knowing her guilt, aware that everything around her has life and vitality: " 'only I am dreary, / And, mother, of my dreariness behold me very weary.' " She submits to slow death:

> Then breaking into tears,—"Dear God," she cried, "and
>   must we see
> All blissful things depart from us or ere we go to THEE?
> We cannot guess Thee in the wood or hear Thee in the
>   wind?
> Our cedars must fall round us ere we see the light
>   behind?"

Part 3 ends on death and Onora's recognition of her sin; Part 4 reveals her still challenging God's will. When she finally dies, it is not out of obedience to God's call, but because earth excludes a woman who defies male authority: Onora perishes "mute for lack of root, earth's nourishment to reach." This Eve also allies herself with Lucifer, and is punished.

The dramatization of the "nun in the east wall . . . buried alive" because she defied male authority is emblematic of woman's condition. The absolute trust the mother has in Onora's allegiance to the nun is pitted against God, father, son, and essentially against priest and bridegroom. The father's apparently gratuitous summoning of his daughter to death, and the punitive killing of her husband, thereby denying her happiness, sex, and love, ultimately render the women powerless against this masculine will. Certainly the desire of patriarchal society to immure woman was becoming a peculiarly personal concern of Barrett's as she lingered in her invalid's room. The strength of the protest against it is vivid here, even if submission is the outcome.

"Rhyme of the Duchess May," however, records a heroine who refuses submission. Although she also dies, her death results from self-assertion for which she feels no remorse. The poem first appeared in *Poems of 1844*, a year after its composition. Barrett wrote it after reading George Sand's work, which may account for this heroine's refusal of courtly and marital economies. Barrett dramatizes medieval marriage as an economic, not affectionate, arrangement. The Duchess May, "a Duke's fair orphan-girl," was ward of her uncle, the earl, who "betrothed her twelve years old, for the sake of dowry gold, / To his son Lord Leigh the churl." But the Duchess May, who loved Sir Guy of Linteged, rejected such traffic in women inherent in the sex/gender economy of marriage. When she refused to marry her cousin, the earl commented, " 'Good my niece, that hand withal looketh somewhat soft and small / For so large a will, in sooth.' " To which his niece astutely replied, in a sing-song nursery rhythm that mocked her uncle's diminution of her, " 'Little hand clasps muckle gold, or it were not worth the hold / Of thy son, good uncle mine!' " Her cousin invoked might as right; he "jerked his breath, and sware thickly in his teeth" that " 'He would wed his own betrothed, an she loved him an she loathed, / Let the life come or the death.' " The Duchess May resisted intimidation and refused to acquiesce, declaring, " '[a] woman's will dies hard' " and " 'orphaned girl and dowered lady, / I deny you wife and ward.' " She married Sir Guy of Linteged at midnight in secret and rode off with him through the "night-storm," reflecting in the natural world the upheaval she had created in the social order.

After three months of marriage Earl Leigh and his son with their forces attacked Linteged:

Down the sun dropt large and red on the towers of
  Linteged,—
> *Toll slowly.*
Lance and spear upon the height, bristling strange in
  fiery light,
        While the castle stood in shade.

For fourteen days, reflecting the red sun, the castle "seethed in blood." The
violence dramatized male rage at woman's assumption of power over her own
life. Lord Leigh gleefully anticipated the moment he would "wring thy
fingers pale in the gauntlet of my mail." Leigh, whose "thin lips . . . scarcely
sheathe the cold white gnashing of his teeth," imagined a cruel revenge. But
the Leighs were not the only ones to assault the integrity of Duchess May.
Sir Guy equally objectified her when he suggested ending the slaughter of his
soldier kinsmen by voluntarily dying and returning his wife to Lord Leigh.
He valued his men's lives over his wife's, although to assuage such betrayal he
pictured an idealized ending to the affair, not the torture Leigh fantasized:

"Then my foes shall sleek their pride, soothing fair
  my widowed bride
        Whose sole sin was love of me:

"With their words all smooth and sweet, they will
  front her and entreat"—
> *Toll slowly.*
"And their purple pall will spread underneath her
  fainting head
        While her tears drop over it.

"She will weep her woman's tears, she will pray her
  woman's prayers"—
> *Toll slowly.*
"But her heart is young in pain, and her hopes will
  spring again
        By the suntime of her years."

    It is a patronizing attitude and a fictional vision; nothing in the
spunky young Duchess suggested such submission of "her fainting head."
When she heard that Sir Guy intended to kill himself and return her to Lord
Leigh, she cried and "Low she dropt her head, and lower, till her hair coiled
on the floor." But her coiling hair suggested strength, not "the fainting head"
of the Duke's picture of her grief. Her grief was short-lived and transformed

into action; she decided to die with her chosen husband. The Duchess's actions affirmed what neither the beloved Sir Guy nor the loathed Lord Leigh understood: she was not an object whose disposition men decide; she was not an object whose fate could be decided by displays of male strength; she was not an object who passively submitted to men's will.

She decided her own fate, jumping to death with her husband. Terrified but determined, once on horseback seconds before death, "she clung wild and she clung mute with her shuddering lips half-shut". Her abundant hair is a symbol of passion, energy, and assertion as she insists "by all my womanhood" and "by wifehood's verity" on dying with her husband, to avoid Lord Leigh. Reminiscent of Landon's "Hindoo Widow," this protagonist is more closely allied to Morris's Jehane in "The Haystack in the Floods": she decides her fate rather than ceding to custom. Unlike the knight in "The Romaunt of the Page," Sir Guy accepts the Duchess's authority. Barrett dramatizes the balance of determination and fear in the Duchess's Pyrrhic victory through the horse's terrified balancing on the tower top "in stark despair, with his front hoofs poised in air" before the three plunge to "the headlong death below."

In the conclusion the narrator, a bell-ringer, thinks on "the ancient Rhyme." He notices a grave: "HERE, UNDEFILED, LIETH MAUD, A THREE-YEAR CHILD, / EIGHTEEN HUNDRED FORTY-THREE." He does not contrast her innocence and the lovers'guilt, but rather likens them:

> Though in passion ye would dash, with a blind and
> heavy crash—
> > *Toll slowly—*
> Up against the thick-bossed shield of God's judgement
> in the field, —
> > Though your heart and brain were rash, —
>
> Now, your will is all unwilled; now, your pulses are
> all stilled:
> > *Toll slowly.*
> Now, ye lie as meek and mild (whereso laid) as Maud
> the child
> > Whose small grave was lately filled.

Although the Duchess May defied patriarchal authority and both lovers defied God in their suicidal leap, the narrator gives his and, he feels sure, God's blessing on them, "I smiled to think God's greatness flowed around our incompleteness,— / Round our restlessness, His rest."

This conclusion, together with the prologue, frames the Duchess May's story: the bell-ringer claims to "read this ancient rhyme" while sitting in a churchyard hearing the bells peal. This story within a story functions as a distancing device, reducing Barrett's apparent responsibility for her unorthodox story. However, the tone relates less to the heroine's triumph than to the grief for her death, suggested by the mood of mourning and the solemn ringing of the bells. The bell-ringers announce, " 'Ours is music for the dead.' " The solemn tone is achieved by Barrett's manipulation of the ballad form and its refrain; by reading the refrain in the middle of each stanza the reader hears the bell toll against the unfolding narrative rather than as a conclusion to each stage.

What is the lament for which the bell tolls throughout this "ancient rhyme"? Like "The Romaunt of the Page" and "The Lay of the Brown Rosary" the poem ends with the death of both man and woman: the knight in "The Romaunt of the Page" seems incompetent to save his life without his page/wife and may well meet as bloody a death as she; the bridegroom dies upon kissing his bride in "The Lay of the Brown Rosary" before she herself declines into death; and in a more triumphant death Sir Guy and Duchess May decide their own fate. These ballads expose the destructiveness to both men and women of the sex/gender economy defined as courtly behavior and often as Victorian ideology.

If these three poems were popular, "Lady Geraldine's Courtship" truly won its readers' hearts in spite of Barrett's apprehension over its modernity: "it is a 'romance of the age,' treating of railroads, routes, and all manner of 'temporalities,' and in so radical a temper that I expect to be reproved for it by the Conservative reviews round". The poem is a strange hybrid: self-consciously modern in theme, yet persistently courtly in rhetoric. Yet Barrett finally allows an assertive heroine to live, even if only within limiting conventions.

In the first part the poet, Bertram, writes to a friend about his love for and apparent rejection by Lady Geraldine; the narrator in the conclusion reveals Bertram's mistake. The poem's modernity is established from the outset:

> She has halls among the woodlands, she has castles by
>   the breakers,
> She has farms and she has manors, she can threaten
>   and command:
> And the palpitating engines snort in steam across her
>   acres,
> As they mark upon the blasted heaven the measure of
>   the land.

The rhythmic repetition of "she has . . . she can" is as ordered as the structured social system that allows for Lady Geraldine's inherited lands and power; however, the movement through the last two lines is analogous to the trains piercing those pastoral country estates. Bertram describes how he and Lady Geraldine discussed at length rural scenes and concerns, books, and the problematics of progress:

> "We are gods by our own reck'ning, and may well
>   shut up the temples,
> And wield on, amid the incense-steam, the thunder of
>   our cars.
>
> "For we throw out acclamations of self-thanking, self-
>   admiring,
> With, at every mile run faster,—'O the wondrous
>   wondrous age!'
> Little thinking if we work our SOULS as nobly as our
>   iron,
> Or if angels will commend us at the goal of pilgrimage.
>
> "Why, what is this patient entrance into nature's deep
>   resources
> But the child's most gradual learning to walk upright
>   without bane!
> When we drive out, from the cloud of steam, majestical
>   white horses,
> Are we greater than the first men who led black ones
>   by the mane?
>
> "If we trod the deeps of ocean, if we struck the stars
>   in rising,
> If we wrapped the globe intensely with one hot electric
>   breath,
> 'Twere but power within our tether, no new spirit-
>   power comprising,
> And in life we were not greater men, nor bolder men
>   in death."

Through Bertram, the poet, Barrett confronts some crucial artistic, social, political, and spiritual issues of her day: To what extent should poetry represent contemporary concerns? What place does the language of industry

have in the rhetoric of poetry? Is progress in and of itself good? What
happens to the soul under technological advance? The poem's modernity is
also expressed in Bertram's entertaining Lady Geraldine by reading not only
from Spenser and the "subtle interflowings / Found in Petrarch's sonnets"
but also:

> At times a modern volume, Wordsworth's solemn-
>   thoughted idyl,
> Howitt's ballad-verse, or Tennyson's enchanted
>   reverie,—
> Or from Browning some "Pomegranate," which, if
>   cut deep down the middle,
> Shows a heart within blood-tinctured, of a veined
>   humanity.

This was a modernity that won Robert Browning's heart.

The poem seemed "so radical" to Barrett because of its
preoccupation with class, dramatized in the union of the poor, low-born poet
with the wealthy and noble Lady Geraldine, which suggests that the life of
the mind makes a poet as rich as an aristocrat. However, it also questions the
premise of courtly love that informed nineteenth-century rhetoric about
women. Thus Bertram resembles a sonneteer in his languishing after a lady
whom he believes totally unattainable, and whose very unattainability fuels
his passion:

> I was only a poor poet, made for singing at her casement,
> As the finches or the thrushes, while she thought of
>   other things.
> Oh, she walked so high above me, she appeared to
>   my abasement,
> In her lovely silken murmur, like an angel clad in wings!

His memory of "the blessèd woods of Sussex . . . / With their leafy tide of
greenery still rippling up the wind" is transformed into "the cursèd woods of
Sussex! where the hunter's arrow found me, / When a fair face and a tender
voice had made me mad and blind!" Bertram exploits the courtly image of
the slaying of the lover by Cupid's "arrow" as he imagines himself one of
Cupid's victims. Lady Geraldine is as beautiful as any troubadour's or
sonneteer's mistress:

> Thus, her foot upon the new-mown grass, bareheaded,
>   with the flowing

> Of the virginal white vesture gathered closely to her
> throat,
> And the golden ringlets in her neck just quickened by
> her going,
> And appearing to breathe sun for air, and doubting if
> to float.

His love for her is platonic:

> And I loved her,
> loved her certes
> As I loved all heavenly objects, with uplifted eyes and
> hands;
> As I loved pure inspirations, loved the graces, loved
> the virtues,
> In a Love content with writing his own name on
> desert sands.

> Or at least I thought so, purely.

He pursues her with humiliating persistence: "Why, her grey-hound followed also! dogs—we both were dogs for scorning—/ To be sent back when she pleased it." And he lives in "endless desolation."

It is not clear how deliberately overt was Barrett's mockery of the attitudes and rhetoric of the courtly lover. What is apparent is that this traditional language of woman worship is what was available to a woman imagining herself as a male poet writing about a woman. This courtly system crumbles, however, when Bertram overhears Lady Geraldine tell a wealthy admirer, " 'Whom I marry shall be noble, / Ay, and wealthy. I shall never blush to think how he was born.' " Bertram, ignorant of her love for him, is also ignorant that she is describing the "wealth" of the poet, equating the poet's genius to an inherited title. A true courtly lover, Bertram upbraids Lady Geraldine for her cruelty, for her delight in her superiority and, in fact, for the very qualities he had been worshiping:

> "What right have you, madam, gazing in your palace
> mirror daily,
> Getting so by heart your beauty which all others must
> adore,
> While you draw the golden ringlets down your fingers,
> to vow gaily
> You will wed no man that's only good to God, and
> nothing more?"

Her response to this tirade is to look up "as if in wonder, / With tears beaded on her lashes, and [say]—'Bertram!'" Traditionally the lady is silent: the lover adores, berates, and desires the lady, and humbles himself with no verbal response. Bertram experiences an extravagant reaction to her thus tenderly naming him, shattering the courtly code: "her gentleness destroyed me whom her scorn made desolate"; he is "struck backward and exhausted by that inward flow of passion":

> By such wrong and woe exhausted—what I suffered
>   and occasioned,—
> As a wild horse through a city runs with lightning
>   in his eyes,
> And then dashing at a church's cold and passive wall,
>   impassioned,
> Strikes the death into his burning brain, and blindly
>   drops and dies—
>
> So I fell, struck down before her—do you blame me,
>   friend, for weakness?
> 'Twas my strength of passion slew me!'—fell before her
>   like a stone;
> Fast the dreadful world rolled from me on its roaring
>   wheels of blackness:
> When the light came I was lying in this chamber and
>   alone.

Not only has the courtly lady spoken in gentleness to her lover, but in a further role reversal, the man, overcome by emotion, swoons at the woman's feet. Lady Geraldine's acknowledgment of love for the poet signals Barrett's dismantling of a literary tradition that rhetorically maintained woman in an idealized, distanced, and unrealistic position; it is as though the knight in "The Romaunt of the Page" had finally understood that it is only a male fantasy to talk of "a small bright cloud / Alone amid the skies" as revealing woman's honor.

But that is not how the poem ends; this ballad, which subverts conventions and in which (finally) the lovers live and the only violence is Bertram's faint, has some puzzling elements. First, Barrett persists in her inability to imagine a woman poet; thus, like "The Poet's Vow," "Lady Geraldine's Courtship" subscribes to the convention of a male poet whose vision is modified or clarified by a female muse. The use of this convention maintains, even in what Barrett saw as the poem's radical temper, a basically conservative vision. Second, there is the episode surrounding the statue,

Silence. This statue, built in a fountain on one of Lady Geraldine's estates, represents man's fantasy of woman at his most adoring and misogynistic: she is a work of art cast in marble; she is called Silence; she sleeps; and she holds a rose, referred to as her "symbol-rose." The statue's origin is in Egyptian mythology, in which the god, Heru P-Khart, was represented as a youth with one finger pointing to his mouth. The Greeks adopted him as their god of silence, Harpocrates, and legend has it that Cupid gave Harpocrates a rose to bribe him not to betray Venus's part in a love affair he happened to witness. The rose, which to the Greeks was a symbol of the male god of silence, and in the courtly love tradition was a symbol of woman, is fused here to represent a silent woman, a woman such as Carlyle admired doing her "silently important" duties and "lead[ing] noiselessly" under man's protection. Bertram and Geraldine disagree over the relation of the essential meaning to the symbolic nature of the statue. Bertram describes Lady Geraldine's beauty, thus aroused:

> Half in playfulness she spoke, I thought, and half in
>   indignation;
> Friends, who listened, laughed her words off, while
>   her lovers deemed her fair:
> A fair woman, flushed with feeling, in her noble-
>   lighted station
> Near the statue's white reposing—and both bathed in
>   sunny air!

Lady Geraldine, linked with the "statue's white reposing," becomes associated with the silent woman: as two women they are "both bathed in sunny air" and beautiful to their admirers. The introduction of the statue seems an irrelevant intrusion except to reinforce the idea of woman as object of man's gaze.

The narrator of the poem's conclusion recalls the scene, however, when Bertram finished his letter in despair; having made such a foolish outburst, he had determined to leave Lady Geraldine's house early in the morning. Looking up, however, he saw Geraldine, whom he described as a silent statue: "Soh! how still the lady standeth! . . . / 'Twixt the purple lattice-curtains how she standeth still and pale!" He saw her "Shining eyes, like antique jewels set in Parian statue-stone!" and recognized how "underneath that calm white forehead" she was "burning torrid"; Lady Geraldine's statuesque quality was emphasized by the movement around her that so contrasted with her own stillness:

With a murmurous stir uncertain, in the air the purple
    curtain
Swelleth in and swelleth out around her motionless
    pale brows,
While the gliding of the river sends a rippling noise
    for ever
Through the open casement whitened by the moonlight's
    slant repose.

Bertram commanded her, "'Vision of a lady! stand there silent, stand there
steady!'" and invoked again courtly rhetoric for " 'the lips of silent passion, /
Curved like an archer's bow to send the bitter arrows out.' " To aid his
illusion of her as a courtly mistress, "Ever, evermore the while in a slow
silence she kept smiling, / And approached him slowly, slowly, in a gliding
measured pace." He could not separate reality from fantasy, and she
concurred with this illusion: "'Bertram, if I say I love thee, . . .'tis the vision
only speaks' " He "quickened to adore her, on his knee he fell before her."
The image of woman as a statue on a pedestal with a man worshiping at her
feet was finally undercut as "she whispered low in triumph" that a poet is rich
and noble, and " 'I shall not blush in knowing that men call him lowly born.' "
The final iconoclastic lines of the poem are given to a woman who refuses
her silent role and, in acknowledging her love, expresses the fact that,
underneath the "calm white forehead" men perceive in women, she does in
fact have passions "ever burning torrid."

The speaking statue acts as a symbol of change, not its enactment.
Although marriage between Bertram and Lady Geraldine may be radical, its
rhetoric is conservative. That Barrett stresses the poem's modernity in such
rhetoric, and creates a male poet as protagonist, suggests that her situation
has certain parallels to a courtly lady's. The conventions of both the Middle
Ages and the nineteenth century make the union of woman and poet
difficult.

Although Barrett wrote a few ballads after this, such as "Amy's
Cruelty" (Last Poems, 1862), she never repeated such concentration and such
strategies again. Aurora Leigh indicates why: reflecting on her success as a
poet, Aurora declares,

My ballads prospered; but the ballad's race
Is rapid for a poet who bears weights
Of thought and golden image.

I do distrust the poet who discerns
No character or glory in his times,

And trundles back his soul five hundred years,
Past moat and drawbridge, into a castle-court,
To sing—oh, not of lizard or of toad
Alive i' the ditch there,—'t were excusable,
But of some black chief, half knight, half sheep-lifter,
Some beauteous dame, half chattel and half queen,
As dead must be, for the greater part,
The poems made on the chivalric bones;
And that's no wonder: death inherits death.

Aurora Leigh speaks to Barrett's conviction that the poet's "sole work is to represent the age, / . . . this live, throbbing age" not to "[trundle] back his [*sic*] soul five hundred years" to medieval times. Aurora's rejection of a poetics that limits woman, "some beauteous dame," as "half chattel and half queen," and one that is "dead" because forged from "chivalric bones," parallels Barrett's own rejection. Although in these medieval ballads and courtly love poems Barrett dramatized Victorian middle-class woman's position in the sex/gender economy of marriage, the medieval context proved constricting for her development as a female poet.

"The Romance of the Swan's Nest," which first appeared in *Poems of 1844*, demonstrates the inadequacy of such a poetics for a woman poet, signaling Barrett's rejection of making poems from "chivalric bones." Little Ellie is refreshingly free from sentimentality, except perhaps for the reference to her "shining hair and face." She has freedom: "Little Ellie sits alone / 'Mid the beeches of a meadow, / By a stream-side on the grass" a mile's walk from home (a freedom comparable to that of the narrator in Barrett's lyric, "The Lost Bower"). It is refreshing in its tactful and open avowal of childhood eroticism:

She has thrown her bonnet by,
    And her feet she has been dipping
        In the shallow water's flow:
Now she holds them nakedly
    In her hands, all sleek and dripping,
        While she rocketh to and fro.

To talk of the poem as relating Ellie's sexual fantasies may be a little crude, but certainly a young girl's stroking her wet naked feet and rocking to and fro thinking of a handsome knight who is riding his red-roan steed to visit her is certainly as suggestive in its way as the more passionate eroticism of "Goblin Market." Little Ellie's fantasies center on the stock features of romance that must have constituted her reading: a noble lover who woos ladies with his lute and kills men with his sword. Ellie imagines he will prefer her to knightly glory, but she will test him, sending him on dangerous missions before finally giving in: "I may bend / From my pride, and answer—'Pardon / If he comes to take my love.' " Merging fantasy with reality, Ellie imagines showing this heroic lover her secret, the "swan's nest among the reeds." However, while Ellie had daydreamed, "Lo, the wild swan had deserted, / And a rat had gnawed the reeds!" What she holds valuable in the actual world is destroyed. Dreaming courtly fantasies, Barrett implies, gnaws at women's energy, sexuality, and identity as the swan has left the nest and the rat eaten the reeds. This poem, placed almost at the end of the volume, repudiates a literary convention that served but ultimately confined Barrett.

The ballads in *Poems of 1844* reflect the popularity of medieval settings for both male and female poets. Thus Barrett is neither writing as a mere poetess nor appropriating a form, such as the epic, seen exclusively as male. The ballads contain, however, a set of conventions that imprison woman as silent object. Barrett moves toward freeing woman from such objectification by an assertion that simultaneously subverts the poetesses' commitment to self-abnegating love. The violence within and the deaths at the end of the ballads represent both the punishment of such assertion and a dramatization of the violence wrought upon both women and men by courtly conventions. The ballads are as assertive as Barrett's reading of Sand on her invalid couch, yet as confining as Barrett's imprisonment in her father's house. They are Songs of Innocence, still imagining Eve as submissive to her Biblical and Miltonic forms, yet initiating a rebellion against both Eve's literary and Barrett's actual confinement, a rebellion that culminated in Barrett Browning's departure for Italy. The *Sonnets from the Portuguese* record the process of this rebellion, and "The Runway Slave at Pilgrim's Point" enacts its triumph.

DEIRDRE DAVID

The Social Wound and the Poetics of Healing

The mind that produced *Aurora Leigh* was praised by the *Westminster Review* in 1857 as one remarkable for 'its abundant treasure of well-digested learning, its acute observation of life, its yearning sympathy with multiform human sorrow, its store of personal, domestic love and joy'. This was a rare moment in an avalanche of negative criticism including the rest of the *Westminster's* review) which roundly condemned Barrett Browning's prolixity, extravagant metaphors, eccentric rhymes, riotous metre, and, most significantly and pervasively, her use of 'unfeminine' poetic language and her choice of poetic subject. She is labelled an 'unchaste poet'. Accused of depicting female types the critics seemed to prefer *not* depicted by a 'poetess' beloved as much for her refined seclusion as she was for her scholarly verse, she had dared to parade before her astonished readers a lascivious aristocrat, a raped working-class girl, and an intellectually independent heroine. She was accused of writing in a 'high fever', of taking the literary field like Britomartis, an assertive, mythological maiden who escaped the sexual advances of Minos by leaping from a rock. Like Britomartis, Barret Browning takes a Spasmodic leap from her rock, not, however, as frantic escape from male pursuit, but to immerse herself in the representation of subjects more usually treated by the novel: utopian politics, female sexuality, rape, urban misery, and the female struggle for professional recognition. In

From *Intellectual Women and Victorian Patriarchy: Harriet Martineau, Elizabeth Barrett Browning, George Eliot* © 1987 by Cornell University Press.

what follows, however, I shall argue that despite the thematic boldness, the daring brutality, and the dauntless reference to female sexuality, *Aurora Leigh* is a strongly conservative poem.

Having chastised Barret Browning for her unfeminine coarseness in figuring rape and references to prostitution, contemporary reviewers also attacked her for creating an implausible figure in Marian Erle, arguing that no working-class girl could possess such language and dignity. Undeniably, Marian is an idealised figure, as Cora Kaplan observes in attributing such idealisation to Barrett Browning's 'aversion to realistic portrayals of working-class women.' What Kaplan neglects to add is that the characters are not only idealised in *Aurora Leigh*, they are hardly characters at all; they possess no finely nuanced and registered shades of consciousness, and apart from *Aurora Leigh* herself who addresses the reader in a language necessarily poetic rather than prosaic, they are emblematic sketches: Romney is a misguided socialist, Lord Howe an aristocratic liberal, Aurora's aunt a gentry spinster. As Virginia Woolf observed, when she assessed *Aurora Leigh*'s formal challenge to the supremacy of the novels of the mid-Victorian period in representing social problems, the character are 'summed up with something of the exaggeration of a caricaturist,' a failing that is unavoidable, Woolf sensibly suggests, as blank verse does not permit that subtle development of character that comes from the effect of one character upon another, nor does it allow for plausible conversation between characters. Crisply summing up the problem, Woolf concludes, 'Blank verse has proved itself the most remorseless enemy of living speech.'

Vigorously employing blank verse and multiple images of degradation and exploitation, Barrett Browning vividly places Marian's rape before the reader, if not in its details then in its absence. Social and literary decorum dictates that Marian's story remain unsaid, yet its marginal status intensifies its volatile content:

> We wretches cannot tell out all our wrong
> Without offence to decent happy folk.
> I know that we must scrupulously hint
> With half-words, delicate reserves, the thing
> Which no one scrupled we should feel in full.

Marian is the victim of man's violence, not merely his seduction, and besides helping to transform her from fallen woman to the 'Marian' figure that she becomes, this emphasis underlines the violence that is a central theme of the poem. Aurora becomes a mother to Marian, making those 'half-words' whole, repairing as much as she is able the injury she has suffered, and in the way of all mothers described by Aurora in evoking her own Italian childhood, 'kisses full sense' into what Marian cannot say. In giving voice and protection to Marian, Aurora rejects a social evil consistently attacked by Barrett Browning: the sexual hypocrisy of respectable women. If there is one place where *Aurora Leigh* takes a radical stand, it is when it daringly deploys erotic imagery and when it refuses to be silent about sexuality.

In an intriguing pattern for a woman who led such a severely sequestered life yet identified with a male poetic tradition, Barrett Browning favours active, phallocentric images for poetic creation. The maker and the subject of the poem are imagined as male and female in *Aurora Leigh*, as we see in the lines that shocked contemporary critics: 'Never flinch, / But still unscrupulously epic, catch/ Upon the burning lava of a song/ The full-veined, heaving, double-breasted Age.' As I suggested earlier, *Aurora Leigh* attempts to mould the thematic content of the Victorian 'female' novel to the form of Classical 'male' epic. Here, Aurora exhorts herself and other poets to 'represent the Age', to employ epic form despite its current literary unfashionability and to catch in the volcanic image of 'burning lava' the voluptuous female time, heaving with nurturing life in its 'full-veined' breasts. Moreover, the image suggests some of the paradoxical mythologisation of women in the Victorian period: the poet must actively create a swiftly moving song out of an age which, even if it is the present one, is also immutably stable in its association to mother earth. Making poetry is straightforward, unflinching, male work, but the female subject of the poem is more complicated: woman is both symbol of the 'heaving' present and of an almost primordial past. Furthermore, *Aurora Leigh*'s self-description as working poet employs an image of poetic action suggestive of thrusting, male sexuality:

> . . . I stood up straight and worked
> My veritable work. And as the soul
> Which grows within a child makes the child grow,—
> Or as the fiery sap, the touch from God,
> Careering through a tree, dilates the bark
> And roughs with scale and knob, before it strikes
> The summer foliage out in a green flame—
> So life, in deepening with me, deepened all
> The course I took, the work I did.

The simile links poetic and organic growth with images of vital, thrusting movement. The poetic/ arboreal sap is 'fiery', it careers, dilates, manifests itself in obtrusions of 'scale and knob', until it blazes, 'strikes out' into green flame.

In 1861 Thackeray rejected one of Barrett Browning's poems, 'Lord Walter's Wife' for the *Cornhill* on the grounds that 'there are things my squeamish public will not hear', hastening to assure her that the wife of Browning and the mother of Pen was sacred to English readers. Barrett Browning's response was to the point: 'It is exactly because pure and prosperous women choose to *ignore vice*, that miserable women suffer wrong by it everywhere.' The poem in question is a spirited attack on male hypocrisy. An engaged man declares to his friend's wife that he finds her 'too fair', and deliberately encouraging his attentions, the woman, Lord Walter's wife, instructs him in the unhappy social truth that men treat all women as sexual commodities to be used and discarded. Had she succumbed to his advances he would no longer find her so desirable. 'Too fair?—not unless you misuse us! and surely if, once in a while, / You attain to it, straight way you call / Us no longer too fair, but too vile.' The poem is vitalised by a woman's anger, felt not only for herself but on behalf of all women who are either deified or degraded by men. Twenty years earlier, in writing to Mary Russell Mitford, Barrett Browning berated respectable women, 'Fair wives of honourable husbands', who will 'shrink from breathing the same air with a betrayed woman', yet will gracefully sit down to dinner with male adulterers.

During the Crimean War, Barrett Browning wrote to an old friend that 'there are worse plagues, deeper griefs, dreader wounds than the physical. What of the forty thousand wretched women in this city? The silent writhing of them is to me more appalling than the roar of the cannons.' In *Aurora Leigh* the wounds are both physical and symbolic: Marian is violently wounded by rape and in a hellish scene of diseased bodies swelling the aisles of the church where Romney and Marian are to be married, all is an oozing 'peccant social wound.' The image of the wounds is crucial not only to the poem, but also to Barrett Browning's work work as woman intellectual/poet. In refusing to ignore the wounds inflicted upon prostitutes, in compelling society to look at the 'offal' it makes of 'fallen' women and also of the poor, and in symbolising social evil as social wound, she creates herself as a ministering healer to an infected world. If society has been cleft in two by a symbolic knife, if women are cleft by rapacious men, then Barrett Browning will, through her poetry, heal the wounds—but not as auxiliary helper in the way the Martineau designed her work to serve male theory. Berrett Browning is a principal actor in the work of healing. She rejects the retrograde function of ancillary usefulness, refuses the role of 'female nurse' to a diseased world—behaves, in fact, in accordance with her actual view of the profession of nursing. As much as she admired Florence Nightingale as an individual, she was sharply critical of the way that nurses enact the 'safe' roles inscribed for them by a male-dominated society: 'Every man is on his knees before ladies carrying lint. . . . if they stir an inch as thinkers or artists from the beaten line (involving more good to general humanity than is involved in lint) the very same men would curse the imprudence of the very same women and stop there . . . I do not consider the best use to which we can put a gifted and accomplished woman is to *make her a hospital nurse.*' In *Aurora Leigh*, Barrett Browning stirs more than an inch as 'thinker' and 'artist' from the beaten line.

If one considers that the image which unifies *Aurora Leigh* is that of maternal nurturance, that Aurora is symbolically suckled by the hills of her Italian childhood, that Romney feeds the great carnivorous mouth of the poor through his Christian socialism, it may seem contradictory to suggest, as I do, that an imagery of wounding is also central to the poem. However, this is obviously less a pattern of contradiction than it is one of dialectical relationship: injury and nurturance are governing concepts which inform each other, and which, in their dialectical turn, direct the entire poem. Contrary to what one might expect, however, the mammocentric imagery does not work in quite the same way as that of wounding because symbolic and literal nurturance possesses its own contradictory implication not always ascribable to the constitutive relationship between wounding and healing. Even Marian's nurturance of her bonny baby is invested with an almost malevolent quality: as she suckles him, she seems to consume him greedily in an image of appropriation, 'drinking him as wine'. Moreover, Lady Waldemar's breast both attract and repel. They are an unspoiled source of life and an image of demonic eroticism: the paradox suggests that contradiction between the deification and degradation of women which Barrett Browning attacks in her poem, 'Lord Walter's Wife.' Lady Waldemar offers a dazzling display of ripe female sexuality:

> . . . How they told,
> Those alabaster shoulders and bare breasts,
> On which the pearls, drowned out of sight in milk,
> Were lost, excepting for the ruby clasp!
> They split the amaranth velvet-bodice down
> To the waist or nearly, with the audacious press
> Of full-breathed beauty. If the heart within
> Were half as white!—but, if it were, perhaps
> The breast were closer covered and the sight
> Less aspectable by half, too.

Proceeding through a sequence of false appearances and concealed truth, the description shows that 'aspectable' things are not what they seem. Nature herself (in the seductive shape of milky breasts) seems to drown out female ornamentation (the pearl necklace), yet the visible ruby clasp indicated Lady Waldermar's embellished sexuality. A single grey hair in her luxuriant bronze tresses contrasts ironically with the symbolism of her amaranth-velvet bodice (the purple colour of a mythical flower which never fades). The display of vibrant sexuality implies its own degeneration, and, significantly in terms of what Lady Waldemar does to Marian, the radiant whiteness of her breasts conceals the dark heart within. Lady Waldemar is what her name implies— the 'weal' which 'mars' all she touches.

The depiction of women in *Aurora Leigh* is framed by Barrett Browning's employment of three interwoven colour images: green, red, and white. The first symbolises the serenity Aurora enjoys in the time she is freed from her aunt's instruction in English womanhood; the other two tend to express, even when employed by Aurora herself, the prevailing nineteenth-century fragmentation of woman into a creature fractured by seemingly irreconcilable, and therefore dangerous, attributes. Sometimes speaking this imagery of fragmentation, Aurora moves from the green, calm (but stultifying) time of her young womanhood to her mature, vibrant, fiery part in building the New Jerusalem:

> I had a little chamber in the house,
> As green as any privet-hedge a bird
> Might choose to build in, though the nest itself
> Could show but dead-brown sticks and straws; the walls
> Were green, the carpet was pure green, the straight
> Small bed was curtained greenly, and the folds
> Huge green about the window which let in
> The out-door world with all its greenery.

No *Jane Eyre* red room this, no symbolic chamber of female anger or prison of female desire, but rather the calm, cool space of the English countryside where, employing the bird imagery that is everywhere in the poem, Aurora describes herself nesting in her green chamber/privet hedge. Some reviewers accused Barrett Browning of melodramatic borrowings from Brontë's novel, of making Romney both St John Rivers and Rochester, the stern seeker of missionary helper rather than sexual partner and the misguided lover blinded by fire. Romney, however, is neither as chillingly austere as St John Rivers nor as passionately vital as Rochester for the obvious reason that he is not, as I have suggested earlier, a character whom we suspect of having much feeling at all. He is a deluded spokesman for Christian socialism who learns that a 'famishing carnivorous mouth,- / A huge, deserted, callow, blind bird Thing' (his image for the poor) needs more than worms in the form of utopian politics to fill it.

The first significant employment of the red/white imagery occurs in Aurora's description of her mother's portrait executed after her death. The face, throat and hands possess a 'swan-like supernatural white life', yet the body wears a red brocade dress, and to the child Aurora the face is 'by turns' 'Ghost, fiend, and angel, fairy, witch, and sprite'. This is the paradoxical female face of so much Victorian art—the angelic sprite who winds her hair around the neck of a knight in Waterhouse's 'La Belle Dame Sans Merci', the fiendish, contorted figure of Hunt's 'The Lady of Shalott', Rossetti's 'Lady Lilith' whose massive neck and powerful jaw forebode an awful female mystery. Confronted as a child by a contradictory representation of her mother, as a woman Aurora must integrate these iconised fragments of Victorian womanhood.

When she hears of Marian's flight from London, Aurora employs the commonplace imagery of purity and whiteness to assure Romney that his lost bride will stay as pure as 'snow that's drifted from the garden-bank / To the open road'. In Marian's own powerful evocation of her despair, however, the imagery becomes more complicated. She describes herself, pregnant and destitute, wandering the roads in France:

> And there I sat, one evening, by the road,
> I, Marian Erle, myself, alone, undone,
> Facing a sunset low upon the flats
> As if it were the finish of all time,
> The great red stone upon my sepulchre,
> Which angels were too weak to roll away.

The raped woman, spoiled yet innocent, soon to give birth to a joyful child from brutal rape, reddened by the blood of defloration literally and symbolically 'engraved' upon her white body, likens the setting sun to a red stone upon her sepulchre. There is a foreshadowing of the end of Hardy's Tess here, a character also figured in the red and white imagery of purity and defloration: Tess sleeps on an oblong slab at Stonehenge, is sacrificial victim to sexual hypocrisy, and is awakened by a strong ray of the rising sun as the police arrive to arrest her for the bloody stabbing of Alex d' Urberville. In Marian's language, the red imagery links the dying day, the exhausted woman, and the weakened angels; all seems to be in a paradoxically fiery decline and suggests a significant contrast to Aurora on her twentieth birthday. A radiant, vital and virginal 'Aurora, fresh from her vernal nest in the morning, foreshadows a depleted, violated Marian at sunset. On Aurora's morning, she is dressed in white, hopefully self-wreathed in ivy as symbol of the poetic power to come: 'The June was in me, with its multitudes / Of nightingales all singing in the dark, / And rosebuds reddening where the calyx split'. The green calyx splits to reveal the ripening rose and suggests the departure of a maturing Aurora from the green enclosure of her room.

If Marian suffers a symbolic fiery ordeal as she feels the weight of 'a great red stone' upon her grave, then Romney suffers a literal one when he is blinded in the fire set by local peasants, incensed by the 'drabs and thieves' he has housed in his Phalanstery. He describes himself as 'A mere bare blind stone in the blaze of day', an image which connects with Marian's evocation of gravestone and sunset (and also an image whose alliterative, jarring assonance recalls the closing of the seventh section of *In Memorium*, 'On the bald street breaks the blank day'). Fusing the traditional myths of poet as witness to a transcendent order and of woman as sympathetic consoler, Aurora repairs the injuries suffered by Marian and Romney.

The informing structure of wounding and healing in *Aurora Leigh* is emphatically etched by imagery of knifing. 'There, ended childhood' declares Aurora on the death of her father. Her life becomes 'Smooth endless days, notched here and there with knives, / A weary, wormy darkness, spurred i' the flank / With flame, that it should eat and end itself / Like some tormented scorpion'. Barrett Browning sustains the imagery of knifing as Aurora describes her aunt's discipline as a 'sharp sword set against my life', her aunt's gaze as 'two grey-steel naked-bladed eyes' searching through her face, and a young man at a dinner party as possessing 'A sharp face, like a knife in a cleft stick'. Moreover, Aurora's sense of injured self is sometimes surprisingly gruesome, even sado-masochistic: 'So I lived' she says, 'A Roman died so; smeared with honey, teased / By insects, stared to torture by the moon'; in London she likens the city sun to the 'fiery brass' of cages used in Druidic sacrifice 'from which the blood of wretches pent inside / Seems oozing forth incarnadine the air'; and in justifying her refusal of Romney, she suspects that 'He might cut / My body into coins to give away / Among his other paupers'.

Knifing and bleeding are prominent symbols in the severe condemnation of female sentimentality which Romney imprudently issues to Aurora:

> . . . Your quick-breathed hearts,
> So sympathetic to the personal pang,
> Close on each separate knife-stroke, yielding up
> A whole life at each wound, incapable
> Of deepening, widening a large lap of life

To hold the world-full woe. The human race
To you means, such a child, or such a man,
You saw one morning waiting in the cold,
Beside that gate, perhaps. You gather up
A few such cases, and when strong sometimes
Will write of factories and of slaves, as if
Your father were a negro, and your son
A spinner in the mills. All's yours and you,
All, coloured with your blood, or otherwise
Just nothing to you.

From Romney's perspective of patriarchal socialism, woman lack the
male faculty of abstraction from personal experience to a general theory of
society: wounded women give up their entire beings at one emotional 'knife-
stroke', leaving no room in their maternal laps for the woes of the world.
Through Romney's sexist sermon, Barrett Browning seems slyly to respond
to those critics who derided the poems *she* wrote about factories and slaves,
and also to a powerful Victorian myth about intellectual women—if women
can only write about what is 'coloured' with their blood, can only think in
terms of 'yours and you', then their minds must be symbolically stained by
the somatic signs of their womanhood. In the success of *Aurora Leigh* and in
her own career, Barrett Browning defies the ugly implication that the
intellectual lives of women must be marred by biological destiny.

In proposing to Marian, the cutting edge, as it were, of Romney's
imagery is deflected from disdain for women's sentimentality to a passionate
plea for the class unity that will be realised through their marriage:

. . . though the tyrannous sword,
Which pierced Christ's heart, has cleft the world in twain
'Twixt class and class, opposing rich to poor,
Shall *we* keep parted? Not so. Let us lean
And strain together rather, each to each,
Compress the red lips of this gaping wound
As far as two souls can . . .

Assimilating Christian and socialist doctrine, Romney aligns the origin of
class antagonism with the fall from unity which originated in the piercing of
Christ's body. Despite the eventual insufficiency of Romney's materialistic
remedy for social evil, Barrett Browning, in deploying this imagery, expresses
that yearning for re-integration of the mythical bond between man and his
world which she, in common with many of her Victorian contemporaries,

believed had been stretched to its most 'gaping' extent in the nineteenth century. Romney acknowledges that fallen, class-conscious man can do little more than 'compress' the wound, and from the manner in which Barrett Browning imagines the Church scene where rich and poor come to witness this 'compressing' marriage, it would seem there *can* be no successful healing. The social body is deeply infected. Employing a language of violence and pestilence which reminds us of the suffering scorpion burnt by flame, the Roman eaten by insects, and the Druidic human sacrifices, Barrett Browning paints a grotesque picture.

The vision is infernal. How could a woman who had been secluded from society until the age of 39, and after that who had resided in Italy under the adoring protection of her husband, a woman who was a mother, who had written heart-rending poems about the untimely death of children and of female self-sacrifice such as 'Isobel's Child' and 'Bertha in the Lane'—how could this revered example of female virtue and delicacy describe that half of the wedding party which comes from 'Saint Giles' in the following language?

> . . . Faces? . . . phew,
> We'll call them vices, festering to despairs,
> Or sorrows, petrifying to vices: not
> A finger-touch of God left whole on them,
> All ruined, lost—the countenance worn out
> As the garment, the will dissolute as the act,
> The passions loose and draggling in the dirt
> To trip a foot up at the first free step!
> Those, faces? 'twas as if you had stirred up hell
> To heave its lowest dreg-fiends uppermost
> In fiery swirls of slime, . . .

As far as one can judge from reading her letters, the closest Barrett Browning ever got to such hellish faces was on a rare cab trip to Shoreditch in search of Flush, dog-napped from Wimpole Street. However, she was very close to such scenes of pestilential misery through her daily reading of newspapers, periodicals and novels of social realism (particularly of Sue, Hugo, and Balzac). Moreover, all readers of *The London Times* in the 1840s would have read uncensored reports of testimony before the various Parliamentary committees investigating conditions in the factories, mines and slum areas of the poor. The reports reveal a hellish world of stench, squalor, and disease, of open privies, of prostitutes and beggars living in dens which resembled animal lairs rather than human dwellings.

In February 1843 Barrett Browning read the entire Report of the Royal Commission on the Employment of Children and Young persons in

Mines and Manufactories (one of its Assistant Commissioners was her close correspondent, R.H. Horne): as a consequence of that reading, she was compelled to write her first poem of social protest, 'The Cry of the Children', which appeared in *Blackwood's Magazine* in August of that year. As an avid reader of virtually every kind of Victorian text, she was no stranger to representation of working-class suffering, and this, of course, is really the point—those faces 'festering to despairs' come from her extensive reading. In itself, the informing relationship between reading and writing in a poet's life is hardly remarkable, but by virtue of the limitations of Barrett Browning's experience, her work was generated more by text than it was by direct observation, and it seems as if these sections of *Aurora Leigh* are the hellish distillation of her readings in the Victorian discourse of the poor.

Let me emphasise that Barrett Browning's vision of the pestilential poor does not necessarily bespeak fear and loathing of the working class (in fact, her vision is governed as much by sympathy as it is by revulsion); the important point here is that her representation of that class is derived from the discourse of the poor with which she was most acquainted. The Parliamentary Papers, in particular, consistently employ a language of the inferno: bodies tumble together in crowded hovels, dunghills dominate the landscape, and all is festering and pestilential. Witnesses to this misery were by no means unsympathetic to what they saw (quite the contrary), but the language of their testimony frequently seems derived from the Christian imagery of hell—a stinking, festering hole. In a complex process of representation whereby the poor are implicitly punished by their own vice, they are imaginatively placed in the topos of the damned.

'Only a person with the wildest imagination' would have used the image of hell to describe the poor, observes Gardiner Taplin in his disparagement of *Aurora Leigh*. This is undeniable, and Barrett Browning was not the only Victorian writer to possess such an imagination. In Chapter 22 of Dickens's *Bleak House* (included in the seventh monthly number which appeared in September 1852) Messrs Snagsby and Bucket go in search of Jo, descending deeper in the depths of Tom-all-Alone's; they pass 'along the middle of a villainous street, undrained, unventilated, deep in black mud and corrupt water—though the roads are dry elsewhere—and reeking with such smells and sights that he, who has lived in London all his life, can scarce believe his senses. Branching from this street and its heaps of ruins, are other streets and court so infamous that Mr Snagsby sickens in body and mind, and feels as if he were going, every moment deeper down, into the infernal gulf.' Barrett Browning, who was working on her 'infernal' sections of *Aurora Leigh* in the early 1850s, was by no means singular in figuring the slums and their inhabitants as hellish, even if she was denied that direct observation of

London alleys which Dickens experienced on his night-time excursions with the Metropolitan police.

In some ways, however, Dickens's surrealistic vision of swelling London streets and grotesque humanity also owes less to direct observation than to a fantastic imagination—or, rather, less to the actual urban scene than to representation of it. Hogarth's 'Gin Lane' could well be a source for Field Lane in *Oliver Twist* and for the scene in *Aurora Leigh* as St Giles's Church when the stinking poor arrive to witness the marriage of social classes. As Oliver is dragged along by the Artful Dodger, the air is 'impregnated with filthy odours' and he sees 'heaps of children, who, even at that time of night, were crawling in and out at the doors, or screaming from the inside . . . little knots of houses, where drunken men and women were positively wallowing in filth'. On the way to St Giles's Church, chosen by Romney as the place for his transgressive convention of rich and poor, Hogarthian bodies invade the streets of Belgravia:

> Lame, blind, and worse—sick, sorrowful, and worse—
> The humours of the peccant social wound
> All pressed out, poured down upon Pimlico,
> Exasperating the unaccustomed air
> With a hideous interfusion. You'd suppose
> A finished generation, dead of plague,
> Swept outward from their graves into the sun,
> The moil of death upon them.

The metaphor of the 'social cleft' is both repeated and literalised as the symbolic wound in the social body literally stinks, presses out its suppurating matter. The people clog the streets, ooze into the church 'in a dark, slow stream, like blood', and Barrett Browning pushes her infernal imagery to a hideous conclusion as the movement of the crowd is likened to that of bruised snakes crawling and hissing out of a hole 'with shuddering involution'. As the stinking poor makes its serpentine procession, the upper classes sit with handkerchiefs to their noses and Barrett Browning aligns her pestilential, carnivalesque imagery with her poetics of healing by having one of the aristocrats observe that the present spectacle, 'this dismembering of society', resembles the tearing apart of Damien's body by horses. The social wound, the ruptured body, the bloody procession, all seem to congeal in a brutal image of the dismembered body/social state. In order to understand how Barrett Browning saw her vocation as poet intellectual in terms of cure for the wounded social body, it necessary to examine her politics etiology, so to speak, and her prescribed remedies. Defilement is the disease and artistic service is the medicine.

SUSANNA EGAN

Glad Rags For Lady Godiva: Woman's Story As Womanstance In Elizabeth Barrett Browning's Aurora Leigh

Tensions between gender and genre remain central to discussion of the writing of nineteenth-century women both because we are now reading the dilemmas embedded in their subject matter and because of the generic choices that they made. For no work can this discussion be more heated at the moment than for *Aurora Leigh*, Barrett Browning's generic anomaly novelized epic, collage, or hybrid novel-poem. *Aurora Leigh* demonstrates close ties with the traditions of novel and poetry, but combines these genres in order to achieve a double purpose: presentation of a narrative familiar to readers of prose fiction and simultaneous subversion of this same narrative by means of a dense imagery more common to poetry. Where the novel works realistically with a broad cross-section of characters and scenes from contemporary life and tells a familiar story of love frustrated and then fulfilled, the poem introduces key images that recur with cumulative semantic power and radically affect the novel's conclusion. (Figurative language essentially constitutes the poetic elevation in a work that is neither condensed nor mellifluous.)

In particular, Barrett Browning uses images of Lady Godiva and of Danae to enrich her treatment of marriage and prostitution and of the woman as artist; for both figures and with both (related) topics, vulnerable nakedness becomes the source of power. One virtue, furthermore, of the

From ESC: *English Studies in Canada* 20, no.3, (September 1994) © 1994 by Carleton University.

presentation of Godiva and Danae as images rather than as narratives (for Barrett Browning's purposes, Danae actually originates in a painting) is their wide metaphoric value; she releases them, as it were, from an arrested iconic pose into the narrative situation of women both in and beyond this work, thus enabling them to describe significantly related but distinctive modes of passive resistance to abuse as well as the political value of that resistance.

Barrett Browning also associates Lady Godiva's hair and Danae's shower of gold with the symbolic mantle of the prophet/poet, thus specifying the particular assumption of power that originates in this work in a woman's initial condition of weakness. That this combination of extreme weakness with remarkable power was central to her purpose becomes clear when we recognize that Marian (the traditional victim in terms both of gender and of class) rather than Aurora is the central determiner of meaning for both these images. Margaret Reynolds points out that "Barrett Browning gave Marian Erle, and not Aurora, a personal appearance which very closely resembled her own. . . . That Marian should be depicted as her author's physical self, while the character of Aurora portrayed her intellectual self-construction in writing, suggests . . . the inevitable duality which Barrett Browning conceived as necessary to the writing woman, a crossbreed, evolving out of a feminine nature and a masculine order." Such double focus that discloses two equally demanding identities has been described as a structural pattern of women's autobiography, reminding us that the issues that are central to *Aurora Leigh* were, of course, central also to Barrett Browning's life. The women figure who welcomes the new dawn is therefore richly composite; she is designed both to represent all her sisters and to refigure a woman's stance in literature.

This, of course, is why *Aurora Leigh* has become so important to feminist critics. Although it was popular when first published, *Aurora Leigh* was largely ignored for many decades after Barrett Browning's death and only reinstated (beginning with Woolf's appreciation) fairly recently. Feminists are placing it back in the literary canon both because of its considerable merit and because it is the *Künstlerroman* of a woman poet. But reinstatement has invited troubled discussion about the hybrid nature of the work, essentially because its genres seem to work against each other: the woman poet creates herself through the process of her poem, which celebrates female power and female subjectivity, and which values her art, in the process, above marriage and motherhood; the novelist, on the other hand, seems to renege on this position and "come down," as Margaret Forster puts it, "on the side of a convenient and melodramatic climax." Aurora's final union with her cousin Romney can be read as narrative weakness and failure. Not only does the poet seem to undervalue her art when she acknowledges her love, but she also seems to value the institution of marriage sufficiently to keep the fallen Marian and her fatherless child outside its hallowed precincts. Kathleen Blake refers to Marian, for instance, as "enshrouded, never to be decked out in nuptial imagery." Barrett Browning's hybrid genre, in other words, both states and denies her responsibility as woman and as poet.

Barrett Browning, of course, was working quite consciously in the main stream of the Romantic tradition: this is surely the origin of the autobiographic enterprise, of the confessional mode, of memory, and of subjective perception, as it is of her evaluation of her creative powers. It is from this tradition that she derives her sense of the poet as by now an acknowledged legislator of mankind, her sense of imagination as indeed a spiritual activity connecting the poet with nature, and her sense of a potential golden age. This last is curiously modified by the ugliness and hypocrisy that she satirizes in contemporary society, but remains realizable in revolution, to which she was passionately committed, and, within the poem, in her concluding vision of the New Jerusalem. It makes sense that a woman poet should look forward for her golden age and not back. We know that childhood for a woman was too often a tight cocoon from which she was not allowed to break. (And we think of Elizabeth Barrett, conveniently immobilized in her father's house, or, indeed, of Mariana in her lonely moated grange waiting for "him" to liberate her.) Woman's golden age is not inherited but to be made by means of the liberating creativity of her own inspired imagination seeking, out of the denials and fragmentation of her gifts, a satisfactory wholeness. Wordsworth's *Prelude* provides a partial model, as (to general distress in the Barrett household) does Byron's *Don Juan*. Epic and satire, both traditionally masculine prerogatives, contribute to the hybrid nature of this work.

More important, Barrett Browning, in dialogue with the literature of her time, fused these "male genres" with what has been called the "female genre' of the novel. She denied that the burning of Leigh Hall and the blinding of Romney Leigh at the end derive from the misadventures of Rochester in *Jane Eyre* (1847). Romney Leigh, however, offering Aurora a partnership in mission at the start is also Jane Eyre's cousin, St. John Rivers. Marian, the lowborn saint who suffers rape and single motherhood, derives from Gaskell's *Ruth* (1853), and may be read in the context of Little Em'ly (1850), Hetty Sorrel (1859), Fanny Robin (1874), and Tess (1891). Barrett Browning's social concerns, in particular the imaginative sympathy with which she seeks to transcend the class system, linking discriminations of class with those of sex, place her work squarely amidst the fiction of Disraeli, Kingsley, Dickens, and Gaskell. We can also draw close parallels, especially on the woman question, between her work and that Mme de Staël and George Sand (from whom, some suggest, she derived the name Aurora).

In her discussion of *Aurora Leigh* in relation to Tennyson's poem *The Princess*, Marjorie Stone points out that assumptions about genre and gender interact and structure both the creation and the reception of literary texts. When women move into male-defined genres and feel their feminine perceptions constrained by male discourse, they necessarily adapt what they find to create new and hybrid forms. The *Bildungsroman*, in particular presents women in a patriarchal culture with problems of narrative and of appropriate language. (The very fact that a woman is speaking in *Aurora Leigh* subverts the masculine forms and tropes that she is using.) As Alice Ostriker has pointed out, "[w]henever a poet employs a figure or story previously accepted and defined by a culture, the poet is using myth, and the potential is always present that the use will be revisionist: that is, the figure or tale will be appropriated for altered ends, the old vessel filled with new wine, initially satisfying the thirst of the individual poet but ultimately making culture change possible." Or, as Jacobus puts it, women necessarily work within a male discourse and therefore must "work ceaselessly to deconstruct it: to write what cannot be written." Stone's reading of *Aurora Leigh* in conjunction with Tennyson's *Princess* richly elaborates both the fun that Barrett Browning had with conventional expectations and the numerous ways in which she appropriated what she needed in order to create the organic form that she so keenly advocated.

The collage, the dialogue, the novel-poem should not, surely, contradict itself, however. The woman poet working so boldly in several male-defined genres should not undervalue her achievement by settling for domestic bliss at the end of the story. Barbara Gelpi looks with care at Aurora's relationship both with Lady Waldemar and with Romney Leigh and suggests that the conclusion of the story is no prelude to Victorian domesticity nor to an autobiographical Barrett/Browning romance; rather, where Lady Waldemar has expressed "the voice of Aurora's own self-distrust, the disabling faithlessness of the inner oppressor," Romney, the blind sea king, becomes a dramatic projection of that (blind) faith that is necessary for artistic creativity. Gelpi is persuasive in her analysis of Romney and Aurora "as the dual expression of a single though ambivalent mind," an analysis that "provides a different, interiorized plot to the poem." Wrestling with the same problem in her excellent essay, "Gender and Narration in *Aurora Leigh*," Alison Case writes about "the mixed narration of *Aurora Leigh*," which allowed Barrett Browning "to create a kind of double teleology for the novel, in which the struggle toward artistic independence and success, the plot of poetic 'ambition,' could be kept relatively isolated from the undermining influence of the traditional love-story, with its emphasis on female passivity and lack of emotional or sexual self-knowledge, its insistence on loving self-abnegation as the proper 'end' of female existence." More recently, Reynolds suggests that "by accepting this part of the ideology of patriarchy, Aurora might be courting a self-silencing; once she is complete as a woman—and resolved as a story—she will not be able to go on with the speaking/writing of the self but will be authored by conventional expectations . . . losing those imperatives of self-determination which were the incentive to narrative in the first place." Reynolds concludes that Aurora's determination to continue her professional career successfully negotiates and avoids this "potentially negative resolution."

I would like to go further. Using the recurring image of Lady Godiva, I would like to suggest that buried within the familiar plot that seems so stereotyped and sexist lies an even more radical enterprise than the development and affirmation of a woman poet or the treatment of prostitution and the dignifying of a fallen woman (which were certainly radical issues for Barrett Browning's contemporary readers). Focussing on the relationship between Aurora and Marian, I suggest that the happy-ever-after conclusion is itself subverted and radical, that it involves no capitulation to male-defined conventions, far less to the notion of the male liberator, but, rather, resolves the tensions inherent in radical issues such as woman's work and woman's power to break away from her helpless (or passive) role as victim. I would like to show how Barrett Browning works safely within the Romantic tradition and within the context of the contemporary novel to effect a new reading of a familiar story from within—creating anew, in Percy Shelley's terms, what has been blunted by reiteration. She does this, furthermore, by focussing on the issue of prostitution, specifically the rape of poor Marian, and the ways in which that reverberates through the poem and is central to its meaning. Woman as narrator and as protagonist, in other words, reverses our expectations of what constitutes helplessness and vulnerability, what constitutes decency and shame (both tied to the issues of woman as artist and woman as wife, or as fallen), and who is the liberator of whom.

Combining the realism of the novel (she wanted to "touch this everyday life of our age, & hold it with [her] two hands" with the charged potency of poetry, Barrett Browning has Aurora Leigh reject various forms of male empowerment in order to assume a prophet's mantle that is both poetic and personal; it is central to the subversive nature of the poetic imagery and to the conventional narrative. Romney, for example, fails to recognize Aurora's role; he belittles her verse in Book Two, telling her that Miriam's song can follow after Moses has seen to the slaying of Egypt. By Book Eight, however, he acknowledges her power and is compelled to describe his own near-drowning from lack of faith while she stood "singing on the shore." Another mantle that Aurora assumes only briefly—when she tells Marian to marry Romney—is that which Aaron, like Elijah, takes off at the moment of death. The woman poet must also be prepared to shed her mantle for other women to wear, but her transmission of power lacks precedents and is problematic, because of the choices seemingly forced on her by gender. So we hear that pretty Kate Ward, nestling into marriage with Carrington, reflecting his soul in truly feminine adoration, insists on his painting her portrait in a cloak like Aurora's. The notion is challenging for Carrington yet also coy; Kate Ward is mistress and muse, not free-standing subject or artist.

The cloak of the prophet, which must pass from one generation to the next, is also in this case a woman's garment to be worn or removed. Aurora/Miriam as prophet needs extraordinary faith in order to sing when Romney/Moses does not believe her power is significant, even though he flounders in the waters, or is comparable to the ungodly Egyptians, if he devalues her role. Aaron is instructed to take off his priestly robe when he is a very old man and about to die and he will pass it on to his sons in their generations as priests of Israel. Neither Miriam nor Aaron, however, provides a sufficiently complex model for Aurora Leigh, who has to choose between poetry and marriage. As a nineteenth-century heroine she cannot, so to speak, wear her cloak and shed it. Nor can she, in shedding for marriage the power that the cloak represents, envisage for herself such hereditary succession as Aaron's. Both the human vulnerability of the everyday life/novelistic heroine, however, and the desired apotheosis of the prophet/poet require the removal of this symbolic garment; Barrett Browning can use the power of poetry but must also, in her "touch [of] this everyday life," reveal her heroine as woman.

So Barrett Browning combines the imagery of the prophet's cloak with the image of Lady Godiva, who, in her helplessness as the wife of a powerful man, sheds her clothing to achieve her righteous ends. Unlike Aaron's or Elijah's, Lady Godiva's undressing is explicitly sexual and therefore dangerous for her; she is valuable to this poem because she risks personal exposure to serve a political purpose, thereby converting female vulnerability to female heroism. Challenged by her tyrannical husband to expose herself in order to help the poor, Lady Godiva does so, her purity ensured both by the covering of her own abundant hair and by the selfless love with which she turns naked submission (like the helplessness of the victim of rape) into creative action (like that of the woman poet). Lady Godiva is not, in fact, passive, and Lady Godiva is effective. Two particular images connected with Lady Godiva recur in *Aurora Leigh*—the belts or crowns that bind and cinch and the hair and clothing that fall free.

Tennyson's Lady Godiva, we may remember, sends a herald out to proclaim that "she would loose / The people," whereupon she "Unclasp'd the wedded eagles of her belt, / The grim Earl's gift. . . . [A]non she shook her head, / And shower'd the rippled ringlets to her knee; / Unclad herself in haste; . . . Then she rode forth, clothed on with chastity." In Tennyson's version, which Barrett Browning certainly knew, the only man who fails to recognize the importance and value of her heroic self-exposure is Peeping Tom, who is struck blind—like Romney Leigh. The woman who asserts her own subjectivity does not remain a helpless object of the male gaze.

Mermin discusses Lady Godiva not in relation to *Aurora Leigh* but as a symbol to Barrett Browning of the ways in which she as a woman could take risks for women's issues and indeed for the wider causes of social reform. She refers, for example, to letters of 1831 indicating Barrett Browning's support for the Reform Bill. When the Anti-Corn-Law League asked her to write a poem in support of their cause in 1845, she wanted to do so. Her father, however, and her brothers, and even her cousin John Kenyon, on whose help she so constantly relied, overwhelmed her with their scorn of women and/or poets involving themselves with politics. Writing in distress to Mary Russell Mitford, she wonders whether she would not indeed be an embarrassment to her family and friends if she took "such a prominent post in the political ground, harp in hand & petticoat down to the ankles. But," she adds, "I am writing ungenerously—I feel I am. *Not like a Godiva.*"

Barrett Browning had Godiva on her mind because of some recent correspondence with Harriet Martineau. Martineau had gone public with the news that mesmerism had cured her of uterine cancer. Barrett Browning wrote to Mitford about her horrified admiration of Martineau's courage: "[I]f she believed that her sufferings were in any way connected with the *conditions of her womanhood*, she was . . . very brave indeed." Her letter of sympathy to Martineau herself produced the response: "I took my part deliberately,— *knowing privacy to be impossible*, & making up my mind to *entail* publicity as the only course faithful to truth and human welfare. I cannot tell you how the thought of *Godiva* has sustained and inspired me." To Mitford, Barrett Browning resumes, "She says, she was prepared for the publicity; & *she thinks of Godiva*. . . . I admire her more than ever. I always did admire the *moral heroic* beyond all things . . . next to genius." If she had failed herself to be a Godiva in 1845, Barrett Browning set out to demonstrate both the moral heroic and genius in *Aurora Leigh.*

The moral heroic is both stated and subverted when Romney Leigh, idealist, social reformer, burdened with money and distinction, fails to persuade the poet to prefer action with him over her heartfelt vocation, and turns to Marian, saintly and persecuted child of the people, for an exemplary marriage across class lines. She will be the heart and he will be the head. In Book Four we have an extraordinary scene of moral and social chaos in the church, and Marian fails to turn up. In fact, she has been persuaded by Lady Waldemar to leave the country, but the point here, in a scene of vivid chaos that anticipates the fire at Leigh Hall and the violent destruction of all Romney's best efforts, is that Marian is unavailable for the rescue that he has had in mind. Indeed, when we next see Marian in the streets of Paris with a baby in her arms, we are tempted to cast Romney, her would-be-saviour, as villain of the piece, the James Steerforth, the Squire Donnithorne, the Alec D'Urberville, wayward, restless, interfering, unaware of what it is that Marian as Marian really needs.

Romney, of course, does not deserve this. He is an honourable man, own cousin to Charles Kingsley or Frederic Denison Maurice. The rescue he attempts, however, is part of the larger scene of prostitution that pervades the work, not the references to or glimpses of prostitutes in the streets that so shocked Victorian mamas, but, rather, the conventional perception of male/female relationships, which is defined in terms of the male heroic. So, we must hastily point out, he is innocent of intended harm to Marian. Lady Waldemar's servant has spirited her away to a brothel in Paris, where she is drugged and raped. This betrayal and violence have actually been anticipated in her story to the poet of how she had fled from her brutal parents after her mother had come upon her suddenly:

> And snatching in a sort of breathless rage
> Her daughter's headgear comb, let down the hair
> Upon her like a sudden waterfall,
> Then drew her drenched and passive by the arm
> Outside the hut they lived in. When the child
> Could clear her blinded face from all that stream
> Of tresses . . . there, a man stood, with beast's eyes
> That seemed as they would swallow her alive.

This, in fact, is the wicked squire, the Peeping Tom, who is dangerous because he sees her only as an object of his desire and not in her own integrity. In Godiva-purity, she flees into what becomes her alternative, marriage to Romney, who does, at this point, rescue her. Her own desires in this rescue, her heartbeats,

> might as well as written on the dust
> Where some poor bird, escaping from hawk's beak
> Has dropped and beats its shuddering wings.

Marian's plight, dramatically compounded by her role as victim of class and of sex, is equivalent to that of Aurora, who is Romney's cousin, more evidently the heart to work with his head, and who suffers no such violence but is exposed instead to the sanctioned prostitution of marriage. Aurora's equivalent danger is quite simply need and convention. Romney's suit is pressed on her as appropriate for the estate, as a duty, and not least as a safeguard against poverty. Her father's sister, her hair braided tight to tame any accidental thoughts, has trained her in the cage-bird life,

> Accounting that to leap from perch to perch
> Was act and joy enough for any bird.

Aurora resists Romney's proposal as she later rejects out of hand invitations to marry other men who would make her respectable and keep her in funds. Resistance, for Aurora, as for Marian, is based on self-respect, and the discovery against considerable odds of a womanstance, independent of compromise, barter, and sale. Aurora, indeed, speaks bitterly of the conventional use of marriage as keeping love to pay our debts with:

> We haggle for the small change of our gold,
> And so much love accord for so much love,
> Rialto-prices.

Such marriage is prostitution, even when described as Lord Howe describes it, as protection from the exigencies of poetic inspiration, which he presents as a rape that, in narrative sequence, anticipates Marian's. Marriage, he tells her, would be a tripod

> To throne such feet as yours, my prophetess,
> At Delphi. Think,—the god comes down as fierce
> As twenty bloodhounds, shakes you, strangles you,
> Until the oracular shriek shall ooze in froth!
> At best 'tis not all ease,—at worst too hard:
> A place to stand on is a 'vantage gained,
> And here's your tripod. To be plain, dear friend,
> You're poor. . . .

Lord Howe's violent metaphor of Apollo-like bloodhounds brutalizing the oracle into utterance connects Aurora with Marian as a fluttering bird or wild fawn in desperate flight. For the poet-prophet, Miriam not Moses, kin to Wordsworth in her struggle to follow her vocation, a marriage of convenience that would protect her even from violence such as this is unacceptable. Lord Howe's proposal stiffens her resolve even as it makes her journey hard. She

> answered slow,—as some wayfaring man,
> Who feels himself at night too far from home,
> Makes steadfast face against the bitter wind.

Lady Waldemar disclaims her part in Marian's ruin, and she may technically be right in doing so. But when we are not our brother's keeper. Aurora says, we are his Cain. The lives and the interconnected rescue and responsibility of Marian and Aurora for each other, by means of which they become responsive and creative reflections of each other, centre on another image that pertains to both of them, describing again for one a physical and for the other a poetic rape and impregnation, and that is the image of the rape of Danae by Zeus.

The painter Carrington invites Aurora's response to two sketches he has made for Danae:

> A tiptoe Danae, overbold and hot,
> Both arms a-flame to meet her wishing Jove
> Halfway, and burn him faster down; the face
> And breasts upturned and straining, the loose locks
> All glowing with the anticipated gold.
> Or here's another on the self-same theme.
> She lies here—flat upon her prison-floor
> The long hair swathed about her to the heel
> Like wet seaweed. You dimly see her through
> The glittering haze of that prodigious rain,
> Half blotted out of nature by a love
> As heavy as fate. I'll bring you either sketch.
> I think, myself, the second indicates
> More passion.

The second Danae, of course, is Godiva-like in her quiet submission, and in the covering of hair. (The second Danae may remind us, also, that the young Aurora blinds herself with the dew of an ivy crown on her birthday, then trails it in dismay at Romney's reaction to her. Meditating on these alternative versions of Danae in prison receiving her god, Aurora too perceives the second as more passionate because "Self is put away." Danae not striving or aspiring becomes the recipient artist-soul. So "We'll be calm,

/ And know that, when indeed our Joves come down, / We all turn stiller than we have ever been."

Similarly, Marian, suffering not seduction but violence from man, indignant that this can be interpreted as shame to her, claims that she has not been raped but murdered, and that, lying (passive) in the ditch, she has discovered embedded in her flesh some coin of price, dropped there by God as payment for her loss. The child is hers alone and she lives no longer as a woman but only through her mother-love. She becomes, in fact, the Virgin Mary, submissive handmaid of the Lord, "Sweet holy Marian," swearing to her purity by the child that she raises up on high. The merging of these myths is harmonious because both Danae and Mary welcome their creative roles and give birth to saviours. The pagan Danae references precede allusion to the Virgin Mary, thus enabling Barrett Browning's treatment of rape to convey both divine and physical impregnation, both poetic and womanly gifts. Danae, in other words, merges the two women and ensures that "Sweet holy Marian" is not rarified but realistic. As Joyce Zonana puts it, "[w]hat Marian calls God's 'coin' is the product of woman's normal biological capacity. It is Marian's female physiology, her 'blood,' that becomes her token of divinity". What is shocking to convention is this interpretation of the fallen woman, who does not go away or die, and does not kill her child, but is sanctified by life and becomes the alter ego whom the poet quests to find. We need to look briefly at Marian as the object of Aurora's quest, and at the yet further reversal of conventional expectations by which the object is shown to be a self-creating subject, like the poet herself.

Writing about her responsibility to speak up on behalf of women, Barrett Browning suggests that the alternative is to be dumb and die. Both the women speak; they tell their stories; they identify their sufferings; resistance to violence takes the form of vocal choice. Reynolds reminds us that "Aurora, as narrator, shows herself to be aware of the various attempts foisted upon her as an individual—and a woman—to write her story for her. . . . Only with the destruction of [these texts] is she released into the possibility of self-construction." Aurora blames herself for not speaking out in anticipation of disaster when Marian disappears. Later, when she finds Marian, she wonders whether to write to Romney, but saves words until she is clear about what to say. Marian, however, now speaks clearly for herself; energetically she reverses the conventional association of innocence in a woman with silence. Aurora is responsible not for Marian's story but for the poetic vision of the New Jerusalem in the glorious dawn with which the poem ends.

But these women are also responsible to each other as respondent to each other's self-creation in resistance, specifically, to Romney. ("The trajector; described by Marian Erle's career," says Reynolds, "inverts the pattern of Aurora's to demonstrate the essential need of the individual (woman) to establish a security of self-recognition." Gelpi's reading of Romney as Aurora's male alter ego opens the whole issue of the Victorian polarities of art and work, especially as their union at the end justifies Aurora's meditation on "the essential prophet's word," which does more for a man "Than if you dressed him in a broadcloth coat / And warmed his Sunday pottage at your fire." Aurora's resistance to Romney begins with his devaluation of her poetry, develops in terms of characterization that move toward self-knowledge, and is central to this issue of the ultimate value of poetry. As Mermin puts it: "Barrett Browning retains the conventional identification of woman with the inner, spiritual, emotional, and subjective sphere: with poetry, and with poems. Instead of switching gender roles she switches the locus of power within them, the novelistic story concluding with an assertion of the primacy of poetry over the novel and of women over men. If power resides in the inner life, it belongs to poetry, and to women and so to the woman poet most of all." We need to bear in mind the commonest Victorian assumptions about appropriate subject matter and treatment against which Barrett Browning makes such bold assertions.

Aurora is responsible for Marian's initial resistance to Romney, though she does not know this until later, because she sows in Marian's mind a self-respecting concern about the nature of Romney's love. Accepting his rescue of her, turning to him in gratitude as to a god, Marian had no thought to ask whether in fact he loved her. Aurora's quest for Marian is not an immediate consequence in the plot of Marian's disappearance but grows, rather, out of Aurora's own malaise, also connected with Romney. Both women, in other words, learn to exercise their words of power in desperate self-definition and in resistance to the ethics and sexual mores of their time. Like Marian, Aurora suffers from Romney's perception of her role; maybe the small shepherd girl asleep among her scattered sheep, he says, does less harm than the overzealous sheepdog who bites a kid. Aurora rejects sleep, rejects pastoral, and claims, as he puts it, that she is breaking mythic turf with the crooked ploughs of actual life.

In actual life, however, Aurora is, as a good Romantic poet should be, lonely. She envies other poets the mothers and wives who reward their efforts. Fighting free of the tight spaces of convention that threaten to bury her alive, she turns herself into a Godiva-poet:

> I drop my cloak,
> Unclasp my girdle, loose the band that ties
> My hair . . . now could I but unloose my soul!

What she does is sell her father's books to realize the money to take her to Italy, her mother's country, to receive herself from "a beaker full of the warm South." Her rejection of language for place of birth, of father for mother, notably includes these realistic and practical concerns that are common to the novel; her ability to uproot herself symbolically depends in part on the common coin that commodifies women like books. (Books, of course, that cater to commercial needs are, like women, soiled.) Such practical matters are not part of the parlance of elevated poetry, but serve in passing to reconnect the genres of this work.

In transition, in Paris, Aurora contemplates the difference between theory and practice, between philanthropy and poetry, which is "the essential prophet's word / That comes in power." Not bread but the word alone conjures up Marian's face, which disappears into the crowd. The recognition, which is mutual, is momentous. Marian's face bursts in upon Aurora's preoccupations like a long-lost face, now dead, floating from the depths to the surface of a pond. The plunge, the splash, and the pursuit are literal and metaphorical simultaneously. The crowd fragments into individual collisions as it absorbs and buries that momentary recognition. The episode is dramatic and bears comparison with Wordsworth's blind beggar,

> Wearing a written paper to explain
> His story, whence he came, and who he was.
> Caught by the spectacle, my mind turned round
> As with the might of waters; an apt type
> This Label seemed, of the utmost we can know,
> Both of ourselves and of the universe;
> And on the Shape of that unmoving Man,
> His steadfast face, and sightless eyes, I gazed
> As if admonished from another world.

Of central importance to Aurora's moment of recognition, however, is the fact that her vision is of a woman's face that also sees her, in other words, is its own subject making its own response. "[T]hose eyes / . . . I do remember, saw me too, / As I saw them, with conscious lids astrain / In recognition." We might contrast with this mirror image the mirroring by Kate Ward of her future husband's soul; such mirroring, after all, is what makes her an appropriate muse and wife. "I've painted her . . . . / The whole sweet face," he writes. "[I]t looks upon my soul / Like a face on water, to beget itself."

Indeed, when Aurora actually finds and grabs Marian in the flower market at dawn, she makes a mistake in trying to lead her home:

Not a word
She said, but . . .
. . . followed closely where I went,
As if I led her by a narrow plank
Across devouring waters, step by step.

The journey is as tense and purposeful as Wordsworth's crossing of the
Simplon Pass, with an enriched reversal of intent as Marian refuses to go
further and Aurora becomes the one to follow:

Then she led
The way, and I, as by a narrow plank
Across devouring waters, followed her,
Stepping by her footsteps, breathing by her breath,
And holding her with eyes that would not slip.

This reversal of roles reiterates the reversal of all expectations. Just as
Romney's offer of marriage to each woman is implicated with the rape of
each, just as Marian's baby, born to woman alone, is an honour from God to
a woman who is pure, so now Aurora's mistaken assumption that she can
rescue Marian becomes Marian's assertive rescue of her. Cooper develops
Marian's role in releasing Aurora from the patriarchal assumptions that
handicap the woman committed to man's work; commenting on the fact that
Aurora begins by "translating" Marian's story, she points out that Marian in
Paris "transforms woman from scorned object to angry subject."
      Failing to recognize her own love for Romney, Aurora has separated
head from heart and art from life. Such dichotomizing, furthermore, limits
both her moral and her imaginative grasp of the situation; she sees Marian's
small, grave-like room and rosy baby only as proof of Marian's guilt and
shame. Failing as compassionate woman and as visionary poet, she mediates,
in other words, between conventional response to such a situation and the
inner reality that Marian manifests as a new revelation. She mediates, also, in
what Blake has discussed as the "self-postponement" of the woman artist,
between the male-desiring Lady Waldemar and the increasingly self-
defining Marian. Aurora herself needs rescuing, and Marian, who has
suffered through external violence and consequent inner madness, has
attained the wisdom that the artist needs, a self-affirming reception of her
shower of gold. Lady Waldemar here becomes the other Danae, reaching
greedily for what she cannot have. Aurora, of course, controls our perception
of this complex character and reveals her own secret desires. She sees Lady
Waldermar's love as of the rialto kind; to declare it in so unmaidenly a

fashion is coarse, like eating garlic. She is a Lamia, a deceiver. She must feign interest in Romney's social work in her attempts to reach his heart, and gives money to his cause to prove her dedication. When gossip at a party describes her, it is as a flower that "neither sews nor spins,—and takes no thought / Of her garments . . . falling off." Far from associating her with Godiva, this crude assessment causes listeners to flinch and draw back their chairs as if they spied black beetles on the floors.

What Marian and Aurora achieve by contrast is a new definition of purity and courage; they step outside the conventions that determine what is garlic, and they assess situations that are conventionally problematic for women in terms of their personal experience. They belong together, furthermore, by virtue of the isolation of their separate predicaments. "I who have written much," Aurora begins, "Will write my story." "I, writing thus," she says at another point, or "[t]oo young, to sit alone . . . I write." The first-person pronoun, the tense shifts that indicates the ongoing activity of translating experience into language, merge with Marian's story. Where she had originally felt that Romney might write his name upon her, as seemed natural, she now speaks for herself: "I, Marian Erle, myself, alone, undone." She invites Aurora to tell her what to say when Romney offers marriage once again, this time to a "ruined maid" with a fatherless child. The selfless generosity of his second offer, of course, suggests one solution to the story that would subvert conventional plotting. But it will not do. For Marian to accept Romney now would make him once again the conventional definer of her identity and reduce her to such conventional definition. (Angela Leighton compares Marian's rejection of Romney here with Aurora's earlier rejection, suggesting that both women assert themselves against the "law of the father." Conventions might indeed be shattered, but she would be respectable and he would be a hero. Aurora tells her to believe his love and marry him. She too is being heroic, but she is not being honest. Here, at the very end, Marian has to reiterate the truly Romantic womanstance in which the traditional object redefines herself as subject because she speaks not out of custom but out of her own inner conviction.

If the novel uses romantic fulfilment as a feature of self-knowledge and as a happy resolution to the complexities of plot, the poetic elements focus on Marian to remind us of the rich palimpsest of issue in this hybrid genre. Barrett Browning elevates the prosaic difficulties of women's daily life and love and work into the domain of high seriousness—of art. At the novelistic level, the story ends "happily ever after" because Marina's rejection of Romney saves the plot from an impossible denouement and releases Romney and Aurora to avow their love for each other. To read it only this way, however, is to ignore the combination of prose fiction with poetry.

Indeed, Marian is unmarriageable and is condemned to a life of sacrificial motherhood, but several important things have happened on Lady Godiva's journey to alter the lot of such fallen women. For a start, the class barrier has been overcome not by marriage but by the profoundly felt sisterhood of these two women. Secondly, Marian's motherhood has been hallowed and sanctified and related very closely to the creativity of the poet. Thirdly, she has reversed roles both with the philanthropic Romney and with the poet Aurora. She who has journeyed through hell and lived to tell her tale is a saviour for them both. And finally, against even the poet's initial assumptions, this is her story. She will not marry Romney, because, much as she admires him, she does not love him. The fallen woman of the Victorian novel turns like the proverbial worm to reject patriarchal assumptions about what might rescue her. She knows what prostitution is and will not sell her soul for a mess of conventional decency. Identified in her creativity with the poet and asserting herself as subject, Marian provides the fullest because all-encompassing possibilities for woman. She is born of the generic mix of prose and poetry. Her story demonstrates transmission of power in womanly community, both the passing of the prophet's mantle and recognition that for the poet and for the woman self-exposing courage calls attention to her power. Surely this celebration of the redefined chastity in which she rides forth clothed constitutes glad rags for Lady Godiva.

TRICIA LOOTENS

Canonization Through Dispossession: Elizabeth Barrett Browning and the "Pythian Shriek"

"How do I love thee? Let me count the ways." Surely no line of Victorian poetry is quoted so frequently, or in such dichotomous contexts, as the opening of Poem 43 in Elizabeth Barrett Browning's *Sonnets from the Portuguese*. Under most circumstances, the line raises a smile, "How do I love this job?" snarls a puffy Boynton cartoon cat, printed on reminder notes; "Let us count the ways," reads a slogan for Arby's fast food. Occasionally, the parody is more pointed. In a *New Yorker* cartoon, for example, an exhausted, beringletted Miss Barrett accepts an abacus—and a reminder to carry the fives—from a bearded Browning. In certain cases, however—in wedding ceremonies, for example, and in Valentine's Day readings—"How do I love thee . . ." evokes a reverent, if edgy, hush. Moved, perhaps in spite of themselves, audiences participate in the ritual invocation of Barrett Browning's verse as a pure and absolute expression of romantic love. Sentimental the *Sonnets* may be, popular culture acknowledges, but they are also sacred.

Are the *Sonnets* sacred as literature, however, or as something else? Moreover, what does their dual canonization as standing jokes and ritual readings have to do with the canonization of Barrett Browning or of her other works? The two questions are interconnected: although the *Sonnets* have long defined E. B. B.'s fame, they themselves have not been defined as

From *Lost Saints: Silence Gender and Victorian Literary Canonization* © 1996 by University Press of Virginia.

suitable objects for critical attention. Most of us think we know the *Sonnets* but how many of us, even students and teachers of English literature, have actually studied them? Like their author, they have come close to being simultaneously canonized and lost.

For a sense of the shape of this paradox, one need only turn to a self-described "living monument in the field of American Letters": Houghton Mifflin's 1974 Cambridge edition of Barrett Browning's *Poetical Works*, which has served many students in the United States as an affordable standard resource. The dustjacket of this volume promises to "meet all the needs of the general reader and student." Its introductory essay, by Ruth M. Adams, clearly numbers canonical revision and editing among those needs: "Who reads Elizabeth Barrett Browning? More people, but not a vast number. Historians . . . will read selectively in *Casa Guidi Windows* and *Poems before Congress. Aurora Leigh* has been rediscovered by those who appreciate its vignettes of society, high and low, its concentration on women, their aspirations to independence and self-sufficiency, and its rejection of mid-Victorian taboos on subject matter. But the audience that is most assured and most numerous consists of those in love or in love with love, who find the *Sonnets from the Portuguese* a full and satisfying expression of their emotions. Certainly some of these sonnets are destined for a modest immortality, but immortality nonetheless."

True to the dustjacket's promises, Adams thus "identifies the [relatively few] poems of Mrs. Browning that have proved of lasting value or interest," assigning to each an authorized audience. With *Casa Guidi Windows, Poems before Congress,* and a few other verses relegated to the historians, lovers of literature are left only *Aurora Leigh* and the *Sonnets*—that is, insofar as they seek only a first reading. For after that, "it is not to *Aurora Leigh*, effective as parts may be, that the reader will return. It is too discursive, too tedious, too platitudinous in most of its sentiments, too much on the level of melodrama in its basic narrative to command respect or liking." Thus, this standard edition of Barrett Browning firmly admonishes against any temptation to reread *Aurora Leigh*: the "living monument" is inscribed with a keep-off sign. Only the *Sonnets* remain, to "give Elizabeth Barrett Browning her modest but secure place as a true lyric poet."

The *Sonnets*, that is—and something else. Having reduced Barrett Browning's canonical claims to a single work, Adams proceeds to locate the cultural value of that work not only in its capacity to offer a "full and satisfying expression" of the "emotions" of "those in love or in love with love" but in its service as clear documentation for the poet's love story: "Directness of communication plus the legend of her own life, assures that [Barrett Browning] will be read both for the pleasure the poems give and

from curiosity about her own romantic love affair with Robert Browning."
The *Sonnets'* glory is that of the legend.

Adams's introduction first appeared in 1974. By 1977, William S.
Peterson was writing that "the chief obstacle to an intelligent understanding
of Mrs. Browning's poetry is the mythological fog which envelops her life."
That cloying fog, which was thickest in the vicinity of the *Sonnets*, was
already beginning to lift. In the slow-moving world of standard pedagogy, as
represented by the Cambridge edition, however, it has yet to dissipate.
Conservative at its first printing, that Adams introduction still stands—and
with it a long-standing tradition that both limits E. B. B.'s claim to literary
recognition to the *Sonnets* and sets up obstacles even to the *Sonnets'* critical
study.

In such a context, Peterson's description of the *Sonnets* as a "dark,
allusive work irradiated with occasional visionary glimpses" might come as a
surprise. So, too, might the *Sonnets* themselves, however. Indeed, so natural
has it become to value—and devalue—the Portuguese sonnets as a simple,
transparent, and thus "full and satisfying expression" of the emotions of
those who are "in love or in love with love," that it is worth pausing here to
reconsider the sequence that Robert Browning termed his "strange, heavy
crown." For recognition of the *Sonnets'* strangeness, heaviness, and eccentric
richness is an indispensable prerequisite for understanding their virtual loss
as works of art.

To gain a sense of what is at stake, one need only focus on the first
action in the sequence. To quote the sonnet in full:

> I thought once how Theocritus had sung
> Of the sweet years, the dear and wished-for years,
> Who each one in a gracious hand appears
> To bear a gift for mortals, old or young:
> And, as I mused it in his antique tongue,
> I saw, in gradual vision through my tears,
> The sweet, sad years, the melancholy years,
> Those of my own life, who by turns had flung
> A shadow across me. Straightway I was 'ware,
> So weeping, how a mystic Shape did move
> Behind me, and drew me backward by the hair;
> And a voice said in mastery, while I strove,—
> "Guess now who holds thee?"—"Death," I said.
> But, there,
> The silver answer rang,—"not Death, but Love."

In a sense, this sonnet offers what Adams's introduction and conventional literary tradition promise: a moving evocation of the power of love and a verse record of the Brownings' courtship. The speaker here is no Every woman, however. Not only does she believe herself to be near death, but she seeks consolation by quoting Theocritus in the "antique tongue." One has to revise and edit a great deal to render such a love generic. Even then, if one expects the speaker to offer a "full and satisfactory expression" of one's own emotion, one may tend not only to read her peril of death as overblown but to flatten the poem's eroticism. The image of Love drawing back the speaker's hair is one whose passionate precision arises from historical specificity. Love's mystic shape is of the speaker's time, not ours. His gesture not only refutes a genuine expectation of death but establishes an intimate claim whose erotic power is deeply, thoroughly Victorian.

Victorian, that is, in the sense of arising from a specific moment in time—but not necessarily Victorian in the sense generally associated with the *Sonnets*. For if the *Sonnets'* speaker is too individual, too historically determined to sing the praises of generic love, her speech itself is surely too abstract, too inwardly focused, and too transgressive or ambivalent to suit readers in search of a representatively quaint historical romantic love affair. Here, too, the drawing back of the hair suggests how such expectations not only overlook the *Sonnets'* very sources of power but block their recognition. For though the *Sonnets* have become justifiably renowned for reversing the courtly tradition of love poetry by speaking romantic desire in a woman's voice, they radically rewrite another famous encounter as well: the courtship of Death and the Maiden.

Much as the lovely, doomed Maiden awaits her lover, only to be overwhelmed by the sinister gallantry of another guest, the *Sonnets'* faded weeping speaker sits in apparent expectation of Death's "mystic shape." When Love arrives in his place, the erotic, gothic struggle that ensues is both new and uncannily familiar. As the medieval maiden insists upon life, Barrett's speaker struggles for death. Love has made a mistake, she insists, or is offering one final test of faith. For God has laid the "curse" of "Nay" on her eyelids, like pennies on the eyes of a corpse. If God offers her a saving "baptism" through the sweetness of Love, he must be presenting it in a self-sacrificial "cup of dole." Death's dew has anointed her forehead, the speaker implies: she is doomed and shriven, promised elsewhere. No (mere) earthly lover should attempt to intervene in the performance of such a promise. Brandishing that equivalent of a "sepulchral urn," her smoldering heart, she warns her would-be lover to back off, lest fire "scorch and shred" him. Her very breath, she assures him, is poison fit to shatter his "Venice-glass."

Like her predecessor, the *Sonnets'* speaker ultimately accepts the substitution of suitors. In place of the heavenly reward she had believed promised by her own "ministering life-angel," whose eyes were fixed "upcast" to the "white throne of God, she accepts an earthly lover, "not unallied / To angels"—a lover who is a worker of lifegiving miracles as well as a poet: "budding, at thy sight, my pilgrim's staff / Gave out green leaves." Now ranked among "God's gifts," her lover proves that "Love, as strong as Death, retrieves as well." The speaker's eventual submission to the "mastery" of this "new angel" is paradoxical, however: she has been crushed low as if by "sword," and yet her conqueror has lifted her up from "abasement." Saved and vanquished at once, she abandons not the conventional modesty of maidenhood but the heroic discipline of divinely ordained asceticism:

> my soul, instead
> Of dreams of death, resumes life's lower range.
> Then, love me, Love! look on me—breathe on me!
> As brighter ladies do not count it strange,
> For love, to give up acres and degree
> I yield the grave for thy sake, and exchange
> My near sweet view of Heaven, for earth with thee.

Perhaps one form of sainthood has been replaced by another . Once "a poor, tried, wandering singer . . . leaning up a cyprus tree," she had told her lover, "The chrism is on thine head,—on mine, the dew,—/ And Death must dig the level where these agree." Now, anointed by a kiss, "the chrism of love, which love's own crown, / With sanctifying sweetness, did precede," she no longer "sings" while weeping. She longs, toward the poem's close, to shoot "My soul's full meaning into future years, / That *they* should lend it utterance, and salute / Love that endures, from Life that disappears!" The patient ascetic has become a noisy prophetess; the deathly ash of her "heavy heart" has been transformed into the fertile (if weedy) "heart's ground" from which the *Sonnets* themselves have been drawn.

"Romantic" this may be—and expressive, no doubt, at least at points, of the emotions of those in love (or in love with love). One cannot help wondering, however, how often close reading may have thwarted readers' recourse to the *Sonnets* for "a full and satisfying expression" of their own emotions. To a reader such a Christina Rossetti, the *Sonnets'* ambivalence about restoration to life and to earthly love may well have been deeply resonant, for example, but what of other readers? As Dorothy Mermin points out, there is a long history of "embarrassment" over the *Sonnets*. Although such embarrassment no doubt has many origins, one may well be the text's capacity to transform would-be condescension into confusion. Expecting a Victorian valentine, one finds instead the "strange, heavy crown" of a difficult, ambitious, and deeply personal art—not to mention the passionate idiosyncracies of a speaker whose angelic lover, in one version of the *Sonnets*, makes her feel "as safe as witches." If the *Sonnets* are embarrassing, it may be because the experience of reading them reveals the extent to which we, and not they, rely upon dreams of simple, innocently sentimental Victorian love. We must question our faith in that love—in that safe form of secular sanctity—if we are to come to terms with the *Sonnets'* strangeness and power.

Styles of Sanctity: Barrett Browning's Early Canonic Crises

Though Elizabeth Barrett Browning came closer to achieving full literary canonicity than any of Victorian England's other female poets, hers was always an unstable cultural presence. Decades of criticism agreed with the *Eclectic Review* that Barrett Browning's existence had done something "in a very emphatic way" to "settle the question" of the "intellectual relation of the sexes." The question was, what? Metaphoric monuments to Barrett Browning's glory tended to teeter between extremes—between evocations of a Comtean honorary "Great Manhood" and of the "eternal," generic category of femininity, for example; or between emphasis on poetic wonder and feminine virtue. Although such instabilities were inherent in any attempt to canonize a woman poet, in Barrett Browning's case they were exacerbated both by the poet's own active role in shaping feminine canonicity and by the complex and at points paradoxical relations between her public and private personae.

Surely few women poets can have been more deeply and explicitly concerned with issues of feminine canonicity than Elizabeth Barrett Browning—or more challenging, during their lifetimes, as subjects for critical attempts at stabilizing the poet-heroine's role. E. B. B. worked actively to enter and shape that role; but first for biographichal and then for political reasons, she rendered her position as a would-be poet-heroine an extraordinarily difficult one.

By fourteen, the "Poet Laureate of Hope End" had already composed an *autobiographia literaria*, "Glimpses into My Own Life and Literary Character." By twenty, she had written the "Fragment of an 'Essay on Woman' ", a work that not only rejected conventional praise for preceding generations of women poets but enrolled its author in a sacred feminine literary canon of her own naming. Indeed, although Deirdre David surely goes too far in implying that responsibility for the Barrett Browning legend lies primarily with the poet herself, E. B. B.'s career could be read as one long succession of attempts to accommodate—and to alter—the shape of feminine literary canonicity. Though only highlights can be sketched here, her career provides an indispensable context for understanding the canonization/ decanonization process that started as soon as Barrett Browning died.

In her second signed volume of verse, the 1844 *Poems*, Elizabeth Barrett entered Victorian literary historiography as not only a strikingly ambitious and intellectual poet but an explicit candidate for feminine literary sanctity. It was an auspicious debut. Throughout much of the nineteenth century, long after her elopement had rendered its inclusion deeply ironic, editions of her complete works still opened with E. B. B.'s dedication of that volume to her father: "Somewhat more faint-hearted than I used to be, it is my fancy thus to seem to return to a visible personal dependence on you, as if indeed I were a child again; to conjure your beloved image between myself and the public, so as to be sure of one smile,—and to satisfy my heart while I sanctify my ambition, by associating with the great pursuit of my life its tenderest and holiest affection."

Sanctifying literary ambition was already a central project for the poet, as the remainder of the volume reveals. In her preface, Barrett speaks as a poet-heroine whose domestic devotion converges with self-abnegating Christian devotion—and blends, almost imperceptibly, with the "patience angélique du génie." Aligning herself with holy visionary predecessors, she celebrates her own multifaceted suffering as the source of glorious "knowledge" and "song." She also insists that she has been "hurried into speech" by "adoration" for divinity, driven to attempt a sacred subject that "fastened on" her "rather . . . than was chosen." "Life," she writes, is a "continual sacrament," and "poetry has been as serious a thing to me as life itself."

Such prose opens the way for "A Vision of Poets," a poetic work in which Barrett not only explicitly addresses "the necessary relations of genius to suffering and self-sacrifice" but evokes an eerie architectural canon whose monuments simultaneously celebrate Romantic genius, Pythian inspiration, and the agonies of Christian sanctity. Instructed by a female figure who comes "forth / To crown all poets to their worth," the masculine poet of the "Vision" imbibes first "starry water" that separates him from humanity, leaving him "holy and cold," and then the vile bitterness of "world's use," "world's love," and "world's cruelty." He awakens within a "great church" in which, "Pale and bound / With bay above the eyes profound," he finds a "strange company" of poet-saints: "Deathful their faces were, and yet / The power of life was in them set—/ Never forgot nor to forget." "Glorified," their faces remain "still as a vision, yet exprest / Full as an action—look and geste / Of buried saint in risen rest."

Only one woman is named among the "poets true, / Who died for Beauty as martyrs do / For Truth—the ends being scarcely two." She is, of course, Sappho; and she is crowned not only with bay but "with that gloriole / Of ebon hair on calmèd brows—." To her as to no other poet, Barrett Browning's narrator speaks directly and in a tone of reassurance: "O poet-woman! none forgoes / The leap, attaining the repose."

Poetic, Christian, and perhaps Marian monuments, the figures in this cathedral of art stand

> All, still as stone and yet intense;
> As if by spirit's vehemence
> That stone were carved and not by sense.
>
> But where the heart of each should beat,
> There seemed a wound instead of it,
> From whence the blood dropped to their feet
>
> Drop after drop—dropped heavily
> As century follows century
> Into the deep eternity.

Soon, however, they sing a harmony that makes them "burn in all their aureoles"—until (in another line that resonates with Browning's "Childe Roland"), "the blood which fell / Again, alone grew audible, / Tolling the silence as a bell."

An angel breaks the silence. In his challenging question, the agonies of the female Pythia, the passion of saints, and the "angelic patience of genius" meet:

> "If to speak nobly, comprehends
> To feel profoundly,—if the ends
> Of power and suffering, Nature blends,—
>
> "If poets on the tripod must
> Writhe like the Pythian to make just
> Their oracles and merit trust,—
>
> "If every vatic word that sweeps
> To change the world must pale their lips
> And leave their own souls in eclipse,—

. . . . .

"If ONE who did redeem you back,
By His own loss, from final wrack,
Did consecrate by touch and track

"Those temporal sorrows till the taste
Of brackish waters of the waste
Is salt with tears He dropt too fast,—

"If all the crowns of earth must wound
With prickings of the thorns He found,—
If saddest sighs swell sweetest sound,—

"What say ye unto this?—refuse
This baptism in salt water?—choose
Calm breasts, mute lips, and labour loose?

"Or, O ye gifted givers! ye
Who give your liberal hearts to me
To make the world this harmony,

"Are ye resigned that they be spent
To such world's help?"
                    The Spirits bent
Their awful brows and said "Content."

Content to writhe like the female Pythia and to drink in suffering and bitterness as if they were the tears of Christ, Barrett Browning's "strange company" accepts not only suffering but suffering in potentially feminine form.

Not incidentally, the strange company also implicitly accepts E. E. B., who stands metaphorically ready for any number of crowns of thorns. Such associations were not lost upon several of the volume's initial reviewers, in whose pages the poet appeared not only as a sacred model whose "pain-perfected" voice offers "Revelations," but as a "Margarita or Perpetua of the Christian mythology." E. B. B. was already beginning to succeed as a sacred poet-heroine of resignation and suffering.

Around a month after the 1844 volume appeared, however, Barrett received her first letter from Robert Browning. She responded; and by so doing, the woman who had publicly aired her "fancy . . . to seem to return to a visible personal dependence" on her father set into motion a series of events that would drive her to an act of filial disobedience of the first order. Barrett had cast herself as seeking to embody the highest traditional values both of feminine submission and of poetic ambition, without openly redefining either in the process. The task would have been impossible to fulfill; her life made it impossible to undertake.

A woman who chooses to take a lover and marry can no longer draw upon the symbolic power of ascetic sanctity. With Barrett Browning's marriage, one kind of saint was lost, though another might be found. Dinah Mulock expressed a sense of both possibilities in her 1851 response to E. B. B.'s "later sonnets," the *Sonnets from the Portuguese*:

To Elizabeth Barrett Browning on Her Later Sonnets

> I know not if the cycle of strange years
>   Will ever bring thy human face to me,
> Sister!—I say this, not as of thy peers,
>   But like as those who their own grief can see
> In the large mirror of another's tears.
>
> Comforter! many a time thy soul's white feet
>   Stole on the silent darkness where I lay
> With voice of distant singing—solemn sweet—
>   "Be of good cheer, I, too, have trod that way;"
> And I rose up and walked in strength complete.
>
> Oft, as amidst the furnace of fierce woe
>   My own will lit I writhing stood, yet calm,
> I saw thee moving near me, meek and slow,
>   Speaking not, but still chanting the same psalm,
> "God's love suffices when all world-loves go."
>
> Year after year have I, in passion strong,
>   Clung to thy garments when my soul was faint,—
> Touching thee, all unseen amid the throng;
>   But now, thou risest to joy's heaven—my saint!
> And I look up—and cannot hear thy song,
>
> —Or hearing, understand not; save as those
>   Who from without list to the bridegroom-strains
> They might have sung—but that the dull gates close,—
>   And so they smile a blessing through their pains,
> Then, turning, lie and sleep among the snows.

> So, go thou in, saint—sister—comforter!
>   Of this, thy house of joy, heaven keep the doors!
>   And sometimes through the music and the stir
>   Set thy lamp shining from the upper floors,
>   That we without may say—"Bless God and her!"

Barrett Browning was to write that this poem had touched her "to the quick." One can imagine why. Its subject remains a saint, yet she is also a treacherous sister who has left those she once comforted to freeze outside the "dull gates" of her private heaven. The "music and the stir" of her "bridegroom-strains" create only songs in which they cannot share. The speaker's blessing may be genuine, but her pain seems no less so.

Nor were metaphoric sisters the only ones Barrett Browning left behind. Viewed from the distance of some 150 years, through the glorious haze of the Browning legend, E. B. B.'s elopement looks like high romance. From the poet's own perspective, and perhaps from the viewpoints of many of her contemporaries, it was nothing of the sort. A necessity it might have been; a suitable story for public narration it was not. Presumably, those who knew enough to be able to recount the circumstance of the Brownings' courtship in the 1850s and 1860s understood the depth of the familial trauma involved and refrained from adding to the Brownings'—and the Barretts'—pain through violations of confidentiality. In any case, articles published in the years leading up to and directly following Barrett Browning's death reveal that even the Americans, who were notoriously enthusiastic reporters or fabricators of biographical information, tended to focus on the Brownings' happy marriage and not on their courtship. The general operating consensus seems to have been that the less said about the whole business, the better.

Legendary lore to the contrary, then, in the decade just after Barrett Browning's courtship, critics initially received the *Sonnets* with muted praise. Individual readers, including poets, may well have been susceptible to the *Sonnets'* "explosion of sealed sensation" than reviews indicated, but the fact remains: reticence, not over-whelming enthusiasm, marked the *Sonnets'* initial public reception. Barrett Browning's canonization would now turn to the public persona, just as the writer herself turned to public poetry. Sonnets (and sainthood) aside, by the time she was suggested for Poet Laureate in 1850, Barrett Browning often emerged in periodical literature not only as a major poet but as a form of national heroine—as what the *English Review* celebrated as England's "Queen of Song."

To the extent that her personal life played a major role in such midcentury idealizations, the focus was often on E. B. B. s' person—or rather, on her near lack of corporeal presence. In 1853, for example, American author George Stillman Hillard wrote, "I have never seen a human frame which seemed so nearly a transparent veil for a celestial and immortal spirit. She is a soul of fire enclosed in a shell of pearl." Hillard's "soul of fire enclosed in a shell of pearl" was to attain an iconicity rivalled only by Mary Russell Mitford's earlier tribute to the young E. B. B.'s "sunbeam" smile.

The power of such characterizations is poignantly suggested by a journal entry of Sophia Hawthorne, Nathaniel Hawthorne's wife. "I was afraid to stay long, or to have Mrs. Browning talk," she notes, "because she looked so pale, and seemed so much exhausted. . . . I do not understand how she can live long, or be at all restored while she does live. I ought rather to say that she lives so ardently that her delicate earthly vesture must soon be burnt up and destroyed by her soul of pure fire." Dutifully revising her own impulsive human worry about Barrett Browning's health into a ritualized evocation of radiance, Hawthorne goes on to call E. B. B. "angelic" and a "seraph in her flaming worship of heart," asserting that "how [Barrett Browning] remains visible to us, with so little admixture of earth, is a mystery."

No sooner was E. B. B. rendered a model Englishwoman and a disembodied "soul of fire," however, than she began to publish works such as *Aurora Leigh*, *Casa Guidi Windows*, and *Poems before Congress*, and thus to induce a new canonic crisis. Drawing at points deliberately upon her status as a cultural model, Barrett Browning explicitly intensified the instabilities and subversive potential of her early conceptions of feminine sainthood. In *Poems before Congress*, the last volume she prepared for publication, the powerful (and once notorious) antislavery poem "A Curse for a Nation" may stand as a kind of counterpole to the earlier "A Vision." Both invoke the imitation of Christ; but where the former focuses upon the crucifixion, the latter aligns itself with the Sermon on the Mount. "From the summits of love a curse is driven, / As lightning is from the tops of heaven," the speaker's Angel urges her. Divine guidance, which had once led the male poet of "A Vision" out of the world and into a pure, canonical realm of passive saints anointed and immobilized by Christ's tears, now leads the female poet "A Curse" in the opposite direction:

> "Therefore," the voice said, "shall thou write
>   My curse to-night.
> Some women weep and curse, I say
> (And no one marvels), night and day.
>
> And thou shalt take their part to-night,
>   Weep and write.
> A curse from the depths of womanhood
> Is very salt, and bitter, and good."

This is visionary poetic sainthood at its most subversive and autonomous, both on the level of sexual politics and on those of national and racial politics as well. It signals the grounds for a second canonic crisis. E. B. B.'s abolitionist speaker does more than direct her curse at the United States; at first she attempts to excuse herself from that duty by arguing that as an Englishwoman, she scarcely speaks from a position of strength in criticizing other countries as unjust: "My heart is sore / For my own land's sins."

When the "saint—sister—comforter" eloped, critics had honored her by extending their reticence to her work as well as her biography. When England's Queen of Song created a divinely inspired speaker who criticized her own country and cursed its ally, criticism often had recourse to a vocabulary of demonic possession. Metaphorically attempting to exorcise the visceral, often bitter passion of *Poems before Congress* from the glorious figure of England's poetic queen, reviewers invoked a canonical counterheroine capable of momentarily possessing their ideal. W. E. Aytoun, for example, explains E. B. B's "poetic aberrations" by insisting that like a "Pythoness . . . under the influence of her Cacodaemon," Barrett Browning has been "seized with a . . . fit of insanity." "Balak," not an angel, has inspired "A Curse for a Nation." Even the poet's friend Henry F. Chorley (who misreads the subject of "A Curse") asserts that she has taken "to its extremity the right of the 'insane prophet' to lose his head, and to loose his tongue." Indeed, as Barrett Browning reported with rueful pleasure, William Howitt actually published a *Spiritual Magazine* article insisting that ever since the publication of *Casa Guidi Windows*, the poet had been "biologised by infernal spirits." Thus, the chanting of the priestess became what Edmund Gosse was to condemn as the "Pythian shriek,"—and, in the process, *Poems before Congress* was set well on its way to being marginalized as "uncharacteristic."

Thus, by the time Barrett Browning died, her significance as a poet and a national, cultural, and political figure was deeply controversial. Her succeeding, highly charged canonization was as conflicted and uneven as any other. Working through an irregular process of accretion, it encompassed a range of watchwords and iconic anecdotes whose combinations could take unpredictable, even contradictory forms. As phrases that achieved iconicity in one decade sifted into the revisionary narratives of another, the poet-heroine's form in one year's schoolbooks radically diverged from her appearance in that same year's literary magazines, lecture halls, or private letters. Here as elsewhere in canonization history, then, periodization is a difficult and often misleading issue. Nonetheless, since shifts in the poet's reception tended to be connected to biographical revelations, that reception may be broken down into several clear, if rough stages. After E. B. B.'s death, she emerges first as a Promethean intellectual; then as a still-powerful "wife, mother, and poet"; then as a great lover whose glory may no longer depend upon her poetry; and finally as an Andromeda (or Peau d'Ane) in Wimpole Street, whose physical and mental frailty adds poignancy to her role as a heroine of nostalgically conceived romance (see Lootens). Each of these figures supplements or competes with rather than fully supersedes her predecessors. Each exercises her own powers; each requires her own silences.

The Poet as Boundary Goddess: E. B. B. as Monitory Model

At first, reverence and perhaps even respect seemed to demand biographical reticence. Fearful of being rendered the "heroine of a biography," Barrett Browning herself had been prepared to balk readers' curiosity long before her marriage. That approach was reinforced not only by the poet's reluctance to discuss her elopement but by her widower's famous insistence upon privacy. It would be years before a full-scale biography appeared and even longer before public release of any significant collection of E. B. B's letters. Early on, when controls on biographical revelation were tightest, a number of narratives conceive of E. B. B. almost exclusively as a poet. Though often muted, they echo throughout the century. In such accounts, if the *Sonnets* are not "revised and edited" out, they are discreetly tucked away, often into dependant clauses, beside or behind the likes of *The Seraphim*. Indeed, given later assumptions about the *Sonnets'* Victorian popularity, it is crucial to note how many articles recount Barrett Browning's entire career without so much as a reference to them.

    The Barrett Browning of such writing is preeminently the "author of *Aurora Leigh*": her literary achievement consists not primarily of lyrics or ballads but of epic, religious, and political verse. She is still England's Queen of Song. What is more, she is often the "ultimate" woman poet—sometimes in the sense of "most characteristics" or "greatest so far," but sometimes, too, in the sense of "final." In this latter role, she is not so much sacred as Promethean: she serves as a female canonical Terminus, a glittering boundary goddess who marks, in the words of an 1862 *Saturday Review* article, "the uniform limits of the female intellect."

    "If Destiny and Nature had intended that a great poem should be written by a woman," asserts the *Saturday Review*, "*Aurora Leigh* would perhaps have proved the creative equality of the sexes." As it is, however, the same journal had already asserted, *Aurora Leigh* "furnishes . . . the most conclusive proof that no woman can hope to achieve what Mrs. Browning failed to accomplish." "Such a combination of the finest genius and the choicest results of cultivation and wide-ranging studies has never been seen before in any woman, nor is the world likely soon to see the same again," writes William Stigand in the *Edinburgh Review*, submitting E. B. B.'s "career" as "some proof of the impossibility that women can ever attain to the first rank in imaginative composition." If a woman of such "singular genius and accomplishments, who devoted herself heart and soul to one of the loftiest of human pursuits" could not succeed at writing great poetry, why should any other woman try?

Thus, E. B. B. has tested and proved the limits of generic womanhood: the more unique her gifts and privileges, the more clearly must her ultimate failure serve as definitive proof of female poetic incapacity. At its most concrete, as in C. B. Conant's 1862 *North American Review* essay, such writing casts Barrett Browning as a woman in spite of herself, a charming overreacher whose "great success is in her failure." E. B. B. attempted to hew out a monumental poetic work, Conant acknowledges; but she remained comparable to a "tender-handed woman" who dared to enter "her husband's shop and mimic his handicraft . . . until, weary of the uncongenial work, she threw down the implements, and stood in the grace of her sex,—lovelier for the pantomime." Thus frozen, Conant's E. B. B. embodies the glories not of poetry but of the feminine—the feminine, that is, as perceived by the critic who looks through (and beyond) a female poet's works: "The fair sculptor 'builded better than she knew.' She has left a perfect statue of herself, a service to womanhood and to the world which cannot easily be over-estimated. Whatever inconsistencies belong to woman, and whatever are incidental to the conflicting position in which Mrs. Browning placed herself, between the impulses of her sex and the avocations of the other, are transparently exposed in her own creations". Properly interpreted, E. B. B.'s futile attempt at "competition with men" hence becomes a "glorious [if inadvertent] success, as a higher illustration than was ever otherwise afforded of what a woman is, and of what she may do in her own exalted and luminous sphere." A monument to True Womanhood glimmers behind Barrett Browning's verse, refuting the poet's own articulated feminism.

At its least flattering, such criticism retains E. B. B.'s role as a marker of feminine poetic limitations without according her even the honor of the noble overreacher. Mortimer Collins, in the *Dublin University Magazine*, for example, equates poetic and sexual license in offering a "weighty lesson for literary ladies." Barrett Browning is "one whom many will doubtless rank the greatest poetess the world has ever known," not only because "morally and intellectually, her life was complete" but because "she also found—how different from her predecessors—the right husband." "She would never have reached so high a point if she had not married a great poet." Barrett

Browning's "achievements," he summarizes succinctly, are "her own"; her "faults" are "of her womanhood." Indeed, even she could not escape the "strange destiny" whereby "women of genius" are "ever impelled to treat topics which men avoid; they must give us 'Jane Eyres,' 'Consuelos,' 'Aurora Leighs.' Perhaps after all, though we have some poetesses whom we should be loth to spare, the production of poetry is not precisely woman's mission. Perhaps, after all, the best poem she can offer us is a crowing child, with beautiful bright hair, pillowed upon her loving breast." Compelled by a strange destiny, even so pure a woman as Barrett Browning is helpless to avoid "erotic speculations" and "grossness." How much more dangerous might poetry writing be to a woman whose life was not "morally and intellectually complete?"

"Wife, Mother, and Poet": E. B. B. as Secular Trinity

Barrett Browning's supreme status, both as woman and as poet, could render her a female canonical Terminus: it could doom her to stand as a glittering monitory figure, hand outstretched toward a dead end at best and a gross erotic swamp at worst. It could also cast her as an inspiration or a prophetess, however. In the first decade after E. B. B.'s death, celebration and silence. often merge in paradoxical canonization attempts. Even as admirers celebrate the poet's marriage, they leave her courtship and elopement unmentioned; even as they glorify her poetic fame, they downplay her verses' controversiality. Powerfully and illogically, such accounts often merge the poet's Promethean power with the holiness of domestic angels as well as of warrior-saints.

At points, such combination required extreme measures. James Russell Lowell, for example, was Professor of Belles Lettres at Harvard when he recorded his condemnation of "the physically intense school . . . of which Mrs. Browning's 'Aurora Leigh' is the worst example, whose muse is a *fast* young woman with the lavish ornament and somewhat overpowering perfume of the *demi-monde*, and which pushes expression to the last gasp of sensuous exhaustion. . . . An overmastering passion . . . must be fleshly, corporeal, must 'bite with small white teeth' and draw blood, to satisfy the craving of our modern inquisitors." Like critics during E. B. B.'s lifetime, Lowell quarantines Barrett Browning, the pure poet-heroine, from the corruption represented by her own work. Metaphorically exorcising E. B. B. from possession by the vampire passions that inspired *Aurora Leigh*, Lowell later insists that he has been far from wishing to injure "the pure and fragrant memory" of Barrett Browning—even as he continues to condemn the "hectic flush" and "unpleasant *physical* excess" of *Aurora Leigh* in visceral terms: "It gives me the same kind of shock I felt once in a dissecting room."

If testimony to Barrett Browning's power as an inspirational figure reaches its most paradoxical in Lowell, it reaches its most poignant in American novelist Elizabeth Stuart Phelps's *Story of Avis*. Here, Barrett Browning's work is divine sustenance, while the poet herself is not only a "saint—sister—comforter" but a herald of the future. Early in the novel, young Avis, who has fled her domestic chores, climbs the highest tree in an orchard and opens *Aurora Leigh*, "that idyl of the June, that girls' gospel, which will be great as long as there are girls in the world to think it so." She experiences a revelation: "Full of the vague restlessness which possesses all healthy young creatures, and the more definite hungers natural to a girl of her temperament, Avis . . . was not without capability of relishing a certain quality of poison, not too fully flavored. . . . But it was silent as a convent in the apple-boughs; the growing day drew on a solemn veil of light; . . . and so the manna fell."

Like her mother before her, Avis is ultimately driven to sacrifice her art for her family. Nonetheless, she retains "her conviction that she might have painted better pictures—not worse—for loving Philip and the children; that this was what God meant for her." This conviction has been inspired by her reading of *Aurora Leigh* and her knowledge of its author's biography. Generations of failed attempts must go into the making of a woman artist, Phelps insists. In the meantime, "In the budding of all young gifts, in the recognition of all high graces, in the kindling of all divine fires, we feel a generous glow. . . . When the passion of our lives has long since wasted into pathos, and hope has shrivelled to fit the cell of care, we lean with increasing ardor on the hearts of those in whom purpose and poetry were permitted to be as one."

Leaning "with ardor on the heart" of Barrett Browning, a whole series of writers, mostly from the 1870s, read the poet's life and works as revelations of a feminine literary sanctity whose glories are both heroic and conventionally domestic. Taken individually, their accounts often pull in different directions; taken as a group, they attempt—and at points attain—a dazzling if ultimately untenable equilibrium between celebrating E. B. B.'s individual poetic genius and her embodiment of the generic glory of Woman.

No single work of this sort is more emphatic or more suggestive than the *Atlantic Monthly* obituary by Barrett Browning's friend and admirer Kate Field. To Field, E. B. B. was "Wife, mother, and poet, three in one, and such an earthly trinity as God had never before blessed the world with." Field's is an active, public, sacred heroine: her "life was one long, large-souled, large-hearted prayer for the triumph of Right, Justice, Liberty."

"Wrong was her enemy; against this she wrestled, in whatever part of the globe it was to be found." Yet she is also saintly in a more private sense. Presenting Barrett Browning's personal life as a matter for public celebration, Field combines veneration for the poet's "great love" with admiration for her great verse. She justifies E. B. B. on all counts, explicitly answering criticism of "A Curse for a Nation" by citing an explanatory letter and implicitly defending the Brownings' elopement by asserting its miraculous effects, both personal and poetic. (It was "destiny" that brought Barrett and her future husband "face to face," Field insists—"a destiny with God in it." "Association with the Brownings . . . made one better in mind and soul," she writes. "It was impossible to escape the influence of the magnetic field of love and poetry that was constantly passing between husband and wife."

In its rush to sanctify both the poet's life and her works, however, Field's essay sometimes loses the balance that renders the canonization of woman and poet fully reciprocal. Granted, even when she is cast as "the glory of all" Casa Guidi and as "that which sanctified all," Field's Barrett Browning still retains some humanity. She is a specific, embodied Glory who prefers an armchair near the door and strews newspaper on the table. When Field asserts that the poet's character was "well-nigh perfect," however, or that she was "so humble in her greatness that her friends looked upon her as a divinity among women," one cannot help becoming uneasy. Is this a woman or a Marian monument? By the end of Field's essay, one scarcely wonders at hearing that the dying poet's "spirit could see its future mission" or even that "an unexpected comet" glared across the sky the night after her death. The only surprise is that E. B. B. should have died at all. "Sinless in life," why should she not have simply been assumed into heaven?

As the "shadow of Mrs. Browning's [sinless] self," E. B. B.'s poetry is as indispensable here as the Holy Ghost whose place it takes in Field's secular trinity. At points, however, it already threatens to become equally insubstantial. Indeed, as the *Sonnets* emerge from the obscurity to which they are still relegated by many of Field's contemporaries, they do so less as texts than as transparent veils over their author's heart: "What wealth of love she could give is evidenced in those exquisite sonnets purporting to be from the Portuguese, the author being too modest to christen them by their right name, Sonnets from the Heart. None have failed to read the truth through this slight veil, and to see the woman more than the poet in such lines as these:—'I yield the grave for thy sake, and exchange / My near sweet view of heaven for earth with thee!'"

Where Field's obituary hovers on the edge of creating Barrett Browning as a Marian model, Samuel B. Holcombe's *Southern Literary Messenger* obituary dives straight into the process. Condemning Field's essay as what one might expect from "an avowedly pantheistic publication" such as the *Atlantic Monthly*, Holcombe nevertheless follows Field's lead in celebrating the *Sonnets*. As he makes clear, Holcombe intends no "elaborate" critical engagement with "Mrs. Browning's idiosyncratic merits and foibles as a poet": his concern is with her "womanly character as exhibited in her writings." That character, we are told, renders her "truly the Shakespeare among her sex." Far from being concerned with Field's "Right, Justice, Liberty," however, Holcombe's female Bard is scarcely dedicated even to the art of poetry. "For her," Holcombe writes, "love was the element of life; her soul was pure and chaste as fire; but the wondrous music of this immeasurable passion penetrated her whole being, and kindled it into an ardent and beautiful flame. In her poems, the passions of love in the maiden heart, the devotion of the wife and the affection of the mother, are severally and fully portrayed."

As Love's music "penetrates" the "whole being" of Holcombe's divinely relative Comtean trinity, it "kindles" her into a kind of poetic virgin motherhood. With her "ardent" soul, "pure and chaste as fire," E. B. B. thus speaks for the ideal "maiden, wife, and mother"—and apparently for no one else. What happens, one might ask, when the same poet adopts the voice of masculine or androgynous angels? Of a runaway slave who strangles the child she conceived through rape? Of the great god Pan? Of an Italian patriot declaring war? Of a factory child? In many of her most daring and influential poems, then, Holcombe's Barrett Browning would seem to have been out of her element.

In a dramatic literary Assumption, Holcombe ends by envisioning the "spirits of Beauty, of Love, of Purity, of Virtue," gathering "around the dying couch of the peerless Daughter of Poesy . . . to convey the soul of their faithful priestess and interpreter into a sphere of being better adapted to her inexpressible tenderness, her generous sympathies, and her richly-gifted mind". The "womanly character" of E. B. B. thus attains full status as a vanishing figure of feminine virtue—at the modest price of being implicitly purified of both fleshly desire and much of the body of her work.

By 1868, accounts of the "shrine" at Casa Guidi had already been trickling in for some time. A poem in the 1868 *Atlantic Monthly* brings E. B. B.'s secular sanctity to new heights, however. Lying near death within Casa Guidi itself, the poem's speaker is "returned to warm existence" by nothing less than a vision of Barrett Browning:

> A fate like Farinata's held me fast
> In some devouring pit of fever-fire,
> Until, from ceaseless forms of toil that cast

Their will upon me, whirled in endless gyre,
The Spirit of the house brought help at last.
. . . .

She came, whom Casa Guidi's chambers knew,
And know more proudly an immortal now;
The air without a star was shivered through
With the resistless radiance of her brow,
And glimmering landscapes from the darkness grew.

Thin, phantom-like; and yet she brought me rest.
Unspoken words, an understood command
Sealed weary lids with sleep, together pressed
In clasping quiet wandering hand to hand,
And smoothed the folded cloth above the breast.
. . . .

The quiet brow; the face so frail and fair
For such a voice of song; the steady eye,
Where shone the spirit fated to outwear
Its fragile house; —and on her features lie
The soft half-shadows of her drooping hair.
. . . .

Who could forget those features, having known?
Whose memory do his kindling reverence wrong
That heard the soft Ionian flute, whose tone
Changed with the silver trumpet of her song?
No sweeter airs from woman's lips were blown.
. . . .

The tablet tells you, "Here she wrote and died,"
And grateful Florence bids the record stand:
Here bend Italian love and English pride
Above her grave,—and one remoter land,
Free as her prayers would make it, at their side.

I will not doubt the vision: yonder see
The moving clouds that speak of freedom won!
And life, new-lighted, with a lark-like glee
Through Casa Guidi windows hails the sun,
Grown from the rest her spirit gave to me.

Released from the physical torments of delirium and the spiritual torments of "the Tuscan Master's hell" by a vision of the "spirit" of Casa Guidi, the speaker seems inclined to believe in divine intercession: if poet-worship heals, why question it?

In the end, though, if anyone outfitted Barrett Browning with a full critical halo, it was Edmund Clarence Stedman. "There are some poets whom we picture to ourselves as surrounded with aureolas, who are clothed in so pure an atmosphere that when we speak of them—though with a critical purpose and in this exacting age—our language must express that tender fealty which sanctity and exaltation compel from all mankind." First published in *Scribner's* in 1873 and then reprinted as a chapter in his *Victorian Poets*, Stedman's "Elizabeth Barrett Browning" clearly attained iconicity: it remained central to Barrett Browning studies throughout the rest of the century and beyond. Ironically, the essay's popularity may even have eclipsed that of many of Barrett Browning's actual works. Open an 1877 volume entitled *Elizabeth Barrett Browning*, for example, and one finds that Stedman, not E. B. B., wrote the contents; check the National Union Catalog for the years just after 1900, and although new editions of *Aurora Leigh* are absent, *Victorian Poets* continues to appear until 1917.

In fact, in certain respects, Stedman literally defined Victorian poetry. As Christopher Ricks has noted in the *New Oxford Book of Victorian Verse*, "The word 'Victorian' had from the start been . . . associated with writers; the OED's first instance of the adjective is Stedman's *Victorian Poets*, and the first sense of the noun is 'a person, especially an author, who lived in the reign of Queen Victoria,' where especially an author means very especially a poet: [Robert] Browning as the 'strongest, truest poet of the Victorians' (1876), and [Alfred] Tennyson as, 'alone of the Victorians,' having 'definitely entered the immortal group of our English poets." As *Victorian* entered the language of literary criticism, then, Robert Browning came along as "strongest and truest," Tennyson, as "alone" among the immortal, and Barrett Browning as "the representative of her sex in the Victorian era."

In Stedman's terms, the honor could not have been higher. "We men are fallen tyrants," Stedman once wrote to a female friend. "What plea I can enter for myself I don't know—unless it be to let my article on Mrs. Browning count in my favor." According to his biographers, " 'A man dictates his faith, or illustrates it, by the opinion he has of woman' was Stedman's version of an old truth. One of the most perfect essays ever written by Stedman was that on Mrs. Browning, and he said it was his tribute to Woman." The Barrett Browning essay is indeed a tribute to Woman, at least insofar as Woman is a lost, sacred literary heroine.

As "tender fealty for sanctity" overrides literary analysis in Stedman's work, the familiar sentimental haze of refused critical engagement settles: "We are not sure of our judgment; ordinary tests fail us. . . . Fire is fire, though shrouded in vapor, or tinged with murky hues. We do not see clearly, for often our eyes are blinded with tears;—we love, we cherish, we revere." Stedman's fealty, which seeks to honor both a poet and a woman, thus canonizes a "soul of fire"—a figure whose "memory and career appear to us like some beautiful ideal." Indeed, so ethereal is Stedman's vanishing monument that she almost disappears before the essay begins: "Nothing is earthly, though all is human," he writes. "A spirit is passing before our eyes, yet of like passions with ourselves."

With Stedman, Browning's biography reached fruition as a full-scale "sacred life." Much like its medieval forerunners, this narrative is a pastiche. Casting Barrett Browning as "England's greatest female poet" and the "most inspired" woman poet of history, Stedman brilliantly rings the changes on her earlier portrayals. The devout invalid with her "cloister-life"; the queen; the "fragile" feminine overreacher; the singer of "liberty, aspiration, and love"; Mazeppa; the chrysalis; the Sibyl; and even the Lady of Shalott are all here—and all subsumed by the portrayal of E. B. B. as a perfect, flamelike secular saint.

Metaphorically linking his subject both to Mary ("all these things she 'kept in her heart' ") and to Christ (she gives "Cry of the Children" from on "the Mount"), Stedman articulates an almost complete paradigm for accounts of Barrett Browning's biography as a secular saint's life. First, there is the "chrysalid state," the intellectual "novitiate" of her "cloister-life," in which the physical isolation and suffering that once won E. B. B. popular reverence are underplayed or condensed and concretized by the dramatic (if apocalyptic) story that she witnessed her favorite brother's death at sea. Next, there is the turning point, the "chief event in the life of Elizabeth Barrett": her marriage, which brings motherhood and the "ripe fruition of a genius that hitherto, blooming in the night, had yielded fragrant and impassioned, but only sterile flowers." Then come the poet's final years in Italy, which pass in a kind of sanctified haze. Her "beautiful character" is now "exhibited" in letters and in friends' tributes—not; it must be noted, in her unnamed final volumes, whose contents sound like "sweet bells jangled." As E. B. B.'s "exhausted frame" becomes "now, more than ever, . . . 'nearly a transparent veil for a celestial and immortal spirit,' " her poetic life, too, declines. Finally, in hagiographic tradition's great deathbed scene, the "enraptured seer of celestial visions" rises to her sure reward.

Stedman's account crystallizes popular watchwords into a coherent narrative; it is echoed in turn by his successors in the project of legend-making. Such echoes may not only encompass Stedman's glorification of E. B. B. but also repeat and extend his dismissal of that poet's later writing. To quote William T. Herridge, "In faltering, hurried accents, over which criticism will draw a kindly veil, she spoke her last words for universal liberty, and then awaited with calmness the divine emancipation of death"—not to mention ascent from the "Mount of Transfiguration."

In contrast to accounts of the poet's final volumes, those of her final hours are explicit and celebratory. After living her final years in "a pure atmosphere of love," Marion Couthouy's dying heroine finds that "supernal Beauty . . . now opened upon her. . . .Was it not a foreshadowing of the Beatific Vision?" On a less elevated note, Elizabeth Porter Gould proclaims Barrett Browning victor of what might be called the female writers' deathbed competition. George Eliot's last moments could not possibly have been as inspirational, Gould insists. The best death had clearly gone to the best woman.

Stedman's work did more than consolidate earlier watchwords into a relatively consistent narrative, however. It also helped catalyze crucial shifts in his time's paradigms of feminine literary sanctity. As his biographers put it, Stedman "cared less for literary than for matrimonial women," perhaps particularly when the literary women were fractious. Confronted with Barrett Browning, who was both literary and matrimonial, he shaped of her life—and of her work, especially the *Sonnets*—a testament to the indispensable "relations of art and marriage, where the development of female genius is concerned". It was by "one of Nature's charming miracles," he writes, that marriage gave Elizabeth Barrett both "a precious lease of life" and a "fellow-artist whose disposition and pursuits were in absolute harmony with her own." Through this naturalized "miracle" alone did the "exalted" Barrett Browning rise "to her height."

Stedman's timing was crucial, both in terms of the developing institution of literary study and in terms of the institution of marriage. According to Raymond Williams, Terry Eagleton writes, "The only sure fact about the organic society . . . is that it is always gone." There is probably another "sure fact": such a society is one in which women know, and are happy, in their places. When "all the laws that governed sexual identity and behavior seemed to be breaking down," a number of anxious late-century critics turned to mid-Victorian England as such a lost society—and, somewhat ironically, to Barrett Browning as its heroine. Stedman's essay heralds this development. In a tone that is not merely evaluative but elegiac, it casts E. B. B. as "the representative of her sex in the Victorian era," endowing her with qualities (including "abnegation, hope and faith") that once "seemed the apotheosis of womanhood." Since her death in 1861, Stedman implies, the "passion flower of the century" has vanished; the "conscious medium of some power beyond the veil" has been silent. As Victorianism came to an end, it seems, womanhood began to go downhill.

With Barrett Browning and her father both dead for more than ten years, references to the Brownings' elopement were becoming less risky. Stedman weighs Edward Barrett Moulton-Barrett's probable reasons for opposing E. B. B.'s marriage, even going so far as to speak of Moulton-Barrett's "utter selfishness" in attempting to forbid the poet and her sister to marry. Still, Stedman alludes to rather than addresses the elopement. Moreover, he suggestively counters E. B. B.'s association with filial disobedience through a familial vision that turns long-standing metaphoric patterns to new uses. "The English love to call her Shakespeare's Daughter," he writes, "and in truth she bears to their greatest poet the relation of Miranda and Prospero." Few literary heroines can have been proclaimed the dutiful metaphoric child of more or greater patriarchs than was Moulton-Barrett's disobedient daughter. "What more beautiful subject for a modern painter," Stedman suggests, "than the girl Elizabeth . . . than this ethereal creature seated at the feet of the blind old scholar [Hugh Stuart Boyd], her face aglow with the rhapsody of the sonorous drama, from which she read of Oedipus, until 'the reader's voice dropped lower / When the poet called him BLIND!' Here was the daughter that Milton should have had!" George Barnett Smith, who was to quote and extend much of Stedman's portrayal of Barrett Browning, would be lured into asserting that she should be termed Shakespeare's daughter rather than Tennyson's sister, thus earning from Henry James the withering suggestion that "it might do to try 'Wordsworth's niece' or 'Swinburne's aunt.' "

To be sure, for Stedman there are still "three masterworks": *Aurora Leigh*, *Casa Guidi Windows*, and the *Sonnets*. Not surprisingly, however, the *Sonnets* play a newly central role in this account of miraculous marriage. For "he is but a shallow critic who neglects to take into his account of a woman's genius a factor representing the master-element of love." Just as the "chief event in the life of Elizabeth Barrett was her marriage," the "height" of her literary achievements was the *Sonnets*. Indeed, the *Sonnets* are not only E. B. B.'s greatest works, but they are the definitive works of women's poetry altogether: "The Portuguese Sonnets . . . are the most exquisite poetry hitherto written by a woman, and of themselves justify us in pronouncing their author the greatest of her sex,—on the ground that the highest mission of a female poet is the expression of love."

As centerpieces of a hierarchical, emphatically gendered aesthetics, the *Sonnets* once more establish E. B. B. as a boundary goddess. Now, however, the boundaries have shrunk. Women poets' "highest mission" is not the writing of epic, religious, or political poetry—not the utterance, in Field's terms, of "one long, large-souled, large-hearted prayer for the triumph of Right, Justice, Liberty." It is, rather, "the expression of love"— and of a love, moreover, that inspires critics with the desire to reciprocate in kind. "When an impassioned woman, yearning to let the world share her poetic rapture or grief, reveals the secrets of her burning heart, generations adore her, literature is enriched, and grosser being have glimpses of a purity with which we invest our conceptions of disenthralled spirits in some ideal sphere."

Such reading recognizes not the labor of art but the passion of confession. As a transparent vehicle for "pure" passion, the woman poet becomes both angel and muse: if "we," who are "grosser beings," adore her, it is in great part because the unveiling of her "burning heart" is a medium for our own visions, our own "conceptions of disenthralled spirits in some ideal sphere."

Poet-Heroine to Romantic Heroine: Barrett Browning's Canonical Transformation and the *Sonnets'* Emergence as Relics

During the time when Stedman's sacred life of E. B. B. was first composed and read, Barrett Browning appears repeatedly as "one of the saints": she is both the "apostle of the true woman's poetry" and a prophet who has conveyed into her sex's "hands what might be called a perfect decalogue of womanly virtue."

Typically, where E. B. B. thus appears as both first among women poets and "supreme among women," the miracles of her verse and of her marriage stand equally balanced. In time, however, this balance was to shift. As the century progressed and Robert Browning's poetic reputation rose, glorifications of Barrett Browning began to be subsumed, albeit slowly and unevenly, by celebrations of "the Brownings." Already caught up by what Richard D. Altick calls "the steady drift of nineteenth-century critical attention . . . away from the work and toward the writer," the attention of Barrett Browning's critics drifts even further, away from the writer and toward Robert Browning's wife.

The project of canonizing a Victorian woman as poet had always been deeply problematic. To create a "sacred life" a narrator must combine wonder and virtue, and in nineteenth-century terms, the wonder of true poetry accorded ill with the virtue of true womanhood. Now, however, celebrations of Barrett Browning's courtship and marriage began to offer an escape from this dilemma—a canonical third term. Replace the wonder of true poetry with the wonder of true love, and the problem is solved. Where E. B. B.'s glory became that of a sacred heroine of romance rather than a poet, critics could easily accord her even the most traditional feminine virtues. Moreover, they could retain her as a literary heroine of sorts: for was her reputation not encompassed by Robert Browning's brilliant fame?

Once, the Brownings' love had been celebrated for its contribution
to Barrett Browning's poetry; now, the poetry would come to be celebrated
for its documentation of the Brownings' love. Rhetorically, the shifts
involved are subtle. Symbolically, they could not be more dramatic. It is
suggestive, for example, that Emily Hickey and Frederick J. Furnivall, who
co-founded the (Robert) Browning Society in 1881, both came to Browning's
works through those of E. B. B. Robert Browning had long been "Mrs.
Browning's husband; Elizabeth Barrett Browning was now becoming Robert
Browning's wife.

Robert Browning's wife, that is, and "Pen" Browning's mother. In
his famous introduction to the 1899 edition of *Aurora Leigh*, Algernon
Charles Swinburne outdid himself in praise for the description of Marian
Erle's baby. His glorification of E. B. B. as maternal poet was scarcely
original, however. In 1890, Sarah Warner Brooks had written that "in Casa
Guidi Windows, tender and serious as the Madonna folding in her arms the
sinless Child," E. B. B. was "enshrined forever." The pattern is familiar.
When, in 1899, E. Windgate Rinder listed the "solicitous tenderness of
maternal passion" among those "elemental things" that would supplement
"literary beauty" in giving *Aurora Leigh* continued life, for example, the
division was implicit: womanly virtues from art; motherhood from poetry.

Thus, eagerness to number the poet's "maternal spirit" among her
work's more enduring qualities did not necessarily lead critics to privilege
those works composed after E. B. B. became a mother. Indeed, by the late
1880s, Anne Thackeray Ritchie had already provided a crucial lead in
sanctifying Barrett Browning as a mother at the expense of *Aurora Leigh*. In
a *Dictionary of National Biography* article published between 1886 and 1887,
Ritchie reports that in the late 1850s, as the Brownings were en route to
London, both the manuscript of *Aurora Leigh* and Pen Browning's new
clothes were temporarily lost in Marseilles. "Mrs Browning's chief concern
was not for her manuscripts, but for the loss of her little boy's wardrobe,
which had been devised with so much tender motherly care and pride."

Reprinted and widely quoted, sometimes in juxtaposition to the
poet's claim to Leigh Hunt that she took more pride in her son than in
"twenty Auroras," Ritchie's story would be repeated as a vindication of
Barrett Browning's womanly priorities, a confirmation, in the words of one
Dial review, that Barrett Browning had been a " 'little woman' who loved
'little things,' " an old-fashioned "fond mother and home-keeping wife" who
was "neither a shrill debater nor a clamorous mover of the previous question
nor a seeker to delve where she should spin," yet who had earned "her place
among the immortals." Such vehement praise marks a canonical model who
is only one step away from going out of style. By 1892 Ritchie herself

anticipates later criticisms of E. B. B.'s mothering by revising the narrative to add a criticism of Pen Browning's clothes.

Despite celebrations of Barrett Browning's maternal purity, however, it is as a lover, not as a mother, that E. B. B. is most dramatically canonized toward the century's end. In such contexts, the *Sonnets* began to take center stage. Marriage might be in crisis, many critics asserted or implied, but the Brownings' love could still symbolize the endangered yet eternal values of that institution at its best. Moreover, as a heroine in such accounts, Barrett could wield the sacred powers both of chastity and marriage. For she had kept "the citadel of her womanhood pure and strong until it was conquered once and forever"; and a miracle had been her reward. "Never such love-evolving life found answer so complete this side the Kingdom of Love."

"Whatever cynicism may say of the folly of matrimonial ideals," writes William Herridge in an 1887 *Andover Review*, Elizabeth Barrett's "choice—unhappily with so few parallels in the annals of literature," needs "no justification before the gaze of an admiring world." Her "matchless" *Sonnets* are more than the "work of a poetess": they are "the psalm of a priestess" of matrimonial love. No one could read them "without being stimulated to a truer chivalry and a more profound appreciation of the sacred mystery of a woman's love." Thus, turning "from the work to a noble personality in the worker," critics could read Barrett Browning's career as recording "in letters of gold those eternal laws which lie behind the changing movements of society, and are the foundations upon which the universe is laid." And turn from the work readers did. If, to many readers, the Brownings seemed invincible during this period, it was clearly because they were "classics in perfect married love, as well as in the realm of poetry." Robert Browning himself, that "patron saint of a study group," basked in a dangerous glory partly derived from his association with Barrett Browning. Even his verse would not remain entirely immune from unfavorable comparisons to the romance of the Brownings' courtship.

No single essay is more crucial in this context than Edmund Gosse's famous introduction to an 1894 edition of the *Sonnets from the Portuguese*. Gosse's touching, if slightly inaccurate, account of a tremulous Barrett Browning slipping up behind her husband to place her love poems in his hands is a moment of true romance: it quickly attained iconicity. Widely quoted and reprinted, both in later editions of the *Sonnets* and in Gosse's own popular *Critical Kit-kats*, the scene still appears, in excerpt, in the notes to Porter and Clarke's scholarly edition of Barrett Browning's *Complete Works*.

As Gosse's introduction demonstrates, glorifications of the Brownings' courtship could spring from sexual anxieties extending well beyond the "marriage question." In the 1870s, Stedman himself had discreetly hinted it "no sacrilege to say" that the *Sonnets'* "music is showered from a higher and purer atmosphere than that of the Swan of Avon." By 1894, when Gosse wrote, a new vocabulary stood ready: not only *feminism* but *homosexuality* had entered the general vocabulary. That "Edwardian development," the "homosexual Shakespeare," had arrived, and with him a new explicitness about the cultural implications of intersections between sexual and literary reputations.

One year before Oscar Wilde's arrest on charges of sodomy, in an era in which "many Englishmen regarded . . . homosexual scandals . . . as certain signs of the immorality that had toppled Greece and Rome," Gosse proclaimed that E. B. B.'s "voluble, harsh, and slight" sonnets had a "curious advantage" over those of her great predecessor. Although "it is probable that the sonnets written by Shakespeare to his friend contain lovelier poetry, . . . those addressed by Elizabeth Barrett to her lover are hardly less exquisite to any of us, and to many of us are more wholesome and more intelligible." If Gosse terms Barrett Browning's "wholesome" *Sonnets* more "intelligible," it is clearly because—to adapt a phrase coined about this time—they express a love that dares to speak its name.

Perhaps, Gosse implies, there is no point in undertaking what Simon Shepherd has termed "the tidying-up of the National Bard's sexuality": "Many of the thoughts that enrich mankind and many of the purest flowers of the imagination had their roots, if the secrets of experience were made known, in actions, in desire, which could not bear the light of day, in hot-beds smelling quite otherwise than of violet or sweetbriar." Still, consolation exists. The *Sonnets* offer an "accredited chronicle" of chaste marital love, "lifted far out of any vagueness of conjecture or possibility of misconstruction." "Built" as they are "patently and unquestionably" on an authorized heterosexual "union in stainless harmony," the *Sonnets* become not so much texts as inspirational edifices, bulwarks of a literary city on the hill.

Significant for setting the *Sonnets* as the culmination of Barrett Browning's career and for establishing heterosexuality as a central source of their redemptive power, Gosse's introduction is no less important for its role in the *Sonnets'* literal and metaphoric transformation into relics, a process that simultaneously raises them to glory and relegates them to the status of objects. As a whole series of charming gift volumes attests, by the century's end, when separate editions of *Aurora Leigh* were going out of print, the *Sonnets'* combined canonization and commodification was well under way.

There is no prettier presentation of E. B. B.'s verse than a certain British Library book whose printed text Gosse mentions in his introduction. Cushioned in its own morocco box, this gilt-edged, tooled volume is a full-fledged reliquary. Inside its front cover, beside the golden text of Sonnet

XIX, is a lock of brown hair behind glass; inside the back cover, a white lock whose contrasting color is somehow moving. Both locks, a note in the volume attests, came from Robert Browning on his deathbed. The white one was his own; the brown one was given to him by Elizabeth Barrett Browning before their marriage. He carried it with him (in a carefully displayed bit of paper) as long as he lived. Next to a letter from Browning's daughter-in-law to Thomas J. Wise stands the volume's centerpiece: the "1847 Reading Edition" of the *Sonnets*.

The brown lock of hair seems to be the real thing, though it was clipped from the wrong Browning's head. If so, it will surely not be the first time that true and false relics have been housed together. For the "Reading edition," with its anonymous "octavo of 47 pages," which Gosse asserts to have been printed through the assistance of Mary Russell Mitford, is a fraud. As Philip Kelley and Betty A. Colley tell it, after Robert Browning's death, the Brownings' daughter-in-law, Fannie, removed a lock of hair from "one of the love letters where it had remained since it had been cut from Robert Browning's head," and presented it to Thomas J. Wise. The honor seemed well merited: "sometime President of the Bibliographical Society, honorary Master of Arts at Oxford, member of the exclusive Roxburghe Club of book collectors, and one of the most learned bibliographers in England," Wise had been an active member of the Browning Society, a correspondent of Robert Browning's regarding the authenticity of Barrett Browning publications, and the compiler of the standard bibliography of Barrett Browning's works. By the 1930s, however, bibliographers John Carter and Graham Pollard had begun to suspect the authenticity of certain publications listed in that bibliography, and had followed a trail of clues straight back to Wise. As it turned out, Wise was a forger. He had actually used the Browning Society's own printer, Richard Clay and Sons, to create his fakes.

Fannie Browning told Wise the hair had come from her father-in-law. Wise, however, "convinced himself it was that of Elizabeth Barrett Browning. He had a box built which was inscribed 'This lock of Elizabeth's hair was held by Robert Browning in his hand while he was dying.' On one of her visits to Hampstead, Fannie—who was at Robert Browning's deathbed—saw the inscription and corrected Wise. He smiled and exclaimed, 'If he was not holding a lock of her hair in his hand, he ought to have done so!' " So much for the power of history to defuse legend. Once more, in literary as in religious canonization, reverence and falsification have gone hand in hand.

Gosse's role in Wise's forgery remains unclear, as does the extent to which one should accord him responsibility for another, more abstract kind of falsification: the process of canonizing the *Sonnets* as chaste, nostalgically conceived Victorian valentines. Since Gosse's essay began as an introduction to the *Sonnets*, there is some justification for his abandoning E. B. B.'s verse after their publication, for example; and though Gosse praises the *Sonnets* as relics, he also analyzes them as verse. Nonetheless, his essay contributes powerfully to a larger pattern of accounts in which the "supreme" *Sonnets* dramatically overpower and marginalize the remainder of E. B. B.'s verse, in great part through claims to a glory that seems at least as much documentary as artistic.

If the *Sonnets* were the "perfection of song," the "very spirit of human love made visible," they were so because they were the "matchless series . . . through which Mrs. Browning has chanted her life's apotheosis." We are unable to tell by which we are most affected," wrote one frank author in the *Literary World*, "the poetry itself, or that wonderful 'apocalypse of soul,' than which no revelation could be more beautiful."

Thus, the *Sonnets* came to be reified as relics of Barrett Browning's "life's apotheosis." The interplay of such canonization and commodification finds its most dramatic and poignant monument in Baylor University's Armstrong Browning Library. At the library's 'architectural focal point," the "Cloister of the Clasped Hands," Harriet Hosmer's bronze cast powerfully renders its subjects' physicality. Spare, small, and irreducibly individual, the Brownings' hands lie in a grasp whose very strength evokes the transience of mortal love. These living hands are lost. To one side of Hosmer's sculpture, a marble wall holds the "O Lyric Love" passage from *The Ring and the Book*, engraved in gold; inevitably, the paired sonnet on the other wall begins, "How do I love thee?" Above and behind the glass case is a painting by John Carroll—a wifty, sentimental scene in which a glamorized Elizabeth leans on Robert's arm. The painting's source? The Eaton Paper Company, purveyors of the perfect stationery for love letters.

Commodified, metaphorically chastened, and offered as antidotes to sexual anarchy, Barrett Browning's love poems became sacred objects; but in the process, in many cases, they may have ceased to be read as poems. As relics of a great love, they were perfect. Like other relics, however, they need not even be particularly attractive in and of themselves. Even when Gosse himself termed them the "purest" of Barrett Browning's works, for example, such praise merely established them as the "least imperfect," the "most free" from "laxity" and "license." The body of the poet's verse was thus metaphorically rendered as less pure than the spirit of her love. Love, not art, created the *Sonnets*' supremacy; the value of the verses was coming to depend on the power of the heroine.

Biographical Revelations and the Hysterical Heroine:
The Browning Letters

Both in terms of reverence and reticence, Robert Browning was a key agent in his wife's canonization, whether as a woman or as a poet. As a popular figure, he came to radiate a cultural glory that blended with and augmented that of his wife; on a personal level, his devotion to E. B. B.'s memory only intensified her already powerful connections to sainthood. The most famous instance of such reverence, which occurred in 1889, was sparked by the following passage, printed in the newly published letters of Edward FitzGerald: "Mrs Browning's Death is rather a relief to me, I must say: no more *Aurora Leigh*s, thank God! A woman of real Genius, I know: but what is the upshot of it all? She and her Sex had better mind the Kitchen and their Children; and perhaps the Poor: except in such things as little Novels, they only devote themselves to what Men do much better, leaving that which Men do worse or not at all." Quick to respond, Browning printed the following scathing reply in the *Athenaeum*:

To Edward FitzGerald

I chanced upon a new book yesterday;
I opened it, and where my finger lay
   'Twixt page and uncut page, these words I read
—Some six or seven at most—and learned thereby
That you, Fitzgerald, whom by ear and eye
   She never knew, "thanked God my wife was dead."

Ay, dead! And were yourself alive, good Fitz,
How to return you thanks would task my wits:
   Kicking you seems the common lot of curs—
While more appropriate greeting lends you grace:
Surely to spit there glorifies your face—
   Spitting—from lips once sanctified by Hers.

From the standpoint of the poet-heroine's canonization, the incident is painful and deeply ironic. For what FitzGerald attacks is not so much the "woman of real Genius" as the author of *Aurora Leigh*; and what Browning understandably defends is not so much the author of *Aurora Leigh* as his wife, whose very kiss confers sanctity.

    Browning died the same year—and with him, not only a certain quality of reverence for his wife's memory, but a certain level of biographical reticence. For Barrett Browning's widower had remained as adamantly devoted to the privacy of his wife's memory as he was to its sanctity: as long as he lived, he ensured that few of Barrett Browning's private papers could appear in print, and he resisted publication of her unpublished verse. When E. B. B.'s letters began to appear, then, they bore the glamor of long-cherished secrets.

"Sweet poet! sweetest lover! unto thee / The great world bows in fond idolatry," wrote Allen Eastman Cross in 1889. The great world was soon to echo his evaluative hierarchy. As Alice Meynell instructed readers one year before the 1898 publication of Frederic G. Kenyon's two-volume edition of the *Letters of Elizabeth Barrett Browning*, Barrett Browning was already coming to represent "a moral, and an emotional excellence, rather than a poetical excellence." She was expected to "live in history" as "a nobly passionate personality rather than as a poet." Barrett Browning's "character" was now "her greatest legacy to the world." Though their estimates of Barrett Browning's poetic achievement vary, reviewers of the Kenyon volumes tend to agree: they praise the woman over her works and the love story over all else.

Stedman's moral had been that if a true woman revealed the secrets of her burning heart in song, generations would revere her. The moral of many stories told toward the century's end was that if such a woman consummated one of the great marriages of all time, that glory would never fade—even though remembrance of her poems might. "A greater gain to humanity than the picture of a good and noble life is the view we obtain of the most perfect example of wedded happiness in the history of literature," one 1897 article ruled. "This, even more than her poems, was the legacy which Mrs. Browning left to her fellow-men." To quote William Cameron, "If her novitiate of suffering was severe, her married life was throughout a period of almost indescribable happiness. . . . Her poetic work is the truest and fairest expression of what she was, and of what she felt. All that was womanly in [E. B. B.'s] work will live, despite every defect of art, in virtue of its womanhood . . . . In the least inspired of [her poems] there was a graciousness of fancy, a sweetness of nature, a tenderness of feeling, a rectitude of intention, which entitles them to respect if it does not ensure them permanence in memory."

The woman must save the work, if it is to be saved at all. "Her spiritual fire and her moral courage will probably redeem in the eyes of posterity her artistic defects," a *Spectator* review predicted. When Carlyle asserts that "no Poem is equal to its Poet," his claim concerns the relations between humanity and art. When Barrett Browning's critics make apparently analogous claims during this period, they tend to be addressing the relations between femininity and art; and they tend to conclude that though it may be fine to be a woman poet, it is better to be the heroine of a romance. As one author optimistically put it, "All Barrett Browning's readers [were] her lovers"; and lovers may adore a heroine without revering her verse.

When R. B. Browning published his parents' love letters in 1899, he unleashed a storm of controversy over rights to privacy; but he also did much to end a long-standing, if muted, scandal of another sort. As the *Saturday Review* put it, justification for Browning's decision to publish was "easily found in the favourable light it throws upon the one dubious act of his father's life. Those who admired Robert Browning most have always wished, in the corner of their hearts, that he had not snatched his wife by a clandestine arrangement from the house of her unconscious father. This wish will never be felt again." Now, irrevocably, what remained of public silence surrounding the Brownings' elopement came to an end. As the details of their courtship finally emerged, the two poets entered "into their glory" as definitive figures of romance.

There is no judging the extent of earlier readers' unease over the Barrett-Browning elopement, of course. Still, the tenor of reviews of the love letters indicates that it may have been strong. Despite the letters' revelations, for example, the best that *Fortnightly Review* writer Eleanor Towle could say was that the Brownings' elopement had been carried out "upon the highest if not the soundest principles." A *London Times* article, reprinted in the *Eclectic Magazine*, was even less sympathetic: "Judging from the evidence of these letters alone, it would seem that the Barrett-Browning story offers no exception to the good common sense rule that in nine cases out of ten a secret engagement is a foolish mistake." Browning should simply have asked for Barrett's hand "as soon as she might recover her health," the review naively suggests. *The Church Quarterly Review* goes even further. The "runaway match" might have turned out "to be the greatest possible blessing to both parties," it acknowledges. Still, only the courtesy of the reviewer prevents "another side to the question of the relationship between the lover and the lady's father" from being aired.

Though the heyday of the poet-heroine (and of poet-heroes) was nearing its end, in the face of such disapproval, romantic sanctification flourished once more in its extravagant forms. Spurred by heated critical controversy over whether the letters should have been published at all, admirers insisted upon their redemptive power. Could anyone expect R.W. Browning to imprison "a visitant angel"? "Of course," H.M. Sanders wrote, "we all agree as to the supreme sacredness of love." Still, it never hurt to have new proof, especially where marital love was concerned. "Marriage as an institution has been under some sharp censures of late," noted a writer for the *Academy*, and "it had in that volume for the most pessimistic readers its sure defence." "When there *are* such depths and heights in a world of sin and limitation," Elizabeth Porter Gould wrote in *Education*, "why should they be hidden, while weak, adulterated and sinful actions are spread out on the housetops?" It would have been no less than "sacrilege to have destroyed such a revelation when it is so much needed to-day."

As more than one writer stressed, literary historiography had particular need of such revelations. "In the unlovely wilderness of much literary biography," the "life of the Brownings" could be "set like an oasis." Thus, "though the publication of such letters goes far to establish a really regrettable precedent, yet with the squalid story of Byron's love affairs paraded in half-a-dozen volumes, with Shelley's scarcely less unhappy marriage-ventures [and George Sand and De Musset's 'liaison'] become public property, . . . it is all but imperative for the credit of humanity that this story should be told."

The Brownings' love story had become a great romance of literary history—and perhaps a greater gift to that history than any mere text could be. As Charlotte Porter put it, "The spiritual beauty of the love revealed in these 'Letters of Robert Browning and Elizabeth Barrett' is so magnetic that it makes their reader, too, this more than half-century later, fall in love with the writers." The Brownings were ideal lovers, the "hero and heroine of the most wonderful love story . . . that the world knows of." Whether cast as "true drama," or as the "poem" that they "devised out of their own lives," their love story became an ultimate, unwritten text, a sacred revelation against which no mere written work could ever hope to compete. Greater than mere history, and as glorious as written romance, it was a "manifestation of true love—a manifestation such as history has never and fiction has rarely if ever paralleled."

Against such a text, the *Sonnets* had little chance. For alongside (or perhaps underneath) the increasing purification and etherealization of E. B. B.—and, by extension, of her verse—there had always been an undercurrent of anxiety about the dangerous bodies of the poet and her texts. "Sonnets they are not," an 1889 *Nation* essay had already asserted, for example, "for they err against all the canons; but they are passionate expressions of love." Compelled to fault the actual writing of "these glorious poems" in that same year, critic John Dennis abandons his generally calm, academic tone to become painfully personal: "It is with a feeling sad almost as that of a father whose daughter's beauty has been marred by some miserable accident, that we are forced, despite our wishes, to note even in this, her most perfect work, . . . strange flaws." In its natural—which is to say ideal—state, the body of E. B. B.'s verse would apparently have been flawless, a fit heir not merely to Milton or Shakespeare but to the critic himself. As it is, however, the "miserable accident" of Barrett Browning's own style has rendered the body of her work that of a disfigured daughter.

"You simply cannot beat in their own way—a way a trifle overluscious perhaps; but so are peaches and pine-apples—the best of the *Sonnets from the Portuguese*," the *Saturday Review* had acknowledged only the year before. Juicy and decadent, these last poetic fruits offer a powerful and suggestive contrast to the *Sonnets'* associations with chaste purity, and a reminder that no canonization is ever uncontested. If one looks beyond the ethereal monuments to womanhood that have served as a central focus of this chapter—and, indeed, of Barrett Browning's reception—one finds other more fleshly figures, who are not only heirs to the Pythia evoked by E. B. B.'s contemporaries but predecessors of the neurotic heroine who is to become Andromeda in Wimpole Street.

That heroine was not long in coming. Whatever the love letters' publication may have done for the Brownings' status as romantic ideals, it did little to enhance the reputation of Edward Barrett Moulton-Barrett, as a surviving son angrily pointed out. With its fairy-tale associations, the word *ogre* quickly became a favorite descriptor for the poet's father. Other characterizations ranged from "odious old gentleman" to a modern-day, unconscious Agamemnon. The resulting transformation of courtship narratives helped catalyze a crucial and damaging shift in Barrett Browning's reputation. It had been one thing for Robert Browning to have "snatched his gifted bride from the arms of Death," and quite possibly the death of a saint. It was another, however, for him to rescue her from the clutches of an increasingly vicious, "degenerate" patriarch. Barrett Browning's canonization as a romantic heroine had already ceased to require that its subject be a great poet; now it began to dispense even with the need to present her as a great woman.

As Moulton-Barrett assumed the guise of a villain, his daughter began to be transformed into a maiden in distress—and the more distress the better. Barrett Browning's literary significance had already been proclaimed to be "a moral, and an emotional excellence, rather than a poetical excellence." Now, perhaps fueled by continuing conservative skepticism about the propriety of the Brownings' elopement as well as by fin-de-siècle fascination with accounts of abnormal feminine psychology, an emerging narrative retained the glory of the Brownings' literary romance while implicitly denying Barrett Browning even personal claims to glory. In the words of one 1899 reviewer, critics began to consider the possibility that E. B. B. had been "made hysterical by her long seclusion."

In some cases, such an assertion could partially exonerate the father; in all, it could heighten the daughter's romantic plight. Once suspected of having "snatched" his wife, Robert could now save her—not merely from death, from membership in the "mournful sisterhood" of single women, or even from her nasty father, but from incipient mental illness. E. B. B., who had once served as the "representative of her sex during the Victorian era," as a lost apotheosis of womanhood, was becoming a true fin-de-siècle heroine, an enchanting neurotic: "In short, this rather plain, thin, faded, hysterical woman was loved for herself as perhaps none of all the world's famous beauties has ever been."

Such evocations of Barrett Browning as hysterical heroine set forth a romantic story whose outlines were to satisfy both adherents of Freud and lovers of damsels in distress. In the twentieth century, of course, Elizabeth Barrett would emerge as Andromeda in Wimpole Street—and as a clear descendent of "Peau d'Ane," the fairy-tale heroine forced to flee her father's lust in Andrew Lang's late-nineteenth-century edition of Charles Perrault's stories. Where E. B. B.'s "supreme" strength had once testified to the limits of feminine poetry or the glories of companionate marriage, her supreme weakness could now testify to the sweet, faintly ridiculous innocence of pre-Freudian romance. By 1903, an *Athenaeum* review of a translation of the *Sonnets* would assert that these works give expression to "what may be supposed to be the emotions of the celestially average good woman in love."

Ultimately, this account would bring E. B. B. to Broadway. If she thrived as a romantic heroine, however, she was in trouble as a poet. For if Barrett Browning's verses were inferior to the poet herself, E. B. B.'s fall from Victorian grace into hysteria scarcely boded well for her critical reputation. There is no more famous evidence of how the legend's fascination with her frailty had come to override interest in her work than the fate of the following passage from G.K. Chesterton: "On the day on which it was necessary for her finally to accept or reject Browning's proposal, [Elizabeth Barrett] called her sister to her, and to the amazement and mystification of that lady asked for a carriage. In this she drove into Regent's Park, alighted, walked on to the grass, and stood leaning against a tree for some moments, looking round her at the leaves and the sky. She then entered the cab again, drove home, and agreed to the elopement. This was possibly the best poem that she ever produced." The truth is, of course, that E. B. B. never "produced" such a poem. Chesterton did. Such are the ironies of canonization, moreover, that his description of it may be the most famous single paragraph he ever wrote. Ironically, Chesterton's account thus offers a double testimony to the overwhelming power of literary legend making. For like Stedman, Gosse, and many others, Chesterton had recorded a number of vivid, specific responses to Barrett Browning's verse. None has been widely reprinted.

As the secular saint's life broke down and the hysterical heroine's romance gained power, critics increasingly (and retroactively) ascribed Barrett Browning's former cultural power, both as a poet and as a heroine, to the innocent enthusiasm (or gullibility) of a feminized, sentimentalized Victorian public. Barrett Browning's early success came to stand for the worst in poet worship. Not incidentally, it was also metaphorically associated with the "nerves," "gushing," and defiance of an influential nineteenth-century female readership. As contempt or condescension toward women readers began to go hand in hand with disdain toward the Victorian public as a whole, such narratives paradoxically accorded literary historians free rein for their own sentimentality. Although Barrett Browning the poet might be made to display all the worst aspects of a culture from which fin-de-siècle criticism sought to break free, Barrett Browning the sentimental heroine still offered romantic or comic relief from analysis of the "real" development of literary tradition.

Certain biographical sketches of the poet's life thus evoke all the quaint, comfortable charm of a Victorianism toward which one might still feel a kind of rueful affection. By 1906, for example, a *London Times* article (reprinted in the *Living Age*) already presents a clear paradigm for the operation of such nostalgia within the shift from canonization to decanonization. "It is the person, not the poet, who lives most," its judgment begins, conventionally enough. "Her poetry as poetry is imperfect. She is an incomplete artist, but a complete woman; and it is as a complete woman that she will stand and endure. When we use the word 'poet' we mean, of course, a professional poet. Every woman is a poet, and she, who was more intensely woman than other women, was, in this way, a past-mistress of poetry." Not surprisingly, the "Sonnets from the Portuguese" "remain her masterpiece— . . . because they are the fullest expression of the woman in her; and, better than these, the best poem that she created, was her own life with her husband." What follows, however, is new and disquieting: "This is perhaps the reason why she is comparatively little read by the present generation; the woman of one age seldom speaks to the 'business and bosoms' of her followers fifty years later."

Thus, having rendered her poetry a secondary concern, E. B. B.'s individual perfection itself falls prey to a form of planned obsolescence. As faith in the Victorian poet-heroine begins to falter, reference to the flawed textual bodies of E. B. B.'s works start to merge with expressions of doubt as to the perfection of their author. Writing on the "Browning-Barrett Love-Letters and the Psychology of Love," Hiram M. Stanley notes that although the "sensuous side" of love, "as might be expected, is chiefly revealed in the letters of Robert Browning," Barrett Browning's sensuous expressions were "vivid" in the sonnets. From him, this assertion is a compliment. From Sanders, however, similar comments on the *Sonnets* take on a different tone: "Never was there a more unmistakable, nor a more intimate personal utterance" than these verses. "Never did a woman make a more entire and outspoken confession of the faith that was in her. Here, if ever, would the discoverer of indiscretions find a secret to be kept inviolate, a rapture for the eyes of the husband alone . . . a confession sacred, holy, incommunicable." Once bared by the *Sonnets*, the "shrine" of E. B. B.'s love was no longer inviolate. On an explicit level, Sander's sexual and sacred metaphors work to absolve readers of the love letters of guilt. Implicitly, however, they question the morality, or at least the modesty, of having published the *Sonnets* in the first place.

Of all such denigrations of the *Sonnets*, none is more striking than that of Browning researcher Elizabeth Porter Gould. Defending the Browning love letters' publication Gould asserts, in *Education*, that they have "been given to the world and have blessed it." "Very little, if any, of our fiction *remains* on such heights. . . . Even poetry, which perhaps is the most genuine expression of the high truth, is not free from the trail of the serpent. But here in this revelation life is *lived*." Deliberately created in the awareness of stylistic good and evil, the *Sonnets* can never be free of the "trail of the serpent." Only letters, presumably written without thought of publication, can express the prelapsarian unselfconsciousness of lived revelation. Thus, in the most extreme instances, the composition of poetry itself becomes a sign of neurosis or sin. The *Sonnets* may still be their author's "supreme" works, but now they embody hysteria or the artistic trail of the serpent.

The Pythia's Return: Fin-de-Siècle Evocations of Hysterical Victorianism

Even the most modest heroine might write love letters, the underlying argument of certain criticisms of the *Sonnets* runs; but there is something wrong with a woman who puts her love into the public form of poetry. Thus, ironically, certain turn-of-the-century criticism both reconfirms mid-Victorian unease over the *Sonnets'* revelations and extends it to far more dangerous ground. For what is immodest now is not so much the exposure of the writer's personal life as that of her artistic labors. Such ironies multiply toward the century's end, as accounts of Barrett Browning's life and works disassociate themselves both from the midcentury criticism that rendered her a poet-heroine and from the later nostalgic canonization that transformed her into an embodiment of the lost Victorian apotheosis of womanhood.

In the *Nation* in 1889, for example, Eugene Schuyler already terms the success of Barrett Browning's early poems "almost inexplicable." E. B. B.

benefited from her era's dearth of good poetry, he suggests; and "then, too, she was a woman—a reason which, in her inner soul, she detested. . . . And then she was admired by women, and placed, as Miss Mitford says, 'in the situation of Wordsworth forty years ago—the foundress of a school of enthusiastic worshippers, laughed at by those who do not feel high poetry.' ".The hysterical heroine is thus issued a mutually reinforcing hysterical audience. Never mind that there were no "Barrett Browning Clubs": with this cut at "enthusiastic worshippers," Schuyler manages to link outmoded reverence for poets with feminine "enthusiasm." His tone of knowing humor would soon become a staple in treatments of the poet's reception.

Aurora Leigh is often central to such revisions. Though it is Barrett Browning's most "important and most characteristic work," A. C. Benson writes, length alone "would prevent" the "undramatic . . . digressive" work from "ever being popular." Why, then, had it sold so many editions? His answer: the poem's autobiographical nature, along with "the comparative mystery in which the authoress was shrouded and the romance belonging to a marriage of poets—these elements are enough to account for the great enthusiasm with which the poem was received. Landor said that it made him drunk with poetry,—that was the kind of expression that admirers allowed themselves to make use of with respect to it. And yet . . . the fact remains that it is a difficult volume to work through." By thus retroactively (and inaccurately) establishing romance at the center of Barrett Browning's popularity, Benson could reinforce his own period's revisionist sentimentality even as he denigrated his critical predecessors, the poem's current admirers, and Aurora Leigh itself.

When Gosse characterizes Barrett Browning's readers in A Short History of Modern English Literature, he does not exempt even the author from the enthusiastic delusions evoked: "Their nerves were pleasurely excited by the choral tumult of Miss Barrett's verse, by her generous and humane enthusiasm, and by the spontaneous impulsiveness of her emotion. They easily forgave the slipshod execution, the hysterical violence, the Pythian vagueness and the Pythian shriek."

Once, Barrett Browning's critics had charged her with metaphorically violating the virtues of Victorian femininity by subjecting herself to the irrational, disturbingly somatic transports of the Pythia; they had proclaimed the results of such inspiration to be out of character. Now, her character has become that of the Pythia, and the mid-Victorian public, whose enthusiasm Gosse so confidently traces to "nerves," is proclaimed to have "easily forgiven" the stylistic wildness that once rendered it so uneasy. Thus the mid-Victorian Pythia returns in a new guise. Still terrifyingly somatic in her inspiration, she is no longer divinely inspired, and no longer separated from E. B. B. herself, as a representative of Victorian womanhood.

As ever, the *Saturday Review*'s representations of literary sexual politics are among the most explicit. As early as 1888, after condemning Barrett Browning's "extravagant and glaring" poetic "defects," a reviewer goes on to cite "the endless gush and the sickening sentimentality, the nauseous chatter about 'womanhood' and 'woman's heart,' and all the rest of it, which she almost invented, but of which the secret by no means died with her." This is strong language from a journal so recently given to panegyrics of old-fashioned femininity. It is clear what kind of readers this reviewer would have us believe welcomed Barrett Browning's verse—and what kind of visceral revulsion the work still evokes.

Earlier critics had defended their poet-heroine by metaphorically dispossessing her of any works that did not seem to speak of "womanhood" or "woman's heart." Now, gallantry moves in the opposite direction, as the *Saturday Review* critic attempts to exonerate a new (potential) poet-heroine from responsibility for E. B. B.'s "endless gush and . . . sickening senti-mentality." "Had Mrs. Browning been at all conscious of the horrible faults of her verse," this author assures readers, "it is probable that she would have been so disgusted as to produce nothing at all, and that would have been a loss indeed." If she could not have helped being a Victorian woman, it seems, a fully conscious E. B. B. would at least have been heroic enough to keep silent.

Like canonization, such decanonization does not go uncontested. In a fine reversal of the *Saturday Review* position, for example, Meynell attempts to separate the true E. B. B. from Victorian womanhood by deploring "that in" Barrett Browning's poetry which "always had more semblance of life than force of life—the faults that came of a too conscious and too emphatic a revolt against her time, a too resolute originality. In another age Elizabeth Barrett Browning would not have needed, or have thought she needed, to spend her strength upon a strained attitude." Just as the *Saturday Review* author's alleged condemnation of sentimentality paradoxically echoes earlier critics' anxieties over fleshly, gushing style, however, Meynell's attempt to accord *Aurora Leigh* only the "semblance of life" actually amplifies initial reviewers' unease at the poem's vitality. Indeed, the poem's greatest flaw turns out to be its "turn of assertion and menace."

In any case, the "Pythian shriek" is now Barrett Browning's: the poet herself is reassimilated to her already decanonized later works—and wished away, as they were. The once sacred embodiment of Victorian womanhood has lost her sanctity. Her final years, which once marked her preparation for an ascent into heaven, now mark her ineluctable descent into personal and poetic decay. Once, the poet-heroine was exorcised; now she herself is the figure who must be driven out if literary history is to remain sane and healthy. We have seen what happened when FitzGerald's letters expressed his relief at Barrett Browning's death. Only a few years later, however, Gosse himself asserted that after 1850 Barrett Browning's "art . . . declined, and much of her late work was formless, spasmodic, singularly tuneless and harsh, nor is it probable that what seemed her premature death, in 1861, was a real deprivation to English literature." Given her production of works such as *Aurora Leigh* and *Poems before Congress*, it seems, the poet's death at age fifty-five only "seemed" premature.

Gosse's magisterial tone is more offensive, because more calculated, than FitzGerald's confessional mode. Its elegiac emphasis on Barrett Browning's personal and poetic decline, however, sounds almost mild in comparison to Harriet Waters Preston's *Atlantic Monthly* essay of 1899. Terming *Aurora Leigh* "socialistic," "sensational," and "ineffective," Preston writes, "Involuntarily, we recall the profane ejaculation of Edward FitzGerald when he heard of Mrs. Browning's death. 'Thank Heaven there will be no more Aurora Leighs!' And while we love the aged Browning all the better for the furious defense he made of his wife's genius against the shade of her incorrigible censor, we know that FitzGerald was right. More Aurora Leighs would have been a heavy misfortune to letters."

Though Preston seems to have read FitzGerald's comment and Browning's reply rather carelessly, hers is a considered opinion. Returning to Stedman's jangled bells metaphor, Preston goes on to imply that *Aurora Leigh* evinces nothing less than progressive mental illness on the part of its author. When the ailing poet went to Italy, "the physical taint remained, congenital and incurable; and . . . the mental taint which inevitably accompanied it was to become increasingly conspicuous in all her published utterances. . . . The woman's voice, ever soft, sympathetic, and musical by the fireside, sounded thin and shrill when uplifted in high argument upon . . . political and social questions. . . . The hysterical note . . . [is not] at any time quite absent from Mrs. Browning's longest, and in some respects most considerable poem. . . . The bells were in truth jangled beyond repair." E. B. B., it seemed, had not died a moment too soon: her "physical taint" might otherwise have further infected literary history, creating a "heavy misfortune to letters." Harriet Waters Preston, it must be noted, was to edit the first Cambridge edition of Barrett Browning's work: the current "living monument" still includes her notes.

Thus, to buy the most accessible *Complete Works* of Barrett Browning is still to buy a monument to legend—complete with keep-off signs in the introduction and prettified Field Talfourd portrait on the front cover. Still, the texts are there for those who choose to go against advice. Loss is a relative term; Barrett Browning has fared better than many. Just as canonical revision and editing ultimately failed to transform Barrett Browning, the dead sinner, into a stable saint, so romantic reverence and literary decanonization ultimately failed to fix E. B. B. as a decorous Andromeda in Wimpole Street. It seems suitable that in 1931, as Barrett Browning languished on Broadway in Rudolf Besier's *The Barretts of Wimpole Street*, she also appeared, in very different guise, in an essay by Virginia Woolf. The architectural canon that houses Woolf's vision of poets is a "mansion of literature." In it, she tracks E. B. B. to her current position, locating her in the downstairs "servants' quarters, where, in company with Mrs. Hemans, Eliza Cook, Jean Ingelow, Alexander Smith, Edwin Arnold, and Robert Montgomery she bangs the crockery about and eats vast handfuls of peas on the point of her knife." Vitality, noise, fearless "vulgarity": though these attributes fit neither the "supreme woman" nor her genteelly neurotic successor, they had been ascribed to the "headlong" poet during her own lifetime. They would emerge once more, later in this century, as sources of a rising literary fame.

JEROME MAZZARO

Mapping Sublimity: Elizabeth Barrett Browning's Sonnets from the Portuguese

For a Renaissance scholar and modernist like Robert B. Heilman, Elizabeth Barrett Browning's sonnet "How do I love thee?" with its "piling up of abstractions and generalizations . . . gives a positive effect of insincerity." It "is as embarrassing as all platform rhetoric." He compares the poem's matter to Goneril's similar protestation of love for her father in Shakespeare's *King Lear*, distorting the inappropriateness of Goneril's emotions for a parent into an attack on Barrett Browning's verse technique. Certainly, as T. S. Eliot remarks in "The Metaphysical Poets" (1921), between Shakespeare and Barrett Browning a change or "dissociation of sensibility set in." No longer, as in the poetry of Edmund Spenser, were emotions to be set off by the poet's constructing an external and conventional emblem or image to which a reader's emotions would sympathetically respond. Rather, as William Wordsworth noted in his Preface to *Lyrical Ballads* (1800), poems and their subjects would rise internally from a "spontaneous overflow of powerful feelings." In the case of the Romantic poets, whom Barrett Browning succeeded, the emotion most often sought was that of the sublime, situated, as religious writers like Robert Lowth held, in terror and shrinkage associated with contemplating divinity, eternity, etc. or, as Wordsworth maintained, in mentally expansive moments amid primitive nature or, as in his "Upon the Sight of a Beautiful Picture" (1815),

From *Essays in Literature* XVIII, no. 2, (Fall 1991) © 1991 by Jerome Mazzaro.

amid the modest and commonplace. Wordsworth's own evocations of the sublime in his poetry in terms of terror, transgressed boundaries, and spatial metaphors have been ably argued, and in *Sonnets from the Portuguese* (1850) Barrett Browning seems intent on adapting the terror and physicality of these metaphors to her own encounter late in life with love. In so doing, she is not always involved, as Heilman infers that she might be, in expressing literary sincerity.

Barrett Browning's interests in sublimity are everywhere evident in her Prefaces. She not only uses them to reject the opinion "that poetry is not a proper vehicle for abstract ideas" but speaks of poetry and its aims in moral superlatives. In the Preface to *The Battle of Marathon* (1819), for instance, she calls poetry the "noblest" human production: it "elevates the mind to heaven, kindles within it unwonted fires, and bids it throb with feelings exalting to its nature." She chooses to model her own work on Homer, "the sublime poet of antiquity," hoping, like him, to awaken audiences "to the praise of valour, honour, patriotism, and, best of all, to a sense of the high attributes of the Deity, though darkly and mysteriously revealed." Seven years later, she invokes the "sublime" Dante, wishing that, in *An Essay on Mind*, "the sublime circuit of intellect . . . had fallen to the lot of a spirit more powerful than [hers]," so that the work's "vastness" of design and "infinite" subject might have been better embraced. Longinus, "the Homer of critics," is invoked in the Preface to *The Seraphim* (1828) to counter a generation of critics who "believed in the inadmissibility of religion into poetry." Stating that "the very incoherences of poetic dreaming are but the struggle and the strife to reach the True in the Unknown," she claims for herself these "sublime uses of poetry, and the solemn responsibilities of the poet." In the 1844 Preface to her *Poems*, she again laments "the tendency of the present day . . . to sunder the daily life from the spiritual creed," having earlier, in her Preface to *Prometheus Bound* (1833), faulted Longinus for not having recognized Aeschylus's creating in Prometheus "the sublime of virtue" which her own verse translation seeks to preserve.

Nor is there any question that, as biographers have pointed out, expansive as well as terrifying moments accompanied the successful suit and daily life on which *Sonnets from the Portuguese* is built. Elizabeth Barrett was thirty-nine at the time of her first meeting with Robert Browning and already a highly regarded poet. She had suffered the deaths of her mother and brother and had reconciled herself to ill health, opium addiction, and the foregoing of many of the rewards that an active life offers. She was reclusive, bookish, contemplative, and intellectual, and, although not the "confined" and "almost hermetically sealed" figure that R. H. Horne describes in *A New Spirit of the Age* (1844), she had turned her thoughts toward death. Now, she was forced by Browning's insistence to consider turning these thoughts back toward life, surrendering her chastity, marrying, and devoting herself once again to the risks and disappointments of an active existence. In doing so, she would be defying a dictatorial father who characteristically would oppose the action and who, since her brother's death, had not reproached her for her part in it. Moreover, by the union, she would be giving up a direct relationship that she had forged with God in order to stand, as Saint Paul observed, in relation to a husband as that husband did to God and as the church does to Christ (Ephesians 5:21–24). Rather than the vividness and gentle agitations of beauty, the conflict, implications, and resolutions of these possibilities affected her deepest being.

There is no question, either, that formally some of the techniques that Renaissance poets used to assert sincerity in their sonnets are used by Barrett Browning in realizing parts of the sequence. With their rigorous *abbaabbacdcdcd* Petrarchan rhyme scheme and Miltonic disregard of line end and division into octave and sestet, the poems suggest that, much as in the sonnets of John Donne and John Milton, violations to form occur because the emotions or thoughts are in excess of or different from what convention allows. The failure of the content of Donne's "At the round earth's imagined corners," for instance, to fit neatly the *abbaabbacdcdee* rhyme scheme that he provides is, in part, a tribute to the forcefulness of the poem's vision of world end and a reinforcement of the destruction and transformation that take place. Both he and Milton accepted the sonnet form as *lingua franca* for ideas and strong emotions and saw their formal violations of it as acceptable, more truly personally reflective weddings of form to content. Barrett Browning, like Wordsworth before her, seems, in contrast, to have to justify not adjustments to form but the very idea of the sonnet as an adequate embodiment of or vehicle for true emotion. Wordsworth's comparisons of the form to a prison which "no prison is" and to what in Milton's hands "became a trumpet" that let him blow "soul-animated strains" are here relevant. At times, in the *Sonnets from the Portuguese*, form and content are so deliberately left at odds to mark not excess but empty and artificial boundaries that periodically, on grounds independent of sincerity, critics other than Heilman have called the competence of Barrett Browning's verse technique into question.

These critics see in Barrett Browning's submissions to a system of measure (line) and closure (rhyme) that does not measure or close and in her appeals for authority and convention to biblical and literary antecedents that do not quite correspond an impetuosity, faulty judgment, or misplaced ingenuity. They cite the "Latinate horrors, strained conceits, and specious supernatural intervention" that generally mar her verse and note, in the failure of these poems to observe line endings and divide neatly into octet and sestet, "the straining muscles and suffused countenance of the prisoner in the strait-jacket." In the much praised Sonnet 5 ("I lift my heavy heart up solemnly"), for example, they are united in pointing out the imprecision of Sophocles's Electra as a correlative for the poet's feelings about her dead brother. Electra is mistaken about Orestes's being dead, and a reader's knowledge of this fact confuses the poem's impression. Critics are similarly embarrassed by the false self-depreciation that occurs in Sonnets 3 and 4 and by images that seem to make sense only as they are explained by the poet's life and letters. They have also objected on occasion to the poet's choice of language and the exaggerated nature of many of her contrasts. These failures in presenting precise correlatives for emotion have led even supporters of her work like Alethea Hayter to call the result a "cornucopia" of "rich confused fruits" and pronounce the "much-praised" sequence "not her best work" because in it "she is dealing with an emotion too new and powerful for her to transmute . . . into universally valid terms."

Moreover, as a result of gender, temperament, or a decision to follow history, the poems do not adhere either to the stereotypes of Victorian romance or to most Renaissance love sequences. Victorian social conventions provided no ready serious models for centering on an active older woman in love. They dictated, rather, that "good" women in love be young, submissive, devout, attractive, patient, helpless, and passive. Their function was to lift "carnal" man into a "higher life." Nor were Renaissance conventions with their cupids, arrows, and love sickness more accommodating. Love did not enter by the eye and take root in the heart. Nor was the speaker—like the speakers of so many older sequences—the initial pursuer languishing in pain at a beloved's cruelty. Rather, as Dorothy Mermin points out, the sequence confounds what "earlier love poetry had kept separate and opposite: speaker and listener, subject and object of desire, male and female." It begins with the sudden intrusion of love and the reasons why it must or should not occur. The sequence then moves to love's acceptance in calls for closeness and union that are repeatedly imaged as occurring between the "darkness" of the speaker's life before love entered and her views of God and eternity. By Sonnet 22, love is accepted, and with the exception of Sonnet 35, the last half of the sequence bears no indications of regret. In Sonnet 35, the speaker wonders briefly whether, having invited disowning, she will miss home and family. It is the sequence's celebration of joy as a reversal of fortune and a joint reflection on real life happiness that prompted its early appeal. In addition to a sign of divine favor, the successful overcoming of impediments, differences, and distances is, as Glennis Stephenson remarks, the substance of "all great love stories" and makes "the consummation, when it occurs, . . . appear all the more moving and perfect."

Nonetheless, while true and significant, the poet's supposed impetuosity and the sequence's failures to adhere to Victorian and Renaissance love conventions explain less some of its oppositions of content and form and occasional absences of sincerity than do Lowth's characterizations of the sublime. In *Lectures on the Sacred Poetry of the Hebrews* (1787), Lowth cites not only the presence of "elevated sentiments" and bright, animated, energetic, and uncommon language but also the reluctance of the text "to fix on any single point." The mind moves "continually from one object to another," suddenly and frequently changing persons, especially in addresses and expostulations and, at times, in the very act of uttering, catches suddenly at a new and sometimes redundant expression that appears more animated and energetic. Likewise occurring at these times are frequent changes or variations in tense. In dealing with deity, Lowth remarks that "nothing . . . is nobler or more majestic" than a description "carried on by a kind of continued negation." Boundaries "are gradually extended on every side, and at length totally removed; [and] the mind is insensibly led on towards infinity." Citing as "the most perfect example . . . of the sublime ode" a text "which possesses a sublimity dependent wholly upon the greatness of the conceptions, and the dignity of the language, without any peculiar excellence in the form and arrangement," he prepares the way for statements like S. T. Coleridge's that "nothing that has a shape can be sublime except by metaphor *ab occasione ad rem*" and the belief that forms like the sonnet might become a series of boundaries whose inability to contain a writer's "utmost faculties and grandest imagery" contributes to a feeling of majesty and the sometimes inexpressible majesty of God.

This emphasis on the sublime would directly affect sincerity by affecting the sequence's ability to create and sustain character. First, character resides in a grammar of coherence, and the sudden shifts in person, tone, tense, emotion, and diction which Lowth details detract from a central identifiable focal point. But even if this point were to be manifest, a common trait of sublimity is a feeling of transport out of one's characteristical focus. In the case of Shakespeare's characters whose transports derive not from sublimity but from passion, Dr. Johnson notes that they so come to act and speak under "the influence of these general passions and principles by which all minds are agitated" that they manifest "nothing characteristical." The choice for an editor's "correctly" assigning speeches to a specific actor hinges on extrinsic evidence. Indeed, sublime transport differs markedly from both the internally consistent unifying voice, lifestyle, outlook, and behavior of the secular Renaissance love sequence and the violations of form and emotionally based meditational transports of its religious poetry. In the sonnets of Donne, for example, the elevated passions of the sestet are prepared for by the octet's equally intense context- and self-defining interactive language and central binding image. Thus, while "escapist," they are, nonetheless, "in character" with the octave psychologically and theologically. In the sonnets of George Herbert, where, as in those of Barrett Browning, the opacity of verbal interaction is weaker and no distanced persona emerges, the degree that a unified or sincere self occurs is gauged outside the poem in weighing the poem's language against the poet's other works or life.

In the opening two sonnets of *Sonnets from the Portuguese*, one can see how these elements of the sublime are incorporated into the sequence. The first sonnet takes the reader from the comfortable and bounded imaginative realm of literary reminiscence into the frightening and unbounded realm of mystical appearance:

> I thought once how Theocritus had sung
> Of the sweet years, the dear and wished for years,
> Who each one in a gracious hand appears
> To bear a gift for mortals, old or young:
> And, as I mused it in his antique tongue,
> I saw, in gradual vision through my tears,
> The sweet, sad years, the melancholy years,
> Those of my life, who by turns had flung
> A shadow across me. Straightway I was 'ware
> So weeping, how a mystic Shape did move
> Behind me, and drew me backward by the hair,
> And a voice said in mastery while I strove, . .
> 'Guess now who holds thee?'—'Death', I said. But there,
> The silver answer rang. . 'Not Death, but Love.'

The poem opens on a figure who thinks of life in terms of art, in this instance, of life as imaged by Theocritus in Idyll 15. The allusion is precise and, indeed, an adequate translation of the Greek. In the Idyll, the lines appear as part of a song that is sung by an accomplished female poet and contrast with the everyday chatter of the two women who pause to hear the singer. Their "dear and wished for years" not only revive briefly the annual return of Adonis from the dead which the original Greek celebrates but also embody return in their being themselves recollection. With their "gift" of recovery, they thus oppose "the sweet, sad . . . melancholy years" of the second quatrain and their implied irretrievable loss that "flung / A shadow" across the speaker's life. This shadow suddenly gives way in the sestet to the awareness of "a mystic Shape" which seems to echo and combine those visionary episodes of Eliphaz in Job (4:12–16), Jacob in Genesis (32:27–30), and Paul in Acts / (9:3–5). It violently draws the speaker "backward by the hair" and eventually reveals itself as Love. In so doing, it rejects her expectations of Death and, by proximity, so merges Love and Death that, coevally as one is led by "mystic" and the calculated incoherence into the realm of the sublime, one is returned to Theocritus and the associations there of love and death with Adonis and Venus and Persephone and Dis. Given Barrett Browning's Preface to *The Seraphim* (1838), one is led, in addition, to Christ's death as love and the Christ-like imagery that will surround the suitor of the sequence.

Moreover, one has in the conflation of referents for the "mystic Shape" an example of the inability to grasp exactly and, therefore, the need to try several metaphors that the sublime occasions. In their edition of *The Complete Works* (1900), Charlotte Porter and Helen Clarke identify the wording of the incident with Athena's action toward Achilles in Book 1 of the *Iliad*. There is, however, in the Barrett Browning telling no anger, a reversal of gender, and no prior acquaintance with the deity. Achilles recognizes the goddess immediately. The incident does seem to suggest what theologians call "catabatic mysticism" (i.e., divinity's approaching the human), and it is the suggestion of such an approach that the verses from Job, Genesis, and Acts make their claims. In *A Philosophical Enquiry into the Origin of Our Ideas of the Sublime and Beautiful*, Edmund Burke calls the Job passage "amazingly sublime," and Job's passing from joy to loss to regained joy parallels the speaker's passage in the sequence from "childhood joy" to the loss of a brother to regained happiness. But here, too, differences exist. In Job, the mystic shape appears *before* not *behind* Eliphaz and draws him forward to the belief that one cannot comprehend and, therefore, should not presume to interpret God's measure. In the parallels from Genesis and Acts, the violence which the figure displays by drawing the speaker backward by the hair is echoed in Jacob's wrestling and Paul's unhorsing and their efforts to know the figure's name in the speaker's query and disclosure. The failure of the sonnet's content, consequently, to fit formal demands is understandable, given the poem's sublime elements.

In the second sonnet, a different kind of confusion associated with sublimity occurs. The suitor is introduced, and the seemingly boundless realm which deity inhabits is imaged as terrifying audible darkness. Deity's opposing Nay, which furnishes the speaker's first effort at dissuasion, is so absolute that even death could not make her feel more closed to the gentleman than she now feels. Expressed as visual exclusion, this sense speaks to the suitor's physical being and, building on the "only" and "all" of the sonnet's opening line, contrasts with the presumed limitlessness of God. Had God so ordained, the poem ventures, as terrifying and vast as the greatest efforts of man and nature are, they would not have been able to prevent the union.

> But only three in all God's universe
> Have heard this word thou hast said,—Himself beside
> Thee speaking, and me listening! and replied
> One of us . . *that* was God, . . and laid the curse
> So darkly on my eyelids, so to amerce
> My sight from seeing thee,—that if I had died,
> The deathweights, placed there, would have signified
> Less absolute exclusion. 'Nay' is worse
> From God than from all others, O my friend!
> Men could not part us with their worldly jars,
> Nor the seas change us, nor the tempests bend;
> Our hands would touch for all the mountain-bars,—
> And, heaven being rolled between us at the end,
> We should but vow the faster for the stars.

In drawing the expanses of personal terror and shrinkage which accompany the sublime when it is associated with deity, the sonnet again displays confusion and incoherence. Phrase is piled upon phrase, and orderly progressions of thought are twice interrupted by qualifying parenthetical matter. First, in line 4, "one" is identified as "God," and then, in a further compounding of confusion, the "curse" of line 4 is identified as a punishment before its exclusionary nature is given. "Amerce," as scholars have pointed out, joins the speaker's fate verbally to those angels of *Paradise Lost* who for Satan's fault are "amerc't / Of Heav'n." Presumably, her similar opposition to divine will by allowing the suit will deprive her of the gentleman's "Christ-like" sight as these angels have been deprived of the sight of God. But one has almost to eliminate the interruption in order to understand the situation fully. These syntactical and sequential confusions lessen as the poem moves in the sestet to a sense of positive expansion associated with the natural sublime and recalls the impediments to "the marriage of true minds" that Shakespeare writes of in Sonnet 116. This move from confusion and incoherence is conveyed in lines which, despite their negations, honor rhyme and formal line end. They restore the worldly and literary senses of order on which the sequence opened and, hence, round off the sonnets from or bridge them to the remainder of the sequence. The sonnets are further separated from succeeding accounts by their being cast in the past tense.

Sincerity in these opening sonnets is not at issue, since the speaker's role in regard to determining significant action remains essentially passive.

She does not choose the appearance of the "mystic Shape" or God's judgment against a courtship. One would suspect that, as the poems deal more with choice, "daily life," and a realm which the lovers inhabit, oppositions of form and content and confusion as signs of sublimity should diminish and more traditional and containable approaches to sincerity appear. This, however, is not the case. Syntax, for the most part, does grow less obscure, but there are in the remaining sonnets only seven—4, 8, 13, 16, 27, 35, and 43—when can be divided cleanly into octet and sestet. Despite the often balanced and dialectical nature of the subjects, there is, moreover, little or no attention paid to rhetorical balance or proportion. Sentences are constructed loosely as in conversation, and interruptions and paddings for the sake of rhyme persist. As in the opening sonnets, one draws from the informality, immediacy, italicized words, and many bracketed phrases the same sense of the speaker's catching suddenly at vastness with new and more animated expressions that Lowth associates with sublimity. But whereas the kind of conflation which occurs in the image of the "mystic Shape" of sonnet 1 seems not to recur, there is in the treatment of subjects, as in Sonnet 25, an amplification or diffusion, "many circumstances being added, and a variety of imagery introduced for the purpose of illustration." Lowth associates this amplification with sublimity, and, as in verses of a song, the differing allusions and metaphors of the "varied robes" extend and ornament the subject, supporting an impression of poetic range and individual versatility.

The changes to the image of the heart as a heavy weight on which Sonnet 25 begins exemplify the practice. As Hayter notes, the image appears to change as if the speaker were unaware "where [it was] leading her, as one [is] in conversation." This "conversational" artlessness continues in the speaker's failures to limit her statements to either quatrain or octet. Line 4 is made to overflow by simile, and line 8, by withholding "my heavy heart" for emphasis, and one has none of the reflection or shifting viewpoint that is customary to the sonnet sestet.

> A heavy heart, Belovèd, have I borne
> From year to year until I saw thy face,
> And sorrow after sorrow took the place
> Of all those natural joys as lightly worn
> As the stringed pearls . . . each lifted in its turn
> By a beating heart at dance-time. Hopes apace
> Were changed to long despairs, till God's own grace
> Could scarcely lift above the world forlorn
> My heavy heart. Then *thou* didst bid me bring
> And let it drop adown thy calmly great

Deep being! Fast it sinketh, as a thing
Which its own nature doth precipitate,
While thine doth close above it, mediating
Betwixt the stars and the unaccomplished fate.

The key to the poem, however, lies not, as Hayter proposes, in the contrasting "heavy heart" and "stringed pearls" of lines 1 and 5 but in the "dance-time" of line 6. The allusion is the Ecclesiastes 3:4 and its mention of "a time to mourn, and a time to dance" and corresponds to Barrett Browning's use of women "stringing pearls" amid "universal anguish" in *Aurora Leigh*. The "heavy heart" of the opening line is, thus, not only, as Hayter conjectures, "the heart as a heavy locket," but more than an item of jewelry: it is, once again, as in Sonnet 1, the heart in mourning, and perhaps even Job's "heart of stone"(41:24). As so often in the sequence, the poet appears to be moved coevally by the death of her brother and the sheltered existence to which women are relegated, and by being so complexly moved, she lends strong support to Angela Leighton's argument for the sequence's dual Muses and to recent feminist interpretations. In regard especially to the former, Leighton notes that "the harsh superimposition of love on grief in the *Sonnets* betrays the extent to which the role[s]" of the dead brother and live suitor are "the same." They are objects of the poet's "imaginative desire to write."

Readers are thus to infer that before the suitor's arrival, the speaker's heavy heart had come to resemble that heart described by God just before Job's submission and the restoration of his good fortune. Sorrows have replaced what, in the brother's company, had been "natural joys," until, in a reference to Luke 24:2, "God's own grace / Could scarcely lift [it]." Here, in a recurrent but not continuous analogy of the suitor's impact to Christ's, the heart/stone becomes the stone of Christ's tomb, and, through the suggestion of redemption through Christ's death and resurrection, the speaker approaches a status similar to that grace which Job enjoys at his trial's end. Immediately, the next line returns to Ecclesiastes and "a time to cast away stones" (3:5). The statement is, as biblical interpreters note, "a metaphor implying the act of marital intercourse." Sinking beneath the surface of what appears to be well water, the heart/stone finds itself being closed over by the suitor. The action not only conveys a wifely Pauline submergence of self to replace the sheltered life of lines 4–6 but, as in a number of sonnets, mediates a middleground "Betwixt the stars and unaccomplished fate." In these differing appearances, the "heart" image offers neither the opening sonnet's conflation of allusions nor a unified binding image by which, as in Donne's sonnets, readers may infer a unified character and sincerity. Rather, it

presents a series or cluster of images loosely associated about a belief in the
determined seasons, life rhythms, contrasts, and accountings of Ecclesiastes.

Along with sonnet 22, Sonnet 43, which Heilman attacks, locates
the place of these seasons as existing, like the Theocritean text of Sonnet 1,
somewhere between divine sublimity and the "daily life" of what Sonnet 22
calls "the unfit / Contrarious moods of men." The sonnets, thus, form part
of a treatment of distance whose romantic development Stephenson touches
on. Not only, as she argues, are the distance between the speaker and suitor
indicative of stages in worldly desire, distances between the speaker and
subsequently the lovers and God indicate stages of heavenly desire. In a kind
of pre-Eliotic "mythic method," Barrett Browning shapes these distances to
a belief that "the contemplation of excellence produces excellence, if not
similar, yet parallel. Again, as elsewhere in the sequence, this "excellence"
includes literary models as well as poetic impulses, and again, Paul's
depictions of worldly and divine love color the models on which the poems
focus. In both sonnets, Barrett Browning endorses Paul's views on marriage's
place, but unlike him, she advocates here not the male priority of Sonnet 25
but parity between the worldly participants. The advocacy reflects what
critics describes as the poet's deep dissatisfaction with women's role in
marriage. Barrett Browning knew that her mother's marriage had not been
happy, and, as Hayter notes, "she had seen too many instances of mistakes
and disillusions, treacheries and tyrannies, in other marriages. Nonetheless,
the poet appears to except from attack her own present circumstances,
having insisted in Sonnet 14 that the suitor's love "be for nought" but "love's
sake only," agreeing with Shakespeare's Sonnet 116 that "love is not love /
Which alters when it alteration finds."

Having accepted the suit as part of God's will and restoration to
grace, she imagines the worldly consequences of its acknowledgment and
fulfillment:

> When our two souls up erect and strong,
> Face to face, silent, drawing nigh and nigher,
> Until the lengthening wings break into fire
> At either curvéd point,—what bitter wrong
> Can the earth do to us, that we should not long
> Be here contented? Think. In mounting higher,
> The angels would press on us, and aspire
> To drop some golden orb of perfect song
> Into our deep, dear silence. Let us stay
> Rather on earth, Belovèd,—where the unfit
> Contrarious moods of men recoil away

And isolate pure spirits, and permit
A place to stand and love in for a day,
With darkness and the death-hour rounding it.

Again, as in Sonnet 25, neither the formalities of line, quatrain, or octet are adhered to. Lines 4 and 8 overflow once more into 5 and 9. The expression "face to face" appears in 1 Corinthians after Paul's description of love as the manner in which one will see when "the imperfect will pass away" (13:4–8, 10) and Exodus 25:18–20 and the ark of the covenant have been suggested as the origin of the souls as two angels standing face to face. Dante, Shelley, Milton, and Blake may have contributed, moreover, to the angels' "lengthening wings break[ing] into fire / At either curvéd point." The angels' being "face to face" measures, in addition, the movement toward parity which has occurred since Sonnet 3 when, because of the pair's difference, their "ministering two angels" could only "look surprise / On one another, as they [struck] athwart / Their wings in passing." Determined to stay on earth where their "pure spirits" will be separated from the unfit moods of men, they accept the world's "darkness and the death-hour," knowing that, in the rightness of their love, whatever "bitter wrong" the earth can do them, their feelings will survive. This knowledge reinforces the closing "natural" sublime of Sonnet 2, where had they had God's approval, "Men could not part [them] with their worldly jars." No longer, it appears, is it deity but the world and her family who pose obstacles ("bitter wrongs") to which their spirits—so long as they do not presume on heaven—are more than a match.

Pauline echoes are again present in the opening lines of Sonnet 43. Involved here is Paul's prayer that the faithful, grounded in love "may be able to comprehend with all saints what is the breath, and length, and depth, and height" of Christ's love (Ephesians 3:17-19). When "feeling out of sight" of such ends, the speaker senses the suitor's less expansive love having metaphorically filled the void. On a different level, the sonnet complements the substitution of the suitor and life for the "visions" and books of Sonnet 26. The human measures of this love occupy lines 5–8, opposing the apostle's revealed Being and Grace in line 4 with man's imagined Right and Praise. Returning by way of contrast to Paul's statements on divine love in 1 Corinthians 13:11 and Ephesians 3:18, the speaker recounts in the sestet a history of her conversion from "old griefs" and "childhood's faith" to a love that seemed to restore her "lost saints" and, should God "choose," will grow better after death:

How do I love thee? Let me count the ways.
I love thee to the depth and breadth and height

My soul can reach, when feeling out of sight
For the ends of Being and ideal Grace.
I love thee to the level of everyday's
Most quiet need, by sun and candlelight.
I love thee freely, as men strive for Right;
I love thee purely, as they turn from Praise.
I love thee with, the passion put to use
In my old griefs, and with my childhood's faith.
I love thee with a love I seemed to lose
With my lost saints,—I love thee with the breath,
Smiles, tears, of all my life!—and, if God choose,
I shall but love thee better after death.

The sonnet is one of those few that theoretically can be divided into quartrain, octet, and sestet, though internally the proportions of the seven ways in which the speaker loves and an eighth manner which she projects are anything but balanced. They run from three to one line in length and do, as Heilman charges, contain a lot of abstractions. Purists, in addition, may object to the near rhymes of "ways" and "Grace," "use" and "lose," and "faith" and "breath." Still, in light of the sonnet's careful demarcations of divine, human, and personal realms, Heilman's complaints of faulty verse technique, insincerity, and platform rhetoric appear excessive. William T. Going's response that "in context" the sonnet "is not 'embarrassing . . . platform rhetoric,' " while promising, raises new questions. Foremost among them is how consistently is the sequence to be read. If, as critics charge, Barrett Browning is unable at times to carry an image through one sonnet, how valid is an approach that insists upon a selective consistency of "former phrases or images"? How much weight, for instance, can be given the poet's possible uses of Achilles in Sonnets 1 and 27 or her return to Theocritus in sonnet 40? Thematically the problem of irreconcilable opposites (Polyphemus and Galatea) seems to have been resolved earlier, and although Lowth mentions Theocritus's elegance and knowledge of Solomon's Song of Songs, he cites neither Idyll 11 or 15. True, Polyphemus's ability to use song to overcome his feelings for the unresponsive sea nymph contrasts with the suitor's unwavering fidelity, but is anything more specifically intended than a general bookishness from which the speaker claims disruption in Sonnet 26?

Readers have experienced, moreover, at least two methods of associative development in the sequence influencing their understanding—conflation and amplification. In Sonnet 43, one has, in addition, an unreconciled refinement of language usage similar to that separating thought and feeling in Eliot's "dissociation of sensibility" and echoing that division of literary and everyday language in Sonnet 1. There are in the poem's three

divisions the mind "elevated to heaven" by its incorporation of Pauline
allusion and religious language ("soul," "out-of-sight," "Being," and "ideal"
rather than social "Grace"); human aspiration in references to "everyday,"
"need," "sun and candelight," and associations of both "Right" and "Praise"
with man; and personal history in the sestet's movement from "childhood's
faith" and "lost saints" to an image of eternity. While recapturing
thematically the sequence's associative "fields" of religion, daily life, and
personal history, the divisions, by their exclusions of one another, result not
in perhaps an intended echo of choral strophe, antistrophe, and epode but in
what nineteenth-century psychologists call a "divided self." Not so much the
abstractions that Heilman cites but the failure of these "fields of
consciousness" to unite into a credible literary voice produces the sonnet's
impressions of insincerity and "embarrassing . . . platform rhetoric." Clearly,
had Barrett Browning been able early to infuse her theological and learned
bent into common speech, the absence of conviction which Heilman
associates with an inability to find "images to realize, to prove her existence"
might not have occurred.

Still, if the objections which Heilman raises in response to Sonnet
43 can be identified with the failure of the sequence's non-sublime poems to
achieve what Louis L. Martz calls "the unity" of a "meditative style," the
other readers'objections to the sequence's formal transgressions and
"careless" verse technique remain unchallenged. Given that the divisions of
the conventional sonnet are best suited in narratives whose lines are familiar
and that, by impeding horizontal movement, they assist vertical self-
definition, a narrative line which chooses to confuse gender roles and refuses
to adhere to Victorian stereotypes or Renaissance conventions must be seen
as novel. The novelty is increased, moreover, by the poet's belief in the
language, if not the actual existence, of a worldly "divided self." For such a
narrative, expository and lyrical strains cannot be expected to occur at pre-
set and regular intervals, and for readers to expect that they should is perhaps
a bit unrealistic. Given the singularity that Barrett Browning assigns to the
suit, it seems unrealistic as well to expect either adherence to
conventionalizing measures and closes or exact correspondence in the work's
biblical and literary allusions. The protagonist is not offered as a new ideal.
Thus, much as imprecision and formal violations function in the sublime
poems to suggest a release from religious preconceptions, imprecision and
formal violations function in these sonnets of daily life to convey release
from social expectations. The poet's success in both endeavors can be
measured positively in the surprise which critics note in their readings of
Sonnets from the Portuguese and negatively in the "embarrassment" and
"Peeping Tom sensations" that they complain of.

DOROTHY MERMIN

The Female Poet and The Embarrassed Reader: Elizabeth Barrett Browning's Sonnets from the Portuguese

"**I** love your verses with all my heart, dear Miss Barrett"—so began Robert Browning's first letter to the poet he was soon to meet, court, and marry. He went on to praise her poems' "fresh strange music, the affluent language, the exquisite pathos and true new brave thought." Such enthusiasm was not unusual then or later in the nineteenth century, for Elizabeth Barrett was a famous and respected writer whose work was considered learned, innovative, obscure, and difficult as well as expressive and moving. Rossetti, Morris, and Swinburne admired her intensely when they were young and impressionable and much Pre-Raphaelite poetry shows her influence. Her poems offered a vital energy, a new and compelling music, a bold engagement with controversial social issues, and a combination of tough wit with passionate intensity that was more like Donne than anything yet published in the nineteenth century. Coventry Patmore found *Sonnets from the Portuguese* "lofty, simple, and passionate—not at all the less passionate in being highly intellectual, and even metaphysical." Her use of the ballad tradition bore fruit in the work of Morris, Rossetti, and others, her poems on social themes were popular and influential, and *Aurora Leigh*, her feminist novel in verse, had a huge success (partly *de scandale*) and still charms readers with its wit, psychological acuteness, social comedy, and exuberant energy. But even with the current interest in female writers most of her

From *English Literary History* 48, no. 2 (Summer 1981), © 1981 by The Johns Hopkins University Press.

poetry is neglected, while from *Sonnets from the Portuguese*—her most lastingly popular work and, next to *Aurora Leigh*, her most considerable poetic achievement—critics avert their eyes in embarrassment.

The poem deserves much more attention from literary historians, however, both because of Barrett Browning's influence on later women poets and because it is the first of the semi-autobiographical, amatory, lyrical or partly lyrical sequences in modern settings that comprise one of the major innovations of Victorian literature. The poetry is much more subtle, rich, and varied than one would guess from "How do I love thee"—the only one of the sonnets that most of us know. The poem's enormous popularity with unliterary (presumably female) readers, along with the even more popular legend of the fair poetess, the dashing poet-lover, and the mad tyrant of Wimpole Street partly account for the repugnance—often expressed as ridicule—that *Sonnets from the Portuguese* is apt to inspire. But the real problem is that the female speaker produces painful dislocations in the conventions of amatory poetry and thus in the response of the sophisticated twentieth-century reader, whose first overwhelming though inaccurate impression of the poems is that they are awkward, mawkish, and indecently personal—in short, embarrassing.

The speaker fills roles that earlier love poetry had kept separate and opposite: speaker and listener, subject and object of desire, male and female. While this produces a rich poetic complexity, it also produces embarrassment, which as Erving Goffman says can arise from the clashing of apparently incompatible roles. Traditionally in English love poetry the man loves and speaks, the woman is beloved and silent. In *Sonnets from the Portuguese*, however, the speaker casts herself not only as the poet who loves, speaks, and is traditionally male, but also as the silent, traditionally female beloved. Insofar as we perceive her as the lover, we are made uneasy both by seeing a woman in that role and by the implications about the beloved: the man seems to be put in the woman's place, and—especially if we recall the origins of the female lyric tradition in Sappho—we may seem to hear overtones of sexual inversion. Insofar as the speaker presents herself as the beloved, however, she transfers the verbal self-assertion and many of the attributes which in poems traditionally belong to the subject of desire, to desire's normally silent and mysterious object. The result is a devaluation of the erotic object that casts the whole amorous and poetical enterprise in doubt. For the object is both the speaker and the text, an identity like that which Browning asserted in his first letter to Elizabeth Barrett: "I do, as I say, love these books with all my heart—and I love you too." The identification troubled her, though she could not entirely disavow it: "There is nothing to see in me," she told him; "my poetry . . . is the flower of me . . . the rest of me is nothing but a root, fit for the ground & the dark." She assumed at first that his love was "a mere poet's fancy . . . a confusion between the woman and the poetry." Many of the sonnets say, in effect: *"Look at me, and you will cease to desire me."* So solicited, many readers turn away.

They turn from a sight that violates both literary and social decorum: a distinctly nineteenth-century woman in the humble posture of a courtly lover. This blurring of sexual roles is established in the third sonnet, which imagines the beloved as a glorious court musician "looking from the lattice-lights" at the speaker, who is just a "poor, tired, wandering singer, singing through / The dark, and leaning up a cypress tree." Later the speaker compares her bewilderment after seeing her lover to that of a rather Keatsian "acolyte" who "fall(s) flat, with pale insensate brow, / On the altar-stair." The traditional poet-wooer, insofar as he describes himself at all, is pale, wan, and weary from unsatisfied desire. Barrett Browning in her essay on English poetry quotes with affection a passage by Hawes that includes these typical lines: "With your swete eyes behold you me, and see / How thought and woe by great extremitíe, / Hath changed my colour into pale and wan." In *Sonnets from the Portuguese,* pallor and weariness belong to the woman both as signs of passion, as in the images of minstrel and acolyte, and—more disturbingly still—as the self-portraiture of an aging woman.

The self-portrait, furthermore, is detailed, unflattering, and accurate. In one of the poem's most vivid scenes from a recognizably nineteenth-century courtship, the speaker gives her lover a lock of hair and reminds him that her hair is no longer dressed with rose or myrtle like a girl's:

> it only may
> Now shade on two pale cheeks the mark of tears,
> Taught drooping from the head that hangs aside
> Through sorrow's trick.

She has "trembling knees," "tremulous hands," and "languid ringlets." This is a literally faithful picture of the poet (whereas Shakespeare's description of himself in the *Sonnets* as marked by extreme old age presumably is not). The unfashionable ringlets and the characteristic droop of the head can be seen in her pictures. Elizabeth Barrett was forty years old when she married (Browning was six years younger) and had been an invalid, grieving and blaming herself for the death of her favorite brother, addicted to opium, and mostly shut up in one dark airless room, for years. The extraordinary biographical accuracy with which the poem depicts its female speaker violates the decorum of the sonnet sequence almost as much as the sex of the speaker does.

As is usual in love poetry, there is much less physical description of the man than of the woman. And his appearance, in significant contrast to her own, is always imaginatively transformed when it is described at all. *Her* hair is just "brown," but *his* seems fit for verse: "As purply-black, as erst to Pindar's eyes / The dim purpureal tresses gloomed athwart / The nine white Muse-brows." We can usually accept her exaltation of her beloved—who is characteristically described as royal, whose color is purple, whose merit knows no bounds—because the terms and images are familiarly literary. She gives no sketch of him to match her cruel self-portrait and apologizes for her ineptitude in portraying him:

> As if a shipwrecked Pagan, safe in port,
> His guardian sea-god to commemorate,
> Should set a sculptured porpoise, gills a-snort
> And vibrant tail, within the temple-gate.

No apology is really necessary, however, for this flattering comparison of the lover to a sexy sea-god or for the disarmingly erotic porpoise.

Sometimes she is herself transformed by her own imagination, but into an object unworthy of desire. Her house is desolate and broken, like that of Tennyson's Mariana. She praises him at her own expense: she is "an out-of-tune / Worn viol," but "perfect strains may flat / 'Neath master-hands, from instruments defaced." His imagination, that is, might be able to transform her even if her own cannot. Earlier she had offered herself as the object of his poems (rather than the subject of her own):

> How, Dearest, wilt thou have me for most use?
> A hope, to sing by gladly? or a fine
> Sad memory, with thy songs to interfuse?
> A shade, in which to sing of palm or pine?
> A grave, on which to rest from singing? Choose.

This extreme self-abnegation is also an incisive commentary on male love poems, however, since the alternatives require not only the woman's passivity and silence but her absence and finally her death. Christina Rossetti makes a similar indirect comment in the lyric that begins "When I am dead, my dearest, / Sing no sad songs for me"—in the dreamy twilight of the grave, she won't hear them. Rossetti's speaker in *Monna Innominata* does define herself within the terms set by male poets, each sonnet in the sequence being preceded by epigraphs from Dante and Petrarch; but her lover goes away and in the last sonnet she is left with "Youth gone, and beauty gone" and "A silent heart," "Silence of love that cannot sing again." Similarly, Barrett Browning's

"Catarina to Camoens" presents Catarina on her death-bed musing over Camoens' poetical praise of her eyes, which she recalls at the end of each of the twenty-nine stanzas; Camoens is abroad and she imagines what he might say about her death and how he might come to praise another woman. This poem was one of the Brownings' favorites, and they called her sonnets "from the Portuguese" in a cryptic allusion to the fancy that Catarina might have spoken them. But the speaker in *Sonnets from the Portuguese* initiates and writes her own poems. She does not choose merely to respond to her lover's words, to be silent, to be abandoned, or to die.

And so the sequence works out terms of reciprocity between two lovers who are both poets. His love calls forth her poems, but she writes them. He is the prince whose magic kiss restores her beauty, which in turn increases her poetical power (in love poems as in fairy tales, women draw power from their beauty). He "kissed / The fingers of this hand wherewith I write; / And ever since, it grew more clean and white / . . . quick . . . When the angels speak." He has the "power" and "grace" to see beyond appearances to her true worth; through her outer self—"this mask of me"—he sees her "soul's true face" and "all which makes [her] tired of all, self-viewed," and still "Nothing repels" him. His attention encourages her to speak, although in an early sonnet she had briefly adopted the conventional female role: "let the silence of my womanhood / Commend my woman-love to thy belief." She says that his poems are better than hers, but we never hear them, and throughout the sequence his role as poet seems to be in abeyance. He let drop his "divinest Art's / Own instrument" to listen to her sad music— "To hearken what I said between my tears"—and although she asks him to show her how to express her gratitude, we don't see him do so. In the final sonnet she offers him the poems, metaphorical flowers in return for his real ones.

The ultimate source of both her attraction and her power in these poems, however, is simply her own desire. What, after all, does a lyric lover traditionally offer as an inducement to love except his love itself? And if desire confers erotic value, then she herself, being poet-lover, must be an object worthy of desire. Her poem can work if she is humble, but not if she is cold.

> Yet love, mere love, is beautiful indeed
> And worthy of acceptation. Fire is bright,
> Let temple burn, or flax; an equal light
> Leaps in the flame from cedar-plank or weed:
> And love is fire. And when I say at need
> *I love thee* . . . mark! . . . *I love thee*—in thy sight
> I stand transfigured, glorified aright,

With conscience of the new rays that proceed
Out of my face toward thine. There's nothing low
In love, when love the lowest: meanest creatures
Who love God, God accepts while loving so.
And what I *feel*, across the inferior features
Of what I am, doth flash itself, and show
How that great work of Love enhances Nature's.

In the quick and subtle reasoning conducted largely through a series of brief analogies, in the flexibility and control with which the verse bends to the argument and to the rhythms of thought and speech, and in the final sonorous generalizations, the poem is more proleptic of Meredith's *Modern Love* than it is reminiscent of Renaissance sonneteers or even of Donne. Like a character in a Victorian novel, she sees herself through another's eyes, but it is the fire of her own love that glorifies her. Later poems in the series develop this realization of the primacy of desire, his and her own. Love me, she says, "for love's sake only"; and, reciprocally, "Make thy love larger to enlarge my worth."

When the speaker looks at herself in the mirror that traditional love poetry holds up to either men or women, she is apologetic and we are embarrassed. But when she expresses desire, she finds strong new images and a new poetic voice, sensuous, witty, and tender.

What I do
And what I dream include thee, as the wine
Must taste of its own grapes . . .

Let the world's sharpness, like a clasping knife,
Shut in upon itself and do no harm. . . .

When our two souls stand up erect and strong,
Face to face, silent, drawing nigh and nigher,
Until the lengthening wings break into fire
At either curvèd point. . . .

She compares her thoughts of her lover to entwined vine-leaves that hide a palm tree, asking him to "renew" his "presence" in terms that suggest a Bacchic rite.

Rustle thy boughs and set thy trunk all bare,
And let these bands of greenery which insphere thee

Drop heavily down,—burst, shattered, everywhere!
Because, in his deep joy to see and hear thee
And breathe within thy shadow a new air,
I do not think of thee—I am too near thee.

Readers don't seem to be bothered by erotic passages like these, which use images—knives, grapes, androgynous angels, palm trees, dolphins—that evoke no inappropriate reminders of either courtly love or Victorian manners. What does embarrass us is the feeling aroused by less erotic sonnets that we are eavesdropping on the lovers' private affairs. This feeling has several sources. One is that the disparity between the female role and the traditional poetic lover's, between this speaker and the remembered voices we dimly hear behind her, makes us aware of much that is unconventional, and we assume that what is not conventional is autobiographical, merely personal, mawkishly "sincere." And of course Barrett Browning herself, like most Victorian readers and writers, valued the appearance of sincerity in poems very highly, and generally achieved it—which is one reason why Victorian readers liked the *Sonnets* better than later generations have. Thus Christina Rossetti takes for granted that if "the Great Poetess" had been unhappy in her love she might have written a different set of sonnets, with a "'donna innominata' drawn not from fancy but from feeling" (interestingly enough, Rossetti says this in a head note implicitly disavowing any autobiographical element in *Monna Innominata*). But women's writing is all too easily read not just as sincere but, more damagingly, as artless and spontaneous. When women's poetry (especially love poetry) is powerful, it is assumed to be autobiographical, and when evidence for this is unavailable, as with Rossetti and Dickinson, critics have deduced it from the poems. And so Barrett Browning's experiments with meter and rhyme were taken as carelessness or ineptitude; even G. K. Chesterton, who found her writing astonishingly "'manly'" and remarked that she is often "witty after the old fashion of the conceit," could not forbear adding that such wit "came quite freshly and spontaneously" to her.

Finally, of course, we know that the story the *Sonnets* tells is true. Elizabeth Barrett was a legendary public figure even before her marriage, by virtue of her poems, her learning, her seclusion, and her sex, and for most readers the personal element has been inseparable from the sonnets since their first publication. We know the story of her courtship, which was largely epistolary and has been available in print since 1899, and the many parallels between the letters and the poems tempt us to assume that the poems were spontaneously produced at the moments they appear to describe.

It is worth noting, however, that the letters themselves don't embarrass us; only the poems do. We are more disturbed by the incongruity we feel between the sentiments and the genre than by the sentiments themselves. Little scenes from Victorian life and characteristically Victorian modes of feeling and turns of phrase give a strange context to the sonnets' erotic intensities and traditional form. They seem to belong in prose fiction instead.

> My letters! all dead paper, mute and white!
> And yet they seem alive and quivering
> Against my tremulous hands which loose the string
> And let them drop down on my knee tonight.

The speaker recalls her dead mother's kiss and her own childish play among the cowslips. When she addresses her lover as "Dear" or "Dearest" or "Beloved" she sounds more like a Victorian wife than a courtly lover: "I lean upon thee, Dear, without alarm." She likes him to call her by the "pet-name" of her childhood. They exchange locks of hair. She wonders if she will miss, when she marries, "Home-talk and blessing and the common kiss," the "walls and floors" even, of home. Barrett Browning's most sympathetic and discriminating critic, Alethea Hayter, says that *Sonnets from the Portuguese* is too intimate, "emotionally . . . naked"—and yet all Hayter's well-chosen examples of unduly intimate passages refer to self-descriptions or incidents, not feelings: her pale cheeks, the lock of hair, the pet name, his letters and kisses. The events of courtship as a Victorian woman experienced them don't seem to belong in sonnets—we haven't seen them there before, have we?—so they must be personal, particular, trivial. We are offended by the publication, implicit in the act of writing poems, of what we feel should be kept private.

The legend that has grown up about the *Sonnets* exploits, distorts, and exaggerates the personal element. Barrett Browning herself worried about the question of privacy, particularly no doubt because the poems concerned her husband, whose aversion to literary self-exposure was extremely strong. In 1864 he explained how and why she showed him the *Sonnets* for the first time three years after their marriage:

> all this delay, because I happened early to say something against putting one's loves into verse: then again, I said something else on the other side . . . and next morning she said hesitatingly "Do you know I once wrote some poems about *you*?"—and then— "There they are, if you care to see them." . . . How I see the gesture, and hear the tones. . . . Afterward the publishing them was through me . . . there was a trial at covering it a little by

leaving out one sonnet which had plainly a connexion with the former works: but it was put in afterwards when people chose to pull down the mask which, in old days, people used to respect at a masquerade. But I never cared.

This is simple and straightforward enough. But Edmund Gosse's silly, apochryphal version of this episode has followed the *Sonnets* through many printings and still appears in the reprinted Cambridge Edition of 1974. Gosse's tale transfers the reader's embarrassment to the poet herself. She came up behind her husband, Gosse reports, "held him by the shoulder to prevent his turning to look at her, and . . . pushed a packet of papers into the pocket of his coat. She told him to read that, and to tear it up if he did not like it; and then she fled again to her own room." Afterwards, says Gosse, she "was very loth indeed to consent to the publication of what had been the very notes and chronicle of her betrothal." But Browning makes it clear that his wife's reticence had been mostly the deferential reflex of his own. In 1846 she had answered his question about what she had been writing recently (almost certainly these sonnets) with a wit and self-possession absolutely antithetical to Gosse's emblematic tale of coyness, self-dramatization, and shame. "You shall see some day at Pisa what I will not show you now. Does not Solomon say that 'there is a time to read what is written.' If he doesn't, he *ought*."

Insofar as the *Sonnets* are autobiographical (and not just spontaneous), however, they inaugurated a new Victorian convention to which almost every significant poet except Robert Browning contributed: the use of autobiographical material in long poems that play specifically "modern" experience against some of the traditions of amatory poetry. Arnold's *Switzerland*, Patmore's *The Angel in the House*, Tennyson's *Maud*, and Clough's *Amours de Voyage* were published in the 1850's, Meredith's *Modern Love* in 1862. Of all of these, only *Sonnets from the Portuguese* does not, so far as we can tell, fictionalize the story or attempt to disguise the personal references. The male poets presented their own experiences and feelings as exemplifying those of modern man, or at any rate the modern sensitive intellectual or poet, but the modern woman's personal experience could not easily be made to carry so heavy a contextual burden. There were no ancestral female voices to validate her own and define by contrast its particular quality. Nor, as Barrett Browning knew, were readers disposed to hear women as speaking for anything more than themselves. Women can't generalize, Romney smugly explains to Aurora Leigh, and therefore can't be poets, and Lady Waldemar repeats the common assumption that "artist women" are "outside . . . the common sex."

The unusual situation of a female poet in love with a male one was not easy to show as representative, but Barrett Browning worked in many ways to generalize and distance her experience. The use of the sonnet sequence, first of all, seems an obvious choice now, but in fact *Sonnets from the Portuguese* inaugurated the Victorian use of the old genre. Although she noted the absence of female Elizabethan poets—"I look everywhere for grandmothers and see none"—the sonnet sequence offered a way to subsume her own experience into a wider tradition. Within the sonnet form itself she curbed the liberties with rhyme and meter for which she was notorious, although she did not keep to the usual structure of the Petrarchan sonnet, allowed herself great variety of tone, and broke up lines in fresh and surprising ways. She reminds us, too, that she is writing poems, not love letters, when a poem represents what she does not say to the lover or suppresses words of his letters that are too private to repeat.

She generalizes her situation most clearly and deliberately through literary allusions, particularly in the first two sonnets, which draw on Theocritus, Homer, Milton, and Shakespeare. *Sonnets from the Portuguese* begins: "I thought once how Theocritus had sung / Of the sweet years. . . ." This refers to the song in the fifteenth idyll which anticipates Adonis' return from death to the arms of Aphrodite and is proleptic both of the speaker's movement from death to love and of the coming of her lover. The speaker "mused" Theocritus' story "in his antique tongue," she says, thus establishing her credentials as a reader of Greek, a serious, educated person. And as she mused: "a mystic Shape did move / Behind me, and drew me backward by the hair"—a typically female image of passivity, no doubt, but taken from the episode in *The Iliad* when Achilles in his wrath is similarly pulled back by Athena. The allusions are deft and easy, the voice that of one who lives familiarly with Greek texts. The second sonnet draws with the same casual confidence on Milton and Shakespeare. Only she, her lover, and God, she says, heard the word "Love"—and God "laid the curse / So darkly on my eyelids, as to amerce / My sight from seeing thee"—a more "absolute exclusion" than death itself. The word "amerce" recalls Satan's description of himself as by his fault "amerced / Of heaven" a highly relevant allusion in the sonnet's context of "all God's universe," "absolute exclusion," and a blinded poet. Then in the background of the sestet we hear "Let us not to the marriage of true minds": if God himself were not opposed, "Men could not part us . . . / Nor the seas change us, nor the tempests bend." The rebirth of Adonis, Achilles' injured love and pride, Satan's exclusion from heaven, Shakespeare's celebration of human love—these and not the stuffy room in Wimpole Street are the context in which *Sonnets from the Portuguese* initially establishes itself.

The poem does seem increasingly to take place within a particular domestic interior, but the space it occupies is symbolical and highly schematic. It is sharply constricted on the horizontal plane but open to heaven above and the grave below. At worst, the speaker is like "a bee shut in a crystalline," in a "close room." In her childhood she ran from one place to another, but the movements she imagines for the future are almost always vertical. Typical repeated words are *down*, *fall*, *deep*, *rise*, *beneath*, and especially *drop*, used eleven times in the forty-four poems, and *up*, used twelve times. Even marriage, leaving one home for another, means that her eyes would "drop on a new range / Of walls and floors." The reader may feel a bit claustrophobic, but the speaker usually imagines enclosure as protection rather than imprisonment. "Open thine heart wide," she says, "And fold within the wet wings of thy dove." The last sonnet sees "this close room" as the place of fruitful seclusion where the lover's flowers throve and her poems unfolded in her heart's garden (like her "great living poetry" of which Browning said that "not a flower . . . but took root and grew" within him).

For the space, which becomes at the end a garden of art, belongs like the story enacted within it as much to Victorian artistic convention as to the setting of Elizabeth Barrett's life. There is a close pictorial equivalent in Dante Gabriel Rossetti's painting *Ecce Ancilla Domini* (1849–50), an Annunciation scene nearly twice as high as it is wide in which the Virgin sits on the bed pressed against the wall, as if cowering away from the tall upright angel who reaches almost from the top to the bottom of the picture and takes up a full third of its horizontal space. In Tennyson's early poems, which often echo through Barrett Browning's, a woman shut up in a house or tower is a recurrent figure for the poet. The speaker of the *Sonnets* is like the Lady of Shalott: people heard her music from outside the "prison-wall," paused, and went on their way. Like the soul in "The Palace of Art," she has "lived with visions. . . Instead of men and women." She inhabits a figurative dwelling like Mariana's moated grange rather than a solid house in Wimpole Street: "the casement broken in, / The bats and owlets builders in the roof." (Elizabeth Barrett twice compared herself in letters to Mariana.) In addition, love offers to her as to Tennyson's sensitive, bookish, imaginative, isolated heroes and heroines an escape from self-imprisonment in a world of shadows. "I will bury myself in myself," says the hero of *Maud* (in an early version he plans to bury himself in his books, which is equally relevant), and Maud's love restores him to life. Like the heroes of *Switzerland* or *Amours de Voyages*, the woman in the *Sonnets* finds her lover more passionate and alive than she is herself. He is not imprisoned; he draws her back to life. (In fact, Browning drew Elizabeth Barrett into marriage, motherhood, society, travel, political engagement—the ordinary social, human world that women often represent to their lovers in Victorian poems: but the poem is less proleptically literary than life was and does not anticipate this outcome.) The speaker has the qualities, then, both of the male Victorian poet as introverted self-doubting lover and of the female figures in which Tennyson embodies passive, withdrawn, and isolated aspects of the poetic character.

The unspecified sufferings and griefs that have marked the speaker's face and almost killed her are also signs not only of Petrarchan love, feminine weakness, and biographical fact (Barrett Browning's long illness and her brother's death) but of the poetical character too, as many Romantic and Victorian poets conceived it. Matthew Arnold's Empedocles, for instance, renounced poetry because isolation and empathy make poets suffer too much. In the 1844 preface to her poems Barrett Browning discusses the volume's two longest works in terms of the woman poet's vocation and special qualifications. *A Drama of Exile*, she says, represents the expulsion from the Garden "with a peculiar reference to Eve's allotted grief, which considering that self-sacrifice belonged to her womanhood . . . appeared to me . . . more expressible by a woman than a man." And in *The Vision of Poets*, she says, she has "endeavoured to indicate the necessary relations of genius to suffering and self-sacrifice"; for "if knowledge is power, suffering should be acceptable as a part of knowledge." Thus by an implicit syllogism, suffering is power: women can be poets precisely by virtue of their womanhood.

Another major point of intersection between conventional and personal, male and female, poet and beloved, occurs in the general area in which *Sonnets from the Portuguese* anticipates the Pre-Raphaelites. Here as elsewhere, Barrett Browning is the precursor, though we are likely to read her through expectations formed by those who followed. Sometimes her accents have a Meredithian wit, quickness, cleverness, and variety, as in the tenth sonnet, "Yet love, mere love." Sometimes the poems resemble Dante Rossetti's *House of Life* in their personifications, marmoreal cadences, archaisms, and heated slow simplicities ("Very whitely still, / The lilies of our lives," or "What time I sat alone here in the snow"), and, more pleasingly, in their striking use of Latinate words ("lips renunciative," "Antidotes / Of medicated music"). The speaker is like the tortured husband of *Modern Love* in her subtlety of psychological analysis, intricate arguments and images, and variations of tone and rhythm that can shift in a flash from formal intensity to broken phrases of the speaking voice. She somewhat resembles the speaker in *The House of Life*, too, with her dark allusions to untellable sins and sorrows. But if she speaks like a Pre-Raphaelite poet, she also resembles such poets' favorite subject, the fatal woman: enclosed, passive, pale, deathly. Like Morris' Guenevere or Rossetti's Lilith, she often seems to be looking at herself in a mirror. Like the wife in *Modern Love*, she breathes poison. From the lover's point of view, she is silent and unresponsive in the earlier sonnets, hiding her feelings from him and speaking to be heard only by the reader.

But she lacks the fatal woman's guile, mystery, and beauty. As speaker she must let the reader hear her, while her bent for self-analysis and formal commitment to lyric self-expression preclude duplicity.

Such persistent doubling of roles accounts for most of the disconcerting strangeness of *Sonnets from the Portuguese*. The speaker is cast as both halves of a balanced but asymmetrical pair, speaking with two voices in a dialogue where we are accustomed to hearing only one. Obviously there are rich possibilities for irony here, but Barrett Browning does not take them—does not appear even to notice them. Nor does she call our attention to the persistent anomalies and contradictions even without irony. This above all distinguishes her from her male contemporaries. The juxtaposition of traditional amatory poetry and the Victorian idea that love should be fulfilled in marriage, combined with the desire of almost every important Victorian poet to write within the context of contemporary social life, inevitably opened up the disjunction between the passionate certainties of literature, and the flawed complexities of life, between the amatory intensity of poetic lovers and the confusion and distractedness of modern ones. Sometimes modern settings produce unintended comedy, as in much of Patmore or the description of Maud's dresses ("the habit, hat, and feather" and "the frock and gipsy bonnet"—"nothing can be sweeter / Than maiden Maud in either"); more often, though, Tennyson, Clough, and Meredith exploit the disjunction between literature and contemporary life through self-denigrating irony. *Sonnets from the Portuguese* might well have become the same sort of poem; at any rate, the love letters, kisses, pet-names, childishness, and ringlets rest uneasily with Maud's dresses on the dangerous edge of bathos. Elizabeth Barrett had planned as early as 1844 to write a long poem about "this real everyday life of our age," which she thought as interesting and potentially poetical as past times had been. While her plan was for a novel-poem and in due course issued in *Aurora Leigh*, *Sonnets from the Portuguese* appears to be an earlier fruit of her growing desire to cast off fictional trappings and write from her own time, place, and social class. But neither *Aurora Leigh* nor the *Sonnets* works ironically.

For Barrett Browning does not want to show up disparities: she wants to find a place within the tradition for modern poems, and especially for female poets—not to mark how far outside it she is. Nor can she mock the sonnet tradition from within as Shakespeare and Sidney could, since she wants to assert her right to use it at all. *Sonnets from the Portuguese* is organized around the double discovery that love's seeming illusions are realities, still accessible, and that one can be both subject and object of love, both poet and poet's beloved. Because she does not use irony to mark the points at which the old and the new come together—she wants to create fusion, not show disjunction—she runs the risk of leaving us disoriented and uneasy instead of releasing us, as Clough and Meredith do, into the ironical recognition of a familiar failure. And since success for the poet in this poem involves a happy ending for the lovers, or at least not an unhappy one, there is no release such as Tennyson and Arnold would give us into the lyrical pain of loss.

Barrett Browning knew that embarrassment always threatens to engulf the woman poet, particularly in an amatory context. In a remarkable emblematic incident, Aurora Leigh celebrates her twentieth birthday by crowning herself with ivy leaves, a playful anticipation of the posthumous glory she covets. Recognizing the potentially ambiguous symbolism that a wreath could bear, she had chosen neither the poet's bay nor the lover's myrtle; but when her cousin Romney comes suddenly upon her he sees the wreath simply as a sign of female vanity, flattering to his sense of male superiority, his contempt for mere artists, his love, and his hopes of marrying her. She is memorably embarrassed:

> I stood there fixed,—
> My arms up, like the caryatid, sole
> Of some abolished temple, helplessly
> Persistent in a gesture which derides
> A former purpose. Yet my blush was flame. . . .

Romney thinks that women cannot be poets. Seen through his eyes, Aurora becomes a work of art instead of an artist, and an archaic, useless one at that. Her aspirations to poetic fame dwindle under his amused, admiring gaze into girlish narcissism. The absolute conflict between her intention and his interpretation immobilizes her: she does indeed become object rather than subject, self-assertive only in the blush that is inherent in her name and the mark of internalized conflict. She marries Romney, years and books later, but by then he has not only changed his mind about women poets; he is blind and cannot see her.

The extreme paucity of good lyric poetry by Victorian women, which is in such striking contrast to their success in narrative, is largely due to the felt pressure of forms, convention, and above all readers' responses that could not accommodate female utterance without distorting it. This is a problem of the female speaker, not just of the woman writer, as we see in *Bleak House*. Dickens wants to give Esther Summerson narrative authority as well as attractiveness and self-effacing modesty, and the incongruity that results suggests to some readers either intentional irony or authorial failure. Women novelists appear more alert to the problem and usually get round it by avoiding first-person female narrators; only Charlotte Bronte faces it squarely, as part of her battle against conventional notions about female attractiveness, passion, and will. (It is significant that Aurora Leigh's rejected lover's character and fate strikingly recall *Jane Eyre*.) One reason that *Aurora Leigh* seems to many readers fresher and more alive than *Sonnets from the Portuguese* is that the novelistic form of the later poem enabled the poet to speak freely, and without arousing significant conflict in the reader, in her own distinctive, distinctively female voice.

LINDA H. PETERSON

Rewriting A History of The Lyre: *Letitia Landon, Elizabeth Barrett Browning And The (Re)Construction Of The Nineteenth-Century Woman Poet*

At the beginning of Letitia Landon's *A History of the Lyre*, a male speaker looks at the portrait of a female poet and meditates on the function of memory and autobiographical self-construction:

> 'Tis strange how much is mark'd on memory,
> In which we may have interest, but no part;
> How circumstances will bring together links
> In destinies the most dissimilar.
> This face, whose rudely-pencill'd sketch you hold,
> Recalls to me a host of pleasant thoughts,
> And some more serious.—This is EULALIE.

At the beginning of Elizabeth Barrett Browning's *Aurora Leigh*, a speaker, now a female poet, meditates on the function of memory and autobiographical self-construction in a simile alluding, I think, to Landon's poem but revising its plot and intention:

> Of writing many books there is no end;
> And I who have written much in prose and verse
> For others' uses, will write now for mine—

From *Women's Poetry, Late Romantic to Late Victorian: Gender and Genre, 1830-1900* © 1999 by St. Martins Press.

As when you paint your portrait for a friend,
Who keeps it in a drawer and looks at it
Long after he has ceased to love you, just
To hold together what he was and is.

Like Landon, Barrett Browning remarks on the importance of memory, which 'hold[s] together' the subject, 'what he was and is'. Like Landon, too, Barrett Browning analogizes portrait painting and autobiographical writing—with L.E.L.'s 'rudely-pencill'd sketch' and its capacity for linking past and present becoming the portrait Aurora Leigh will create in verse to construct a coherent poetic self and a new vision of the woman poet.

Yet these opening passages are significantly different. In *A History of the Lyre*, it is the male lover who holds the poetess's sketch and contemplates it for 'a host of pleasant thoughts' and the construction of his *own* history and identity, whereas in *Aurora Leigh* it is Aurora who writes of herself for her 'better self'. Landon's analogy between autobiography and portrait painting gets subordinated to a simile ('As when') as if Barrett Browning means to subordinate the traditional function of women's memoirs to the more pressing need of the woman poet. There is a shift, in short, from a male viewer to the female poet, from art produced to satisfy masculine desire to art for the sake of the female poet, from a literary tradition of biographical memoirs *about* women poets to a new tradition of autobiography *by* women writers (hinted at in the next allusion of *Aurora Leigh*—the one in lines 9–13 to Wordsworth's *Immortality Ode* and *Prelude*, the latter published just six years before Barrett Browning's poem). Barrett Browning, I shall argue, corrects Landon's opening passage—and, more broadly, the preface to and plot of *A History of the Lyre*—by taking (auto) biographical forms identified with the Romantic *poetess* and reconfiguring them to serve the development of the Victorian woman *poet*. In these corrections she revises the constructions of the poetess as they appeared in Landon's works and in a spate of biographies about Landon published in the two decades before *Aurora Leigh*.

Like many of Landon's poems, these biographies reproduce—indeed, they help to construct—the myth of the Romantic poetess. As Glennis Stephenson has pointed out, biographies of the poetess invariably associate her work with her body and depict it 'as the intuitive and confessional outpouring of emotion':

Words like 'gushing' and 'over-flowing' abound in [the works of Landon and Hemans] . . . . These women are . . .

fountains, not pumps. The flow is from nature, not art. Usually
the creative woman in these poems is betrayed and abandoned,
and finds that with the loss of love the flow dries up.

Thus a poetess like Landon came to exemplify a debased or inferior form of
Romanticism—'Wordworth's "spontaneous overflow of powerful feelings"
which, rather than being recollected in tranquility, [were] immediately
spewed out on the page'. Angela Leighton has further pointed out that
'although L.E.L. insists on art as an overflow of the female body, she also
frequently freezes the woman into a picture, a statue, an art object'—
something that occurs at the beginning and end of *A History of the Lyre*. 'Such
frozen postures', Leighton notes, have 'a way of turning the woman into a
form of sexual or artistic property for the man.'

   These views of the poetess—as improvisatrice, as statue or art object
produced for man's pleasure, as abandoned woman—go back at least as far as
the first nineteenth-century autobiography of a woman poet, Mary
Robinson's *Memoirs* (1801). In the *Memoirs*, Robinson, an actress turned
writer, describes numerous scenes in which she dresses up and performs for
her audience, usually depicted as male. Her daughter and editor Maria
Robinson specifically links her mother's poetic production with
improvisation. Maria recounts scenes, for example, in which her mother
'poured forth those poetic effusions which have done so much honour to her
genius and decked her tomb with unfading laurels'—poems like 'Lines to
Him Who Will Understand Them', in which Robinson bids farewell to
Britain for Italia's shore; or 'The Haunted Beach', inspired by Robinson's
discovery of a drowned stranger; or 'The Maniac', written, like Coleridge's
Kubla Khan, in a delirium excited by opium. And, of course, Robinson was
the archetypal abandoned woman, the first of several mistresses of the Prince
of Wales, left in the lurch without financial support or social protection when
another woman took his fancy.

   Robinson's combination of improvisation and performance
influenced the next generation of women writers, even though her
autobiography was *not* an exemplary narrative. Generically, her *Memoirs* are
chroniques scandaleuses, the tales of a popular young actress who became the
Prince's mistress and later turned professional writer when he abandoned
her. The next generation, including Hemans and Landon, sought to avoid
the scandal and self-aggrandizement of this form of life-writing. Thus they
did not publish their own autobiographies; rather, in good early Victorian
fashion, they let their lives be written for them—by family members, close
friends, and other women writers who could testify to their feminine as well
as literary virtues. None the less, we can trace the influence of Robinson's

Memoirs in the biographies of Landon (and, to some extent, Hemans)—and in precisely the features that Stephenson and Leighton single out: the poetess as improvisatrice, gushing forth her effusions like a natural spring; the poetess as statue, frozen into an artistic posture for the benefit of the male viewer; the poetess as abandoned woman, achieving fame perhaps but losing in love.

Such depictions of Landon began as early as 1839 with Emma Roberts's 'Memoir of L.E.L.', included in the posthumously published *The Zenana and Minor Poems*. According to Roberts,

> While still a mere child, L.E.L. began to publish, and her poetry immediately attracted attention. . . . [S]he rushed fearlessly into print, not dreaming for a moment, that verses which were poured forth like the waters from a fountain, gushing, as she has beautifully expressed it, of their own sweet will, could ever provoke stern or harsh criticism.

Laman Blanchard, who brought out *The Life and Literary Remains of L.E.L.* in 1841, similarly treats her poetry as natural productions: 'Just as the grass grows that sows itself'. Like other biographers who would follow, Blanchard associates Landon herself with the title character of *The Improvisatrice*, noting that the heroine of that poem was 'youthful, impassioned, and gifted with glorious powers of song; and, although introduced as a daughter of Florence . . . she might be even L.E.L. herself; for what were the multitude of songs she had been pouring out for three years past, but "improvisings"?' When William Howitt published his biographical *Homes and Haunts of the Most Eminent British Poets* in 1847, he, too, associated Landon with her *Improvisatrice*, noting that 'the very words of her first heroine might have literally been uttered as her own:—

> "Sad were my shades; methinks they had
> Almost a tone of prophecy—
> I ever had, from earliest youth,
> A feeling what my fate would be."

Such associations had, of course, been encouraged by Landon herself who, after translating the poetical odes in Madame de Stael's *Corinne*, took to appearing publicly in the Sappho-Corinne mode, dressed in Grecian costume with her hair done à la Sappho, and who continued writing and rewriting the Sappho-Corinne myth, including the archetypal version in *A History of the Lyre*.

The myth of the poetess as *improvisatrice* had certain advantages: it linked her to the cult of genius and her work to inspired rather than mechanical or pedantic production. But it also had disadvantages: in its emphasis on the poetess's natural genius and her youthful, sometimes even infantile poetic effusions, it tended to restrict the poetess to a youthful, immature stage of development and to mitigate against more mature, serious writing. All of the major nineteenth-century women poets—Robinson, Hemans, Landon, Barrett Browning, Rossetti—were infant prodigies, young geniuses who could recite hundreds of lines of verse as children (Hemans), or who composed poems and stories almost before they learned to hold a pen (Landon), or who published volumes of ambitious verses in early adolescence (Robinson, Hemans, Barrett Browning, Rossetti). This myth of youthful genius, as Norma Clarke has pointed out, tended to work against the development of the woman poet's career—and serious treatment of her poetry—once she moved beyond youth into maturity or middle age.

Despite the identification of Landon with the Improvisatrice of 1824—and later with Erinna (1826) and Eulalie, the poetess of *A History of the Lyre* (1829)—Roberts and Blanchard both insisted that readers should not simply equate Landon with her imaginary poetesses—particularly not with the tragic Sapphic poetess who achieves fame but is unlucky in love. Roberts, who lived with her at 22 Hans Place, insisted that Landon was not a solitary, melancholy genius, but a cheerful, domestic woman: 'It may indeed be said, to L.E.L.'s honour, that she retained, to the last moment of existence all the friends thus domesticated with her, those who knew her most intimately being the most fondly attached'. The tales of unrequited love were, in Roberts's view, 'the production of a girl who had not yet left off her pinafores, and whose only notion of a lover was embodied in a knight wearing the brightest armour and the whitest of plumes'. Blanchard declared that

> no two persons could be less like each other in all that related to the contemplation of the actual world, than 'L.E.L.' and Letitia Elizabeth Landon. People would in this, as in so many other cases, forgetting one of the licences of poetry, identify the poet's history in the poet's subject and sentiments, and they accordingly insisted that, because the strain was tender and mournful, the heart of the minstrel was breaking.

On this point they were taking their cue from Landon who, in the preface to the volume that includes *A History of the Lyre*, wittily disclaimed the biographical link that so many of her readers assumed: 'If I must have an unhappy passion, I can only console myself with my own perfect unconsciousness of so great a misfortune'.

Yet such disclaimers of Sapphic tragedy, most written after Landon's mysterious death by an overdose of prussic acid and intended to offset rumours of suicide, have the strange effect of reinforcing the third feature of the myth of the Romantic poetess—that of model or statue, of the poetess as a performer who strikes a pose for the pleasure of her audience but to her own detriment. The plot of *A History of the Lyre* reinforces this notion. Like many of Landon's works, it reproduces the Sappho-Corinne myth: it tells the tale of an inspired poetess, half-Italian, half-English, who spends her daytime hours in solitude, awaiting inspiration, and her nights in company, performing for her audience and winning great fame. She meets a man who listens and gazes raptly but who, in the end, abandons her for a more conventional, domestic Englishwoman. In *A History of the Lyre* the Englishman tells the tale of his encounters with Eulalie and of his eventual marriage to Emily. Landon adds the touch of having the poetess Eulalie create her own statue—'a sculptured form' that becomes a funeral monument:

> 'You see', she said, 'my cemetery here:—
> Here, only here, shall be my quiet grave.
> Yon statue is my emblem: see, its grasp
> Is rais'd to Heaven, forgetful that the while
> Its step has crush'd the fairest of earth's flowers
> With its neglect'.

This conclusion recognizes that the poetess sacrifices herself in performance for men: for their erotic pleasure, obviously, but also for their corporate benefit in that she does not interfere with (or intervene in) the patriarchal structures that allow Eulalie to die solitary and Emily, her passive, domestic counterpart, to marry and reproduce English culture. In *A History of the Lyre*, far more than in earlier poems, the poetess becomes complicit in her own death.

Of the early biographers, only Howitt seems to have noticed the element of self-sacrifice and self-destruction in Landon's life and work. Although he presents it only as a possibility, he speculates that L.E.L. must have seen her fate 'from earliest youth' and understood the destructiveness of the poetic myths she was creating:

> Whether this melancholy belief in the tendency of the great
> theme of her writings, both in prose and poetry; this irresistible
> annunciation, like another Cassandra, of woe and destruction;

this evolution of scenes and characters in her last work, bearing such dark resemblance to those of her own after experience; this tendency, in all her plots, to a tragic catastrophe, and this final tragedy itself,—whether these be all mere coincidences or not, they are still but parts of an unsolved mystery.

Despite the tentative phrasing, Howitt was not a believer in 'mere coincidences'. His treatment of Landon's death makes it clear that he found foreshadowings in her poetical and fictional work, of her tragic end. He recognized, as I believe Elizabeth Barrett did also, that Landon's self-construction as a Sapphic poetess destined her for an early death, that she more or less wrote herself into that fatal plot.

Elizabeth Barrett was a careful reader (and admirer) of Landon's poetry, and she read carefully as well Blanchard's 1841 biography of the poetess. In a letter to Mary Russell Mitford, she compared Landon with Hemans, concluding that 'if I had those two powers to choose from—Mrs Hemans's and Miss Landon's—I mean the *raw* bare powers—I would choose Miss Landon's'. Yet Barrett also believed that Landon had not fully realized her promise or power. To Mitford she further commented, 'I fancy it would have worked out better—had it *been* worked out—with the right moral and intellectual influences in application'.

Barrett Browning's most sustained commentary on Landon's work comes, as I shall argue here, in the opening books of *Aurora Leigh*, where she acknowledges, yet rejects, the self-construction of the poetess who preceded her. In these books she gives to Aurora those 'right moral and intellectual influences' and shows, in the later books of the poem, how the life of the woman poet might 'work out better' with them.

I have already suggested that, in allusions to *A History of the Lyre* and *The Prelude*, Aurora determines to write an autobiography for her own poetic development, as Wordsworth had done and Landon had not. Her allusion to Wordsworth's poetry —

> I, writing thus, am still what men call young;
> I have not so far left the coasts of life
> To travel inland, that I cannot hear
> That murmur of the outer Infinite
> Which unweaned babies smile at in their sleep . . .

—claims partnership with an undebased Romantic tradition and a masculine form of autobiography. Aurora Leigh is still young enough that she recollects Wordsworthian joy and, more importantly, that her autobiography may usefully trace 'the growth of a poet's mind' and provide evidence, to adapt Wordsworth's phrase, that 'May spur me on, in [wo]manhood now mature, / To honorable toil'. This turn to a Wordsworthian form of autobiography swerves away from Landon's view of the poetess as erotic object or as performer for the pleasure and benefit of men.

In the opening books of *Aurora Leigh*, Barrett Browning also abandons the model of the female poet as improvisatrice. In Book I Aurora admits that young poets often write spontaneously and effusively:

> Many tender souls
> Have strung their losses on rhyming thread,
> As children, cowslips.

Although she figures such rhyming as natural, she is not content to remain in this immature artistic state:

> Alas, near all the birds
> Will sing at dawn—and yet we do not take
> The chaffering swallow for the holy lark.

In Books II and III, often taking the lark as her counterpart, Aurora traces her development beyond the stage of natural effusions toward that mature poetic production of which Wordsworth wrote in *The Prelude*. At the end of this sequence she notes:

> So life, in deepening with me, deepened all
> The course I took, the work I did.

As she traces Aurora's career, Barrett Browning includes many details of plot that specifically recall Landon's life, thus suggesting that she means to treat the life of the Romantic poetess as a stage in the development of the Victorian woman poet—as ontogeny recapitulating phylogeny. This treatment allows Barrett Browning to acknowledge the achievement of the Romantic poetess but with the implication that she, representative of the next generation, will progress further. For example, in Book III Aurora moves to an attic room in London, to 'a certain house in Kensington' and 'a chamber up three flights of stairs'. Barrett Browning never lived in a writer's garret, but Landon certainly did—at 22 Hans Place in an attic space invariably described in the biographies as a 'homely-looking, almost uncomfortable room, fronting the street, and barely furnished'.

So, too, Barrett Browning makes Aurora a hack writer of prose as well as an aspiring poet. It was Landon, not Barrett Browning, who churned out reviews for the *Literary Gazette* and whose biographers mention, usually

as evidence of her wide reading, her enormous prose production. Like
Landon, Aurora works 'with one hand for the booksellers / While working
with the other for myself / And art'. Even Aurora's popularity with her
readers suggests Landon's early career. The fanmail 'with pretty maiden
seals' from girls with names like 'Emily' or the 'tokens from young bachelors,
/ Who wrote from college' recall both the sweet, domestic bride of *A History
of the Lyre* (also named Emily) and the anecdote related by Edward Bulwer
Lytton and repeated in virtually all of L.E.L.'s biographies about admiring
young male readers:

> We were young, and at college, lavishing our golden years, not
> so much on the Greek verse and mystic character to which we
> ought, perhaps, to have been rigidly devoted, as 'Our heart in
> passion, and our head in rhyme'. At that time poetry was not yet
> out of fashion, at least with us of the cloister; and there was
> always in the reading-room of the Union a rush every Saturday
> afternoon for the 'Literary Gazette'; and an impatient anxiety to
> hasten at once to that corner of the sheet which contained the
> three magical letters 'L.E.L.' All of us praised the verse, and all
> of us guessed at the author. We soon learned it was a female, and
> our admiration was doubled, and our conjectures tripled. Was
> she young? Was she pretty? And—for there were some embryo
> fortune-hunters among us—was she rich?

　　　　Such details in Book III not only allude to Landon's life but signal
more generally, I think, the determination of Aurora, like other Victorian
women writers, to pursue a professional career. In the 1820s, 1830s, and
1840s many women writers, like Landon and Roberts at 22 Hans Place,
Harriet Martineau in Fludyer Street, and George Eliot at 142 The Strand,
moved to lodgings in London to signal their professional aspirations, and
they were not above writing reviews, translating foreign literature, or doing
other hack work to provide the financial means needed to support their
literary careers. Aurora's life as a 'city poet' represents this new, if not quite
glorious stage in the nineteenth-century woman writer's professionalization.
　　　　The differences from Landon's life are also significant, however—
most notably Aurora's unsullied reputation and her unwavering
commitment, despite early fame, to produce high art. Landon's reputation
had come to ruin (or close to it) with rumours of illicit liaisons with William
Jerdan, editor of the *Literary Gazette*; William Maginn, the heavy-drinking
Irish journalist associated with *Blackwood's* and *Fraser's*; and Daniel Maclise,

the painter. Although they name no names, the early biographers acknowledge these 'atrocious calumnies', in Howitt's phrase, invariably to refute them. None the less, the biographers admit that Landon's public persona, 'the very unguardedness of her innocence' and her lack of concern 'about the interpretation that was likely to be put upon her words', contributed to the problem, as did the life histories of her fictional poetesses. Eulalie in *A History of the Lyre* confesses that she is more like the 'Eastern tulip' with its 'radiant' yet short-lived colours than the pure 'lily of the valley' with its 'snowy blossoms'. In contrast, Aurora can say unequivocally,

> I am a woman of repute;
> No fly-blow gossip ever specked my life;
> My name is clean and open as this hand,
> Whose glove there's not a man dares blab about
> As if he had touched it freely.

As she begins her career, she self-consciously resolves to live 'holding up my name / To keep it from the mud'.

More important to artistic development, Barrett Browning revises Aurora's attitude toward fame and sustained poetic achievement. Eulalie, like Erinna before her, laments that she has lost the desire (or perhaps that she lacks the ability) to sustain her work:

> I am as one who sought at early dawn
> To climb with fiery speed some lofty hill:
> His feet are strong in eagerness and youth
> His limbs are braced by the fresh morning air,
> And all seems possible:—this cannot last.
> The way grows steeper, obstacles arise,
> And unkind thwartings from companions near.

But whereas Eulalie laments that early fame has proved a fatal opium—

> I am vain,—praise is opium, and the lip
> Cannot resist the fascinating draught,
> Though knowing its excitement is a fraud,

—that she can 'no longer work miracles for thee [fame],' and that now 'Disappointment tracks / The steps of Hope,' Aurora determines that she will progress beyond simple 'ballads', the form identified with female poetesses, and work her way up through the generic ranks that have long challenged English male poets: from pastoral through epic. Indeed, one can read the opening monologue of Book V as Aurora's challenge to Eulalie's tragic lament in *A History of the Lyre*. It presents a counter-argument that women poets can indeed 'last' as 'The way grows steeper, obstacles arise, / And unkind thwartings from companions near.' It imagines women poets treating 'The human heart's large seasons', from 'that strain of sexual passion' to 'the great escapings of ecstatic souls', not just Landon's more simple romantic and domestic love. Significantly, too, Barrett Browning turns Eulalie's admission of inadequacy into Romney's assertions of the female poet's limitations. In *Aurora Leigh* it is the male critic who denigrates the woman poet's abilities and achievements, not the woman poet who initiates her own destruction.

What Barrett Browning does not alter or avoid is Landon's psychological insight that the female longs for, perhaps even needs, the approval of her male reader. In *A History of the Lyre* Eulalie performs for large audiences but in particular for the pleasure of the Englishman who follows her about for a year; when he leaves Italy without offering marriage, she more or less 'hang[s] [her] lute on some lone tree, and die[s]'. L.E.L.'s arrangement of these details is significant: Eulalie, in a long monologue reproduced by the male speaker, laments the ill effects of fame, and praises the virtues of 'the loveliness of home' and 'support and shelter from man's heart'. When the monologue ends, he abruptly states, 'I soon left Italy; it is well worth / A year of wandering, were it but to feel / How much our England does outweigh the world'. We might read this hiatus simply as an acknowledgement that poetic genius is unsuited to domestic life. Landon seems to have intended, however, a stronger link between the continuing work of the female poetess and the continuing approval—including love—of her male audience.

Aurora confronts the issue of male approval in Book V, where she lays out her plan for progress up through the generic ranks and then identifies the primary obstacle to that progress:

> —I must fail
> Who fail at the beginning to hold and move
> One man—and he my cousin, and he my friend.

Aurora fears 'this vile woman's way / Of trailing garments', yet determines, unlike Landon's poetess, that it 'shall not trip me up'. If Landon framed the issue in erotic and romantic terms, Barrett Browning re-frames it in poetic and aesthetic terms. Aurora admits her loneliness as a woman writer and her envy of male artists who are rewarded with love, whether the love of a mother or of a wife. But the need for love, we should note, is not peculiar to the *woman* artist; it affects male artists like Graham, Belmore, and Mark

Gage, all of whom rely on domestic affection. Aurora expresses her desire for
Romney's approval in rather different terms from those of L.E.L.—that is, in
terms of the poet's vocation and specifically the female poet's terrain: Is her
work, contrary to what Romney believes, equal to that of the social activist?
Shall the woman poet be confined, as in Romney's view at the end of Book
IV, to 'the mythic turf where danced the nymphs', or shall she treat the whole
range of human experience and passion that Aurora details at the beginning
of Book V? In Barrett Browning's poem it is Aurora's view, not Romney's
opinion or Landon's precedent as a poet of lyric love, that finally determines
the career of the woman poet—and the plot of the remainder of the poem.

After Book V, very little of Landon's life and work informs *Aurora
Leigh*—except, of course, that Barrett Browning revises the conclusion to *A
History of the Lyre* (a conclusion some biographers thought Landon had
enacted in her life). Eulalie, Sappho-like, dies an abandoned woman; Aurora
lives to marry Romney. Eulalie's history is told only after her death, by her
male admirer; Aurora Leigh's is written at the peak of her power by the poet
herself. If the marriage ending of *Aurora Leigh* has been controversial among
contemporary feminist critics, primarily for seeming to succumb to the
conventions of the marriage plot, it looks different in its historical and
generic contexts. In the context of women's autobiography, it represents a
determination to write one's own life and not let others construct one's life
history. In the context of biographies of the nineteenth-century woman poet,
it represents a writing against a prior tradition, a rejection of Landon's dying
for (male) pleasure, and a progression from the poetess to the woman poet.

Barrett Browning is famous for having written, 'I look everywhere
for grandmothers and see none'. Perhaps Landon, born in 1802 only four
years before her, was too close in age to be considered a literary
'grandmother'. Perhaps Dorothy Mermin is right that, in making such a
comment, Barrett Browning was ignoring 'the popular "poetesses" who
adorned the literary scene', as they did not represent 'the noble lineage with
which she wished to claim affiliation'. Perhaps between the statement to
Robert Browning in 1845 and the writing of *Aurora Leigh* a decade later, she
owned up to the existence of women writers who had influenced her, if only
(or primarily) as negative examples. Whatever the case, when Barrett
Browning came to write her autobiography of the new woman poet, she
framed its plot and some of its features in terms of the female literary figures
of the preceding generation. If in revising *A History of the Lyre*, she lets
Eulalie's lyre stay hanging on a tree and gives Aurora instead a Gideon's
trumpet, 'a clarion' to press 'on thy woman's lip', she none the less acknowledges, in the scope and density of her allusions, the importance of Letitia
Landon's work in the history of nineteenth-century women's poetry. Like it or
not, the Romantic poetess was one progenitor of the Victorian woman poet.

MARGARET REYNOLDS

Love's Measurement in Elizabeth Barrett Browning's Sonnets from the Portuguese

And the king called his three daughters to his side and asked them each in turn: "How much do you love me?" 'Right,' panicked the eldest daughter who was a good housekeeper, 'think expensive.' "I love you," she said, "more than gold and purple, more than frankincense and myrrh, more than the spices of the Indies." And the King was pleased. 'Heigh ho,' thought the second daughter, who had read her French feminist theory, and knew exactly where she was. And she answered him: "I love you more than liberty, more that sight, more than sense, more than life itself." And the king was pleased. Turning to the third daughter, he asked again, "How much do you love me?' And the third daughter said, "I love you as meat loves salt." "As meat loves salt?," said the King, "As meat loves salt? That's not very poetic"—and he turned her out of the palace.

My story, as you will guess, concerns, as all the stories do, the tale of the youngest daughter who riddles, and yet who speaks the truth about love's measurement. Except that, in this case, she started out as the eldest. Elizabeth Barrett Browning, famous as a daughter, famous as a lover, famous as a poet of love; each of these attributes apparently separate, and yet, in fact intimately connected, leading directly from one to another, all three tied together by the question of who you love, how to place a value of love, and how that value is spoken, accounted for, balanced in the books.

From *Studies in Browning and His Circle* 21 © 1997 by Baylor University.

In the myths, in the fairy tales, this is always the question: how much is love worth, how many secrets will Psyche endure, how long a silence will Griselda maintain, how many shirts can love weave out of nettles, how big, how deep, how wide, how much do you love me? In love, lovers become stockbrokers tallying up the size of their investment in the beloved like Puccini's Mimi, "I have so many things to tell you, or one alone, but big as the sea, like the sea, profound and infinite. . . ." They become accountants compiling an inventory of the beloved's charms, like St. Preux in Rousseau's *La Nouvelle Héloïse*, "We will pass over the fact that the painter omitted several of your beauties. . . . He hasn't included that barely perceptible mark which is under your right eye, nor that which is on the left side of your neck . . . . O God, is this man made of bronze? . . . He has forgotten the little scar which is under your lip. . . . They become misers, counting out their expenditure on the beloved, like Oscar Wilde listing his debts incurred for Lord Alfred, "The Savoy dinners—the clear turtle soup, the luscious ortolans wrapped in their crinkled Sicilian vine-leaves, the heavy amber-coloured, indeed almost amber-scented champagne—Dagonet 1880, I think, was your favourite wine?—all still have to be paid for." And they become the monotonous register, endlessly ringing up accounts of love like the old song Barthes quotes, "Love makes me think too much," before he goes on to explain, "At times, . . . a fever of language overcomes me, a parade of reasons, interpretations, pronouncements. I am aware of nothing but a machine running all by itself, a hurdy-gurdy, whose crank is turned by a staggering but anonymous bystander, and which is never silent."

A hurdy-gurdy, ticketing and pricing up love's claims, which has only become louder, more insistent in the years which intervene between us and the Brownings. All you need is love, love makes the world go round, where did our love go, everybody loves somebody sometime, love is never having to say you're sorry, what's love got to do with it?

When Robert Browning and Elizabeth Barrett fell in love, like most lovers, they weighted up their experience. With our wise retrospect it looks as though Robert Browning was testing out the ground for romance even with his very first letter, "I love your verses with all my heart, dear Miss Barrett . . . I do, as I say, love these Books with all my heart—and I love you too" . . . and early on he tried the measure of one of the world's great love stories by referring, pretty inappropriately given the mature ages of Elizabeth and Robert to Romeo and Juliet. If, as Daniel Karlin has argued, it was the story of Perseus rescuing Andromeda chained to the rock, which was to become the yardstick in Robert's mind for the tale of these middle-aged lovers, in Elizabeth's private versions of her own story it was not myth, but fairytale which provided the balancing scales. As the characters in their romance develop, as the dramatis personae take their places, she images them in her letters as modern-day incarnations out of the Brothers Grimm or the Arabian Nights. Of herself she says, "I have no spell for charming the dragons"; of her father, " 'If a prince of Eldorado should come with a pedigree of lineal descent from some signory in the moon in one hand, & a ticket of good-behaviour from the nearest Independent chapel in the other' . . . . 'Why even then,' said my sister Arabel, 'it would not *do.*' "; of Miss Mitford she writes, "She is one of the Black Stones, which, when I climb up towards my Singing Tree & Golden Water, will howl behind me & call names."

In Barrett Browning's *poetic* account of the courtship, *Sonnets from the Portuguese*, which she was writing during the years of 1845 and 1846, the literary allusions are typically numerous and diverse, drawn from classical writers such as Theocritus, Homer and Sophocles, from Petrarch and Shakespeare, through to her own immediate predecessors and contemporaries, Felicia Hemans, L.E.L., and Alfred Tennyson. But the tone and the imagery which colors the *Sonnets* is derived from a fairytale stock; there are palaces inhabited by her princely lover, gifts of ruby crowns and golden thrones, magic kisses which wake the enchanted Sleeping Beauty or which make the hand they touch grow cleaner and whiter, there are forlorn ladies sitting chained and alone in the snow, and bright ladies who give up acres and degree, and all for love. Also borrowed from the patterns of fairy tale are the repetitions, revisions and reprises which make up the shape of *Sonnets from the Portuguese*. Scenes are returned to, themes are reiterated, and these patterns, these numberings, these measurements, allow Elizabeth Barrett to work out, rather as Cinderella tries on the glass slipper, whether or not her romance fits.

At first, she gives an account of herself which seems to make her into an ugly sister. It is not that she is too large, and needs to chop off bits of her person to cut herself down to size, but that she is too small. In the third sonnet, Barrett Browning marks out the differences between her speaker-self and her poet-beloved. It is a class difference, a difference of social degree and place, and a difference, quite literally, in height, because he is envisaged looking out of a window and *down* on her:

> Unlike are we, unlike, O princely Heart!
> Unlike our uses and our destinies . . .
> . . . Thou, bethink thee, art
> A guest for queens to social pageantries,
> With gages from a hundred brighter eyes
> Than tears can make mine, to play thy part

Of chief musician. What hast *thou* to do
With looking from the lattice-lights at me,
A poor, tired, wandering singer, singing through
The dark, and leaning up a cypress tree?. . . .

In Sonnets VIII to XII the woman-speaker again takes up this
question of worth and value, setting up a long quarrel with herself designed
to reckon up the possibilities of exchange between herself and the beloved.
"What can I give thee back," she asks in Sonnet VIII, "O liberal / And
princely giver, who hast brought the gold / And purple of thine heart . . . in
unexpected largesse? am I cold, / Ungrateful, that for these most manifold /
High gifts, I render nothing back at all? / Not so; not cold,—but very poor
instead. . . . "

In the next Sonnet she asks, "Can it be right to give what I can
give?" which is only tears and sighs. "We are not peers," she says, "so to be
lovers: and I own, and grieve, / That givers of such gifts as mine are, must /
Be counted with the ungenerous. . . . " Then she cheers up a bit, opening
Sonnet X with "Yet, love, mere love, is beautiful indeed / And worthy of
acceptation. She goes on, "There's nothing low / In love, when love the
lowest," and so on to Sonnet XI beginning "And therefore if to love can be
desert / I am not all unworthy" which brings her to the conclusion, in Sonnet
XII, that her own offering of "mere love" is not so modestly valueless after
all: "Indeed this very love which is my boast, / And which, when rising up
from breast to brow, / Doth crown me with a ruby large enow / To draw
men's eyes and prove the inner cost . . . ."

Themes of measurement, value, worth, exchange and commerce run
throughout *Sonnets from the Portuguese*, but this is one of the most sustained
run of examples, and it ends, significantly with this Sonnet, Sonnet XIII:

And wilt thou have me fashion into speech
The love I bear thee, finding words enough,
And hold the torch out, while the winds are rough,
Between our faces, to cast light on each? —
I drop it at thy feet. I cannot, each
My hand to hold my spirit so far off
From myself—me—that I should bring thee proof
In words, of love hid in me out of reach.
Nay, let the silence of my womanhood
Commend my woman-love to thy belief,
Seeing that I stand unwon, however wooed,
And rend the garment of my life, in brief,

By a most dauntless, voiceless fortitude,
Lest one touch of this heart convey its grief.

Here, Barrett Browning's speaker turns her beloved into one who, like the King who began my story, who wants her to say, to speak, to name, to count her love. "How much do you love me?" is the unsaid question which precedes this poem.

Like the third daughter in my story, like Cordelia in *King Lear,* Barrett Browning's speaker won't answer. "Love, and be silent," says Cordelia; "Let the silence of my womanhood / Commend my woman-love to thy belief," says Barrett Browning. Like Cordelia's, her silence is heroic, "a most dauntless, voiceless fortitude." Cordelia refuses to speak because speaking love is a transgression of the laws of anatomy: "I cannot heave my heart into my mouth." Barrett Browning refuses to speak because speaking love improperly breaks off the right bond between the individual's body and soul: "I cannot teach / My hand to hold my spirit so far off / From myself— me—that I should bring thee proof / In words, of love hid in me out of reach." There is something wrong with this demand, "How much do you love me?"—*something wrong*, which has to do with the body—with the woman's body—with the relationship between a woman's body and spirit which, when in right conjunction, makes her who she is.

When the King asks his daughters "How much do you love me?" he reveals how much he loves them. He reveals that they, in his eyes, have no individuality, they are nothing, except what can be measured in relation to him. They are commodities, valuable to the King only insofar as they bring worth to him, only insofar as they aggrandize him, increase him, augment him, by loving him—a lot. The King's daughters, women in general, are then, in Irigaray's terms, "goods," and with these goods, a man may go to market: "For woman," she says, "is traditionally use-value for man, exchange-value among men. Merchandise then . . . . Women are marked phallically by their fathers, husbands, procurers. This stamp[ing] determines their value in sexual commerce."

In *King Lear*, of course, this is immediately obvious. When Cordelia fails to speak, or rather, speaks in a riddle—"I love your Majesty according to my bond, no more nor less"—she instantly loses her value. No longer Lear's jewel, her "price is fallen," she is now not fit for the market, but is given to France with nothing, for nothing, as nothing. This is the problem. If a woman is a commodity in the market-place then she cannot be a dealer. She is an object with, or without, value. She is not a subject with something to sell, except maybe herself. She certainly is not an equal who can wrangle, and bargain, haggle and trade, backed up by the securities of individual worth.

But this is the old law of the father. Elizabeth Barrett Browning, unlike Cordelia or the third daughter in my story, was a child of the nineteenth century, born in an age of commerce and enterprise, trade expansion and Empire, investment and interest and profit. She knew that she was supposed to be the raw material, but she wanted to be the dealer; and there weren't going to be any middlemen in her transactions. In the early sections of *Sonnets from the Portuguese* she plays out the old version of the measuring fairytale. She treats herself as a commodity and works out her price, her value, how much she is worth, before she allows the question, which makes her worthless, to be asked. But in the latter part of the *Sonnets* she sets up a new relation, a new version of sexual commerce, where she is an equal trader, driving a hard bargain.

In real life Elizabeth Barrett made it clear to Robert that this was going to be the way of it right from the start. He may have been trawling for romance; she was setting up a business deal. In her first letter, written in reply to his first letter of January 10, 1845, she wrote: "You meant to give me pleasure by your letter—and even if the object had not been answered, I ought still to thank you. But it is thoroughly answered. Such a letter from such a hand! Sympathy is dear—very dear to me: but the sympathy of a poet & of such a poet, is the quintessence of sympathy to me! Will you take back my gratitude for it?—agreeing too that, of all the commerce done in the world, from Tyre to Carthage, the exchange of sympathy for gratitude is the most princely thing?"

After that, he shouldn't have been surprised at what happens in the *Sonnets*. At Sonnet XVIII the speaker gives the beloved a lock of hair. Well, fair enough, this is in all the fairytales and myths too, and we know very well what it means. From the story of Samson to the *Rape of the Lock*, from Rapunzel to that other Victorian story of merchants and sexual commerce, Christina Rossetti's *Goblin Market*, the cutting off, the stealing, the selling, the giving away of hair, of a piece of the self, symbolizes the commodification of the body, the sale of the self into another's power, the prostitution of the individual's autonomy. And because, for the most part, commodification is a woman's problem, it is usually women who lose their hair. *Not this time.* Barrett Browning's speaker gives away her hair in the best fairytale tradition: "I never gave a lock of hair away / To a man, Dearest, except to thee . . . "— *but then* she demands one back again. "The soul's Rialto hath its merchandise; / I barter curl for curl upon that mart, / And from my poet's forehead to my heart / Receive this lock which outweighs argosies. . . ."

From this point on in the Sonnet sequence, the speaker-lover and the listener-beloved are construed as equals whose exchange, whose commerce, must be mutual: "If I leave all for thee, wilt thou exchange / And be all to me. . . . " At Sonnet XXI the speaker even goes so far as to turn around the beloved's unspoken question "How much do you love me?" and makes him do the speaking which she had refused: "Say over again, and yet once again / That thou dost love me. Though the word repeated / should seem 'a cuckoo-song'. . . . Say thou dost love me, love me, love me—toll / The silver iterance!—only minding, Dear, / To love me also in silence with thy soul."

There is a paradox here. In silence, according to the riddle of the third daughter, according to Cordelia and, it would seem, to Barrett Browning herself, lies the truest love. But a womanly silence is not going to get the *woman-poet* very far. If a woman keeps silent she risks, first of all, objectification, commodification, she does not speak out herself, but can only be spoken. And if a poet is silent, how then is she a poet? And a poet is what Barrett Browning is, therefore she has to speak. When Elizabeth Barrett chose to make a sonnet sequence out of the story of her love, she was self-consciously re-writing her poetic inheritance. What *should* happen in the sonnet sequence, what does happen in Petrarch, in Spenser and, give or take a mysterious young man, in Shakespeare, is that the *male* poet speaks as the feeling subject, and the *female* beloved just *is*, as the silent object. Man does, woman is. Traditionally women, as objects, as commodities accruing to increase the worth of man, have only been allowed to speak to flatter. Their speech is about the King, they must say how much they love him, and not about themselves. And this prohibition, this hijacking of women's speech, denies woman's identity and selfhood. This is exactly what Virginia Woolf observed when she described the debilitations in the old law of the father which betrayed the woman writer, which turned a woman into an Angel who was only allowed to speak of a man to say *how much she loved him*: "Directly . . . I took my pen in my hand to review that novel by a famous man, she [the ideal Angel in the House] slipped behind me and whispered: 'My dear, you are a young woman. You are writing about a book that has been written by a man. Be sympathetic; be tender; flatter; deceive; use all the arts and wiles of our sex. Never let anybody guess that you have a mind of your own. Above all, be pure.' And she made as if to guide my pen. . . . "

Barrett Browning didn't want anyone to guide her pen. She made her sonnet sequence in a style different from that of her predecessors. This time, in the *Sonnets from the Portuguese*, the speaking subject is clearly a *woman* and a poet. Her beloved is in a different style too, he is also a poet and a speaking subject. By the end of the sequence of forty-four poems they are equal. The exchange between them is mutual, the rendering of gifts is equivalent, their commerce is measured out and balanced on either side. In the last Sonnet, she recalls what he had given her over the period of courtship: "Beloved, thou hast brought me many flowers / Plucked in the garden, all the summer through / And winter, and it seemed as if they grew / In this close room. . . . " And she gives also in return: "So in the like name of that love of ours, / Take back these thoughts which were unfolded too, / And which on warm and cold days I withdrew / From my heart's ground. . . ." Her gift, as befits a poet, is her own poetry, and the wreath of sonnets which she weaves for him, becomes her beloved as appropriately as the poet's own attribute of a laurel crown.

This is a new text for Barrett Browning, a new speaking. But in order to say it she has to revise the old scripts, and to learn a new vocabulary, a new lexicon. The subtext in the question from the fairytale, "How much do you love me?," is the crippling dependence of the daughter on the father. She is a thing, a thing which belongs to him, to be used by him. And *abused* by him. "Incest," according to Lacan, "is bad grammar." And Barrett Browning had to learn to speak proper. Angela Leighton has shown how Barrett Browning so strangely threw off her "filial reverence" for her poetic grandfathers, at exactly the same time as she threw off her dependence on her own father. In fact, her poetry and her relation to her father were always closely connected in her own mind. She dedicated her 1844 volume of poems, the volume which immediately preceded, and precipitated Browning into her life, to her father with these words: "Somewhat more faint-hearted than I used to be, it is my fancy thus to seem to return to a visible personal dependence on you, as if indeed I were a child again; to conjure your beloved image between myself and the public, so as to be sure of one smile,—and to satisfy my heart while I sanctify my ambition, by associating with the great pursuit of my life, its tenderest and holiest affection. Your EBB." ". . .[I]ts tenderest and holiest affection"—"How much do you love me?," the father asked. And in 1844 Elizabeth Barrett Barrett answered as the eldest daughter. As Elizabeth Barrett *Browning*, which she became in 1846, she learned to speak of her father only according to her bond, no more, no less—and the eldest daughter became the youngest daughter after all.

The *Sonnets from the Portuguese* mark a radical change in the character of Elizabeth Barrett's poetry, or rather, in the character of Barrett Browning's poet. In the earlier work, her first-person poetic personae are either male, as in *Lady Geraldine's Courtship*, or sexless, as in *A Vision of Poets*, so that she does not contravene the law of silence for women. In the *Sonnets*, however, a *woman* speaks, and she speaks as a *poet*, the equal of a man-poet, fit to barter and compete with him. Early on in the exchange of letters between Barrett and Browning, she had written that she envied Browning because he was " 'masculine' to the height—and I, as a woman, have studied some of your gestures of language & intonation wistfully, as a thing beyond me far!"

Well, old habits die hard, and flattery is not the worst of them. But in 1845 there was some real reason for anxiety in her assessment of herself as that strange anomaly called "woman-poet." Only three years earlier in 1842, Mary Anne Stodart had written in an influential book, called *Female Writers: Their Proper Sphere and Powers of Usefulness*, that man is high while woman is low: "We can see the man of high poetic genius delighting in the wide-rolling ocean . . . . We can see the poet watching with high exultation the bold and fearless eagle, as in steady grandeur, it rises from the earth and gazes unappalled on the splendours of the noon-tide sun; but woman, gentle woman, will sooner bend over the turtle-dove, admire its beautiful form, its delicate plumage, read the quick glances of its eye, and with responsive readiness give meaning to its tender cooing."

No wonder Barrett Browning needed to invent a new woman-poet, a high, wide, strong woman-poet who could speak without cooing. This is what she did in the *Sonnets from the Portuguese*. Angela Leighton calls the *Sonnets from the Portuguese* "self-celebrating," and so they are. It is a poem to the beloved, and a song of myself.

And it didn't stop there. In her later poems, Barrett Browning continued with this speaking-out woman-poet persona. In *Casa Guidi Windows*, in *Aurora Leigh*, in *A Curse for a Nation*, even in a late poem like *Lord Walter's Wife*, she takes on the role of the woman who speaks out, not to flatter, or measure for someone else's benefit, but for herself. In this way she marked out a path for the woman poets who followed her and admired her example, Christina Rossetti and Emily Dickinson, for instance, and Barrett Browning herself knew that that was part of the politics of her new speaking self. In 1861 she wrote, rather unfavorably, to her friend Isa Blagden about a new volume of Adelaide Procter's poems, then she added: "This is all between you and me—I admire her personally—and there's goodness and grace in what she writes. . . . It would, in fact, be *horrible* for me to be heard nibbling at another woman's poems. I would as soon that people said I dyed my hair."

I used to think that this comparison was just funny. Now, remembering the question of hair, what it means, who you give it to, what of yours it gives away, I wonder if the fairytale context is not here too. Barrett Browning hasn't given this lock of hair away, but she wants to be seen in her true colors. Extracting herself from the economy of the father, whether that demanded by a real father, or that imposed upon her by her poetic fathers and grandfathers, meant that Barrett Browning could transform herself from the dependent daughter who competes with her sisters, into an independent self who can speak for her own kind.

But, you may say, the *Sonnets from the Portuguese* was first of all a private document. And so it was. The poem was not intended for publication, and it was not meant for public consumption. It was her own measure that Elizabeth Barrett weighed up. Which is exactly what happens when, in the

penultimate Sonnet, number XLIII, she seems, perversely, to get around to
answering that old question.

> How do I love thee? Let me count the ways.
> I love thee to the depth and breadth and height
> My soul can reach, when feeling out of sight
> For the ends of Being and ideal Grace.
> I love thee to the level of everyday's
> Most quiet need, by sun and candle-light.
> I love thee freely, as men strive for Right:
> I love thee purely as they turn from Praise.
> I love thee with the passion put to use
> In my old griefs, and with my childhood's faith.
> I love thee with a love I seemed to lose
> With my lost saints,—I love thee with the breath,
> Smiles, tears, of all my life!—and, if God choose,
> I shall but love thee better after death.

Nine times she says, "I love thee" in this Sonnet, and not once is
whatever she says about "thee" at all. Every bit of this Sonnet is a measure—
note "count," "depth," "breadth" and "height"—but it is a measure of the
self, of who the woman-poet is and will be, how she can be valued. The
Sonnets from the Portuguese may not have been designed as a public statement,
but here she escapes an old regime where she was enjoined to silence or
riddles, and she transforms herself into a speaking subject who can take her
own story to market. In this commercial frame, the title *Sonnets from the
Portuguese*, which refers both to E. B. B.'s poem on the Portuguese Catarina
in "Catarina to Camoëns," and hints of translation, may have yet another
meaning to add to its many, for these *Sonnets* then become goods, foreign
imports, argosies, brought across the seas from another trading nation,
"from the Portuguese."

In her book on fairytale Marina Warner tells the story of
Donkeyskin, which is a variant on the "How much do you love me?" King-
and-daughter story, and which, in many ways, parallels Elizabeth Barrett
Browning's private and public stories about herself. After giving birth to a
girl-child Donkeyskin's mother dies, making her husband promise that he
will only marry again if he can find a wife as beautiful as herself. He searches
the four corners of the globe but fails, until one day it occurs to him that his
own daughter is indeed as beautiful as her mother. Pressing her to marry
him, the King thus asks the question of his daughter "How much do you love
me?" and, aware of the taboo in his demand, she is condemned to silence.
Advised by a fairy godmother, Donkeyskin flees disguised as a bear in one

version, in the skin of a magic donkey that defecates gold in another, and seeks humble work as a skivvy in the palace of a neighboring king. There, one day, the Prince chances to espy her in the privacy of her hovel, or pigsty, or grubby kitchen and. . . . the rest is history. According to Warner this story is not now as familiar to us as, say, Cinderella or Sleeping Beauty, because, during the eighteenth and nineteenth centuries it was either omitted from the major folk tale collections altogether, or it was bowdlerized and the key reference to incest was taken out. *Why* is the question. Because, says Warner, it was too real, too close to home: "It is when fairy tales coincide with experience that they begin to suffer from censoring rather than the other way round. . . . [Donkeyskin's] predicament [is] at one and the same time a ridiculous, unsuitable extreme of invention which will give children ideas, and at the same time veracious and adult, and children are no longer to be exposed to such knowledge."

If we lost the story of Donkeyskin during the nineteenth century, we acquired the story of Elizabeth Barrett at the end of it. I suspect that one reason why her own story has become one of our modern myths is because it so closely resembles the archetypes we know. Like Donkeyskin, Elizabeth Barrett was asked a taboo question, twice over, once by her father, and once by her poetic forefathers. Like Donkeyskin she set a value on herself, transformed herself, changed her class, took herself to the labor market, and found her Prince because she found herself. She thus became a fairytale heroine. And the later versions of her story, in their strange skewed way, often put back the elements of the tale that we might otherwise leave out.

Rudolf Besier was not entirely on the wrong track in his 1930 "comedy" *The Barretts of Wimpole Street* when he made the horrible father pursue Elizabeth with the obligatory question:

> Barrett: You're not frightened of me? (*Elizabeth is about to speak—he goes on quickly*) No, no. You mustn't say it. I couldn't bear to think that. (*He seats himself on the side of the sofa and takes her hands.*) You're everything in the world to me—You know that. Without you I should be quite alone—you know that too. And you—if you love me, you can't be afraid of me. For love casts out fear. . . . You love me, my darling? You love your father? . . .
>
> Elizabeth: (*in a whisper*) Yes.

Nor was Besier entirely wrong when he ended the play with Father Barrett's planned revenge on Flush,—for Flush the dog, the animal alter ego, is left over as a remnant, a reminiscence of the disguise of furry skin borrowed by the heroine who will transform herself and escape into a new life. Virginia Woolf also took up Flush's point of view, but it only works because he is a ready-made trig point for measuring our Elizabeth Barrett Browning's story. The same is true of Lily Wilson, used as a litmus paper to test out the color of the Browning's romance in Margaret Forster's novel *Lady's Maid*.

The story of the Brownings' lives has become our modern fairytale. And Elizabeth Barrett Browning's *Sonnets from the Portuguese* has become the official record of that fairytale. Of course, Browning wrote poems out of it too, and what could be more potent than that tiny fragment, "O lyric love, half angel and half bird / And all a wonder and a wild desire . . . . "? But it's Barrett Browning's poems that stick with us as the true measure of love in poetry. Think how many of her first lines are familiar even to those who never read poetry: "the face of all the world is changed, I think, / Since first I heard the footsteps of thy soul . . ."; "And wilt thou have me fashion into speech / The love I bear thee. . ."; "If you must love me, let it be for nought / Except for love's sake only . . ."; "When our two souls stand up erect and strong . . ."; "How do I love thee? let me count the ways. . . ."

Accessible enough to be used by everyone, sentimental enough to be felt by us all. Since 1846, or more particularly perhaps since 1899 when the so-called Browning love letters were published, the Brownings' romance, and Barrett Browning's poems have become the true measure of romantic love.

And you find them in the strangest places. The American popular pianist Liberace recited "How do I love thee" as part of his stage act. In Erich Segal's 1960s weepy called *Love Story*, made into a blockbuster film with Ali McGraw and Ryan O'Neal in the early Seventies,—remember that "Love means never having to say you're sorry" . . . ?—it was a Barrett Browning poem that the doomed Jennifer read out at her hippy wedding, "when our two souls stand up erect and strong." Theirs was a pretty traditional story of heterosexual love thwarted by a heavy-handed father—the boyfriend is actually called Oliver Barrett, and there's a running joke about "no relation" to Elizabeth Barrett Browning. But other prohibitions draw the Brownings in as their yardstick: "We are closer married" than the Brownings were, said the lesbian poets Katherine Bradley and Edith Cooper who wrote together as Michael Field. The writer Radclyffe Gall gave Una Troubridge a copy of Besier's *The Barretts of Wimpole Street*, in 1943, and when Hall died shortly thereafter, Troubridge had inscribed on the plaque on her tomb in Highgate Cemetery, "And if God choose, I shall but love thee better after death. . . Una." In 1950, Violet Trefusis sent her one-time lover Vita Sackville-West a book, and Vita replied: ". . . you sent me a book about Elizabeth Barrett Browning. Thank you darling generous Lushka, and you gave me a coal-black briquet. . . which always burns in my heart whenever I think of you.

You said it would last for three months, but our love has lasted for forty years and more." The book was Frances Winwar's *The Immortal Lovers*, published in that year. Violet knew her message would be clear. Even now we can read her measure.

One hundred and fifty years ago Elizabeth Barrett and Robert Browning were married at St. Marylebone Church. The numbers are clear enough. From a quarter to eleven to a quarter past eleven. The twelfth day of the ninth month of the year eighteen forty-six. The ninety-first time of their meeting. Five people present. One hundred and fifty years on we remember that event. Today thousands of people know of it, then . . . . five. And that half-an-hour that contained five people is as nothing compared to the tiny infinitesimal moment which we can never know. The moment which contained only *two* people, the moment of seismic reaction written on their skin, in their gut, which Elizabeth Barrett and Robert Browning knew what they were to one another.

Now their flesh is dust. And their words, work, work on their words, words on their work, speaks volumes, covers page, encompasses the planet. Passion is volatile. We bring all our weights and balances, pulleys and tapes, and fail entirely to make the count. The thing we would price up is minute, and yet it fills all this space. Smaller than small, bigger than big. Love will not be measured.

> And the first soul called to the other first soul and asked:
> "How much do you love me?"
> And the other soul said, "How do I love thee?
> Let me count the ways. . . . I love you one moment's kiss,
> forty-four sonnets, and one hundred and fifty years."
> And both souls were satisfied.

GLENNIS STEPHENSON

The Vision Speaks: Love In Elizabeth Barrett Browning's "Lady Geraldine's Courtship"

Among Elizabeth Barrett Browning's contemporaries, one of the popular poems in her 1844 collection was "Lady Geraldine's Courtship." The ballad was warmly admired by Carlyle, Martineau, and the Rossettis, among others, and frequently singled out for particular praise by the critics. Barrett Browning, who had written the poem hastily to meet a publisher's deadline, was amused and surprised by its success and believed that it had attracted "more attention than its due." Modern critics have wholeheartedly agreed, and done more than enough to compensate for any overindulgence on the part of nineteenth-century readers. The poem now rarely attracts critical attention, and, when it does, it is usually dismissed as no more than a particularly uninspired example of Barrett Browning's early ballad romances.

But "Lady Geraldine's Courtship," the last of the romances to be written, actually bears only the most superficial resemblance to the other ballads; both thematically and stylistically, the poem reveals a significant advance in Barrett Browning's treatment of the main subject of this group of poems: the subject of love. The other early ballads almost consistently focus on the failure of love; the heroines are repeatedly frustrated in their attempts to establish lasting and satisfying relationships by the intervention of death, the inconstancy of their lovers, or—most importantly—the passive roles imposed upon them by conventional notions concerning the proper behavior

From *Victorian Poetry* 27, no. 1, (Spring 1989), © 1989 by West Virginia University.

for women in love. Even when Barrett Browning does write of a happy, although short-lived, union in "Rhyme of the Duchess May," she makes little attempt to suggest the nature of the love which drives May to elope with Sir Guy. She sweeps right past the initial joys of love and fixes firmly on its eventual sorrows. The other early ballads may be primarily concerned with romance, but the romances they present are rarely emotionally complex.

In "Lady Geraldine's Courtship," Barrett Browning is interested in bringing love to life for the reader, not in tracing the reasons for its demise. For the first time, the nature of a successful romantic relationship becomes the focus of her attention, and the relationship is shown to succeed primarily because the heroine is not confined to that restrictive position of passive and silent beloved against which Barrett Browning's earlier female character so vainly rebelled. There is a new emphasis on the woman's potential to be the active subject in a narrative, the "lover" rather than merely the "beloved"— an emphasis which leads to a deliberate confounding of traditional lovers' roles. The title itself, "Lady Geraldine's Courtship," piquantly raises this issue in providing us with no context by which to ascertain whether this is grammatically an objective or subjective genitive: it could equally mean "The Courtship of Lady Geraldine (by Bertram)" or "Lady Geraldine's Courtship (of Bertram)." The poem at large demonstrates that the genitive leans more to the subjective than the objective and that Geraldine is the active lover. Along with this new emphasis on woman as lover rather than beloved, there is a movement away from a preoccupation with plot to a concern with relationship and a resulting interest in experimenting with sensuous language to convey the physical and the spiritual nature of the relationship; "Lady Geraldine's Courtship" consequently marks an important turning point in Barrett Browning's conception and treatment of the question of love.

The main narrator of this romantic tale is Bertram, a poor poet who is invited by the wealthy and powerful Lady Geraldine to Wycombe Hall. Lady Geraldine and Bertram spend many hours discussing such topics as the primary importance of the soul and the basic nobility of all men, and Bertram comes to believe she is sympathetic to his radical social theories; he falls in love with her, but assumes his passion to be hopeless. One morning, he overhears Geraldine tell an overly persistent suitor, an earl, that she will marry only a wealthy and noble man. "I shall never blush," she claims, "to think how he was born." Bertram, misunderstanding her words, angrily rushes into the room, denounces her for scorning the common man, and declares that he has dared to love her. His passionate tirade over, he hears Lady Geraldine say his name, and swoons away at her feet; when he awakens in another room he begins to write the letter to a friend which comprises the main body of the poem. In a brief conclusion, Barrett Browning adopts an omniscient narrator to describe Geraldine as she comes to Bertram's room and declares her love for him and the poem ends with Bertram kneeling before Geraldine while she whispers triumphantly. "It shall be as I have sworn. / Very rich he is in virtues, very noble—noble, certes; / And I shall not blush in knowing that men call him lowly born."

This "Romance of the Age," which replaces exotic landscapes and ancient days with the Victorian drawing room, may not be as colorful as "A Romance of the Ganges," or as thrilling as "The Romaunt of the Page," but it is psychologically far more interesting. In the other early ballads, Barrett Browning generally employs an omniscient narrator, but rarely takes advantage of the opportunity this provides to suggest the thoughts and feelings of her characters or to explore their emotional responses to each other; as is usual in traditional literary ballads, the events of the story take precedence over the developing inner lives of the characters. In "Lady Geraldine's Courtship," the inner life predominates; the poem "has more mysticism (or what is called mysticism) in it," Barrett Browning wrote to Mary Russell Mitford, "hid in the story . . . than all the other ballad-poems of the two volumes." It is actually more like a dramatic monologue than a ballad: Bertram's perceptions, and in particular his responses to Geraldine, become of far greater significance than the actual events he describes.

The main narrative, the letter written by Bertram, is complicated by the presence of three different perspectives. First, there are the two perspectives provided directly by Bertram. The young man who records the events of the preceeding days is painfully aware of his love for Lady Geraldine and believes she scorns him as lowly born; his resulting bitterness and cynicism frequently emerge to color his narrative. He is trying, however, to convey not only his present unhappiness, but also his thoughts and feelings as he lived through these experiences. Consequently, as he becomes caught up in his memories, Bertram also appears as the idealistic romantic, smitten by the woman he sees as representative of "all of good and all of fair." These two perspectives rarely emerge as distinctly as I have presented them, and as a result, the young poet's narrative is sometimes marked by contradiction or ambivalence; descriptions of lingering tenderness can be quickly succeeded by, or mixed with, the bitter recriminations of a lover scorned.

Bertram's dual perspective, however, does not dominate the poem completely. Barrett Browning actually creates two distinct strands of narrative: Bertram's story, which is given directly, and Geraldine's, which must be deduced. As Bertram describes Lady Geraldine and recalls what she said and did, the reader pieces together a second, and more accurate, underlying narrative which tells of Geraldine's responses to, and growing love for, the young poet. Since Bertram tells the story, his narrative obviously

appears to dominate the text, but Barrett Browning continually distances the
reader from his perspective and encourages the construction of the
alternative narrative. Geraldine never becomes lost as the silent passive
object in Bertram's story; she is too clearly established as the active speaking
subject in her own.

In attempting to distance the reader from Bertram, Barrett
Browning ensures that he does not always appear as a sympathetic character.
His most objectionable feature stems, somewhat paradoxically, from his most
admirable. Bertram's democratic views allow for no distinction to be made on
the grounds of birth, wealth, or social position. The primary importance of
the soul and the irrelevance of worldly trappings is a subject of which he
never tires. It forms the basis for both a scornful summary of British social
law and an ironic lecture on the "wondrous age" of progress which is more
concerned with the development of iron than the development of man's
spirit. As he indicates when, enraged, he suggests Lady Geraldine needs to
show "more reverence . . . not for rank or wealth . . . / But for Adam's seed,
MAN!", he is convinced of the basic nobility of all men. Everyone, he
grandly announces, is stamped with "God's image," and has "God's kindling
breath within."

But Bertram is an inverted snob. Although his scorn for Lady
Geraldine's fashionable friends seems to be justified, he nevertheless
frequently appears to have a weighty chip on his shoulder. He is much too
quick to dismiss the wealthy and nobly born with disdainful generalizations.
Barrett Browning's attempt to distance the reader from Bertram is perhaps
overly successful when she depicts him storming into the room to denounce
Geraldine. In Bertram's presence, Geraldine displays the conventional signs
of love: she trembles and is alternatively flushed and pale. Bertram's response
is unforgivable, even if his pride has been hurt; he is just too smug: "'tis so
always with a worldly man or woman / In the presence of true spirits," he
sneers, "what else can they do but quail?."

Not surprisingly, the peasant poet has not proved to be one of
Barrett Browning's more popular creations. Edmund Stedman, for one,
found him unbearable. In "Lady Geraldine's Courtship," Stedman wrote,
Barrett Browning succeeded only in "showing us how meanly a womanish
fellow might act"; Bertram, he assures us, is a "dreadful prig, who cries,
mouths, and faints like a school-girl, allowing himself to eat the bread of the
Philistines and betray his sense of inequality, and upon whom Lady
Geraldine certainly throws herself away." Stedman's response is extreme,
however, and his understanding of the poem questionable. Barrett Browning
does not aim to create a strong and spotless white knight for Geraldine, and
Bertram comes alive for the reader so vibrantly precisely because his eager
idealism is so endearingly flawed.

Barrett Browning also encourages the continual construction of Geraldine's alternative narrative by revealing Bertram to be an unreliable narrator and a poor interpreter of Lady Geraldine. Initially he seems to attribute her flattering attentions to a taste for poetry and sympathy with his democratic views. After overhearing her conversation with the earl, he assumes that she is no better than her companions and has only been idly amusing herself. He was no more, he tells his friend with bitter regret, than a momentary diversion, a household pet like her greyhound, a dog whose antics are encouraged when it is convenient but who is scorned and sent home as soon as he becomes tiresome.

Geraldine's response to the earl never misleads the reader. Her attraction to the poet and her scorn for society's values are immediately recognizable as soon as she singles Bertram out with an invitation to Wycombe Hall. The invitation, extended in the presence of her friends, results in a sudden telling silence. Geraldine colors, and although Bertram interprets this as a momentary blush of shame, her subsequent words indicate it is more likely to be a flush of anger. "I am seeking," she says with cold deliberation, "More distinction than these gentlemen think worthy of my claim"; "these gentlemen" are obviously thinking quite the opposite, and her cool polite formality only thinly veils an aggressive challenge to their arrogant pretensions.

Geraldine's attraction to Bertram becomes even clearer after his arrival at Wycombe Hall. On the very first morning of his visit, she leads him and her other guests directly to the statue of Silence in her garden. Her following commentary on the statue suggests that this scene has been carefully staged—and staged entirely for Bertram's benefit. She is eager to demonstrate that she too is unimpressed by outer show and concerned only with spiritual excellence. While the typical statue of Silence has her left hand's index finger on her lips to say "Hush," Geraldine's Silence is asleep; her finger has fallen on her cheek and her symbol rose is held only slackly. This particular interpretation of the conventional form, Geraldine says, suggests how "the essential meaning growing may exceed the special symbol." The statue may no longer display all the expected attributes of a typical figure of Silence, but it has become a truer representation of the concept of silence. This, she continues, "Applies more high and low. / Our true noblemen will often through right nobleness grow humble, / And assert an inward honour by denying outward show." Bertram gives Geraldine no opportunity to continue and to explain how the concept applies to the low— although he might have found this instructive. His favorite topic has just been raised, and in he jumps, determined to prove Geraldine wrong. The result is a verbal tug of war. While Geraldine is vainly struggling to convey a personal conviction to Bertram, he views the discussion purely on a general level. "'Let the poets dream such dreaming! madam, in these British islands / 'Tis the substance that wanes ever, 'tis the symbol that exceeds.' " Geraldine is not about to give up, and insistently returns the subject to the personal:

> 'Not so quickly . . . I confess, where'er you go, you
> Find for things, names—shows for actions, and pure gold
> for honour clear:
> But when all is run to symbol in the Social, I will throw you
> The world's book which now reads dryly, and sit down with
> Silence here.'

While the reader may see a subtle message of encouragement for the young poet in Geraldine's argument, Bertram misses the point entirely. He may hold democratic views in theory, but—quite understandably—the possibility that the wealthy and powerful Lady Geraldine might be romantically interested in him, a lowly born poet, never enters his mind. Before Bertram can recognize that she not only seriously accepts his democratic theories but is quite prepared to put them into practice, Geraldine must literally become the active subject in the narrative. She must take the initiative and explicitly declare her love.

As this resolution to the poem indicates, the active role of lover in "Lady Geraldine's Courtship" is not restricted to Bertram; the roles of lover and beloved are as interchangeable as the positions of narrative subject and object. This is one of the most significant ways in which "Lady Geraldine's Courtship" differs from Barrett Browning's previous medieval ballads—and possibly one of the reasons it is "A Romance of the Age." Although the earlier ballads focus primarily on the female perspective, they show the roles of men and women to be firmly, and often fatally, fixed according to traditional standards. As Dorothy Mermin has shown, the women in these poems are generally passive and powerless; the men do all the choosing and the acting. The women who do attempt to step out of their assigned roles— to become the active subjects or lovers in their own narratives—inevitably meet with disaster. Barrett Browning now moves away from these early ballads and in the direction of the later poems by suggesting an interchangeability of roles in the lovers' relationship and showing a hero and heroine who are equally suited to the roles of both lover and beloved.

Initially, the reader no doubt approaches the poem with the standard expectation that Bertram will appear as the lover and Geraldine the beloved, and the opening stanzas seem to confirm such as assumption by placing Bertram in the most conventional of lover's roles: the troubadour, the poet-lover "singing" to the beautiful noble lady whom he apparently has no hope of winning. The most notable features of this traditional lover are his romantic deification of the beloved and his accompanying conviction of unworthiness. Bertram quickly demonstrates he conforms to the type. There is an important distinction, however, between the inequality present in social roles and lovers' roles, and the difference is made quite clear when Bertram first describes Lady Geraldine to his friend:

> There are none of England's daughters who can show a
> prouder presence;
> Upon princely suitors' praying she has looked in her
> disdain.
> She was sprung of English nobles, I was born of English
> peasants;
> What was *I* that I should love her, save for competence to
> pain?
>
> I was only a poor poet, made for singing at her casement,
> As the finches or the thrushes, while she thought of other
> things.
> Oh, she walked so high above me, she appeared to my
> abasement,
> In her lovely silken murmur, like an angel clad in wings!

When Bertram considers the social inequality which divides him from Lady Geraldine, his tone is bitter; with those numerous alliterative p's, he almost seems to be spitting out his scorn for the system. He is echoing the views of the majority, not his own, but is convinced that these are the views that will prevail; he has little hope of seeing his dream of a more democratic world realized. Gradually, however, the bitterness disappears and is replaced by a sense of wonder and reverence. The language softens as he dwells on a vision of Geraldine, who first appears to him in that highly traditional role of an angel from heaven, silent save for the murmur of her silks. Bertram as social creature may have little use for class distinctions, but as Barrett Browning shows, the experience of romantic love inevitably creates its own set of distinctions, its own levels of inequality. Bertram as poet and lover sees Geraldine as a superior being not because he is dazzled by her wealth and position, but, quite simply, because he loves her.

The romantic deification of the beloved emerges throughout Bertram's letter. At first, he believes that he loves Geraldine because she is a

Platonic form of ideal beauty and he, as a poet, "could not choose but love her." "I was born to poet-uses," he tells his friend,

> To love all things set above me, all of good and all of fair.
> Nymphs of mountain, not of valley, we are wont to call the Muses;
> And in nympholeptic climbing, poets pass from mount to star.

When he overhears Lady Geraldine's conversation with the earl, however, and the hopes he has unconsciously been harboring are dashed, Bertram recognizes that he had loved Geraldine not just as a "heavenly object"—in the same way he "loved pure inspirations, loved the graces, loved the virtues," but also as a woman. Her declaration, therefore, is particularly painful for him; not only does Geraldine confirm his belief that she would never marry such as he, but her apparent arrogance also detracts from his image of her perfect goodness; the beauty seems to be detached from the virtue. His vision of Geraldine no longer appears to match the reality.

Geraldine feels as unworthy of Bertram as he does of her, and is not above indulging in a little nympholepsy herself. She has woods in Sussex, she announces when inviting the young man to Wycombe, with "some purple shades at gloaming / Which are worthy of a king in state, or poet in his youth." The royal purple she believes to be equally suited to king and poet, and by directly equating the two, she explicitly reveals her attitude towards Bertram. While he is the lowly poet worshipping the divine lady, she is the young girl adoring the superior soul with his great poet-heart. As they sit among the daisies on the hillside and Geraldine encourages Bertram to speak on the spirit or pleads with him for a poem, she becomes like a schoolgirl eager to learn from, and please, her teacher. And when she finally goes to Bertram's chamber, her sense of unworthiness is unmistakeable. "Dost thou, Bertram, truly love me?" she asks in wonder, "Is no woman far above me / Found more worthy of thy poet-heart than such a one as I?"

The experience of romantic love, Barrett Browning suggests, precludes any possibility of a conviction of equality in a relationship. It is the lover's belief in the infinite superiority of the beloved that, when love is discovered to be returned, results in that elevating sense of wonder which later pervades the *Sonnets from the Portuguese* and which is experienced by both Bertram and Geraldine in "Lady Geraldine's Courtship."

Bertram's angry tirade is the means by which Geraldine learns he returns her love, and it is apparently his declaration of love, not his bitter recriminations, that she primarily hears and to which she eventually responds. When the passionate flow of words abruptly ends, she looks up "as if in wonder, / With tears beaded on her lashes, and said—'Bertram!'—It was all." The joyful surprise and wonder experienced by Bertram upon discovering Geraldine loves him are described less directly but in more detail. When Geraldine comes to his chamber—surely a daring step—she is silently smiling, crying, and blushing. She approaches Bertram with "her two white hands extended as if praying one offended, / And a look of supplication gazing earnest in his face." There can be little doubt what her presence means. Consequently, Bertram is simply unable to believe that she is really with him. He assumes he is dreaming, conjuring up a "vision . . . of mercies;" the implications of her actual presence would be overwhelming. As Geraldine glides closer to him, he desperately clings to his conviction that she is a vision; "No approaching—hush, no breathing!" he pleads, "or my heart must swoon to death in / The too utter life thou bringest, O thou dream of Geraldine!." Only when Geraldine touches him and with "both her hands enfolding both of his" says, "Bertram, if I say I love thee, . . . 'tis the vision only speaks," is he forced to acknowledge her actual presence. For both the reader and Bertram, Geraldine rises far above the traditional role of the angelic beloved, passive, silent and unobtainable in her perfection; the vision and the woman merge.

Although "Lady Geraldine's Courtship" ends with Bertram kneeling before Geraldine in the conventional pose of the lover adoring his lady, for the greater part of the poem he is actually the lover only in the most figurative sense. His letter is full of the images commonly associated with love-melancholy. Love is seen as a wound inflicted by Geraldine in the alternately blessed and cursed woods of Sussex. The arrows which inflict the wound come from Geraldine's hypnotic eyes which "undo" Bertram and draw him on, and from her "lips of silent passion, / Curved like an archer's bow to send the bitter arrows out." Like the most conventional of lovers, Bertram is left "mad and blind" with an almost painfully acute sensitivity to the presence or voice of his beloved. He reads the poems of Petrarch, among others, to Geraldine and avoids the company of her guests whenever possible, preferring to languish alone and listen to Geraldine's "pure voice o'erfloat the rest" or to muse over the poems of Camoëns, another lover cruelly separated from his lady by society. Shakespeare's Rosalind could teach this particular lover little.

Although Bertram is certainly a perfect literary lover, his only active courting of Geraldine is contained, ironically, in the angry lecture to which he subjects her. As he listens to Lady Geraldine and the earl, he literally sees red; he feels within him the "conventions coiled to ashes" and suddenly becomes quite capable of openly speaking his mind. He reveals not only his anger, but also his love, and his lecture on the equality of all men gradually becomes a series of bitter compliments to Geraldine on her "lovely spirit face" and "voice of holy sweetness." As Bertram's passions build and Geraldine does not respond, he quickly works up to a full declaration of his feelings:

> Have you any answer, madam? If my spirit were less earthly,
> If its instrument were gifted with a better silver string,
> I would kneel down where I stand, and say—Behold me! I am worthy
> Of thy loving, for I love thee. I am worthy as a king.

This climactic moment is tinged with irony for the reader; Geraldine has already vainly tried to indicate to Bertram that he is indeed, in her eyes, the equal of a king.

Geraldine is far more active in the role of lover than Bertram. She may even be seen as the female version of that noble Duke on a red roan steed that Barrett Browning's other early heroines, such as Little Ellie in "The Romance of the Swan's Nest" and May in "Rhyme of the Duchess May," either dream about or love. Bertram, conversely, with his tears, his tenderness, and his sensitivity, displays numerous "feminine" qualities which are appropriate to both lover and beloved. Geraldine's more active role is, admittedly, partly the result of the differences in their social positions. In spite of all Bertram's theories, he could never initiate the relationship. It is essential that Geraldine should make the first move and invite him to Wycombe. Nevertheless, throughout the poem Barrett Browning continually undercuts the importance of social position.

This was, indeed, Coventry Patmore's major objection to the poem. Quite certain that such an ill-matched pair as Geraldine and Bertram could never be happy, Patmore as self-appointed marital expert reminds us just how strongly early nineteenth-century society would object to such a "mesalliance." Geraldine would be forced to relinquish her "*station in society*," he observes with distaste, and this point is not made clearly enough in the poem. If Barrett Browning meant to show the nobility of Geraldine, he writes,

> in leaving the condition in which she had passed her life, for the sake of passing it hence forward in the unsophisticated company of an uneducated poet, and his friends and relations, she ought, in order to have brought out her meaning artistically, to have

shown that the Lady was not only fully aware of the sacrifice she was making, but that she was also capable of enduring it to the end, with all its trying circumstances of social contempt and dissonance of habits.

Patmore is obviously more concerned with the effects of social position than the effects of love. The middle-class reading public, though it could accept the romantic notion of the marriage of a man to his social inferior—a Cinderella or a Pamela—still reacted strongly against the idea of a highborn woman stooping to conquer. This was precisely because such a situation implies an active sexuality on the woman's part. Barrett Browning does not hesitate to create an actively sexual heroine and, despite the grim mutterings of such critics as Patmore and Stedman, she successfully romanticizes the feminine plot of desire. Patmore's objections to the story surely stem from his uneasy recognition that Barrett Browning is quite clearly showing how unimportant social standing can become once a woman is permitted to feel normal sexual desire.

As Barrett Browning undercuts the importance of social position in the poem as a whole, so she minimizes its significance as a cause of Geraldine's active love-making. Geraldine is a strong woman with an independent mind and a healthy disregard for convention; in courting Bertram she is as defiant as he would be in courting her. And her active wooing is not confined to the obvious examples of inviting Bertram to Wycombe and going to his chamber to declare her love; she attempts to win him in various subtle ways. Once she has the poet at Wycombe, she continues to pay him particular attention. Repeatedly, she coaxes him to join her and her friends, and, when he lingers behind, apparently draws on all her charms to encourage him. Her conversation is always obviously directed to Bertram and her other guests seem forgotten. In the midst of a large gathering, Geraldine manages to transform the time she spends with Bertram into intimate moments.

This sense of intimacy pervades "Lady Geraldine's Courtship" and clearly reflects Barrett Browning's primary concern with the nature of Bertram and Geraldine's love. The poem may be, as she explained in a letter, "a 'romance of the age,' treating of railroads, routes, and all manner of 'temporalities,' " but the romance is far more important than the railroads. For the first time in her career, Barrett Browning has shifted her interest away from the excitement of plot and has concentrated specifically on the nature of a romantic relationship.

As Barrett Browning becomes more interested in the intricacies of love than of plot, she also searches for new ways to convey the nature of the love she describes, and, to a great extent, she relies on the effects of highly sensuous language and imagery. The rendering of sensuous experience in "Lady Geraldine's Courtship" becomes a true register of both erotic and emotional attraction, and a means of providing the reader with access to the inner lives of her characters. There is little sensuous description in the previous ballads, a telling reflection of the frustration of desire pervading the poems, and when it does occur, it usually suggests desire displaced. There is more of the sensual, for example, in Duchess May's caressing the red roan steed on which she escapes from that abhorrent—yet sexually magnetic—villain, Lord Leigh than there ever is in her relationship with the stiff picture-book knight she marries.

In "Lady Geraldine's Courtship," an abundance of sensuous description brings the love of the poet and the lady alive for the reader, and it clearly establishes that, despite Bertram's nympholeptic leanings, he does not love an ideal or a vision, but an actual woman. There are two sides to Geraldine's character—the regal, awe-inspiring lady, and the playful, often child-like woman. Bertram apparently finds her highly desirable in both roles. As the high-born lady, Geraldine is kingly, princely, and owns vast properties; it is not her wealth or position that attract Bertram, however, but the power and strength they bestow upon her, her consequent ability to "threaten and command." This Geraldine is associated with luxurious surroundings, the "crimson carpet" and the "perfumed air" and the finest jewels in the land. When she rejects her numerous suitor, she deals with them as "imperially as Venus did the waves." Her demonstration of power and control enables Bertram to feel more acutely her superiority—and the attitude of worship is, for both him and Geraldine, erotically satisfying.

As she demonstrates when inviting Bertram to Wycombe, Geraldine can play the role of the grand lady with great style. She deals with the obvious disapproval of her friends with a "calm and regnant spirit," and when she leaves the room, resembles "one who quells the lions." Her magnificence leaves Bertram quivering with silent pleasure. Even in this scene, however, she reveals the other side to her character when she softens visibly as she turns to Bertram. Lady Geraldine, lion-tamer, is replaced by Geraldine, lover. Sharp coldness is succeeded by an overflowing warmth, a welcoming smile, and an almost flirtation tone when she says:

> I invite you, Mister Bertram, to no scene for worldly speeches—
> Sir, I scarce should dare—but only where God asked the thrushes first:
> And if you will sing beside them, in the covert of my beeches,

I will thank you for the woodlands,—for the human world,
at worst.

While Geraldine as lady is most closely associated with courts, castles, and
ancient halls, Geraldine as woman and lover is associated with these
woodlands, with hills, forests, swans, and fawns. She appears as an integral
part of the natural sensuous world, and as Bertram writes his letter, the sound
of the woods that he connects with Geraldine haunts him as much as her "fair
face" and "tender voice."

Since this face and voice drive Bertram "mad and blind," it is fitting
that his sensuous perceptions of Geraldine are revealed primarily through
visual and aural images. The sound of Geraldine as she moves is seductively
rendered by such alliterative and onomatopoeic phrases as "lovely silken
murmur" and "sudden silken stirring." While primarily aural, these images
also embrace the tactual, and this mingling of the senses is particularly
appropriate since the sound of Geraldine is something Bertram feels
intensely. His vision of Geraldine as angel may initially suggest he resembles
the poet of the traditional romantic lyric with its masculinist plot of distance
and desire, but the sensuous imagery he employs eliminates the traditional
sense of separation and emphasizes instead a sense of intimacy and the
unmistakable proximity of a flesh and blood woman. Bertram registers an
acute, almost physical sensitivity to Geraldine's presence; the sound of her
arrival, he records, "touched my inner nature through."

Geraldine's voice has a similar effect. Unlike the other women,
whose voices Bertram scorns as "low with fashion, not with feeling,"
Geraldine has a "pure" and "tender" voice of "holy sweetness" which turns
"common words to grace." Her "sudden silver speaking" can leave Bertram
weak and helpless, and he is easily bound by her "silver-corded speeches."
The effect of Geraldine's voice is never shown more clearly than at the
climax of his passionate tirade:

> But at last there came a pause. I stood all vibrating with
> thunder
> Which my soul had used. The silence drew her face up like
> a call.
> Could you guess what word she uttered? She looked up, as
> if in wonder
> With tears beaded on her lashes, and said—"Bertram!"—It
> was all.

The passage is reminiscent of Herbert's "The Collar," in which the raving of
the rebellious soul ends with a simple call from God. Bertram's violent rush

of passion is subdued by a single word. He is struck by the "sense accursed and instant, that if even I spake wisely / I spake basely—using truth, if what I spake indeed was true." The sound of Geraldine's voice crushes him, in spite of his previous conviction that his anger is justified, he suddenly instinctively feels he is wrong. Geraldine's feelings for Bertram are obviously conveyed through her voice, and Bertram is therefore left thoroughly confused; the message that he seems to detect in the voice is completely at odds with his rational estimation of the situation. At this climactic moment, it is perhaps not so surprising that he should faint away at Geraldine's feet.

Geraldine's appearance is clearly as captivating as her voice, and Bertram frequently interrupts the flow of his letter to dwell on the vision of her beauty. Every smile and every movement is lingered over and described in detail; even the movement of her garments is noted when Bertram remembers her wandering in the gardens:

> Thus, her foot upon the new-mown grass, bareheaded, with the flowing
> Of the virginal white vesture gathered closely to her throat,
> And the golden ringlets in her neck just quickened by her going,
> And appearing to breathe sun for air, and doubting if to float,—
>
> With a bunch of dewy maple, which her right hand held above her,
> And which trembled a green shadow in betwixt her and the skies.

Once again the tactual emerges. The passage may have a primarily visual appeal, but Bertram still conveys the impression that he is actually feeling the wetness of the maple, the pressure of Geraldine's foot on the grass, and the soft flicker of her hair on her neck—Barrett Browning is already well aware of the potential sexual suggestiveness of woman's hair and will later use such images to even greater effect in *Aurora Leigh* and *Sonnets from the Portuguese*.

It is the effect of the eyes, however, that is most fully explored in "Lady Geraldine's Courtship." Geraldine's "shining eyes, like antique jewels set in Parian statue-stone," Bertram claims, "undo" him. That steady serene glance which can quell in a moment can also appear soft and inviting. When she turns and looks at Bertram, he remembers, "she drew me on to love her / And to worship the divineness of the smile hid in her eyes." Those deep blue eyes "smile constantly, as if they in discreetness / Kept the secret of a happy dream she did not care to speak." Geraldine's eyes, like her voice, reveal her love, and Bertram consequently finds her glances a mystery.

The visual and the aural finally become merged in the description of Geraldine singing. As Bertram and Geraldine sit alone on the hillside, they often tire of books and grow silent. The silence gives Bertram a pleasant, yet disconcerting, awareness of Geraldine's presence which is "felt with beatings at the breast." Geraldine, apparently similarly disturbed, breaks the silence by bursting into song. "Oh to see or hear her singing!" Bertram writes,

> scarce I know which is divinest,
> For her looks sing too—she modulates her gestures on the tune,
> And her mouth stirs with the song, like song; and when the notes are finest,
> 'Tis the eyes that shoot out vocal light and seem to swell them on.
>
> Then we talked—oh, how we talked! her voice, so cadenced in the talking,
> Made another singing—of the soul! a music without bars.

Geraldine herself becomes the song, and what is sung is indistinguishable from the singer; Bertram responds with the senses and the spirit.

Both the presentation of Geraldine as song and singer and the mingling of the sensuous and the spiritual in this central passage become a reflection of Barrett Browning's larger concern within the poem to create and celebrate a successful romantic relationship. The lines which traditionally divide poet from lady, subject from object, lover from beloved, and sensuous from spiritual gradually dissolve and, as they do, the barriers which left Barrett Browning's earlier heroines frustrated, able to find satisfaction in love only by accepting God as substitute-beloved, are overcome. As Barrett Browning's first detailed evocation and dramatization of a growing love, "Lady Geraldine's Courtship" marks a crucial turning point between the early ballads, with their pessimistic and rather superficial handling of romance, and such later works as *Sonnets from the Portuguese* and *Aurora Leigh*, with their more mature and complex investigation of the experience of love.

MARJORIE STONE

A Cinderella Among The Muses: Barrett Browning and the Ballad Tradition

In their 1867 edition of *Bishop Percy's Folio Manuscript*, John H. Hales and Frederick J. Furnivall picture the ballad before the Romantic revival as a "Cinderella" among the Muses:

> She had never dared to think herself beautiful. No admiring eyes ever came near her in which she might mirror herself. She had never dared to think her voice sweet. . . . She met with many enemies, who clamoured that the kitchen was her proper place, and vehemently opposed her admission into any higher room. The Prince was long in finding her out. The sisters put many an obstacle between him and her. . . . But at last the Prince found her, and took her in all her simple sweetness to himself.

Some readers might pause over the class and gender-inflected assumptions in this ingenuous fairy story of a gallantly patronizing "Prince" taking a low-born maiden "to himself," not to speak of the cultural hegemony implied, given that the "Prince" was English and so many of the ballads were Scottish. But few would dispute the importance of the union Hales and Furnivall so fancifully describe. Every student of Romantic poetry is aware of the profound significance of the ballad revival, reflected in Bishop Percy's

From *Victorian Literature and Culture* 21 (1993) © 1993 by AMS Press.

Reliques of Ancient English Poetry, in Sir Walter Scott's "minstrelsy," and above all in the *Lyrical Ballads* published by Wordsworth and Coleridge in 1798.

Yet the ballad is seldom recognized as an important Victorian genre, even though it attracted major and minor poets throughout the nineteenth century. G. Malcolm Laws, Jr.'s catalogue of Victorian literary ballads is longer than his catalogue of Romantic ballads. As Law suggests, the ballad was held in particular esteem by Pre-Raphaelite poets like D. G. Rossetti and Swinburne. Tennyson, like Hardy after him, also employed innovative variants on the form throughout his long career, in works such as the "The Sisters," with its refrain "O the Earl was fair to see!", "The Lady of Shalott," the immensely popular "Lady Clara Vere De Vere," "Edward Gray," "Lady Clare," "Locksley Hall," "The Revenge: A Ballad of the Fleet," and "Rizpah." Ballads are particularly numerous in his 1842 *Poems*, reflecting their prominence in a period marked by the success of Macaulay's *Lays of Ancient Rome* and the continuing sway of Sir Walter Scott's ballads and narrative poems. The ballad has an even higher profile in Elizabeth Barrett's 1844 *Poems*, commended by the *English Review* for containing "some of the best ballad-writing" encountered "for many a day." Indeed, Barrett's "peculiar skill" in "this species of poetry," a form she had made "peculiarly" her own, was frequently praised in the reviews of the two volumes that established her as Tennyson's rival in 1844. Although Barrett was no "Prince," she too took that "Cinderella" among the Muses, the ballad, to herself—not so much because of its "simple sweetness" but because its energy, its frank physicality, its elemental passions, its strong heroines, and its sinewy narrative conflicts allowed her to circumvent the passionless purity conventionally ascribed to the middle-class Victorian woman. In her own appropriations, the lowly maiden is used to interrogate the inscriptions of sexual difference it appears to encode.

For a number of reasons, some having to do with the ballad genre itself, others with the general approach to Barrett Browning's works, her achievement in the ballad form is insufficiently appreciated today. Even recent feminist critics tend to disparage her ballads, ironically by placing them in the context of a separate "feminine genre" of ballad-writing which is, in Dorothy Mermin's words, "sentimental" and "retrogressive." This essay will argue for a different perspective on the Victorian ballad and Barrett Browning's ballads in particular. Her revisionary innovations in the genre can be more fully appreciated when we re-situate her ballads in the matrix of the Romantic ballad revival and the tradition it produced, ranging from Bishop Percy to the Pre-Raphaelite poets and Thomas Hardy. By considering the intertextuality of a number of her ballads, and by reconstructing the horizon of expectation against which they were written and read, I hope to show how poems like "A Romance of the Ganges," "The Romaunt of Margret," "The Poet's Vow," "The Romaunt of the Page," and "Rhyme of the Duchess May" echo and adapt the motifs and conventions of traditional ballads and Romantic narrative verse in ways that point forward to the ballads of the Pre-Raphaelite poets.

I use "intertextuality" here in the broad sense it has come to have as the prescriptive definitions of structuralism and semiotics have yielded before the recognition that repertoires of anonymous social and literary codes cannot be easily extricated from traditional questions of particular sources and influences. Some of the conventions and motifs Barrett deploys in 1838 and 1844 ballads were so widely disseminated and frequently imitated that they undoubtedly are intertextual in the stipulative sense emphasized by Roland Barthes and others. Yet the border between this form of intertextuality and identifiable influence is often difficult to determine. Like the words analysed by Antony Harrison, many of Barrett Browning's ballads also involve "self-consciously intertextual uses of precursors" to expose ideological values and presuppositions.

Barrett Browning's more self-conscious intertextuality is particularly apparent in her modification of what Nancy K. Miller terms "female plots"— that is, the plots that "culture has always already inscribed" for women, plots reinscribed in "the linear time of fiction." Like Charlotte Brontë, Barrett Browning has often been faulted for her handling of plot. Mermin observes that it was fortunate Barrett Browning did not write novels because she "had no gift for inventing plots" and the stories in her ballads are "invariably silly," if "entertaining." But in many instances, the "silly" stories that Mermin objects to in Barrett's 1838 and 1844 ballads are no more absurd than the plots they play against in the traditional ballads collected by Percy, and in Romantic ballads and narratives written by Gottfried Bürger, by Scott, and by Wordsworth and Coleridge.

The revisions in several of Barrett Browning's ballads cast additional light on her complex adaptation of plots and motifs in precursor texts. These revisions also indicate that, contrary to prevailing assumptions, Barrett Browning engaged in careful and often extensive rewriting of some of her ballads, both at the manuscript stage and after they had appeared in periodicals and annuals. Her alterations in the ballads, like the significant textual changes she introduces in successive editions of her other works, point to the need for a modern scholarly edition of her poems. This essay considers some of the changes she made in "The Poet's Vow" between its first publication in 1836 and its appearance in subsequent editions of her works, and in "The Romaunt of the Page," between the manuscript draft, its initial publication in the 1839 *Findens' Tableaux*, and its republication in the

1844 *Poems*. In the case of "The Poet's Vow," her revisions serve to extend the critique of Wordsworth readily apparent in the initial version of the poem—a critique she effects in part by drawing on the plots and motifs of the old anonymous ballads in the Percy collection. In "The Romaunt of the Page," however, it is certain of the Percy ballads themselves that she most directly writes against.

As in the case of "Rhyme of the Duchess May," the most substantial revisions in "The Romaunt of the Page" expand the role and motivation of the poem's male protagonist, revealing how Barrett Browning progressively complicated her "female plots" by portraying their intersections with the social systems that create and encompass them. The changes in "The Romaunt of the Page" and "Rhyme of the Duchess May" thus look forward to the last of the 1844 ballads to be written, "Lady Geraldine's Courtship," with its male protagonist Bertram, and to *Aurora Leigh*, where the conflicts between Romney's reformist socialist ideals and his conservative assumptions about gender are portrayed at some length. In short, Barrett Browning shows how the "female plots" constructing Aurora as a subject are inseparable from the gender plots of Romney and his society, thereby establishing an ideological nexus she first began to explore in her ballads.

The 1844 poems brought before a wide public, both in England and America, two of Barrett's ballads previously published only in the 1839 and 1840 editions of *Findens' Tableaux*: "The Romaunt of the Page" and "The Lay of the Brown Rosary." Several new poems identified as "ballads" by contemporary reviewers also appeared in 1844, most notably "Rhyme of the Duchess May," "Bertha in the Lane," "Catarina to Camoens," "The Romance of the Swan's Nest," and "Lady Geraldine's Courtship." These poems were acclaimed by general readers as well as critics. Barrett was highly amused by "an account in one of the fugitive reviews of a lady falling into hysterics" after reading "Rhyme of the Duchess May," and a similar story of a "gush of tears" down "the Plutonian cheeks of a lawyer" as he read "Bertha in the Lane." As Mermin notes, "Barrett's ballads were her most consistently popular poems in the nineteenth century." They were often reprinted in selected editions of her poems, while particular favourites, such as "Rhyme of the Duchess May" and "Lady Geraldine's Courtship" were republished separately in illustrated editions until well past the turn of the century.

The vogue for ballads in the mid-Victorian period inevitably led to parodies like those in the frequently reprinted "Bon Gaultier" *Ballads*, published in 1845 by Sir Theodore Martin and W. E. Aytoun. One of its later editions included a parody of "Rhyme of the Duchess May" entitled "The Rhyme of Lancelot Bogle." Such parodies no doubt contributed to the relatively low profile of the ballad in modern constructions of the Victorian poetical canon—and, in Barrett Browning's case, to the disappearance of her ballads from literary history altogether. The assumption that a popular *literary* work is necessarily of little artistic value has lingered longer in the case of Victorian poets than in the case of novelists such as Dickens or Wilkie Collins.

Paradoxically, in the case of popular literary ballads, the effects of this assumption have been exacerbated by narrow definitions of the genre that privilege the anonymous or "authentically" popular folk ballad over literary "imitations." J. S. Bratton shrewdly notes the limitations of such constraining definitions in the case of Francis J. Child's enormously influential collection, *The English and Scottish Ballads*, and detects the "same assumption of the innate superiority of the traditional ballad" in studies of the literary ballad by Albert B. Friedman and Anne Ehrenpreis. But Bratton's study risks perpetuating some of the very assumptions it criticizes in focusing on the Victorian popular ballad and reclassifying some literary ballads as popular. Thus it attempts a "redrawing of the line which separates 'art' and 'popular' poetry," rather than a questioning of the line itself. In shifting this line, Bratton gives no attention to Barrett Browning's very popular literary ballads. Such omission is typical of literary histories published between 1900 and 1980. Her ballads have particularly suffered from definitions of the genre privileging the "authentic" folk form because they move farther away from this model than literary ballads like Keats's "La Belle Dame Sans Merci" and D. G. Rossetti's "Sister Helen."

These general assumptions about the popular literary ballad seem to underlie Alethea Hayter's 1962 dismissal of Barrett Browning's ballads as "synthetic" confections with a "certain narrative sweep and excitement" appealing to "people who did not normally read poetry at all." Hayter adds in extenuation that Barrett Browning "never really took them seriously," supporting this conclusion with the well-known lines in *Aurora Leigh*:

> My ballads prospered; but the ballad's race
> Is rapid for a poet who bears weights
> Of thought and golden image.

Traces of Hayter's disparaging tone persist in recent feminist reinterpretations. Thus Angela Leighton approaches one of Barrett's earlier poems, "A Romance of the Ganges," and "The Lay of the Brown Rosary" as "ballads which Elizabeth Barrett wrote in response to a demand . . . for morally educative poems" directed toward "a primarily female readership." Leighton finds these "confused and precipitate" ballads to be of psychological interest only, like "The Romaunt of Margret," first published in 1836 in the *New Monthly Magazine*. Kathleen Hickok similarly dismisses "The Lay of the Brown Rosary" as "an uninspired jumble," "The Romaunt of Margret" as completely conventional, and "Rhyme of the Duchess May" as a spasmodic poem.

In a series of articles subsequently incorporated into *Elizabeth Barrett Browning: The Origins of a New Poetry*, Mermin was the first to reinterpret Barrett Browning's ballads as poems providing "a covert but thorough-going reassessment, often a total repudiation, of the Victorian ideas about womanliness to which they ostensibly appeal." "Beneath their apparent conventionality," Mermin persuasively argues, the ballads sceptically examine "the myths and fantasies of nineteenth-century womanhood," including "the virtues of self-repression and self-sacrifice" they seem to affirm. At the same time, however, Mermin doubts that Barrett Browning herself was entirely aware of the subversive elements in her own poems. "Almost all her ballads cry out to be read as feminist revisions of old tales," but they were not interpreted as such by Victorian readers, Mermin emphasizes. "Elizabeth Barrett told the old stories in a style and tone that gave no hint of revisionary intention, and she discarded the ballad form without discovering how to use it effectively against itself."

Helen Cooper and Glennis Stephenson assume a more thorough-going revisionary intent on Barrett's part: Cooper in reading Barrett's medieval ballads as an examination of "the sexual economy of courtship and marriage" and Stephenson in analysing their subversion of "chivalric conventions" and gender roles. Nevertheless, like Mermin, they emphasize the limits of Barrett's revisionism and approach it within the context of a feminine genre of ballad writing which is "squarely in the tradition" of Letitia Landon. Cooper suggests that Barrett followed Landon and Felicia Hemans in using her ballads to explore "issues of domesticity" and that their publication in annuals "apparently located" them in "a female genre." Similarly, while Stephenson explores the "complexity" of "The Lay of the Brown Rosary," she argues that Barrett tended to "devalue" all of her *Findens'* ballads.

There is good reason to question some of these assumptions and their critical implications. In the first place, they depend upon categorizations that are not clearly evident in many early and mid-Victorian references to the ballad. Early Victorian concepts of the ballad seem to have been remarkably broad and inclusive, both in terms of genre and in terms of gender. Neither Barrett Browning nor the majority of her readers seem to have approached her ballads in the context of a separate, feminine tradition. Barrett Browning also took her ballads more seriously than some of her playfully disparaging remarks about the *Findens'* contribution and herself as a "writer of ballads" indicate. More importantly, she clearly did sometimes consciously use the ballad form "against itself" in complicating or subverting traditional ballads, and some Victorian readers, at least, recognized how much she was writing in the wake of Bishop Percy and his imitators.

Recent discussions of Barrett Browning's works by Mermin and Cooper separate her "romantic ballads" with their female protagonists from works such as "The Poet's Vow," even though this poem has stronger formal affinities with the ballad genre, as narrowly defined, than works like "The Lay of the Brown Rosary." Resituating her ballads within the matrix created by the Romantic ballad revival requires an approach less marked by such artificial distinctions. A relatively broad operative definition of the ballad also seems called for, since conceptions of the ballad were more amorphous and comprehensive in the early Victorian period than they became after Child's collection of "authentic" ballads appeared. Many of the works described by Barrett's reviewers as ballads might more probably be classified as romances or romantic tales today, in particular "Lady Geraldine's Courtship," with its subtitle "A Romance of the Age." In *Romantic Narrative Verse*, Hermann Fischer acknowledges the difficulty of distinguishing between these forms, and he traces some of the historical and literary developments that contributed to their amorphousness by the 1830s and '40s. Among much else, Fischer points out that when Scott attempted to describe the new genre of "romantic poetry" or romantic verse narrative in 1813, he did "not distinguish between [sic] ballads, lays and romances"; moreover, Scott's own poetical works reflect an "eclectic mixture" of conventions from "the ballad and romance tradition." Scott's eclecticism led to "rich variations of subject and form" in romantic narrative verse, with the result that "the 'genre' was constantly being extended and becoming vaguer in definition," until its "ramification" led to what Fischer terms its "dissolution." Although Fischer acknowledges that variants on such verse were "repeatedly resurrected by poets such as Macaulay, Matthew Arnold, Tennyson and Browning," he describes it as an exhausted and merely popular form after 1830. Barrett Browning is not included among the few women writers he dismisses as Scott's prolific imitators.

Barrett Browning's titles for her "ballads" ("romaunt," "lay," "rhyme," "romance") and her references to these works in her letters suggest that for her, as for many of her contemporaries, these terms were loosely synonymous. Harriet Martineau, for instance, similarly refers to these works in a letter to Barrett as "your Rhyme, Romaunt, lay-style of poems." Thus I use the term "ballad" here as Barrett Browning and other Victorians used it, to refer to all of her narrative poems with clear affinities either with the characteristic features of the ballad form (the ballad stanza, the refrain, dialogue, tragic and/or topical subject matter) or with the larger tradition of "minstrelsy" and Romantic narrative verse. I have made an exception, however, in the case of the group of narrative poems with dramatized speakers, including "Catarina to Camoens," "Bertha in the Lane," "Lady Geraldine's Courtship," "The Runaway Slave at Pilgrim's Point," "Void in Law," and "Mother and Poet." These works were sometimes described as "ballads," and they share many characteristics with both folk ballads and the ballads of the Romantic revival: there are clear echoes of the old Scottish ballad, "Lady Bothwell's Lament," in "Void in Law," for example. But since this group of poems displays even stronger affinities with the developing form of the dramatic monologue, I have chosen to approach them elsewhere, and made only incidental comments on their ballad traits below.

Barrett Browning often expressed her love for "the old burning ballads, with a wild heart beating in each!" The old Scottish ballads were praised by the historian Henry Hallam for their "Homeric power of rapid narration," and it should not be forgotten that, as James Borg notes, "the ballad was viewed as the prototype of the epic" in the early nineteenth century. As Barrett herself puts it in her survey of English poets from Chaucer to Wordsworth, "The Book of the Poets," the ballad is "a form epitomical of the epic and dramatic." Given this assumption, it is unlikely that Barrett saw her ballads—even her ballads for *Findens'*—as mere diversionary exercises in a "feminine" genre. On the contrary, she may well have approached her ballad writing as a natural preparation for the writing of epic, a view that her own career subsequently bore out as she moved from writing simpler to more elaborate ballads and narratives between 1836 and 1844, culminating in "Lady Geraldine's Courtship," which she clearly saw as the prototype of *Aurora Leigh*. The significance of her ballads in her own eyes is further reflected in the prominence she gives them in planning the contents of the 1844 *Poems*.

Unfortunately space did not permit Barrett to include a survey of the "anonymous & onymous ballads" in "The Book of the Poets," as she explained to Mitford. "We must not be thrown back upon the 'Ballads,' lest we wish to live with them for ever," she fondly observes as she passes them by. Barrett does find room, however, to speak of "the *réveillé* of Dr. Percy's '*Reliques* of English Poetry,' " which sowed "great hearts" like Wordsworth's with "impulses of greatness." Barrett acquired her own copy of Percy's *Reliques* in 1826. Her love of the Percy ballads was shared by Mitford and some of her literary acquaintances, as Mitford's own comments and Robert Willmott's 1857 edition of the *Reliques* indicate. "The Book of the Poets" also alludes to the "Scottish Minstrelsy" inspired by the *Reliques*. Scott's epic narrative *Marmion* is one product of Scottish minstrelsy that enters into the intertextuality of Barrett's 1844 ballads, contributing to the resonance of her depiction of a woman disguised as a page and a nun buried alive in "The Romaunt of the Page" and "The Lay of the Brown Rosary" respectively. The pronounced Gothic strain in the "The Lay of the Brown Rosary" also owes something to Scott, although it reflects more closely the lingering influence of "Lenora," the immensely popular German ballad by Gottfried Bürger that was so important a prototype for Wordsworth, Coleridge, Scott, and Southey in the 1790s, as Mary Jacobus and Stephen Parrish have shown. Fischer notes that the influence of German works like Bürger's ballads contributed to the public taste between 1798 and 1830 for "the outwardly sensational and exaggeratedly thrilling" and for "rebellious amoral 'heroes,' " a taste fully exploited by Byron in his romantic tales.

It is important to note that Barrett's contemporary reviewers were quick to link her ballads to such precursors in the larger ballad tradition. After reading "The Poet's Vow" in October 1836 in the *New Monthly Magazine*, Mitford wrote to Barrett, "I have just read your delightful ballad. My earliest book was 'Percy's *Reliques*,' the delight of my childhood; and after them came Scott's 'Minstrelsy of the Borders,' the favourite of my youth; so that I am prepared to love ballads. . . . Do read Tennyson's 'Ladye of Shalot.' " *The Spectator* noted the resemblance of "The Romaunt of the Page" and "The Lay of the Brown Rosary" to the "old ballads," while *The Critic* described them as "revivals of the old English ballad, to which Miss BARRETT appears to be extremely partial." Similarly, John Forster compared "Rhyme of the Duchess May" to the Scottish border ballad "Edom o' Gordon" included in Percy's *Reliques*; while Sarah Flower Adams in the *Westminster Review* observed of the same poem, "it has all the rapidity of action of 'Leonore,' [and] the descriptive power of Scott and Campbell, united with the deep pathos of the earlier Scottish ballads."

It was not Scott and company, however, who were the most important precursors for Barrett the balladist, but Wordsworth and Coleridge. As Charlotte Porter and Helen A. Clarke noted in 1900, ballads such as "The Poet's Vow" belong to "the totally modern class of symbolic ballads" of which "The Ancient Mariner" is such a notable example. Mary Howitt, whose ballads Barrett often praised, was similarly influenced by "The Ancient Mariner" in works such as "The Voyage of the Nautilus" and "The Old Man's Story," although these poems are less "symbolic" than Coleridge's or Barrett's. Like Elizabeth Gaskell, who echoed Coleridge in depicting the fallen woman Esther in *Mary Barton*, Barrett was particularly drawn to "Christabel," with its sinister symbolic mother-daughter relationship and its highly innovative irregular metre. Jacobus observes that many of the *Lyrical Ballads* are like "Christabel" in releasing "subconscious impulses" in "dramatic confrontations." Much the same can be said of two of Barrett's ballads that echo "Christabel," "The Lay of the Brown Rosary" and "Isobel's Child." The latter, published in 1838, resembles Coleridge's poem in its loose ballad form, in its Gothic imagery and setting, and in its symbolically indirect treatment of the dark undercurrents in a mother's possessive love for her dying infant. Sara Coledridge was one Victorian reader who noticed that "Isobel's Child" was "like 'Christabel' in manner."

Barrett Browning's focus on abandoned or betrayed women in early ballads such as "The Romance of the Ganges' has reinforced the assumption that she was writing primarily in a sentimental female tradition. But such figures were a staple in traditional ballads such as "Lady Bothwell's Lament," in German ballads by Bürger like "The Lass of Fair Wone," and in lyrical ballads by Wordsworth such as "The Mad Mother" and "The Thorn." "The Runaway Slave at Pilgrim's Point," which Barrett Browning referred to as a "long ballad", adapts motifs from "The Lass of Fair Wone" and the "The Thorn," as well as from "The Mad Mother": one manuscript version of "the Runaway Slave" was entitled "Black and Mad at Pilgrim's Point."

It is ballad traits, "The Runaway Slave" reveals how much Barrett Browning's interest in the form was, like Wordsworth's as Tilottama Rajan describes it, "social not antiquarian." Indeed, the conflation of the traditional ballad and the topical, polemical broadside ballad that Rajan discerns in her Bakhtinian reading of Wordsworth's lyrical ballads may have been one reason why Barrett Browning saw Wordsworth as a greater poet than Scott. Scott was not a "great poet" in her view, though she conceded that he was highly accomplished in "poetical-antiquarianism." Like Wordsworth, Barrett Browning was interested in using the ballad form to create a community of readers cutting across classlines and, in the case of "The Runaway Slave," sexual and racial divisions.

Particularly in her later career, however, Barrett Browning was inclined to be more radically polemical than Wordsworth in her appropriation of the ballad for political purposes. "The Runaway Slave," with its abolitionist agenda, and the 1854 political ballad, "A Song for the Ragged Schools of London," follow Shelley's more than Wordsworth's example. In the latter Barrett Browning is clearly writing in the tradition of the topical broadside ballad, using the form as Shelley had used it in "Song to the Men of England" and "The Mask of Anarchy," and as it was widely used by the Chartists in England during the 1840s. As I have argued elsewhere, "A Song for the Ragged Schools" adapts and strategically revises Shelley's rhetorical tactics in "A Mask of Anarchy" to reach an audience more female than male. Its inspiration was also woman-centered. According to Robert Browning, the ballad was originally written to help raise money not for the ragged schools in general, but for "the 'Refuge for young destitute girls' " which Elizabeth's sister Arabella helped to "set going"—"the first of its kind."

Like "A Song for the Ragged Schools," Barrett's earlier, less polemical ballads of the 1830s and 1840s seem designed to appeal to a community of women readers. Although "Lady Geraldine's Courtship" with its male protagonist skilfully combines an appeal to both male and female readers, Barrett Browning seems to have written many of her ballads as a woman speaking to women, not like Wordsworth, as a "man speaking to men." William Herridge observed in 1887 that her ballads "appeal with especial force to the author's own sex, and strike almost every note in the scale of woman's thought and emotion." As Herridge's terms suggest, it was not to the feelings alone that Barrett Browning's ballads appealed, even though she praised the ballad form to Horne because "all the passion of the heart will go into a ballad, & feel at home." "Her narrative ballads have a swift directness and an impressive pictorialism which hold the imagination and stir the blood," James Ashcroft Noble observed. The "swift directness," most apparent in "Rhyme of the Duchess May," may have been acquired in part from her early immersion in ballads by Byron such as "The Destruction of Sennacherib." The pictorial quality reflects the influence of both Byron and Scott. But the vivid scene-painting, most apparent in the "Rhyme of the Duchess May," never impedes the narrative movement, as it so often does in Scott's narrative verse. Unlike Scott's narratives and unlike Wordsworth's "lyrical" ballads, Barrett Browning's ballads typically exhibit a strong narrative propulsion, despite the fact that she herself did not value narrative as the highest element in poetry. "It is the story that has power with people," she acknowledged.

Nevertheless, within this strong narrative propulsion, the convolutions and excesses that disrupt or exaggerate "plausible" sequentiality register Barrett Browning's critique of the plots encoding women's lives in the texts of precursor balladists, both "anonymous & onymous." As Nancy Miller points out, often plots seem "plausible" because they embody the assumptions of the dominant ideologies that determine the conditions for their constant reiteration. Barrett Browning's transformations, like Hardy's in "The Ruined Maid," undermine such plausibility and the ideologies that sustain it. Rajan observes that, because the ballad is a "cultural palimpsest inhabited by traces of more than one ideology," it "functions as a psychic screen on which desires having to do with ideological authority and hermeneutic community are projected and analysed. Barrett Browning's ballads function in precisely this way in their strategic revisions of conventions, motifs, and in some cases, precursor texts familiar to early

Victorian readers. Most notably, in her ballads of the 1830s and '40s, Barrett employs the starker power structures of medieval society to foreground the status of women as objects in a male economy of social exchange and to unmask the subtler preservation of gender inequities in contemporary Victorian ideology. Thus, like some of the modern women writers discussed by Patricia Yaeger, she engages in "a form of textual violation that . . . overgoes social norms by doubling them, by making them visible."

In many cases, her transformations were simply ignored by Victorian reviewers, who imposed the old "plausible" plots of praisable female behavior on her revisionary narratives. But such responses to the ballads cannot be taken to prove a lack of revisionary intention on Barrett's part. Nor do such reviewers necessarily speak for the large body of female readers who may have read Barrett's ballads otherwise. For instance, in Eliza Fitzgerald's copy of Barrett Browning's poems now in the Armstrong Browning library, one of the passages marked most heavily in "The Romaunt of the Page" stresses the courage of the woman-page in meeting the Saracens.

Often the narrative convolutions in Barrett Browning's ballads draw the reader's attention to ironies intensified by her transformative allusions to earlier works. In this respect, her ballads are again very different from Wordsworth's. Despite Wordsworth's democratizing project in the *Lyrical Ballads*, Rajan detects an "elision" of political and social concerns in his reduction of "narrative to a lyric tableau that constructs the world in terms of feeling rather than events or situations." The result is an apolitical "hermeneutics of sentimenalism" that privileges archetypal and universal feeling over political, social, and gender differences. Barrett Browning's focus, on the contrary, is on configurations of plot and character that foreground ideologically grounded gender differences in their intricate intersections with other hierarchies of power: humanity over nature, God over humanity, knight over page, parent over child, priest over nun, and, in "The Runaway Slave," master over slave.

"The Poet's Vow," the 1836 ballad in which Barrett Browning most noticeably echoes the *Lyrical Ballads*, illustrates this striking difference between her handling of the ballad form and Wordsworth's. As Cooper suggests, "The Poet's Vow" is a critique of the Romantic ideology positing nature as female, "the silent other." Possessed by the conviction that mankind has afflicted Earth with the curse of the fall, the nameless and representative poet referred to in the poem's title vows to forswear contact with humanity, consecrating himself to communion with nature instead. Publicly declaring his vow, he bestows his "plighted bride" Rosalind upon his "oldest friend" Sir Roland, offering his own lands as Rosalind's dower.

Declining to be the object in this male exchange, the betrayed Rosalind, still "half a child," rejects the "cruel homily" the poet has found in "the teachings of the heaven and earth." Years later, after the poet alone in his hall has withered within from "rejection of his humanness," Rosalind dies and instructs that her bier be placed before his "bolted door": "For I have vowed, though I am proud, / To go there as a guest in shroud, / And not be turned away." On her breast, like a Lady of Shalott who refuses to be judged merely by her "lovely face," she bears a scroll:

> I left thee last, a child at heart,
>   A woman scarce in years.
> I come to thee, a solemn corpse
>   Which neither feels nor fears.
> . . . .
> Look on me with thine own calm look:
>   I meet it calm as thou.
> No look of thine can change *this* smile,
>   Or break thy sinful vow:
> I tell thee that my poor scorned heart
> Is of thine earth—thine earth, a part:
>   It cannot vex thee now.

As Mermin suggests, the echoes of Wordsworth's "A Slumber Did My Spirit Seal" are "unmistakable," reflecting Barrett Browning's recognition of the "unprivileged position of woman" in the Romantic myth of a female nature. To speak with the voice of nature is to speak with the voice of the dead—or, as in Wordsworth's poem, with the voice of the male poet who chooses to commingle with nature and the dead. In either case, the individual woman is buried.

The crucial difference, of course, in Barrett Browning's rewriting of the Romantic man-nature love relationship is that in "The Poet's Vow" we *do* hear the voice of the still unburied Rosalind speaking from her scroll as an individual woman, not as a mythic female presence articulated by a male poet. Rosalind speaks, moreover, with the passion and bitterness of the betrayed women who so often appear in the ballads collected by Percy. She bears a particularly striking resemblance to the dead Margaret in "Margaret's Ghost" who appears at her lover's bedside to indict him for betraying his plighted troth. By superimposing a traditional ballad plot of human love and betrayal on Wordsworth's representation of the poet's love for nature, Barrett Browning foregrounds the narrative conflicts he deliberately elides in his identification of Lucy with the earth and in his deliberate focus on apparently universal feelings rather than on the drama of conflicting human desires.

In substantially revising "The Poet's Vow" first for her 1838 volume, *The Seraphim, and Other Poems*, and then for her 1850 *Poems*, Barrett Browning intensified both the narrative conflicts between the poet and Rosalind, and the forcefulness and passion of her ballad heroine. In the process, she also extended her subtle critique of Wordsworth. For example, in both the *New Monthly Magazine* version and the 1838 version of the poem, the section entitled "The Words of Rosalind's Scroll" begins with, "I left thee last, a feeble child / In those remembered years." In revising, Barrett Browning removed the emphasis on Rosalind's feebleness and made it clear that, though she was "a woman scarce in years" like Wordsworth's Lucy when her lover consigned her to her fate, she now speaks as a woman with a woman's desires and a woman's strength. The revisions also intensify Rosalind's bitter scorn for the poet's "sinful vow." In both the *New Monthly Magazine* version of "The Poet's Vow" and in the 1838 version, the second stanza of Rosalind's scroll ends with the lines, "My silent heart, of thine earth, is part / It cannot love thee now," not with the forceful declaration, "I tell thee that my poor scorned heart / is of thine earth—thine earth, a part: / It cannot vex thee now." The syntactic doubling in the revised version, "of thine earth—thine earth," undoes Wordsworthian ideology by simultaneously exaggerating and contradicting the identity of woman with nature that he assumes in the Lucy poems.

"The Poet's Vow" provides a further critique of Wordsworth in demonstrating the limited redemptive influence of recollections of early childhood. Barrett Browning's deletion of "those remembered years" is logical, given that the past is not remembered in any living way by her poet. Other revisions serve to emphasize the memories that the poet *should* have shared with Rosalind. For instance, in the *New Monthly Magazine* and the 1838 versions, Rosalind instructs her nurse to gather "little white flowers. . . Which I plucked for thee" and place them on her bier, whereas in the revised version she refers to the flowers "*he* and I" plucked "in childhood's games." The flowers thus bear a message for the poet, as the scroll more overtly does. But, as the passionate scorn of the scroll's words indicates, Rosalind has little faith in the efficacy of the flowers or memory alone. Nor is she herself moved chiefly by the tender recollection of childhood in addressing the poet as she does. Barrett Browning's revisions to "The Poet's Vow" make it clear that it is passion, not memory, that motivates Rosalind. Thus the lines "I have prayed for thee with the wailing voice / Thy memory drew from me" in the two earliest versions of the poem are replaced with, "I have prayed for thee with bursting sob / When passion's course was free."

Yet another dimension to Barrett Browning's intertextual debate with Wordsworth is apparent in the epigraph from "Lines Left upon a Seat

in a Yew-tree" which she added to the poem in 1838—"O be wiser thou, /
Instructed that true knowledge leads to love." In Wordsworth's poem, this
advice is prompted by the example of a hermit who withdrew from the world
and died in the pride of his solitude. Moralizing upon this example, the poet
instructs the reader to "be wiser." In "The Poet's Vow," however, it is the
Wordsworthian poet himself who withdraws into the pride of solitude and
who therefore needs instruction. In effect, then, Barrett Browning turns
Wordsworth's advice back on the poet's own example.

Other revisions in "The Poet's Vow" serve to emphasize the ironic
contradiction between the poet's "vow" to mate himself with the "touching,
patient Earth" and his broken vow to Rosalind. Significantly, the poet's
description of Rosalind as his "plighted bride" does not appear in the *New
Monthly Magazine* version of the poem. Rosalind's declaration of *her* vow to
appear as a corpse before the poet's bolted door ("For I have vowed . . .") is
an even more notable addition to the poem. In both the *New Monthly
Magazine* version and the 1838 version, no vow on her part is mentioned as
she less forcibly states, "For there, alone with the lifeless one, / The living
God must stay." The emphasis on Rosalind's vow in the revised version
foregrounds both the ambiguities of the title and the narrative doublings that
the poem's convoluted plot enacts. Not only is the poet's vow itself doubled,
given that the poet breaks his vow to Rosalind in making his vow to the
Earth. The figure of the poet is also doubled, as Rosalind employs her scroll
to carry out her own vow. In implying that the representative poet of the title
may be female, Barrett Browning subverts the traditional assumption that
the poet is male—an assumption that the poem initially seems to perpetuate.
More telling, perhaps, we may note that of the two poets in "The Poet's
Vow," it is the woman whose words are more powerful in their effect. She
becomes "Triumphant Rosalind!" when the words of her text and the text of
her body combine to "wring" a cry from the "long-subjected humanness" of
the poet who has "vowed his blood of brotherhood / To a stagnant place
apart."

Such passages in "The Poet's Vow" point to its parallels with
Tennyson's "The Palace of Art," where the proud and sinful soul of the
speaker becomes "a spot of dull stagnation." In fact, this is one of several
passages in the revised version of "The Poet's Vow" that points to the
influence of Tennyson's 1842 *Poems*. But the influence also seems to have run
in the other direction. For instance, Barrett Browning's description of the
solitary poet looking down from his lattice to see "Three Christians" going
by to prayer may have influenced the ending of "The Two Voices." Whatever
the pattern of mutual influence may have been, it seems clear that,
independently of each other, Tennyson and Barrett were engaged in writing

strong critiques of Romantic solipsism in the 1830s. Indeed, Peter Bayne aptly describes "The Poet's Vow" as "the ethical complement" of "The Palace of Art" in its treatment of "the cardinal sin of isolation from human interests." But of the two, "The Poet's Vow" is the more pertinent and telling critique of the major Romantics because Barrett Browning's representative poet is a lover of nature, whereas Tennyson's protagonist in "The Palace of Art" is a sterile aesthete and a lover of art, a type that less often appears in Romantic poetry.

Barrett Browning's focus on the poet's love of nature in "The Poet's Vow" reflects her critique of Coleridge as well as Wordsworth. This critique is accomplished principally through an echo of "The Rime of the Ancient Mariner" that calls in question Coleridge's vision of the mariner's redemption. After the poet looks down from his lattice on the "Three Christians" going by to prayer in "The Poet's Vow," he observes a bridal party and then a little child watching the "lizards green and rare" playing near the wall. All of these sights leave him unmoved—even the child who remains "Unblessed the while for his childish smile / Which cometh unaware." The spontaneous release that comes to the Ancient Mariner when he blesses "unaware" the watersnakes does not come to Barrett Browning's poet. The child's spontaneous response to Nature's beauty cannot undo the effects of a crime against the poet's own humanity originally motivated by a misplaced love of Nature. This passage points to the revisionary intent of Barrett Browning's poem and to her reasons for making her alienated figure a poet who sins against his "humanness" rather than a mariner who sins against nature, as in Coleridge's poem. Despite its use of supernatural incidents, "The Rime of the Ancient Mariner" powerfully reinforces the idea expressed elsewhere in the *Lyrical Ballads* by Wordsworth: that nature and natural feeling, defamiliarized by the poet, offer redemption from sin. The poem is therefore in keeping with Coleridge's well-known description in chapter fourteen of the *Biographia Literaria* of the complementary aims that he and Wordsworth had in focusing on the supernatural and the natural respectively. But the poet's feeling of fusion with nature that brings redemption in "The Rime of the Ancient Mariner" becomes the very source of alienation in "The Poet's Vow."

This alienation is only overcome in the poem's conclusion when the "wail" of the poet's "living mind" fuses with Rosalind's "senseless corpse." While "earth and sky" look on "indifferently," God smites the poet with his own "rejected nature," and he joins Rosalind, his fellow poet, in death, as William joins Margaret in her grave in the Percy ballad after her ghost has haunted him. "They dug beneath the kirkyard grass, / For both one dwelling deep." Despite the tone of reconciliation here, one is more struck by the note of revenge in the conclusion to "The Poet's Vow," again typical of many Percy ballads like "Margaret's Ghost" or "Thomas and Annet," which concludes with a double murder and a suicide. In Barrett Browning's rewriting of the Romantic poet's communion with nature, the supernatural joins "Triumphant Rosalind" in recalling the arrogant male poet to a recognition of her humanness as well as his.

The focus on female subjectivity in the second half of "The Poet's Vow" is intensified in Elizabeth Barrett's other ballads of the 1830s, among them, "A Romance of the Ganges," "The Romaunt of Margret," and "The Romaunt of the Page." As Hickok implies, the first of these has much in common with the exotic poems of "pseudo-Oriental sentimentalism" popular in the early nineteenth century: poems such as Letitia Landon's "The Hindoo Girl's Song." "A Romance of the Ganges" has even closer affinities with the traditional ballad, however. Although the poem was written to accompany an illustration in the 1838 *Findens' Tableaux: A Series of Picturesque Scenes of National Character, Beauty, and Costume*, Barrett downplays the exotic elements of "costume," setting, and nationality. Instead, as in "The Poet's Vow," she focuses on the burning passions of love and revenge so pervasive in the old ballads. But in "A Romance of the Ganges," these passions are exclusively female, as the male lover becomes no more than an absent catalyst for the narrative conflict between the betrayed Luti and her unwitting rival Nuleeni. With a further twist, Barrett transforms the two women of "A Romance of the Ganges" from rivals in love into accomplices in revenge, much as Tennyson does in "The Sisters," a ballad which she later praised. Thus Luti leads the child-like Nuleeni to vow to "whisper" to her bridegroom on her wedding day, "*There is one betrays / While Luti suffers woe.*" And to her "little bright-faced son" when he asks, "What deeds his sire hath done," Nuleeni vows to whisper, "*There is none denies, / While Luti speaks of wrong.*"

When Nuleeni, in wondering innocence, softly asks why Luti would wish to define a "bride-day" with a "word of *woe*" and a sinless child's ear with a "word of *wrong*," her fellow maiden cries out:

> "Why?" Luti said, and her laugh was dread,
> And her eyes dilated wild—
> "That the fair new love may her bridegroom prove,
> And the father shame the child!"

As Mermin notes, we begin to see in "A Romance of the Ganges" the "strong, angry heroine who dominates" most of Barrett Browning's ballads. Indeed, Luti's cry for revenge registers an unrepentant excess that is formal as well as emotional, for her fierce declaration appears in four extra lines that spill over the limits of the eight-line ballad stanza that Barrett employs elsewhere in "A Romance of the Ganges." It is as if the river flowing in insistent monotone through the poem's constant refrain, "The river floweth on"—resisting as well as marking each stanza's containment—has suddenly risen in angry overflow. As the refrain implies, and the narrative makes clear, Luti's bitterness and grief flow from herself to Nuleeni. Thus, the curious use of the female pronoun without a clear referent in the first stanza proves justified: "The wave-voice seems the voice of dreams / That wander through her sleep: / The river floweth on." The pronoun in the final line—"She weepeth dark with sorrow"—is similarly ambiguous, in its possible reference to both Luti and Nuleeni. Luti could be any woman, the poem implies, and her sorrow every woman's.

In the earlier ballad "The Romaunt of Margaret," the "running river" in which the protagonist encounters the shadow of her own darkest fears murmurs a parallel story of betrayal and "failing human love." The shade that rises from the river to confront Margret torments her with the thoughts that the love of her brother, her father, her sister, and her lover— all, all will prove inconstant. The poem derives some of its power from the haunting effect of its relentlessly darkening images: the sound of "silent forests" growing between the pauses of the shade's voice; the recurrent trembling of its movement on the grass "with a low, shadowy laughter"; the shadows falling "from the stars above, / In flakes of darkness" on Margret's face—until finally she drowns herself in despair, fusing with her dark double and, ironically, with the inconstancy of the river, in death. But even more of the power of "The Romaunt of Margret" derives from the ambiguities which Barrett subtly develops. Were Margret's dark doubts justified or not? Does she suffer from the inconstancy of others' love or the inconstancy of her own faith in love? Is the love of the knight who has given her no sign but an apparently heartfelt "look" a "transient" love because he is unfaithful or because he is dead? "The wild hawk's bill doth dabble still / I' the mouth that vowed thee true" "the shade whispers with grisly relish. As Hayter suggests, lines such as these give "The Romaunt of Margret" "the true sadness of the old ballads" and their "genuine cold grue."

The narrative frame of the poem, presenting an anonymous minstrel singing the "wild romaunt" of Margret to the accompaniment of a harp, suggests how closely and consciously Barrett was writing within the tradition revived by Percy's *Reliques*. Indeed, she may have felt particularly drawn to the minstrel tradition because, although Bishop Percy declared in the first edition of the *Reliques* that no "real Minstrels were of the female sex," the fourth edition adopted by Willmott acknowledged that there "seem to have been women of this profession" for "no accomplishment is so constantly attributed to females, by our ancient Bards, as their singing to, and playing on, the Harp." In "The Romaunt of Margret," the minstrel's sex is not revealed. But the intensity of the narrator's response to Margret's fate in the poem's concluding stanza—"Hang up my harp again! / I have no voice for song"—may imply that the minstrel too is a woman.

Cooper observes that the minstrel's apparent identification with Margret manifests the "confused relationship of the narrator to her tale" and her inadequacy to conclude her story. The minstrel's declaration, "Hang up my harp again!" is a conventional framing device, however. More importantly, it marks Barrett's movement into a deliberately ambiguous coda in which she develops the *Doppelgänger* motif at a metanarrative level as the minstrel concludes—but does not resolve—the tale of Margret's dark inner conflicts:

> O failing human love!
> O light, by darkness known!
> O false the while thou treadest earth!
> O deaf beneath the stone!
> Margret, Margret.

The minstrel's final series of laments can be read either as a reflection of her keen identification with Margret's anguish in the face of "failing human love," or as her condemnation of Margret's own failing love. In effect, then, the minstrel mirrors the division within Margret herself embodied throughout the poem in the refrain, "Margret, Margret."

In its subtle double depiction of the dialogue of the mind with itself, "The Romaunt of Margret" justifies Cornelius Mathews's observation that Barrett's handling of the ballad form is "subjective." Yet, at the same time, like Wordsworth's complex narrative frames in the *Lyrical Ballads*, the narrative frame in "The Romaunt of Margret" undermines the inscription of the writer as transcendental subject. What we encounter instead is the divided post-Romantic subject that Loy D. Martin has related to the production of the dramatic monologue. The dramatic elements in "the Romaunt of Margret" are highlighted by one reviewer's comment, "We know not anything much newer or more striking, than the *prima intenzione* of 'Margret'; save, . . . in 'the Notion' (as the Americans might call it) of Mr. Browning's 'Pippa.' "

"The Romaunt of Page" is a less "subjective" ballad than "The Romaunt of Margret," yet ultimately it is a more complex one that achieves its effects by subtly revisioning the conventional figure of the woman-page so prevalent in the drama, in ballads and in Romantic narrative verse. As Dianne Dugaw suggests in *Warrior Women and Popular Balladry, 1650-1850*, the female page has many features in common with the transvestite heroine who appears in the "Female Warrior" ballads popular throughout the seventeenth and eighteenth centuries, ballads in which a woman disguised as a man follows her lover to war or to sea. Barrett Browning was undoubtedly familiar with one of the most famous of the female warrior ballads, the variant on "Mary Ambree" included in Percy's *Reliques*. In illuminating the social and historical conditions that explain the immense popularity of the "Female Warrior" ballads among all social classes, Dugaw's study indirectly suggests why a literary ballad like "The Romaunt of the Page" had such a widespread appeal at a time when popular ballads like "Mary Ambree" were dying out because of an increasingly inflexible "semiotics of gender."

Mitford revealed her critical acumen in making "The Romaunt of the Page" the lead poem in the 1839 *Findens' Tableaux of the Affections: A Series of Picturesque Illustrations of the Womanly Virtues*. She also singled it out in the "Preface" and praised it privately to Barrett: "Let me say, my sweetest, that the 'Romaunt of the Page' (which is a tragedy of the very deepest and highest order) always seems to me by far the finest thing that you have ever written; and I do entreat and conjure you to write more ballads or tragedies—call them what you will—like that; that is to say, poems of human feelings and human actions." Reviews of the 1839 *Findens'*, with the exception of *The Literary Gazette*, were equally laudatory, describing "The Romaunt of the Page" as "full of fancy and originality," "shewing true and original genius," "a poem with the spirit of the elder and better day of poetry in every line of it," "full of the early spirit of English poetry." As the last two descriptions indicate, like Mitford, reviewers linked "The Romaunt of the Page" to the early ballads recovered in the Romantic revival. Henry Chorley was atypical in relating the poem to the exclusively female tradition of Hemans's "Records of Woman" in his *Athenaeum* reviews of *Findens'* and of the 1844 *Poems*. Chorley's association seems somewhat justified: the conclusion of "The Romaunt of the Page" may have been influenced by Hemans's ballad "Woman on the Field of Battle." But there is much more reason to interpret "The Romaunt of the Page" as an ironically allusive adaptation of narrative and character configurations in both Scott's *Marmion* and some of the Percy ballads, "Child Waters" definitely, and perhaps "The Not-Browne Mayd" as well.

In "Woman on the Field of Battle" Hemans pictures a "gentle and lovely form" with "golden hair" slain on the battlefield, much as Barrett's woman/page is slain by the Saracens. A passage in the manuscript of "The

Romaunt of the Page," not included in either the *Findens'* or the 1844 version of the ballad, may echo Hemans's poem, as Barrett describes the slain page with the wind lifting "aside her golden hair" to "show the smile beneath it fair." Only one motive could have led a woman to such a death, Hemans declares in her ballad: not glory, but love, which "Woman's deep soul too long / Pours on the dust." Love is also a motive contributing to the fate of Barrett's heroine, but in this case its only one element in a subtle mix of circumstances, motives, and passions. Whereas Hemans presents a static, sentimental tableau of womanly sacrifice, showing no interest in the narrative that leads up to it, Barrett develops an ironic series of narrative conflicts in which a knight and a lady are alike victimized by a system of gender relations in which women function as objects of exchange.

These conflicts and the passions that accompany them were intensified by the substantial revisions Barrett made in "The Romaunt of the Page" for its reissue in the 1844 *Poems*, revisions unnoted in existing interpretations of the poem. Chorley observes in his review of the 1844 *Poems* that she "much simplified" "The Romaunt of the Page" in revising the *Findens'* version. But the observation is inaccurate. While Barrett did eliminate some of the archaic diction, along with the interesting epigraph from Beaumont and Fletcher ("The trustiest, loving'st, and the gentlest boy / That ever master had"), she made the narrative itself fuller, more complex, more ironic, and more conflicted by developing the psychology of the knight and the page. Nevertheless the knight, because he is so ideologically blinded by the very system that victimizes him, emerges as more culpable than the page in both the *Findens'* and the 1844 version. He is as unchivalric and ungrateful as Child Waters, and although unwittingly, he betrays his lady as much as Marmion betrays his woman-page Constance. Significantly, a reference to the knight speaking "kindly" to the page in the manuscript is deleted in the published versions of the poem.

Using an *in medias res* construction, Barrett begins with a knight and a page returning from "the holy war in Palestine," where the page has saved the knight's life "once in the tent, and twice in the fight." In the manuscript the knight is nameless, while in the *Findens'* version he becomes Sir Hubert—but the poet refers to him by name only once, as if to stress his role as a representative knight. As thoughts of home fill the minds of both, the nameless page recalls the dying prayer of his mother, while the knight points out to the page that, although he has proven himself in battle, he is too silent to serve well in the bower of the knight's lady. The page leads the knight to speak more of his lady: is she "little loved or loved aright," asking a question that takes a more pointed form than it does in the manuscript, where this line appears simply as "And tell me if that loved aright"? Gloomily, the knight explains that he does not even know what his lady looks like—that he married her in haste and darkness before leaving for Palestine, out of a sense of obligation to his friend Earl Walter, who lost his life in avenging the honor of the knight's own dead father. When the Earl's wife died, she sent for the knight and asked him to marry her daughter, the "sweet child" made "an orphan for thy father's sake." Bitterly the knight recalls how his bride rose from the ceremony "[a]nd kissed the smile of her mother dead, / Or ever she kissed me."

In revising "The Romaunt of the Page" for her 1844 *Poems*, Barrett greatly expanded the knight's inset narrative of the marriage forced on him by circumstance and the chivalric code—a narrative reversing the conventional plot in which a knight or a "stranger (to all save the reader)," as Robert Browning facetiously remarked, wins a bride because the father owes his life or some other debt to him. In the *Findens'* version and in the manuscript, Earl Walter is a nameless "Baron," and stanza 16, the first half of stanza 17, and stanza 19 do not appear; while very different versions of stanzas 15 and 18 present a brief narrative of the actions and circumstances leading up to the marriage. The additions in stanzas 17 and 19 create sympathy for the knight and develop his motives and passions with some psychological depth as he declares that it would have been better if he had avenged his own father and died rather than have "murdered friend and marriage-ring / Forced on my life together."

Responding with tears of grief to the knight's tale, the page explains that his own sister was married as the knight's lady was but that she "laid down the silks she wore" and followed her new husband to the "battle-place" "[d]isguised as his true servitor." The knight reacts with a "careless laugh":

> "Well done it were for thy sister,
>   But not for my ladye!
> My love, so please you, shall requite
> No woman, whether dark or bright,
>   Unwomaned if she be."

Here again, Barrett's revisions intensify the conflict between her two characters and, in this case, emphasize the ideological system of "true womanhood" she is critiquing. In the manuscript, the knight simply laughs "loudly." In *Findens'*, his laugh is "gay," not "careless," and the last three lines of his declaration are briefer and less unequivocal: "No woman bright, my love requite / Unwomaned if she be." In the manuscript, the last line is still less extreme—"if she loved not womanly." The revisions indicate that, in the knight's eyes, any wife who follows her husband to battle disguised as a page destroys the very core of her womanhood.

This is a dogma that the page strongly questions in another passage that Barrett revised to intensify the conflict between the knight and the page:

> "Your wisdom may declare
> That womanhood is proved the best
> By golden brooch and glossy vest
>   The mincing ladies wear;
> Yet it is proved, and was of old,
> Anear as well, I dare to hold,
>   By truth, or by despair."

In the manuscript, the first line of this passage simply reads as "It seems that everywhere." In *Findens'* it is "Some wisdoms may declare." But in the 1844 version, Barrett makes it plain that it is the knight's limited "wisdom" that the page is questioning. The last three lines of this passage are also more emphatic in the 1844 version. In the manuscript and *Findens'* there are only two lines: "And yet 'tis almost proved as well / by truth . . . or by despair" in the manuscript, and the equally tentative "Yet almost is it proved as well" in *Findens'*. In the 1844 version, however, the page emphasizes how true love is "proved" both in the present and "of old."

As the page passionately defends his hypothetical sister's actions to the scornful knight, Barrett presents her ironically paradoxical vision of the "womanly virtues" the 1839 *Findens'* was meant to celebrate:

> "Oh, womanly she prayed in tent,
>   When none beside did wake!
> Oh, womanly she paled in fight,
>   For one beloved's sake!—
> And her little hand, defiled with blood,
> Her tender tears of womanhood
>   Most woman-pure did make!"

Such a combination of heroic valor "in fight" and womanly devotion is also quite typical of the "Female Warrior" ballads that Dugaw explores, but in early nineteenth-century variants on these, as in "The Romaunt of the Page," insistent "gender markers" like Barrett's phrase "little hand" became much more common.

Little hand or not, such a woman-servitor is wholly unacceptable in the eyes of Barrett's knight, who reiterates his belief in a more conventional type of womanly virtue that hides behind a veil. "No casque shall hide her woman's tear," he declares, in an ironically prophetic, punning line that does not appear in the manuscript. According to the knight, womanly virtue is "[s]o high, so pure, and so apart" from the world that it shines like "a small bright cloud / Alone amid the skies!". When the page asks, what if his lady "mistook thy mind / And followed thee to strife," he asserts that he "would forgive" her and "evermore / Would love her as my servitor / But little as my wife." The revision of "mistook thy will" (in the manuscript) to "mistook thy mind" in the first published version indicates what the page is up against here: not a mere matter of will, but of mindset or ideology. In such a context, the "strife" the page refers to is as much marital as martial.

When the little cloud that provokes the knight's comparison disappears behind a blacker one, the page sees the Saracens approaching. But while "the page seeth all," "the knight seeth none," presumably because his eyes are still dazzled by what Barrett scornfully referred to as the "cloud-minding theory" of true womanhood. As Stephenson has shown, the poet emphasized in her letters to Mitford that the chivalric theory of idealized womanhood was as confining for women as the "pudding-making and stocking-darning" theory. "'Twas a stroke of policy in those ranty-pole barons of old to make their lady-loves idols, and curb their wives with silken idleness," another Victorian woman astutely remarked. The sterility of the chivalric ideal of passive womanhood is dramatically revealed in "The Romance of the Swan's Nest," in many ways the counterpart of "The Romaunt of the Page." In this depiction of a young girl's fantasies, the female who opts for the conventional lady's role of inspiring rather than following her knight—of being his idol rather than his disguised page and "servitor"— is as bitterly betrayed as her more active opposite. As Cooper suggests, Little Ellie's fate in "The Romance of the Swan's Nest" shows how "dreaming courtly fantasies . . . gnaws at women's energy, sexuality, and identity" as insidiously as the rat gnaws at the reeds surrounding the empty swan's nest in the poem's ending.

"The Romaunt of the Page" concludes with the page sending the blind knight on ahead to safety, while the loyal "servitor" drops her disguise, and the embittered wife exclaims,

> "Have I renounced my womanhood
>   For wifehood unto *thee*,
> And is this the last, last look of thine
>   That ever I shall see?
>
> Yet God thee save, and mayst thou have
>   A lady to thy mind,
> More woman-proud and half as true
>   As one thou leav'st behind!"

Disillusioned by earthly love, Earl Walter's daughter turns to God's love and faces the "Paynims," a "Christian page" who taunts the enemy as boldly as any knight might do. "False page, but truthful woman", she dauntlessly dies beneath the scimitar, meeting its downward sweep "[w]ith smile more bright in victory / Than any sword from sheath."

Mermin observes of this conclusion that the protagonist of "The Romaunt of the Page" "succumbs to an ideal of 'womanly virtues' that the poet both scorns and shares" in that she chooses "a woman's fate—unrecognizing, self-sacrificing death." Hickok similarly views the poem as "a sentimental tale of extreme wifely devotion and self-sacrifice," although one used to "arraign the maleficence of current nineteenth-century notions about women." Certainly, some Victorian readers interpreted "The Romaunt of the Page" in sentimental and conventional terms; for example, Thomas Bradfield cited the "cloud" metaphor for woman's honor out of context as proof of Mrs. Browning's "profound admiration of the devotion so characteristic" of medieval women.

What such readings do not address, however, is the fact that Barrett's heroic page never acts more like a man, in conventional terms, than when she is "truthful woman." Even her smile flashes like a sword. Moreover, her motives are mixed rather than "pure" in that, like so many ballad-women, she is driven as much by revenge as devotion. In revising "The Romaunt of the Page," Barrett progressively intensified the woman-page's more vindictive motives. Thus, in the manuscript version, the page wishes her knight may find another lady "More woman-proud, yet all as true / As one thou leavest behind." In *Findens'*, she wishes him a lady "More woman-proud, not faithfuller / Than one thou leav'st behind!" The change from "not faithfuller" to "half as true" is startling, bringing out the anger implicit in line 250, where "ride on thy way" is substituted for the more tender address "my master dear" appearing in the *Findens'* version. The page's possessive pledge to be near to her master as "parted spirits cleave / To mortals too beloved to leave" has a rather ominous note to it as well, intensified in the revision from the *Findens'* version, "as parted spirits are near / The thrice beloved they loved here." Does the outraged wife plan to bless her husband from above, like Catarina, or to haunt him? Perhaps the thought of her will indeed haunt him when he arrives home and realizes that the page who sacrificed himself for him was also the wife he so fiercely resented—a quite probable narrative extrapolation that is not considered in interpreting the page's sacrifice as "unrecognized." He may be "a knight of gallant deeds," as he is introduced in the revised 1844 version. (In *Findens'* he is simply "a knight upon a steed.") But he may discover, as the reader already has, that in this particular "romaunt," the page and not the knight performs the "gallant deeds."

The ironies permeating "The Romaunt of the Page" are intensified when Barrett's revisioning of the lady-page figure is read against its prototypes in ballads like "Child Waters" and "The Not-Browne Mayd" and in Scott's *Marmion*. The immediate inspiration of "The Romaunt of the Page" was the illustration Mitford sent to the poet, picturing a woman disguised as a page, wearing a very short skirt and hiding behind a tree in the foreground, while a knight rides away from her in the background. But it is clear that the conventions of the old ballads and "Child Waters" in particular were in Barrett's mind when she composed the poem. Apologizing to Mitford for the length of her "long barbarous ballad," she quips, "I ought to blush—as ladyes always do in ballads—'scarlet-red.' " Then she adds, "By the way, the pictured one pretty as she is, has a good deal exaggerated the ballad-receipt for making a ladye page—Do you remember?—'And you must cut your gowne of green / An INCH above the knee'!—She comes within the fi fa fum of the prudes, in consequence."

The "receipt for making a ladye page" cited here is Child Waters's own, in the ballad of the same title. Hardly the conventional model of chivalry, he instructs his female companion Ellen, swollen with child by him, to cut off her skirt and her hair and run barefoot as his "foot-page" by his side. He is not even "so curteous a knighte, / To say, Put on your shoone." Nor is this the end of Ellen's ordeals. At Child Waters's bidding, she must run by his side into the "north countrie," swim a swollen river, stable and feed his horse, find him a paramour to spend the night with (while she lies at the foot of the bed!), and then feed his horse again. Finally, as she is moaning with labor pains in the stable, Child Waters's mother hears her, the gallant knight in his "shirte of silke" arrives to see the babe born, and, like Griselda, Ellen is rewarded. Child Waters tells her to be of "good cheere": he will marry her. But the poem ends before the marriage takes place.

The frankly physical treatment of Ellen's ordeals supplies an interesting subtext to the declaration of Barrett's knight that, if his lady followed him as his page, he would love her as his "servitor" but not as his wife. In other respects, however, "The Romaunt of the Page" works against, not with, the text of "Child Waters" by reversing its plot and making marriage the beginning and cause of the page's ordeals, not the end. Moreover, the "Romaunt" shifts the focus in its title and its narrative perspective to the woman-page rather than the knight. In Barrett's ballad, it is the knight who is tested and found wanting, not the woman who is tested and rewarded.

A testing of woman's devotion similar to that appearing in "Child Waters" appears in "The Not-Browne Mayd," in which the minstrel depicts a "SHE-HE" debate between a Baron's daughter and a "squyer of lowe degre" in order to defend women against the men who malign their constancy. As the squire repeatedly tells his lady that he is a "banyshed man" who must go the "grene wode" alone, she vows that she will give up and endure all to be with him: she will sacrifice her good name; she will fight by his side, though "women be / But feble for to fyght"; and she will cut her hair and her "kyrtel by the kne" as he requests. He then denounces her as a light woman who would vow such for any man, much as the knight denounces any woman who would follow him into battle in "The Romaunt of the Page." But after further protestations on the "not-browne mayd's" part, and further testing, the squire declared her to be a constant woman—and reveals that the entire dialogue has been based upon a ruse. He is not a banished man; indeed, he is an Earl's son who vows to marry her. The gender conflicts in the poem are not really resolved, however, since the lady is left questioning the "wyle" her lover has used with her as well as the constancy of men. "[O]ne of the most beautiful & true of our Ballad-poems, is the antique original of the 'Notte browne Mayde,' " Barrett observed in 1843, objecting to Matthew Prior's version of it in "Henry and Emma"—a modernization that "desecrated" the original.

Marmion more directly suggests the perils that attend the woman who proves her love by following her knight as his page, although Scott's text depicts the old story of women suffering from male falsehood, whereas Barrett's shows both sexes suffering from a false ideology. When Constance breaks her religious vows to follow Marmion disguised as "a horse-boy in his train," he treats her as such, making her not only his servitor but also his whore. Marmion suggests why, in the more prudish 1830s, Barrett was careful to have her heroine marry her knight before following him as his page. Betraying his promise to marry Constance, Marmion pursues the wealthy young Clara instead. Clara is forced to flee to St. Hilda's convent and a novitiate's veil in order to elude him, so that Marmion's wickedness almost leads to the symbolic burial of one woman and the literal burial of another, when Constance is immured alive in the dungeon walls of Lindisfarne Monastery for breaking her vows. Like Barrett's page, the forsaken Constance is constant in love, and in revenge. Before she goes to her doom, she gives up the information that will prevent Marmion's marriage to Clara and bring about his downfall. The passages describing Constance's vow to take revenge are among the most powerful in Scott's entire poem, and it is highly likely that, given the immense popularity of Marmion, they influenced Barrett's depiction of her lady-page. Certainly the subtle counterpoint she creates in "The Romaunt of the Page" between the narrative action and the memorial chant for the dead Lady Abbess—"Beati, beati, mortui! / From the convent on the sea"—seems to have been suggested by Marmion. Scott's epic is similarly structured by a counterpoint between *Marmion*'s military exploits and the quieter scenes depicting the Lady Abbess of St. Hilda's travelling to Lindisfarne Monastery, with the sounds of her nuns' voices carrying across the wave much as the dirge of St. Mary's nuns is carried from the convent "on the sea" in "The Romaunt of the Page." Significantly, this prophetic dirge first interrupts the narrative at the point where the lady disguised as a page blushes "sudden red" as ladies in ballads conventionally do and confesses to the knight that his lady's bower is "suited well" to her. As in the case of Scott's Constance, however, female desire is checked by death. In *Marmion*, the Abbess of St. Hilda is one of three church authorities who condemn Constance to her living burial in the walls of the monastery. In "The Romaunt of the Page," the link between the Abbess and the page is forged in two lines Barrett appears to have added to her conclusion: "Dirge for abbess laid in shroud / Sweepeth o'er the shroudless dead."

Barrett's adaptation of elements in *Marmion* is even more apparent in "The Lay of the Brown Rosary," the ballad in the 1840 *Findens'* that, next to "The Romaunt of the Page," was one of her most popular works before the 1844 *Poems* appeared. "The Lay of the Brown Rosary" is a ballad that anticipates Charlotte Brontë's *Villette* in its adaptation of Gothic conventions to represent intense psychic conflicts. Like Brontë, Barrett symbolically develops the figure of the buried nun popularized by Scott's *Marmion* and other works. But whereas Scott's central focus in *Marmion* is male and military, Barrett's, like Brontë's after her, is on the conflicts of female desire with institutionalized repression that speak so powerfully in the interstices of his narrative through the narrative flashbacks and the monastic interludes that link Constance with Clare. The *Doppelgänger* motif linking Onora, the heroine of "The Lay of the Brown Rosary," with the defiant cursing nun, buried alive for her sins, makes this poem a "subjective" ballad like "The Romaunt of Margret," but it is a more daring work, too complex in its play of intertextual allusions to consider fully here. Along with *Marmion*, "The Lay of the Brown Rosary" also seems to draw on Faust, "Christabel," Bürger's "Lenora," and possibly some of the Percy ballads, fusing elements from these texts in a highly original way with Barrett's own innovations, among them the heroine's dream, which she herself thought of as "rather original in its manner." Any analysis of "The Lay of Brown Rosary" is further complicated by the extensive revisions made in the poem between its first appearance in the 1840 *Findens' Tableaux* and its publication in 1844: among others, the change of the heroine's name from Lenora (a direct link with Bürger's ballad) to Onora.

"Rhyme of the Duchess May" also reflects Barrett's adaptation of motifs from Bürger's "Lenora," in this case, as we have seen, creating a connection readily detected by the *Westminster* Reviewer Sarah Flower

Adams. By echoing Lenora's swift, dark gallop to the bridal bed of the grave with the ghost of her slain lover, Barrett subtly foreshadows the fate of the orphan Duchess May and her newly-wed husband Sir Guy of Linteged as they flee to his castle, evading her guardian, the Earl of Leigh, and the cousin whose hand in marriage she spurns: "Fast and fain the bridal train along the night-storm rod [sic] amain." Reminiscent of "Lenora" too, "The Duchess May" depicts what one Victorian critic aptly described as a "dark bridal" concluding with a "double death-ride." Facing certain defeat after a fourteen-day siege by the Leighs in which his castle has "seethed in blood," the anguished Sir Guy seeks to save the lives of his loyal men by riding from his castle tower to a sacrificial death—accompanied, against his will, by his young bride, who leaps into the saddle with him at the last minute. Contemporary readers were especially taken by this spectacular and novel climax, which Mermin astutely interprets as "in effect a bold, bizarre sexual consummation"—even if it does occur three months after the Duchess's actual marriage to Sir Guy.

"Rhyme of the Duchess May" adapts situations and scenes from the old Scottish ballad "Edom o' Gordon" as well as from Bürger's "Lenora," although its "double death" leap was probably suggested by Benjamin Haydon's painting, "Curtius Leaping into the Gulf." The hero of "Edom o' Gordon" is not the brutal border raider referred to in the title but the fiercely loyal Scottish lord's wife who takes a stand on her castle walls and valiantly resists Gordon and his men in her husband's absence. Like the "Female Warrior" in the Percy variant of "Mary Ambree," who also mounts the walls of a besieged castle and "all undaunted" faces the enemy, the Scottish wife in "Edom o' Gordon" may have provided Barrett with an image of heroic womanhood like that "miracle of noble womanhood" later introduced by Tennyson into the "Prologue" to *The Princess*. But she rejects the futile and passive sacrifice of the Scottish lord's daughter in the old ballad, who is lowered over the castle walls in a "pair o' sheits"—only to be spitted on "the point of Gordon's spear" until "the red build dreips" over her yellow hair. Instead, she depicts a more active and heroic sacrificial leap on the part of the Duchess, whom she made more forceful and willful in revising her poem. As in the case of "The Romaunt of the Page," Barrett's revisions to "Rhyme of the Duchess May" also intensify and complicate the psychological and narrative conflict between the newly-wed wife and husband. The most substantial addition to the Berg draft greatly expands upon the complex mix of nobility and blind condescension in Sir Guy's treatment of the Duchess as a representative woman, who "will weep her woman's tears" and "pray her woman's prayers." This addition makes Sir Guy less a stock character and more a prototype of Romney in *Aurora Leigh* and, like Barrett's most significant addition to "The Romaunt of the Page," it reveals her growing interest in representing female lives in the context of ideologies of gender. Other revisions in "Rhyme of the Duchess May" refine the artistry of the verse form itself, as Barrett employs the poem's unusual stanza and the refrain, "Toll slowly," to create both the pulsing, headlong rush of passion and action and the stillness of deathful peace pervading the ballad's frame story of a reader in a churchyard, beside the grave of a three-year-old child.

This reader is like yet different from the minstrel who narrates the tale in "The Romaunt of Margret." In revising "Rhyme of the Duchess May," Barrett more fully developed the narrator's ambivalence towards the "burning" intensity of the passions the poem presents. She also altered the date on the child's grave from 1453 to 1843, the year in which she was writing. The divided framing subject here is thus not an anonymous traditional minstrel but the modern narrator/reader herself or himself—the connection between the two effectively implied by Barrett's depiction of the narrator as a reader in "Rhyme of the Duchess May." We might consider too that the medieval scenes and gender relations Barrett depicts in her "ancient rhyme" may have seemed paradoxically quite modern in the early 1840s, when the medieval revival was in full swing and the earl of Eglinton had recently staged a mammoth tournament, attended by tens of thousands, on the grounds of his castle, and featuring "knights on horseback in full armour, a Queen of Beauty, jesters, heralds, pavilions and a banquet"—all turned into a "fiasco by two days of torrential rain."

Deborah Byrd suggests that Victorian women poets like Barrett Browning turned to the Middle Ages because it was envisioned "as a time in which at least some women had control over their property and destiny and the courage to venture into the 'male' arenas of politics and war." There is much truth in this. The women Barrett Browning encountered in the Percy ballads and even in Scott's romances were not yet confined by what Mary Poovey has analysed as the cult of the "proper lady." In fact, in its frankly physical depiction of strong, heroic, or long-suffering women like Ellen in "Child Waters," the traditional ballad, that "Cinderella" among the Muses, very often was not the bashful maiden Hales and Furnivall quaintly imagined. At the same time, however, Barrett Browning was no celebrator of the often brutal and violent gender and human relations that prevailed in the Middle Ages when a "black chief" was "half knight, half sheep-lifter"—like Edom o' Gordon and his kind—and a "beauteous dame" was "half chattel and half queen." Thus she both echoes and strategically revises traditional ballads in order to dramatize the crudely overt power structures of the society that also produced the chivalric idealization of women. These power structures are blatantly apparent, for instance, when the younger Lord Leigh threatens to take the Duchess May in marriage over the "altar" of her husband's corpse: "I will wring thy fingers pale in the gauntlet of my mail . . .

'Little hand and muckle gold' close shall lie within my hold, / As the sword did, to prevail." If, as Michel Foucault suggests, a changing "technology of power" transformed brutal and external social constraints into more internalized and carefully concealed "humane" forms by the nineteenth century, ballads like Barrett Browning's reverse that strategic transformation in their depiction of gender relations.

Barrett Browning's later ballads typically use contemporary rather than medieval settings. The often noted progression in her ballads from medieval to modern contexts is manifested not only in "Lady Geraldine's Courtship" but also in the very interesting unpublished "The Princess Marie," in the "Sonnets" notebook now in the Armstrong Browning Library, dating from the 1842–44 period. This unfinished poem in ballad stanzas focuses on Princess Marie, daughter of King Louis Philippe of France. Phillip Sharp, who supplies a helpful account of its historical context, along with a somewhat unreliable transcription of the manuscript, describes "The Princess Marie" as a "domestic poem about a head of state." But what really seems to have interested Barrett in the Princess Marie was not her relation to Louis Philippe, but her skill in sculpture and the human cost of her devotion to her art. Thus, "The Princess Marie" is not only a ballad in which Barrett Browning turns to contemporary subjects but also one anticipating her focus on the woman-artist in *Aurora Leigh* and in the powerful late ballad-monologue, "Mother and Poet."

Although they move farther away from their prototypes in the old English and Scottish ballads and the narrative verse of the Romantic Revival, most of Barrett Browning's ballads after 1844 continue to exhibit some of the features considered in this essay: in particular, the ironic manipulation of traditional ballad plots and motifs (often through narrative reversals or doublings), the focus on female subjectivity and the conflicts of female desire, and the exploration of ideological links between the "female plots" shaping women's lives and the gender plots of encompassing ideologies. The female perspective, complicated by lingering ironies, is apparent in the deceptively simple "Amy's Cruelty," for instance, where Barrett Browning explores female as well as male possessiveness in love. The manipulation of traditional ballad conventions is perhaps most evident in the often praised "Lord Walter's Wife." Like "The Not-Browne Mayd" in the Percy collection, "Lord Walter's Wife" contains elements of the debate or flyting match concerning female constancy. Yet typically, Barrett Browning subverts conventional expectations by dramatizing the contradictions and sexual double standard in male perceptions of women and by again showing a man tested and found wanting, not the woman he flirts with and condemns.

The ironies in "Lord Walter's Wife" are more direct than those in "Amy's Cruelty" and in many of Barrett Browning's earlier ballads. Indeed, they were too direct for William Thackeray who, in his well-known exchange with Barrett Browning, considered the poem too frank in its "account of unlawful passion" to be published in the *Cornhill Magazine*, "written not only for men and women but for boys, girls, infants, sucklings almost," as he emphasized with histrionic hyperbole. Perhaps Thackeray was in part responding to the omniscient narrative perspective in "Lord Walter's Wife" that clearly identified the poem's voice with Barrett Browning herself—that is, with "Browning's wife and Penini's mother," to use his own words. Barrett Browning had published ballads before "Lord Walter's Wife" that treated "unlawful" passions even more frankly—most notably, "The Runaway Slave at Pilgrim's Point." But she had used dramatic speakers in these poems. The license these speakers gave her was no doubt one reason why, like Robert Browning, she was attracted to dramatic poetical forms, and to the dramatic monologue in particular.

Barrett Browning's ballads, with their paradoxical combination of the medieval and the modern and their strong, transgressive women, had an influence on subsequent writers that remains to be explored. Their impact on the Pre-Raphaelite poets, in particular, is often acknowledged in passing, yet still largely uninvestigated. Over a century ago, Arthur Benson commented on Mrs. Browning's "fancy for pure romantic writing, since developed to such perfection by Rossetti," singling out for praise "The Romaunt of the Page" and "Rhyme of the Duchess May." In 1900, Porter and Clarke, editors of her complete works, similarly observed that "Rossetti and others of the pre-Raphaelite brotherhood" had followed Barrett Browning in writing "modern ballads," "archaic in diction and suggestion" but striking "new themes." "But her ballads were first," Porter and Clarke remind us. "They are miracles of sympathetic reproduction of an old genre in new substance." Hayter suggests one reason why the influence of Barrett Browning on the Pre-Raphaelites was "forgotten," despite Porter and Clarke's reminder, in noting how critics after 1900 characteristically apologized for and dismissed the many traces of "Mrs. Browning" in the works of D. G. Rossetti and William Morris. As long as this subtle work of cultural "forgetting" lies unanalyzed and unopposed, and as long as Barrett Browning's ballads continue to be excluded from standard surveys of Victorian poetry, while the Victorian ballad itself remains a form denigrated for its very popularity, there will be a missing link in the history of the ballad revival that continues to influence a wide range of writers today. Bob Dylan, whose "Desolation Row" is now studied alongside T. S. Eliot's "The Waste Land," might describe himself too as a "writer of ballads."

MAUREEN THUM

Challenging Traditionalist Gender Roles: The Exotic Woman as Critical Observer in Elizabeth Barrett Browning's Aurora Leigh

The critical reception of Elizabeth Barrett Browning has been characterized by remarkable gaps and silences. Her poems dedicated to Robert Browning, particularly her *Sonnets from the Portuguese*, have never been eclipsed. Her Sonnet 43, "How do I love thee?" is one of the most anthologized and best known nineteenth-century love poems. But her novel poem, *Aurora Leigh*, presents a very different picture. Celebrated after its publication in 1857, the "novel poem went through thirteen editions in England by 1873. After the turn of the century, however, the work was disregarded. Writing in 1978, Cora Kaplan cites Virginia Woolf's comment, made over forty years previously: "Fate has not been kind to Mrs. Browning as a writer. Nobody reads her, nobody discusses her, nobody troubles to put her in her place." Kaplan continues: "Virginia Woolf's comment is almost as true today as in 1932." Only in the past two decades have critics, following Kaplan's lead, begun to reassess *Aurora Leigh* and to recognize the novel poem as one of Barrett Browning's major achievements.

Nevertheless, despite their renewed interest in this long-neglected work, critics have not yet abandoned the somewhat deprecatory and apologetic stance evident even in Kaplan's fine introduction. With few exceptions, critics have regarded *Aurora Leigh* as a powerful but essentially imperfect work. It is flawed, they argue, by the author's lack of critical

From *The Foreign Women in British Literature: Exotics, Aliens, and Outsiders.* © 1999 by the Greenwood Press.

distance from her protagonist, by her failure to come to terms analytically and intellectually with the issues she raises, and by her unconscious antifeminism and woman-hating.

Aurora Leigh is seen as a highly personal, confessional statement, restricted to the relatively narrow scope of the author's subjectivity. Author and narrator are viewed as fully identical. Neither is regarded as capable of coming to terms with wider social, historical, and philosophical issues. While admitting that the narrator, Aurora Leigh, is an unconventional figure and that the author expresses her discontent with the patriarchal status quo, critics have nonetheless seen Barrett Browning as incapable of challenging the patriarchal mindset and its underlying assumptions. Neither the author nor her protagonist is viewed as capable of escaping from the imprisoning framework of a dominant ideology. Imprisoned within a confining mindset, both suffer, critics contend, from a sense of alienation they share with most nineteenth-century women writers and intellectuals. Their exclusion from culture's hegemony leads to self-alienation and to debilitating feelings of helpless resentment and suppressed rage. One comes away from a survey of critical literature with the impression that although *Aurora Leigh* may be a literary masterwork, it is in some ways still a period piece, a Victorian heirloom whose author is so immersed in traditionalist views of women and in personal conflicts about her own femininity that she is unable to think her way out of patriarchy.

This study argues for a very different reading of *Aurora Leigh*. Barrett Browning demonstrates a far greater analytical and critical understanding of the complex traditionalist and feminist issues she raises than previous critics allow. Her critical stance vis-à-vis an entrenched status quo is particularly evident in her use of hitherto unrecognized ironic distancing techniques through the mediation of her fictive narrator, Aurora Leigh. Despite their undeniable similarities, Aurora Leigh is not simply a thinly disguised Barrett Browning in fictive garb. On the contrary, unlike the British-born poet, Aurora is an exotic outsider, born in Italy, raised in an isolated mountain setting, and orphaned at an early age. She is not merely an autobiographical figure, identical to the author. Aurora not only speaks a different language but also, due to an unconventional upbringing, has a set of assumptions very different from those of her British counterparts. She observes British culture with the defamiliarizing and critical eyes of a foreigner. Even as an adult, she never completely loses her sense of strangeness or her critical view of masculinist codes.

Barrett Browning's foreign-born narrator, an outsider to British culture provides the estranged perspective that M. M. Bakhtin refers to as "experimental fantasticality." A key subversive strategy of carnivalized literature, "experimental fantasticality" involves, in Bakhtin's words, "observation from some unusual point of view, from on high, for example, which results in a radical change in the scale of the observed phenomena of life." In the case of *Aurora Leigh*, the defamiliarizing perspective is provided by the little foreign child who has been orphaned and who enters England for the first time at the age of twelve. She views with uncomprehending eyes a world familiar to the British reader. Her dislocated perspective is not the evidence of neurotic self-alienation as critics contend. Instead, her view from the "outside" becomes the locus for a culturally relative critique of contemporary British and European customs and attitudes, particularly attitudes toward women.

Book One of *Aurora Leigh* provides a particularly clear illustration of Barrett Browning's subversive and critical strategies. It traces the childhood development of the Italian-born narrator and from the outset, depicts the child as an outsider to mainstream values and conventions. After her mother's death, Aurora is raised by her father in an isolated setting among the mountains of Italy. She is thus removed from the expected acculturation processes that prepare women to play traditionalist roles within contemporary European and British culture. An unconventional tutor, her father provides her with an equally unconventional education. Her upbringing apart from contemporary society sets the stage for her subsequent role both as outsider and as defamiliarizing foreign observer.

After her father dies, the orphaned child enters British society as a naïve foreigner. Her uncomprehending observations, charted in retrospect by the adult narrator, defamiliarize and shed critical light on the contemporary British norms from the double perspective of the unknowing child and the knowing—but equally unconventional—adult. Barrett Browning uses the doubled perspective to question patriarchal codes and values and to demonstrate both their limitations and their injuriousness as controlling forces in women's lives.

In Book One, the author moves beyond a sharp criticism of the status quo to suggest an alternative paradigm for female education and development. Basing her argument on the premise that traditional gender roles are not grounded in natural law but are socially constructed, the author posits an alternative, nontraditional model for the construction of female identity. She places this unconventional model—embodied in her protagonist—in direct opposition to traditionalist views of women's nature and women's roles as restricted exclusively to the domestic sphere, to motherhood, and to childrearing.

In the first part of Book One, Barrett Browning carefully sets up a test case that will permit her to engage in an acerbic, yet concealed critique of patriarchal norms. She depicts her protagonist's formation of consciousness as an outsider to mainstream culture, and as a result her later views of British society will, by necessity, be estranged and unfamiliar. It is no accident that Aurora Leigh's education parallels that of Rousseau's fictive model of child development in *Emile, or On Education* (1762). Rousseau also provided a test case, but it is restricted to male education. Emile, Rousseau's pupil, is intentionally kept apart from and educated outside mainstream culture. In depicting Aurora's education, Barrett Browning provides a female counterpart to Rousseau's pupil and appropriates Rousseau's revolutionary model of education for women as well as for men.

The striking parallels between the two texts suggest that Barrett Browning, like many other nineteenth-century feminists, intentionally used Rousseau as her point of departure. Rousseau posits a "negative" education of the child who is raised in isolation from society according to a nontraditional pedagogical model. From birth to age five, the child, Emile, is kept apart from institutions, prejudice, authority, and traditional models of childrearing; from five to twelve, he grows up in close association with nature; from twelve to fifteen, he develops his intellect as his tutor begins to educate his mind; and finally, from the ages of fifteen to twenty, he receives his moral and religious education, and he travels in preparation for marriage to a suitably educated young woman, Sophie.

Aurora Leigh's development parallels Emile's stage by stage. From birth to age four, she grows up in Italy in the care of her Italian mother and thus apart from British institutions and prescribed models of female education. Her mother's death leaves her without a female mentor, who could form Aurora Leigh according to traditionalist paradigms. Having removed her to an isolated mountain setting where she remains from ages four to thirteen, her father, like Emile's mentor, Rousseau, provides his pupil with a nontraditional education. After her father's death, from ages thirteen to twenty the orphaned child undergoes a continuing formation of consciousness, which, like Emile's, includes the education of her mind, her religious training, and her travel to foreign countries.

Despite clear parallels, however, Barrett Browning takes issue with Rousseau's educational treatise in one crucial area: his singularly unenlightened views of women. In the "Sophie" chapter of *Emile*, Rousseau makes the traditionalist case that women are submissive, "passive and weak" creatures whose role according to "natural law" is to bend to the "active and strong" male. The resulting "inequality" of men and women, unlike the inequality created by difference in social class, is not an artificial, "unjust, man-made inequality" but is based on "well-grounded general laws," which are "established by nature."

Barrett Browning departs radically from the eighteenth-century philosopher by appropriating his exclusively masculinist model for the education of her female protagonist. Because of her unconventional upbringing, Aurora Leigh, as a test case, resembles Rousseau's male child, Emile. In contrast to Rousseau's Sophie, Aurora is a stranger to, not a product of, traditionalist views of women's education.

Nor only her foreign birth and her "hybrid" parentage—her father is a "cold" British northerner, her mother a warm, emotional Italian woman—but also her mother's death and her father's unusual tutelage play decisive roles in creating a child who falls outside societal norms. Her mother's death is certainly a painful and traumatic experience. But contrary to critical consensus, her mother-want is not to be seen solely or even primarily in negative terms as producing the narrator's traumatized, unstable, and even "diseased" personality. The absence of a female mentor means that the child is unencumbered by the "female" education her mother would have provided. The orphaned child has no female guide who would initiate her into—and shape her according to—socially and culturally prescribed pattern of female behavior. Her mother would, in the narrator's words, have "reconciled and fraternized my soul / With the new order" by "kissing full sense into empty words." These retrospective reflections express the narrator's understandable longing for the comforts of a normative upbringing; at the same time they suggest that were her mother alive as guide and model, Aurora Leigh would, like any other young woman, be conditioned through love and example to accept these conventional forms and "empty words" without question.

In the absence of her mother and female mentor, the enigmatic portrait, painted after her mother's death, plays a significant role in defining—or better, resisting all definitions of—women's roles for the motherless child. The portrait played a pivotal role in numerous critical studies that argue that the picture demonstrates the author's reaffirmation of masculinist codes and patriarchal stereotypes as well as her concomitant neurotic dividedness as a woman. Thus, viewing the portrait as a symbol of the child's unhealthy and fearful relationship with her dead mother, some critics argue that the images she sees on the portrait cripple the child emotionally and mentally and cause her to detest women, particularly mother figures. Others see the projected images on the portrait as the uncritical reaffirmation of male-defined images of women. The author and her narrator project "male defined masks and costumes" of a "dead sign system," which she attempts in vain to "revive." The "horrified" and "confused" child remains transfixed before this "object of worship, desire repugnance and fear." The portrait is seen to signal the poet's and Aurora's inability to escape the oppressions of patriarchy and to question its binary views of women's identity as angel or demon, Madonna or Eve, virgin or whore, nurturer or destroyer.

Critics have failed to note that the mother's portrait *resists* traditionalist views of women, and that the binary images the child projects upon the portrait not only are self-canceling but also fail to adhere to the surface of the portrait. Thus, the pure and motherly Madonna and the threatening, snakey-locked Medusa, a mythical destroyer and fatal woman, are united in a single, paradoxical woman as a "still Medusa with mild milky brows." The author depicts Medusa as having attributes associated not with violence, death, and destruction but with mildness, maternity, and motherhood. All the images the child has gleaned from her reading are presented as a similar self-canceling conflation of antithesis.

In faulting the author for reaffirming patriarchal stereotypes, critics have failed to note that for the narrator, these iconic images are little more than a masquerade of external forms. No single image, whether positive or negative, Madonna or Medusa, remains clearly etched upon the enigmatic surface of the portrait, "which did not therefore change / But kept the mystic level of all forms." These traditionalist icons not only cancel each other but also fail to adhere to the blank screen of the portrait; they are but a passing and shifting picture upon the face of immortality where—as in the paradox of the motherly Medusa—their "incoherencies . . . are represented fully, mixed and merged." Far from reaffirming stereotypes, the portrait puts into question the rigid images and the literary cliches that fix female identity in preconceived forms.

In this context, Aurora's status as an orphan taps into what Kimberley Reynolds and Nicola Humble refer to as the "orphan-convention, with its established traditions of social critique and alienation." Unencumbered by the usual restraints of a fixed nuclear family, orphans had an unusual freedom and autonomy to develop in unconventional ways. Their anomalous position allowed them to serve as vehicles "for radical comment." Aurora is no exception.

While Aurora's mother shapes the child's development by her absence, the father plays a crucial role in forming Aurora's unconventional views of women's nature and women's roles by providing the child with an unconventional education. After his wife's death, he removes his four-year-old daughter to a remote mountain setting where she develops in direct contact with a sublime natural landscape from which she draws sustenance. The father's flight from civilization and his desire to raise his child in unmediated contact with nature and the divine have clear Rousseauistic echoes. But unlike Rousseau, who, for fear of cultural contamination, initially refuses to have his child read any book other than *Robinson Crusoe*, the father stresses the importance of the cultural traditional as an essential part of the child's education. This does not mean that he gives his child a traditional upbringing. A nurturing mentor to his little daughter, he is the anti-type to the oppressive, patriarchal tyrant and to Barrett Browning's own despotic father. Refusing to acknowledge the gender barriers and prescribed notions governing a woman's education, he gives his daughter the education traditionally reserved for sons: "He wrapt his little daughter in his large / Man's doublet, careless did it fit or no."

Contrary to a traditionalist approach even in men's education, her father does not inculcate or enforce a received view of knowledge. Nor does he regard the cultural heritage as an accumulation of sacred and authoritative texts to be venerated unconditionally. He approaches tradition with the mind of a skeptic and teaches his daughter a critical method of thinking: "He sent the schools to school, demonstrating / A fool will pass for such through one mistake, / while a philosopher will pass for such, / Through said mistakes being ventured in the gross / And heaped up to a system." He encourages his daughter to question received notions, and he gives her the intellectual tools and analytical strategies required to question cultural norms and thus to dismantle patriarchy itself. Her father is a liberating figure who provides his daughter with the means to argue her way out of patriarchy.

With her father's death, Aurora now enters British society as a defamiliarizing outside observer whose estranged perspective sheds critical light on cultural norms. She is an orphan, a child with an unconventional upbringing, a foreigner who speaks a different language. She looks at what appears to the British to be "normal" with the astonished eyes of a stranger, unversed in the customs she observes. The child's experience is narrated in retrospect by the adult narrator, now a writer and an unconventional adult who has continued to view the patriarchal world through the estranged eyes of the cultural outsider. Thus, the reader is presented with a doubled perspective. The unconventional adult looks back on the child's experience and comments acerbically on the wider implications of a conditioning process the child resists even though she does not fully understand its implications. The dual perspective allows the author—through the vehicle of her protagonist's narratorial voices as child and as adult—to present an unfamiliar and critical view of the conventional education designed for women.

The author also challenges the fixed binaries according to which her contemporaries constructed female—and male—identity. In portraying the child's encounter with her aunt, Barrett Browning exposes the binary paradigms represented by the Madonna-Eve, angel-demon polarity, as incomplete, reductionist, and distorted projections of womanhood. The meeting between Aurora Leigh, the exotic foreign child, and her aunt, the assiduous enforcer of normative attitudes, is a staged encounter between two patriarchal icons of womanhood: the stereotypical exotic other—the *femme fatale* and violator of normative codes—and a dark, negative figure who is clearly intended as the distortion or transmogrification of the "angel in the house." Like the double-voiced narrative, the critique operates simultaneously on two levels. The foreign child epitomizes the exotic "other" in her most innocent and harmless of forms. She observes the aunt, a representative of British womanhood, with alienated eyes and thus provides an unfamiliar view of socially sanctioned images of women. At the same time, Aurora's aunt who represents the conventional British outlook, observes an exotic intruder who is paradoxically her own flesh and blood. The interplay of mutually elucidating perspectives allows the narrator to question the stereotype of the exotic *femme fatale*, ludicrously seen in a little child, and to challenge the image of the angel in the house, who appears as a soured, embittered figure. Having failed to live out the domestic ideal, the aunt now appears in a dreadful caricature as the accomplice of patriarchy, imposing on others the very norms that have warped and dehumanized her.

In her negative depiction of the aunt, the author is not targeting helpless spinsters; on the contrary, by turning the angel in the house image on its head, she unmasks this conventional image as an unnatural, frigid, and harmful contraption. In the aunt, all the virtues and positive values generally associated with this feminine icon appear in her anti-type as negations of life, as sterile and harmful conventions. In her shaping of herself according to preconceived images of middle-class womanhood, in her internalization of patriarchal values, and in her conditioned responses, the aunt is shown to have warped or killed all her human impulses: "She stood straight and calm / Her somewhat narrow forehead braided tight / As if for taming accidental thoughts / From possible pulses; brown hair pricked with gray / By frigid use of life."

By reversing the expected image of the angel in the house, Barrett Browning demonstrates the frightening results of adhering to a code that imprisons women in a distorted view of femininity. The author targets less the enforcer figure herself than the pernicious conditioning process that produces such accomplices in the patriarchal "project." The author anticipates such twentieth-century critiques of enforcer figures as one finds in Margaret Atwood's parablelike novel *The Handmaid's Tale*, in which women are enlisted in a tyrannical project to oppress and exploit other women.

Barrett Browning implicates an entire series of interesting influences and factors that converge in the figure of the aunt, including the Church as a traditionalist institution. The Church uses "Christian doctrine" to underwrite the patriarchal status quo, preaching conventional views of women's roles—"inhuman doctrines"—that are "enforced at church." This conditioning process produces women whose sinless veneer conceals suppressed hatred, anger, and resentment, "the gall of gentle souls." Interestingly, Barrett Browning gives an astute analysis of the mechanisms of oppression and unconscious suppression that have, erroneously to my mind, been seen as preventing the author from seeing patriarchy in a critical light. Patriarchal conventions are seen as forming an ideological prison that traps its victims, dehumanizes them, and converts them in turn into avid enforcers of inhuman codes. Shaped by this injurious process, the aunt has "lived / A sort of cage-bird life, born in a cage, / Accounting that to leap from perch to perch / Was act and joy enough for any bird." The consequence of this imprisonment is that love has been displaced by duty, Christian charity by resentment, and maternal feelings for an orphaned child by an irrational and persistent hatred.

The aunt, unaware of the paradox of her own position as a victim who victimizes in turn, now attempts to program Aurora Leigh as she has been programmed. Aurora's comment demonstrates her insight into this vicious cycle: "I, alas, / A wild bird scarcely fledged, was brought to her cage". Because of her role as cultural enforcer who hates those who fall outside the culturally sanctioned norms, the aunt appears through the eyes of the child as a harmful, threatening creature, with her "two grey-steel naked-bladed eyes" that "stabbed" through Aurora's vulnerable face.

Citing the aunt and other negative female figures in the novel poem, critics have charged the author with woman hating and unconscious antifeminism. What the figure of the aunt illustrates, however is not the author's antifeminism but her recognition that women who play stereotypical roles frequently act as accomplices who perpetuate the patriarchal conditioning process. In her negative portrait of the aunt, the author is not rejecting women, femininity, or maternity; instead, she is rejecting distorted images of women and the patriarchal ideology on which they are based.

The social and religious conditioning designed to create conventional women not only dehumanizes those who play the game and follow the codes but also produces a distorted view of outsiders and foreigners who resist or violate these codes. By examining the aunt's perception of her niece, Barrett Browning explores the mechanisms of cross-cultural stereotyping and dismantles the ethnocentric image of the exotic woman as *femme fatale*. For the aunt, English women are the absolute norm, "models to the universe."

From the moment the child arrives, the ethnocentric aunt attaches fixed, negative labels to her niece as a foreigner and violator of normative codes. Aurora Leigh appears upon her aunt's doorstep as an abandoned, suffering, bereaved child. She is the exotic other rendered innocent and harmless. But the stereotype shapes the aunt's perceptions so profoundly that she searches Aurora Leigh's face for traces of the evil and demonic *femme fatale* whom she hates with a consuming passion and whom she sees as a threat to the social and psychological norms she has adopted and internalized.

Seen from the aunt's perspective, Aurora Leigh's Italian mother has led the child's British father to violate the terms of his inheritance, according to which the family fortune cannot be inherited by a child born of a foreign wife. Thus, Aurora is penniless after her father's death, a ward of the aunt who has inherited the fortune. Rather than blame her brother for marrying a foreigner, the aunt focuses on her brother's Italian wife as an interloper, a temptress and destroyer who has "fooled away / A wise man from wise courses." Not only has she deprived the aunt "of the household precedence," but she has "wronged his tenants, robbed his native land, / And made him mad, alike by life and death."

Now that her brother's wife has died, the aunt shifts the blame to her thirteen-year-old niece standing on her doorstep. She therefore greets Aurora with suspicion and hatred, and she rejects the girl's displays of affection: "There, with some strange spasm / Of pain and passion, she wrung loose my hands / Imperiously, and held me at arm's length." She searches for a "wicked murderer" in the child's "innocent face." For the aunt, the exotic other is an emblem for the transgression of social codes, a stranger capable not only of sexually illicit behavior but also of robbery and even murder. As Aurora's case demonstrates, the guilt or innocence of those who are targeted plays little role in the injurious mechanisms of cultural stereotyping.

In describing Aurora's education at the hands of this enforcer of normative codes, the author sheds critical light on the conventional conditioning process designed to produce stereotypical women. The child is forced to read a "score of books on womanhood," the very number suggesting the collusion of writers, and of the publishing industry, in reinforcing masculinist codes. Designed to inculcate traditionalist responses, the books "boldly assert" a woman's "right of comprehending husband's talk / When not too deep," as well as "Their rapid insight and fine aptitude, / Particular worth and general missionariness, / As long as they keep quiet by the fire / And never say 'no' when the world says 'ay,' / For that is fatal—their angelic reach, / Of virtue, chiefly used to sit and darn, / And fatten household sinners—their, in brief, / Potential faculty in everything / Of abdicating power in it." Accepting a woman's traditional role requires nothing less than the silencing of her individual voice and the denial of her intellect—in short, her complete abdication of agency, power, and autonomy.

In depicting her protagonist's development and critiquing the aunt's attempt to shape her in traditionalist molds, the author does more than simply undercut normalizing forms of female education. She also offers an alternative model for female identity based on the premise that human identity is not preordained by "nature" but is instead socially and culturally constructed to a marked degree. Although she adopts Rousseau's revolutionary model of the education process, Barrett Browning contests the philosopher's traditionalist argument that women are by nature subordinate and inferior to men. Women, like men, she argues, are capable of dramatic changes in their social and cultural roles. She thus makes the implicit case that nature and natural law are not skewed in favor of the male. In arguing that the concept of nature and natural law can be changed, Barrett Browning implicitly makes the case that nature is a culturally relative projection, in her words, something that we "name" Nature, rather than something that exists in its own right separately from our mental projections. She thus anticipates twentieth-century anthropological arguments that the nature-culture dichotomy is a culturally relative construct, not a universal value-free paradigm on which universal "laws of nature" may be based.

In the final part of Book One, the natural world of the English countryside is both an empirical reality and a mental territory representing a nongendered view of nature. When Aurora discovers an alternative model for female identity, her dawning insight is depicted in metaphorical terms as her departure from the artificially segregated domestic sphere of the house and her entry into a natural landscape beyond gender.

The development occurs in stages. Upon her arrival in England, the homesick child had responded negatively to the foreign landscape, which appeared at first to be diametrically opposed to the sublime setting in the mountains of Pelagria where she had been raised in close contact with nature. There, for nine years, surrounded by "God's silence", she had drawn sustenance from nature, "growing like the plants from unseen roots." After her father's death, she discovers that the universe has "turned stranger." To the foreign child, the "frosty cliffs" and "mean red houses" of England appear to represent a society devoid of human connection: "The ground seemed cut up from the fellowship / Of verdure, field from field as man from man."

Aurora is indeed cut off from sustaining human contact and from nature. Stifled and straitjacketed by convention, the child is all but imprisoned in her aunt's house. She is even denied the sight of nature, previously her source of strength. Obedient to her aunt's wishes, the child "sat in just the chair she placed, / With back against the window, to exclude / The sight of the great lime-tree on the lawn, / Which seemed to have come on purpose from the woods / To bring the house a message." Even when she is imprisoned in the domestic territory of the aunt, as the echo of Coleridge's "This Limetree Bower My Prison" suggests, the child hears the implicit call of a natural world beyond the conventions of the house and the narrowness even of the attached garden.

Summoned by the natural world, which penetrates the house and her room, the child gradually moves out of the imprisoning domestic confines into the garden and then beyond the garden into a wider world that stands in symbolic opposition to the narrowly defined domestic space over which her aunt presides. Nature is portrayed as entering the house and thus as eroding and overrunning the artificial barriers that separate the domestic sphere from the wider external and public world.

The mental process of Aurora's awakening is portrayed in physical terms: Aspects of the natural landscape appear to penetrate the confines of the house, as the window of her room lets in the "outdoor world with all its greenery." The green of nature, spilling into her room, draws her outdoors. As she begins to see the English countryside with new eyes, she is freed, she discovers, not only from the stifling interior of the house but also from the shackles of a confining worldview.

Aurora Leigh's flight into the natural landscape is not simply an escapist, romanticized retreat from reality. On the contrary, it marks her entry into a mental, emotional, and philosophical territory not governed by gender-differentiated norms of behavior. Nature for Rousseau was classless but gendered. That is, according to Rousseau, class distinctions were not based on natural laws; they were man-made and hence artificial. Gender distinctions, by contrast, were ordained by nature and thus a direct outgrowth of natural law. Barrett Browning takes issue with this distinction, arguing that nature is not antifeminist; instead, it represents a symbolic substratum, a hypothetical territory beyond both class *and* gender. Nature does not underwrite inequalities based on sex any more than it underwrites injustices based on social class. Thus, when Aurora enters this hypothetical territory, she discovers a new alternative view of female identity.

Barrett Browning portrays nature and a natural law as shaping her protagonist's formation of consciousness. But she also stresses the complementary role of the cultural heritage. Unlike Rousseau, who restricts the child's reading for fear of leading him astray, Barrett Browning portrays Aurora as discovering the freeing power of the cultural heritage through her father's books that she finds in the attic of the house. The cultural heritage is clearly a patrimony, a legacy from Aurora Leigh's *father*. The author thereby indicates her knowledge that the written records that constitute Western cultural tradition are male-centered and for the most part male-authored. Nevertheless, rather than discard the heritage because of its unavoidable bias, Aurora appropriates the male tradition when she discovers literature as an apt vehicle to express her unconventional view of women's nature. Rousseau argues that women are the better for having their education severely restricted, for he sees the cultural heritage, like civilization itself, in a negative light. Barrett Browning, by contrast, sees the restrictions in a woman's education as a deprivation. Significantly, it is Aurora's encounter with the poets, whom Plato banished from his Republic for their anarchistic and potentially subversive tendencies, that allows Aurora to develop a new view of herself and her place in society: "my soul / At poetry's divine first finger-touch, / Let go conventions and sprang up surprised."

By the end of Book One, Aurora Leigh has learned not only to discard "conventional gray glooms" but also to reject the claims of a male-centered ideology. She emerges as a young woman capable not only of criticizing patriarchal views of women but also of fashioning for herself an alternative identity as a woman writer. During a debate with her cousin Romney, she demonstrates her critical skills, contesting his traditionalist stance point by point. This "courtship" scene is surely an intentional smiling yet serious parody of the traditional "debat d'amour," the sparring courtship that imitates verbally the rituals of male-to-male combat. During this intellectual and amorous sparring match, Aurora rejects every cliché of Victorian womanhood voiced by her would-be suitor and cousin. She also rejects his offer of marriage. Even though it would make her wealthy, marriage to Romney would confine her to a conventionally feminine role as his helpmate. She decides instead to make her own way, as poet and writer, living in poverty in a small garret in London. The subsequent narrative charts Aurora's progress as a woman whose choice of an unconventional profession causes her to transgress traditional barriers, to flout restrictions imposed upon female behavior, and to speak, successfully, in a public voice even while living in a society that consistently relegated women's achievements primarily to the domestic, nonpublic sphere.

In assessing Aurora Leigh's unconventional stance, critics have been consistently troubled by her marriage to her cousin Romney at the conclusion of the narrative. It is viewed as a conventional happy ending and as a capitulation, if not an abject self-abnegation by a formerly heroic protagonist who at the last minute relinquishes all she has gained in order to reinsert herself into patriarchy. This "happy ending," however, only *appears* to provide a pat, socially sanctioned answer to all the difficult questions raised in the novel poem. The terms of Aurora's marriage are as unconventional as her education and her career. In a traditional marriage, the woman of the nineteenth century was expected to subsume her public, economic, and social identity into that of her marriage partner. As Glennis Stephenson has ably demonstrated, the marriage Barrett Browning portrays does not reinstate patriarchal values. Instead, the author provides for a marriage on very different, exceptional, and nontraditional terms. In Stephenson's words, Aurora and Romney "define their new roles and functions and expand the very boundaries of love itself." Barrett Browning is not a separatist. She insists on including love and even marriage in her view of the potentialities of male-female relationships. But she does so, as Stephenson argues, by providing an alternative model replacing "the socially and culturally established form of male-female relationship with a new form of relationship which allows women to play a vital active role and which preserves female autonomy."

The marriage by no means represents a conventional closure. Instead, it is the point of departure for what is depicted throughout the novel poem as a continuing and difficult process of self-discovery. It does not represent a pat solution to the problems raised by Aurora Leigh's anomalous form of identity within an essentially patriarchal context. Her protagonist provides the paradigm for an alternative form of female identity and of marriage. But this future process cannot be mapped in all its many possible variables. The lyric—and problematic—vision at the conclusion of the novel poem is not intended as a roadmap for a territory already explored and charted. It is, rather, the adumbration of a future potentially based on the author's personal experience, an experience that by contemporary standards and within a late-nineteenth-century patriarchal context was admittedly exceptional.

ANNE D. WALLACE

"Nor in Fading Silks Compose": Sewing, Walking, and Poetic Labor in Aurora Leigh

T he November 1993 conference, "Elizabeth Barrett Browning and
Victorian Culture," opened with readings from a drama based on *Aurora
Leigh* and continued with eleven presentations, in a total of forty-two, on
Barrett Browning's novel-poem. The MLA Bibliography tells a similar story.
Of 142 Barrett Browning entries from 1981 through early 1995, thirty-one
name *Aurora Leigh* as a specific object of study, more than any other single
Barrett Browning title. Such a concentration of effort may be problematic,
but there it is: *Aurora Leigh* is the text of the moment in Barrett Browning
studies. Our primary concern, as revealed by both these conference
presentations and other recent scholarship, is to describe *Aurora Leigh*'s
position in the contemporary discussion of women and in our current
discussion of gender.

Like Susan Brown and Laura C. Berry at the 1993 conference,
readers often approach such a description through genre study, regarding
Barrett Browning's poem as a simultaneous reiteration and explosion of
established genres. Marjorie Stone, in her comparative study of *Aurora Leigh*
and Tennyson's *The Princess*, articulates the critical rationale for this
approach:

> assumptions about gender interact in complex ways with the
> assumptions about genre that structure the creation and

From *English Literature History* 64, no. 1, (1997) © 1997 The John Hopkins University Press.

reception of literary texts. Analyzing the writing of texts, feminist critics have explored the ways in which women write between existing genres or adapt male-defined genres such as the bildungsroman to their own needs and rhetorical purposes, often creating new hybrid genres. Analyzing the reception of literary works, they have shown how the privileging of certain genres, the use of misleading categorization by genre, and the formulation of generic features in female or male terms have functioned to perpetuate the marginalization of women's writing.

In adopting such methods, we may pursue the questionable course of reading a text in the ways it says it wishes to be read. Certainly *Aurora Leigh* explicitly sets out a necessary connection between genre revision and gender revision, so that our work along this line functions conservatively (at least with respect to *Aurora Leigh*'s aesthetic proposals) rather than otherwise. Nonetheless, in this essay I too follow *Aurora Leigh*'s suggested methodology, and our current critical bent, to the end of addressing what seems a more immediate problem.

Given Stone's expression of our general perception that gender and genre "interact in complex ways," our conclusions about these interactions in Barrett Browning's poem reduce to the curiously simple dichotomy Stone then implies: subversive hybridization or continuing marginalization. Stone's own work exemplifies the celebratory argument that Barrett Browning's hybridization of epic, romance and novel successfully subverts dominant categories: "Setting up a dialogue of genres to reinforce her dialogue of genders, she challenges the 'violent order' of gender and genre hierarchies: turning men into compulsive nurturers and women into knights-errant, substituting Aurora for Achilles, bringing plain Miss Smith face to face with Homer's Helen and Homer's heroes. Dierdre David represents what currently seems the only alternative. Pointing to the often-questioned end of the poem, she concludes that "the novel-poem *Aurora Leigh* becomes a form-giving epithalamium for the essentialist sexual politics formed primarily through Barrett Browning's very early apprenticeship to male modes of intellectual training and aesthetic practice. In this poem we hear a woman's voice speaking patriarchal discourse—boldly, passionately, and without rancour.

Nowhere in Barrett Browning studies, whether genre focuses the discussion or not, does there seem to be any way around one of these two resolutions of *Aurora Leigh*'s conflicted representations of gender. That *Aurora Leigh*'s constructions of gender are conflicted is well-accepted, and, like most other critics, neither Stone nor David suppresses the poem's difficulties in the progress of her interpretation. But all finally press for what I regard as unfruitfully restrictive "solutions" to these difficulties. I wish to argue that we cannot, after all, choose either the essentialist endgame, or the revisions of genre / gender most prominent in the early books, as the final disposition of the poem. In particular, *Aurora Leigh* resists a conclusive reading of its attitudes toward the crucial relations among women, work and writing.

I suspect that this resistance plays a large part in our repetitive interrogation of Barrett Browning's poem, for it refuses our own desires. It is surely obvious to anyone working in literary criticism that these relations among women, work and writing form an ideological nexus at which we now, in late twentieth-century literary culture, most vigorously seek resolution. For many of us, this is no abstract or "purely literary" matter. Women writers paid (albeit indirectly) for what we write, we feel an immense, personal, at times desperate need to limn clearly and so shift the cultural constructions that inflect our own lives. Feminist readers of various persuasions, pressuring textual constructions of gender, seek some overriding principle by which the apparent paradoxes of Barrett Browning's narrative might be settled. Traditionally, however, our discussions ignore the important connection between the issues of women and artistry, and of women and paid labor, confining "work" to professional writing itself and not relating (except by opposition) that work to other kinds of work, laborious or professional, paid or domestic. I want to return our attention to this connection by reading gender against the genres which metaphorize art as "labor." Thus, rather than considering the genres most prominently "named" by the poem— poem, novel, epic, lyric, bildungsroman and kunstlerroman—I turn to the *sotto voce* genres of georgic and its early nineteenth-century extension, peripatetic.

A reading of these genres, made available for us in *Aurora Leigh's* linked representations of sewing and walking, foregrounds the relationship between the poem's shifting valuations of "women's work" and its accompanying efforts to regender poetic labor. Georgic and peripatetic valorize common, materially productive labors, and metaphorically associate these labors with the work of the poet, firmly attaching the characteristics of "good labor" to poetic composition. Any poem that invokes these genres in representing a woman poet necessarily undertakes a larger task: since georgic and peripatetic have already gendered "labor" and "writing" as masculine, the poem must now re-define the relations among women, work and writing, selecting for its celebration a material labor commonly practiced by women.

In the case of *Aurora Leigh*, as we shall see, this labor is sewing, a kind of work done by almost all women, of all classes, both as unpaid domestic labor and as paid public employment. But here, as one might suspect, further complications arise from mid-nineteenth-century English ideologies of labor. In Nancy Armstrong's influential commentary on eighteenth-century conduct books, she describes the codification of "an absolutely rigid distinction between domestic duty and labor that was performed for money," a distinction still plainly governing representations of women's work in Barrett Browning's time. Domestic duty, as Armstrong maps the category, is private, unpaid, and offers the appearance of leisure, which is to say that women's good work is precisely not "labor." If, as Armstrong suggests, this boundary between domestic work and labor is "a distinction on which the very notion of gender appeared to depend," then revaluing women's work in order to regender poetic labor would dismantle not just an effect, but a foundation of constructed gender.

It is in the negotiation of these difficulties, indicative of complex interactions indeed between gender and genre, that *Aurora Leigh*'s irresolution on the crucial relations among women, work and writing becomes evident. In its first two books, Barrett Browning's poem sets up a deliberate opposition between the female/domestic labor of sewing and the masculine/artistic "labors" of walking and writing. This opposition, sensible enough given Victorian domestic ideologies, also follows a traditional definition of poetry by means of its difference from "lesser," specifically domestic, arts. Anne Finch's "The Spleen" (1701) perhaps most memorably sets out this poetics. "Whilst in the Muses' paths I stray," her frustrated poet tells us,

> My hand delights to trace unusual things,
> And deviates from the known and common way;
> Nor will in fading silks compose
> Faintly th'inimitable rose,
> Fill up an ill-drawn bird, or paint on glass
> The Sovereign's blurred and undistinguished face,
> The threatening angel and the speaking ass.

To a certain extent, Barrett Browning's poem follows this account, in which embroidery (and glass-painting, and all the leisurely domestic arts they stand for) not only mocks but displaces poetry's truth-telling mimesis, its practice preventing the practice of poetry. But in *Aurora Leigh*, sewing is not only a leisurely, decorative, domestic art, but a productive labor of women working for wages in public, rather than domestic, economies. Moreover, the poem's extended metaphorical representation of poetry as walking relies not on the tradition of contemplative poetry embodied in Finch's straying lady, but on

Wordsworthian peripatetic, in which fatherly pedestrian-poets' laborious, materially productive walking performs intellectual and moral cultivation.

Peripatetic inevitably implicates its source-genre, georgic, and here the reader may notice the possibility of a more positive reading of sewing. Some eighteenth-century georgics include passages in which domestic sewing functions as a labor imitative of agricultural cultivation and so *imitative*, in a positive sense, of poetry. But *Aurora Leigh*'s attention to sewing as public wage-labor, and its proposal of a woman poet who imagines herself as one of Wordsworth's pedestrian-poets, suggest further complicating connections between sewing and walking and poetry. Peripatetic, like georgic, figures a common material labor—walking in peripatetic, farming in georgic—as cognate with the "labor" of poetry-writing, and constructs these labors' mutual function as cultivating forces in the poet's/laborer's society. If sewing appears as productive labor, and if women may be walking poets, then no simple opposition between women's domestic work and men's public, cultivating, poetic work may be drawn. Nor may women's sewing be seen as merely imitative of men's cultivating labors. Rather, it must be recognized as yet another possibly cognate labor, a potentially cultivating agency in itself.

The poem deliberately carries these complications forward. *Aurora Leigh* interleaves sewing imagery with the vegetative imagery central to peripatetic and georgic, producing images of poets' mantles, of pricking roses and ivy, of green-clothed rooms bridging domestic interiors and poetic paths. This kind of imagery pervades the early books of the poem, and while it never fully displaces negative interpretations of sewing, it leaves sewing, walking and poetry problematically entangled. Marian Erle's story sets out the full dimensions of this entanglement. For Marian, whose labor as a seamstress proves a stable economic support, sewing also resurrects the moral harvest she first gathers in walking and poetry, and functions as the saving cultivating labor that preserves her past into a potential future. In Marian's story, indeed, it seems as if Barrett Browning might be constructing sewing as georgic labor, using the same tactics of juxtaposition and replacement that Wordsworth used to construct peripatetic—"adapting a male-defined genre," in Stone's terms. But that adaptation, if underway, is broken off, the negative force of the first oppositions never fully denied. The last two books of *Aurora Leigh* rarely image either sewing or walking as the sister-labor of poetry; metaphors of material agency give way to those of transcendent love. The apparent impossibility of either exchanging or separating male and female labors suggests an ideological impasse, in which the poem's varying pressures on the categorical boundaries of art, labor and gender leave us with no clear solutions to the problems it describes. The reading that follows sets out the successive stages of the developing deadlock:

a thorough devaluation of women's work, a reconstruction of women's work as materially and artistically valuable, and a tacit refusal to use the rhetorical weapon so constructed.

Barrett Browning saturates *Aurora Leigh* with references to sewing, a term I will use broadly to indicate the multiple overlapping categories of processes, materials and products of sewing named by the poem. Varieties of sewing mentioned in the poem include tying, stringing, darning, pricking, knitting, stitching, wrinkling, pressing, wreathing, twisting, spinning, embroidering, netting, braiding. As we would expect, these things are done to threads, yarns, silks, brocades; they produce or are wrought on veils, gowns, shrouds, skirts, mantles, fringes, baldaquins, stoles, shoes. But literal sewing expands quickly, and everywhere, into metaphor. Children hang on their mother's skirts like living ornaments; hair is braided or "pricked with grey"; conscience becomes wrinkled, duties are smooth-pressed; a distant horizon becomes a "witch's scarlet thread"; talk is a different, masculine thread, while women may string pearls and rhymes and cowslips alike; nets of money catch the metaphorical lioness-poet; ivy is wreathed and twisted and worn as a pricking crown. By my own rough count (of instances, not necessarily discrete images), there are more than fifty such references in the first two books alone.

Such an extensive and various system of imagery refuses any single reading, but its earliest consistent use is decidedly negative. In Aurora's account of her education, sewing provides the primary symbols of conventional limitations on women's lives. Aurora's first image of her aunt shows her aunt's "somewhat narrow forehead braided tight / As if for taming accidental thoughts / From possible pulses; brown hair pricked with grey / By frigid use of life." The image's connection of braiding and pricking with intellectual and emotional confinement corresponds with the following account of the aunt's "cage-bird life," defined in part by her clearly insufficient expression of Christian charity in "knitting stockings, stitching petticoats / Because we are of one flesh after all / And need one flannel." Submitting to her aunt, Aurora lets her "prick me to a pattern with her pin": she braids her own curls and follows a course of education that keeps her learning metaphorically and literally in skirts. The sciences are "brushed with extreme flounce"; she copies costumes from engravings for her drawing lesson, learns to spin glass (a decorative art), and reads instruction manuals which show a proper woman's "angelic reach / Of virtue, chiefly used to sit and darn, / And fatten household sinners." Last of all she learns to cross-stitch, producing a miscolored shepherdess whose "round weight of hat" reminds her of the tortoise shell that crushes the "tragic poet," Aeschylus.

Helena Mitchie, drawing out the psychosexual implications of such representations, connects sewing's status as inferior artistry with Freudian repression, reading sewing as "a way of repressing and controlling the self," particularly in "the sacrifice of physical self and the repression of bodily urges." Placing Aurora in the company of Maggie Tulliver and Caroline Helstone, Mitchie argues that "sewing is the tiny and fragile channel into which their creativity and their sexual energies must be poured to maintain feminine decorum." Even if one wishes to avoid the possible anachronisms of such a reading (a reading I feel is at least partially justified by the passage above), the traditional poetic devaluation of sewing is plainly in play here. The final image, particularly, recalls Finch's rendering of embroidery as a false art that distorts its subjects while displacing (in this case "killing") the true art of poetry.

At this point, however, Aurora breaks off her account of her education to add a general denunciation of women's work. I want to attend to this "aside" in detail, unfolding the various ways in which it compounds the simpler opposition of sewing and poetry:

> By the way,
> The works of women are symbolical.
> We sew, sew, prick our fingers, dull our sight,
> Producing what? A pair of slippers, sir,
> To put on when you're weary—or a stool
> To tumble over and vex you . . . "curse that stool!"
> Or else at best, a cushion where you lean
> And sleep, and dream of something we are not,
> But would be for your sake. Alas, alas!
> This hurts most, this . . . that, after all, we are paid
> The worth of our work, perhaps.

"Symbolical," although ironic and, in this limited context, perhaps no more suggestive than Finch's "composed" gestures toward a possible conflation of sewing and poetry. Mitchie suggests that the sheer weight of the poem's references to sewing implies such a conflation. Repressed though they are, "leisure-class sewers" like Aurora seam the texts, leaving "a trace of the heroine's physical presence." Thus, despite Barrett Browning's particularly "sinister" figuring of Aurora's whole body into fabric to be marked and pricked, Mitchie postulates the simultaneous elevation of sewing as epic figure: "female occupations, however, [sic] trivialized by the culture are—to use Browning's idiom—the fabric of the poem."

Perhaps because of her focus on the (Freudian) body, however, Mitchie does not notice the grounds on which these implicit connections eventually become explicit, grounds indicated by this passage's shift away from "leisure-class sewers" toward paid needlewomen. Here the products of sewing shift from purely decorative to more utilitarian items, domestic furniture unregarded by the men of the household but nonetheless designed for their use (specifically, their comfort). At the same time, explicitly economic language drives us toward a perception of sewing's public potential as production and paid labor.

These rhetorical moves underscore other effects of Barrett Browning's mass of specialized sewing terms: we are constantly being reminded that there are many different kinds of sewing, with different interpretative potential, and that the issues raised by variant terms include, rather prominently, issues of class. In the common shorthand of nineteenth-century British novels, for instance, the relatively simple distinction between "fancy" and "plain" work signals the difference between Maggie Tulliver, who has mastered only the plain hemming that earned some money during her family's indebtedness, and Lucy Deane, who (like Aurora) has been trained for a respectable upper-middle-class "lady's" station and plays at pretty embroidery.

These class differentials are further complicated, as we might expect, because they are attached to issues of feminine virtue by the "separate spheres" clause of domestic ideologies. As Maggie's case partially demonstrates, women who sew for money, whether doing plain or fancy work, may read as virtuous in their devotion to the family they help support, or in their desire to maintain themselves without resorting to various forms of prostitution (including loveless marriage). But these women also read as sexually vulnerable, apparently as a result of a combination of innocence, passion, beauty, poverty, and a lack of both male protection and female supervision. In this ideological double-bind, paid sewers' sexual virtue seems threatened both by the inadequacy of their pay, which makes them vulnerable to various seductions, and by the fact that they are paid at all, the acceptance of money for a properly domestic task mimicking prostitution. As Nancy Armstrong observes, even that most genteel of paid women, the governess, still violated that harsh line between "domestic duty" and paid labor, "a distinction so deeply engraved upon the public mind that the figure of the prostitute could be freely invoked to describe any woman who dared to labor for money." That women's domestic sewing is not paid for at all, on the other hand, is precisely the sign of domestic sewers' "worth," both in the sense of economic well-being and in that of sexual / social respectability.

So one meaning of Barrett Browning's economic language in this passage, not a surprising one given the indictment of middle-class women's education that precedes it, is its literal claim that domestic sewing is "worthless" in domestic terms as well as in the market terms in which it is figured. Providing neither pleasant decoration, useful furniture, nor emotional connection, women's domestic sewing serves only to support men's sleepy fantasies "of something [women] are not, / But would be for your sake." But the figuring of domestic worth in the language of production and pay also identifies domestic sewers with those who are paid for their labor. Our attention is drawn, briefly but uncomfortably, to the sexual economies of domesticity: a respectable married woman's unpaid work is always, silently, sexual as well as domestic. The distanced but suggestive signs of the pillow, sleep, and dreams of women may help extend our covert recognition of this possibility. Thus the domestic and paid varieties of sewing implicate each other in an involuted field of negative values ranging from low pay to sexual failure or promiscuity.

The apparently simple terms "works" and "work" which frame Aurora's aside amplify its reciprocal devaluations of domestic and paid sewing. Raymond Williams notes the stable, extremely broad function of the word "work" from its Old English origins to the present day as "our most general word for doing something, and for something done." The "predominant specialization to paid employment" as a dominant meaning of "work" occurred gradually, Williams says, as "the result of the development of capitalist productive relations," presumably from the late eighteenth century forward (he implies rather than names the period). Williams offers "one significant example" of this usage: "an active woman, running a house and bringing up children, is distinguished from a woman who *works*: that is to say, takes paid employment." A paragraph or so later, he recurs to this example as he more fully describes the specialization of the term: "*Work* then partly shifted from the productive effort itself to the predominant social relationship. It is only in this sense that a woman running a house and bringing up children can be said to be *not working*. As Williams's repetition suggests, the exclusion of domestic labor from the status of "work" is not just "one significant example," but *the primary* rhetorical distinction effected by the simultaneous processes of industrialization and the increased ideological separation of private and public spheres. The possible movement between a general sense of "work" as a productive effort, a sense essentially cognate with older meanings of "labor" and "toil," and a specialized sense of "work" as paid labor (allied to the more specialized "labor" as productive of *value*) provides the ironic force of Barrett Browning's usage: women's work is not, in one sense, work at all.

There is, however, a further detail of the usage of "work" which Williams does not explore. From the fourteenth through at least the late nineteenth centuries, "work" also meant sewing, in the expanded sense I have employed throughout this essay. The *OED* places this definition of "work" (substantive) sixteenth in its extensive list of possibilities: "The operation of making a textile fabric or (more often) something consisting of such fabric, as weaving or (usually) sewing, knitting, or the like; *esp.* any of the lighter operations of this kind, as distinctively feminine occupation; also *concr.* the fabric or the thing made of it, *esp.* while being made or operated upon; needlework, embroidery, or the like." The tone of this entry, with its implicit equation between "lighter" and "feminine," speaks to the traditional distinctions made above. But it also tells us that even while "work" changed to exclude women's domestic labor, it retained another specialized sense, one defined as feminine and, despite the depreciating tone, vital to certain public as well as domestic economies.

It is in this sense that nineteenth-century novels so often use the word "work," unqualified by any explanation as to the *kind* of work at hand. Adjectives modifying the kind of sewing—plain, fancy, or even "company," as in Elizabeth Gaskell's *Wives and Daughters*, are common, and context generally adds a gloss. We know, for instance, that Dinah Morris has been hemming a sheet when she "let[s] her work fall" to speak of her call to preaching, and that Hetty Sorrel's basket of "little workwoman's matters," which Arthur Donnithorne's advances make her drop, holds sewing implements because she is returning from her lessons with the lady's maid. But the unadorned word "work" nonetheless plainly carries an understood meaning, "sewing," which would be unavailable in a twentieth-century text.

Moreover, in nineteenth-century fictional accounts of domesticity, sewing "stands in" for almost all domestic labor. As in the ideal middle-class practice of housekeeping, in which all signs of actual physical labor were to be kept from view, cooking, water-carrying, cleaning, washing, and so forth, are relentlessly elided. *Adam Bede* offers a few moderately extended discussions of a wider range of domestic work, but these are constrained by class boundaries. Mrs. Poyser, Dinah and Lisabeth, although fully respectable, fall just below the classes of women defined by their laborious maintenance of an *appearance* of leisure. Occasionally, nursing appears, offering pathetic scenes of self-sacrifice, or child care provides charming views of maternal emotion. Both Gaskell's Ruth and Barrett Browning's Marian Erle engage in such domestic work—and, interestingly, in both cases the visible labor is done by a woman who earns money by sewing, a woman already in the "working" classes. But I believe we may state more strongly Mitchie's observation that sewing is "perhaps the most common feminine occupation" of leisure-class heroines: the most common meaning of "work," as read in the nineteenth-century and applied to a middle-class respectable woman, is "sewing."

I have played out Aurora's aside to such an extent in order to establish the comprehensiveness of the poem's early devaluation of "the works of women." Aurora's indictment of sewing as constraining, superficial, trivial, spiritually retrograde, fatal to poetic arts, and economically worthless, constitutes an indictment of women's work in every sense. The needlewoman working for pay, the domestic sewer darning her family's clothing, the (apparently) leisured lady embroidering items both useful and decorative, all are discounted, the very variety of their cheapening enforcing the most negative views of women's work and women's worth. This indictment operates, moreover, at every rhetorical level, literal, figurative, and linguistic. Paradoxically, this same conflation of domestic and paid sewing opens the door to new interpretations of the most positive sort, as peripatetic intervenes in the generic structure of the poem. As Book I closes, however, what we *feel* is the sharp contrast between the enforced worthlessness of sewing and the deliberately chosen, excursive possibilities of walking.

Barrett Browning narrativizes Aurora's growing self-consciousness, and particularly her identity as a poet, as an increasing ability to walk alone outdoors, literally outside the domestic realm defined by sewing. Her poetic walks begin, Bunyan-like, with dreams of walking. In the early morning or before she goes to sleep, Aurora looks out of her window, seeing beautiful grounds which nonetheless limit her vision. She can only imagine the lane, "sunk so deep" beyond the bounding trees that "no foreign tramp / Nor drover of wild ponies out of Wales / Could guess if lady's hall or tenant's lodge" lies inside the line of woods. Although the negative syntax reinforces their purely speculative existence, these poor or working walkers from outside England proper suggest the possibility the poem will open; that Aurora will walk and work in foreign lands, becoming a tenant instead of a lady. But at the moment, we remain focused on the smaller possibility that she will walk out of her house. "Then, I wakened up," Aurora writes, "More slowly than I verily write now, / But wholly, at last," taking actual walks in a lane she no longer has to imagine:

> It seemed, next, worth while
> To dodge the sharp sword set against my life;
> To slip down stairs through all the sleepy house,
> . . . and escape
> As a soul from the body, out of doors,—
> Glide through the shrubberies, drop into the lane,
> And wander on the hills an hour or two,
> Then back again before the house should stir.

In the following lines, we learn that the only activity that gives Aurora comparable relief from the constraints of domesticity is reading. The juxtaposition alone suggests some equivalence between walking and reading, but Aurora makes it explicit by metaphorizing her reading as walking. She describes her reading as following

> The path my father's foot
> Had trod me out, which suddenly broke off,
> . . . alone I carried on, and set
> My child-heart 'gainst the thorny underwood.

On her path of reading Aurora finds the classics, a hodgepodge of "books bad and good," and finally poetry, in which she recognizes her own potential identity as a poet. Walking then becomes a sign, in both her practice and her metaphors, of writing as well as reading, and so of her vocation, her livelihood, and her art.

But Aurora does not always walk alone. Besides her "unlicensed" morning walks, Aurora also walks, by her aunt's permission, with her cousin Romney, sometimes with his painter friend Vincent Carrington as well. When she is in this company, another potential interpretation of her walking threatens Aurora's construction of herself as pedestrian-poet. Aurora claims that she and Romney walk not as "lovers, nor even friends well-matched; / Say rather, scholars upon different tracks, / And thinkers disagreed." But she cannot completely evade the meaning implied by her disclaimer, the traditional meaning of a woman's rural walks with a man as "courtship," "engagement," even "sexual intercourse." Aurora holds this old country meaning at bay by shaping the natural images gathered on their walks into argument against Romney's social philosophy—a Wordsworthian tactic in full accord with her vision of herself as pedestrian-poet. But the possibility of reading their walking as a courtship which might lead to Aurora's complete domestication challenges Aurora's interpretation of her deliberate, solitary walking as poetic labor.

The poem makes this challenge explicit in Book II. Aurora, taking one of her solitary walks on the morning of her twentieth birthday, crowns herself with ivy "to learn the fell" of the laurel wreath to which she aspires. What this walk means to her, plainly enough, is agency and aspiration, specifically the power to work and succeed at poetry. Unexpectedly, however, Romney joins her, engaging her in a long conversation on art and women's proper roles which rather rapidly resolves into a proposal of marriage—the natural result, to his mind, of walking with Aurora all this time. When Aurora rejects his proposal, her aunt appears to continue the confrontation, demanding that Aurora consider before she gives a final answer. The impasse between them ends with the aunt's death and Aurora's decisive rejection of Romney's financial support (which, to do his character full justice, he offers without expectation of their marriage).

The plot of Book II opposes Aurora's poetic walks, open-ended walks intended to continue into the future, to the courtship walk favored by Romney and her aunt, which would end with marriage, "stopping" Aurora's youthful walking. The supporting imagery sets up this opposition a bit differently, rendering domesticity as clothing, especially long dresses, that hinders walking. Both the narrative description of Aurora's walk and the three-way debate that follows rely on images of women's work (here, quite appropriately, the results of women's work, the sewn "works" themselves) and of walking to realize the difference between protected domesticity and the physical, moral, and economic effort of an independent, potentially artistic life. As Aurora leaves the house, she does not stop "even to snatch my bonnet by the strings, / But, brushing a green tail across the lawn / With my gown in the dew," hurries to her self-coronation as poet. The images convey both the potential for constraint by a tied bonnet and a gown that must be dragged through the wet grass, and Aurora's refusal of that constraint, even a partial reversal as the gown becomes an instrument of path-making. Romney's language, on the other hand, emphasizes the propriety of domesticating clothing. He advises her to keep her aspirations in bounds since "even dreaming" of great or lasting fame "[b]rings headaches, pretty cousin, and defiles / The clean white morning dresses." Rather paradoxically, he identifies poetry as a kind of decorative sewing (different somehow from those white dresses) that accomplishes no

> work for ends, I mean for uses, not
> For such sleek fringes. . .
>   as we sew ourselves
> Upon the velvet of those baldaquins
> Held 'twixt us and the sun.

But the point of both figures is the same: women's work gains its only worth through the very thing that renders it useless, its restriction to the cleanly private sphere. Even when Romney presses her to accept the fortune he meant to give her through her aunt, he seems concerned not so much to give her personal autonomy as to remove any taint of labor or earned money from her work at poetry:

> Dear cousin, give me faith,
> And you shall walk this road with silken shoes,
> As clean as any lady of our house
> Supposed the proudest.

If Aurora must walk and write, then Romney wants to be sure that she remains a lady, kept stainless by the silks of domesticity.

Aurora, of course, rejects Romney's consignment of her life to "ease and whiteness," using the figure of walking as poetry to assert her art as both moral and laborious.

> I would rather take my part
> With God's Dead, who afford to walk in white
> Yet spread His glory, than keep quiet here
> And gather up my feet from even a step
> For fear to soil my gown in so much dust.
> I choose to walk at all risks.

As the language of this passage suggests, Aurora's formulations most often connect walking with the transcendent spiritual mission of poetry. Romney's best social reforms mean nothing, she asserts, "Unless the artist keep up open roads / Betwixt the seen and the unseen." Nonetheless, Aurora's exchanges with Romney also make it plain that her work must be public, worldly, and paid work. Her figure of the road-opening artist comes just after Aurora argues that her poetic vocation constitutes "Most serious work, most necessary work / As any of the economists';" a little later, she comments pointedly on Romney's implied offer to "pay [her] with a current coin / Which men give women," the domestic coin which precisely is *not* coin and, to Aurora, has no value.

Interestingly, it is Aurora's aunt who engages in direct discussion of the relations among money, marriage, and poetry. Interestingly, too, when she hears that Aurora has turned Romney down, the aunt first accuses her niece of too great a reliance on her status as a leisured lady, and figures that reliance as greed for fancy work. "Are they queens, these girls?" she asks, complaining that "They must have mantles, stitched with twenty silks" laid before them by their suitors "before they'll step / One footstep for the noblest lover born." Aurora, asserting her own interpretation of walking against this image of walking as an approach to domesticity, responds, "But I am born . . . / To walk another way than his." Her aunt turns the metaphor again, telling Aurora that "A babe at thirteen months / Will walk as well as you," and then asking if Aurora thinks herself "rich and free to choose a way to walk." Despite her own desire to read Aurora's walking as courtship, as an avenue to respectably unpaid domesticity, the aunt here explicitly sets out the economic dimension of the figure, raising the specter of public, paid work: Aurora's walking potentially means an out-of-doors economic independence.

Ellen Moers and Helena Mitchie both have commented on the function of walking for women in nineteenth-century fiction, and specifically in *Aurora Leigh*, as an assertion of self, a physical effort that provides an outlet for otherwise repressed physicality and may signal the woman's struggle for personal independence. Mitchie classes walking as the most common "pastime" of leisure-class heroines, but also notices the possible interpretation of walking as domestic work, work leading toward the desirable domesticity of marriage: "Aimless as the heroine's walking sometimes appears to be, it beats out a path toward marriage and physical fulfillment; it is an important effort on the part of the heroines to influence the direction of the novel and of their lives." Clearly, however, Book II of *Aurora Leigh* asserts an alternative reading of walking. Barrett Browning's construction of Aurora's walking follows the conventions of Wordsworthian peripatetic: walking coincides with the writing of poetry; both walking and writing are figured as labor, materially and economically productive; and both traditionally are identified with the masculine.

William Wordsworth derives peripatetic from classical georgic, replacing Virgil's virtuous farmer with a moralizing pedestrian. One may think here of the many Wordsworth poems in which pedestrian narrators and characters link poetry, material economies, and moral renovation. "The Old Cumberland Beggar," "Michael," "The Brothers," "When to the attractions of the busy world"—the list is quite long and includes both Wordsworth's earliest publications and his two book-length poems. While these poems vary in their emphasis on particular aspects of peripatetic's rhetorical equations, they participate in a common strategy. Juxtaposing agriculture with walking, and then representing walking's greater effectiveness as a cultivating agent, Wordsworth transfers the multiply-cultivating powers of Virgil's farmer to the Wordsworthian pedestrian-poet. Aurora's beliefs about poetry's power to effect reform correspond to peripatetic's expectation that the labors of the pedestrian-poet will mediate cultural conflicts, reconciling old and new, rural and urban, public and private, poor and rich. As the rhetoric of *The Excursion* claims far-reaching effects for the Wanderer's discourse, so *Aurora Leigh* asserts the potentially culture-wide effect of Aurora's poetry.

As one might suspect from this brief overview, Wordsworth's pedestrian-poet, like Virgil's farmer, is male. Certainly there are women walkers in Wordsworth's peripatetics. They often appear as members of the discursive community necessary to produce poetry, and are sometimes represented as uttering the raw materials of its composition. Joanna's laughter echoes among the mountains and, recalled by her companion, impels his inscription of the rock and his composition of "To Joanna"; "The Solitary Reaper," singing as she walks the field, becomes the subject of the passing poet. Significantly, however, these women walkers' utterances are usually wordless, and are always re-narrated to us by a male pedestrian-poet. Even when the woman of "There is an Eminence" names a mountain after her poet-companion, the reader reads it in the poet's first-person voice:

> . . . She who dwells with me, whom I have loved
> With such communion, that no place on earth
> Can ever be a solitude to me,
> Hath to this lonely Summit given my Name.

Although the woman names, she does not narrate or make poetry. In the rhetorical constructions of these closing lines, the impetus for her naming becomes the male poet's active love of her, which creates a permanent sense of community for *him*. He then narrates the act of naming into a first-person poetic event, the attachment of "my Name" to the Eminence (these disturbingly egoistic capitals are Wordsworth's). Interestingly, Wordsworth's revisions of the last line further submerge the woman's power of speech: in the earliest published version of this poem, the last line reads "Hath said, this lonesome Peak shall bear my Name."

Significantly, too, Wordsworth's women walkers rarely participate in any public, materially productive activity. Most, like the "dearest Maiden" of "Nutting," or Emma of *Home at Grasmere*, remain inarticulate companions in the metaphorical cultivations of walking, never shown "laboring" at anything but walking, their economic condition simply not an issue. One of the few exceptions is "The Solitary Reaper," whom we see "at her work, / And o'er the sickle bending," and whom we may infer earns a livelihood. But this inference is possible precisely because the poem is completely silent about the Reaper's material well-being. Instead, the male pedestrian-narrator draws our attention to her wordless, exoticized song, and to his own emotional use of the music. In Book I of the *Excursion*, Margaret works in her garden and spins flax, and the poem associates both productive labors with path-making. But her cultivation fails, the garden falling into ruin, and her poverty steadily increases, her flax spinning insufficient to keep her from illness and death. In fact, the poem frames Margaret's most extensive walking, her accustomed wanderings in the fields near the cottage, as simultaneous sign and cause of her growing neglect of her garden (and her child, who is left to cry inside the cottage while she walks). For Margaret, as for Wordsworth's various female vagrants, walking functions not as productive cultivating labor, but as a sign of economic and moral failure. With the possible exception of the Reaper, then, Wordsworth's women walkers may strive, but do not succeed, at material labor and economic self-sufficiency.

Since genre always carries all its interpretative baggage, there is a level at which Barrett Browning's use of peripatetic implicitly reinforces the differences between male and female work, hardening the distinction between walking and sewing, between public, paid work (or "works") and domestic labor. But *Aurora Leigh*'s representation of a woman pedestrian-poet, its crucial placement of her as narrator, and its recurrence to the possibility of her walking being materially and economically productive, necessarily shifts and opens peripatetic, using peripatetic conventions to unsettle the gender distinctions the mode implicitly supports.

Although the poem's use of peripatetic is concentrated in its first three books, the figure of Aurora as the Wanderer's successor persists in plot and imagery. Aurora first figures her travels in Europe as a walking tour, wondering whether selling her manuscript "Would fetch enough to buy me shoes, to go / A-foot." Both her search for Marian in London and her chance meetings with her in Paris are accomplished on foot (and have the character of arduous walking as well). And despite the disappearance of walking images from the poem's conclusion, a typically Wordsworthian scene of Aurora walking and "musing," "imagining / Such utterance" from the faces of poor Florentian women, occurs as late as the end of Book VII.

More importantly, Aurora does not merely emulate Wordsworth's pedestrian-poets, but succeeds both at poetry and at economic self-sufficiency. From the beginning of Book III, with scarcely any lapse in reader's time between her peripatetic resolutions and the beginning of their fulfillment, we learn that Aurora's poetic achievements have gained admirers and critics. While she generally sets aside others' praise for the products of her writing, driving herself on toward her own standards, she nonetheless claims success through the process itself:

> *I* prosper, if I gain a step, although
> A nail then pierced my foot: although my brain
> Embracing any truth, froze paralysed,
> *I* prosper. I but change my instrument;
> I break the spade off, digging deep for gold,
> and catch the mattock up.

Typically, Aurora speaks of spiritual matters: she defines the "I" of this passage as "the conscious and eternal soul" rather than "the doublet of the flesh." But, also typically, she figures these spiritual gains in terms of labor and economic value—prospering, digging, gold. Indeed she does not cast off the doublet of flesh, the material metaphor, in her rhetoric of poetic gain. When we read the next words, "I worked on," we are well aware of their reference to the self-cultivation of poetic labor. But we are also well-prepared to follow their other implications into the succeeding passage, in which Aurora describes earning money by writing prose: "being but poor, I was constrained, for life, / To work with one hand for the booksellers, / While working with the other for myself / And art." Although inheritances from her aunt and her father (his books, which she sells to get to Europe) give Aurora some support, she works for pay in the public (literally published) world in order to survive. How well she does this may perhaps be measured by her ability to take Marian in when she finds her in Europe: although Italy may not have been as expensive as England, Aurora nonetheless becomes the sole support of a family of three.

By now it is no doubt obvious that the apparent opposition between walking and sewing in *Aurora Leigh* must be complicated by a field of more positive relations. Aurora's linked poetic and material achievements are, by definition, "women's work," and yet are public, cultivating, artistic, self-sustaining. If women's work makes poetry, then poetry may be sewn—or, to play the peripatetic rubric back into georgic, to sew is to sow. And if sewing itself reads as material and economic production, if even domestic sewing is figured as wage-labor, then sewing becomes "work" in every sense of the word, a construction fully capable of supporting these rhetorical links to walking and writing.

If, without recognizing peripatetic, one only reads classical georgic in *Aurora Leigh*, a part of this revaluation is still possible. In English georgics of the late eighteenth century, sewing is one of the figures through which women may (briefly) enter the otherwise decidedly male preserve of cultivation. One important example is the passage in Book IV of William Cowper's *The Task*, which begins satirically but rapidly settles down to a serious celebration of laborious, secluded, middle-class rural life. This book, "The Winter Evening," extols the virtues of a family gathered to "Fireside enjoyments, homeborn happiness, / And all the comforts that the lowly roof / Of undisturbed retirement, and the hours / Of long uninterrupted evening know." First among these is the women's work at hand:

> here the needle plies its busy task,
> The pattern grows, the well-depicted flower,
> Wrought patiently into the snowy lawn,
> Unfolds its bosom; buds, and leaves, and sprigs,
> And curling tendrils, gracefully disposed,
> Follow the nimble finger of the fair;
> A wreath that cannot fade, of flowers that blow
> With most success when all besides decay.

Here is a woman's form of cultivation, embroidery yielding a kind of permanent decorative harvest, and rhetorically identified with "the task," that is, both the general task of cultivation by the private rural farmer lauded by Cowper and Cowper's own poetry-writing, as signaled by the title of his poem. The difficulties of carrying this identification to the point that *Aurora*

Leigh does, however, are manifest. Not only is the women's work merely imitative of actual cultivation (and then only of the growing of feminized flowers), but it is confined to the presumably leisurely evening hours of "enjoyments," "comforts," and "retirement."

Susanna Blamire makes similar identifications, and practices similar containments, in her "Stoklewath; or, The Cumbrian Village," which valorizes the life of rural villagers. It is only when "The morning toils are . . . completely o'er" that "The daughter at the needle plies the seam," while her mother goes to check the "long webs" of bleaching linen spread by the stream. Blamire's brief portrait of two old women at their spinning wheels, mourning the loss of old values, figures revolutions industrial and political as the end of spinning, weaving, and home-sewing: "the world's turned upside down," Margaret says, "And every servant wears a cotton gown, / Bit flimsy things, that have no strength to wear." Although the moment is humorous, it seriously identifies women's work with the conservation of culture, and sets out spinning as discursive. But once again, although these women are engaged in productive work, work actually associated with factory labor in their talk, Blamire prefaces the section in which their portrait appears with the comment that "From noon till morn rests female toil." It seems astonishing that Blamire excludes sewing, spinning, and textile manufacture from the realm of "toil," but she clearly does, and that exclusion makes it impossible to make a full identification between women's work and men's cultivation.

In both georgics, typically, the ideological lines between women's work and men's, and between the domestic enclosure and the more public world of farming, hold firm. In *Aurora Leigh*, Aurora deliberately undertakes work that is traditionally male, and succeeds at it. More importantly, however, the early books of *Aurora Leigh* change not only the gender of the worker, but the gendering of the work. Barrett Browning's use of peripatetic alludes to the possibility of reconstructing "sewing," as Wordsworth does "walking" (a similarly improbable move, given earlier ideas about walking), as genuine georgic labor, redrawing women's work as true cultivation. In her crossing of the vegetative imagery common to georgic and peripatetic with sewing imagery, and in Marian Erle's tale, Barrett Browning seems bent on just such a reconstruction.

In georgic and peripatetic, the details of vegetative images signify the nuances of cultivation's success. Lush vegetation, plants let go to seed, weeds overrunning gardens, orderly gardens—these kinds of images characterize the cultivator's work and so, in the extended meaning of cultivation, indicate the quality and success of poetic work. Assisted by the sheer pressure of her constant references to sewing, Barrett Browning reconfigures this conventional signification to implicate sewing in a three-way conflation. The prime locus of vegetable images is Aurora herself, the poet constantly figured as plants ranging from seaweed to roses. In Book II, the ivy wreath she chooses to signify her dedication to poetry seems opposed to the rose, the emblem Romney uses to emphasize her sexual / generative blooming and potential for married love. Both images, however, carry traces of sewing with them. The ivy's "serrated" leaves and long vines suggest the scissors and needles and threads of sewing; Aurora wreaths and twists the vines around a comb to form a crown. Although the poem emphasizes the scarlet color and budding or mutlifoliate forms of the rose, the thorns are always there too, mimicking the pricking needles of the seamstress. Similar vegetative images connect Aurora and Marian. Appearing as a rose, a nettle (again a pricking plant), a buttercup, an arranger of lilies, Marian the seamstress bears a figurative resemblance to Aurora the poet, providing another extended juxtaposition of walking and poetry with sewing. Implications of women's work, together with Aurora's success as poet, not only shift our sense of these vegetative images in the early books, but potentially undermine Book IX's almost frantic recurrence to rose imagery in its claims for marital love.

Similarly, the occasional appearance of sewing or clothing as the agents or accourtrements of the poet makes it impossible to distinguish completely between the inadequate, restricted work of women and the desirable, cultivating, masculine labors to which Aurora aspires. Just before Aurora figures her reading as following her father's path, for instance, she speaks of the "large / Man's doublet" of his learning, in which he wraps his girl-child, "careless did it fit or no." We twice hear that Kate Ward regards Aurora's cloak as the emblem of her poetic prowess. In Book III she asks Aurora for the pattern of the cloak, and in Book VII Vincent Carrington reports that Kate insisted on wearing a cloak like Aurora's for her portrait, suggesting that Kate sews or has sewn the copy she wears for the sitting. And the women around Leigh Hall give Romney a copy of Aurora's poems "bound in scarlet silk, / Tooled edges, blazoned with the arms of Leigh." Certain figures of this sort imply the inferiority of sewn poetry. Dubious poets may string rhymes "As children, cowslips;" a "smell of thyme about my feet" means true admittance to the company of poets, while "the rustling of [their] vesture" happens in a dream of such community. To some extent, however, the presence of adjacent vegetative imagery reinflects the implication by alluding to georgic.

The "green room" passage of Book I demonstrates the importance of peripatetic and its walking images to *Aurora Leigh*'s conflation of vegetation, with its implication of poetic harvests, and sewing. This passage is the second of two textual bridges between Aurora's description of her domestic education and her first dreams of walking out alone. The first is a description of Romney's early relations with her, including her aunt's encouragement: "At whiles she let him shut my music up / And push my needles down" to walk out with him. But this kind of walking leaves the gap between men's and women's worlds as broad as before: when Romney ventures to touch Aurora, "dropp[ing] a sudden hand upon my head / Bent down on woman's work," she shies away from his protective male affection. How she finds her way out is through a rhetorical transformation of woman's work into man's, sewing into sowing, and then into walking.

> I had a little chamber in the house,
> As green as any privet-hedge . . .
> > the walls
> Were green, the carpet was pure green, the straight
> Small bed was curtained greenly, and the folds
> Hung green about the window which let in
> The out-door world with all its greenery.
> You could not push your head out and escape
> A dash of dawn dew from the honeysuckle
> But so you were baptized into the grace
> And privilege of seeing . . .

The green fabrics of Aurora's domestic space, the carpet, bed hangings, and curtains, become continuous with the green plants of the outdoor world, the province of the male pedestrian-poet. By pushing through the green-hung window and on through the second green curtain, the honeysuckle, the inmate baptizes herself into poetic vision—and sees, just before the passages about the "deep lane" quoted earlier, a mass of vegetation, a lime, broad lawns, shrubs, acacias, elms, arbutus, laurel. This vegetable curtain keeps her from seeing the lane; she actually will see the path only by actually walking. But Aurora's movement into poetry hinges on a conflation of sewn fabrics and cultivated vegetation that gives her access to walked paths.

    This reconfiguration of imagery closely resembles Wordsworth's rhetorical strategies: juxtapose and conflate the metaphorical terms, and then replace one with the other. The problem seems to be in the last move. That is, to reconstruct sewing as true georgic labor, sewing should replace cultivation, or walking, or both, and this does not happen in Aurora's story. In Marian Erle's story, however, sewing functions as a salvation from walking.

    Aurora twice retells part of Marian's life story. In both cases, the stories are framed like Wordsworthian peripatetic: the narrator seeks or encounters another person while walking, recalls or hears that person's story, and then retells it to the reader. Wordsworth generally asserts a symbiotic relationship between narrator and character as necessary to the production of poetry. For instance, "while" the narrator of *The Excursion* walks to the ruined cottage to meet the Wanderer, he recalls how he reencountered his old friend on the road, recollects the time they spent walking together when the narrator was a child, tells the story of the Wanderer's life; arriving at the cottage, he hears (and recounts to us) the story of the cottage, which the Wanderer learned in his repeated visits (on foot, of course) as a peddler. The narrator explains his desire to tell us these stories as a desire to "record in verse" the Wanderer's "eloquent speech" and high moral views. The Wanderer, he claims, is one of the "Poets sown / By Nature" who lacks only "the accomplishment of verse" to be recognized as a poet in the world's eyes. Poetry results, then, from the joint efforts of the two walkers, the natural philosopher and the versifier.

With respect to this collaboration, Marian more nearly resembles Wordsworth's leech-gatherer or his old Cumberland beggar, walking characters who less consciously articulate moral lessons, than his magisterial Wanderer. But like the narrator of *The Excursion*, Aurora must perform laborious, searching walks through the poor quarters of London and the streets of Paris to find Marian before she can tell her story. In the latter case, once Aurora finds Marian, first one and then the other must serve as guide to the place where the story will be told, leading and following as if they walked "by a narrow plank / Across devouring waters, step by step." And like the narrators of Wordsworthian peripatetics in general, Aurora draws attention to the collaborative requirements of poetry and to her own "poeticizing" of Marian's moral content:

> She told me all her story out,
> Which I'll retell with fuller utterance,
> As coloured and confirmed in after times
> By others and herself too . . .
> I tell her story and grow passionate.
> She, Marian, did not tell it so, but used
> Meek words that made no wonder of herself
> For being so sad a creature.

Equally striking, despite some obvious differences, are the similarities of Marian's childhood to the Wanderer's childhood. Like the Wanderer, Marian is born to parents who earn a marginal existence with agricultural labor, and whose livelihood requires walking—in Marian's case, constant tramping in search of "random jobs / Despised by steadier workmen." Like the Wanderer's, too, Marian's outdoor life, although materially impoverished, provides moral instruction reached by walking. Having learned very early to "walk alone,"

> This babe would steal off from the mother's chair,
> And, creeping through the golden walls of gorse,
> Would find some keyhole toward the secrecy
> Of Heaven's high blue . . .
> This skyey father and mother both in one,
> Instructed her and civilised her more
> Than even Sunday-school did afterward

This is, of course, pure Wordsworth, as is the quick contrary validation of Marian's book-learning. Significantly, her experience of books outside of the ineffectual Sunday-school comes to her through manifestly Wordsworthian peddlers whom she meets on the road:

>   Often too
> The pedlar stopped, and tapped her on the head
> . . . .
> And asked if peradventure she could read:
> And when she answered "ay," would toss her down
> Some stray odd volume from his heavy pack,
> A Thomson's Seasons, mulcted of the Spring,
> Or half a play of Shakespeare's torn across
> . . . .
> Or else a sheaf of leaves (for that small Ruth's
> Small gleanings) torn out from the heart of books,
> From Churchyard Elegies and Edens Lost,
> From Burns, and Bunyan, Selkirk, and Tom Jones

The conflation of book-leaves with plant leaves, again straight out of *The Excursion*, turns tramping Marian into a harvester, a participant in cultivation and (note the particular texts named) in poetry. Nor does she merely accept what she is given, but selects and recomposes it, becoming an active cultivator: "she weeded out / Her book-leaves, threw away the leaves that hurt . . . And made a nosegay of the sweet and good."

At this point Marian's story functions like pure peripatetic. Even her despicable parents, so unlike the Wanderer's upright, settled family, feel the expected moral influence of walking in rural lands:

> though perhaps these strollers still strolled back,
> As sheep do, simply that they knew the way,
> They certainly felt bettered unaware
> Emerging from the social smut of towns
> To wipe their feet clean on the mountain turf.

But in the end Marian's walking leads not to greater moral wisdom, nor to the Wanderer's economic self-sufficiency, but to continued dependence and endangered virtue. Marian proves useless at most odd jobs, and walking cannot remedy that insufficiency. "In this tramping life," Aurora tells us, "Was nothing to be done with such a child / But tramp and tramp." This materially unproductive circuit irks her abusive parents, and eventually Marian's mother tries to sell her to a man, driving Marian to flight and illness.

That Marian's walking should lead toward a possible loss of virtue matches the traditional association of women's walking and sexual straying, an association not significantly altered by the masculinist constructions of peripatetic. What saves Marian, the figure that replaces walking as generator of moral and economic value, will not now surprise us: it is, of course, sewing. Though Aurora ironically revoices the parents' view that nothing can be done with Marian but to "tramp and tramp," the next lines show Marian's way out:

> And yet she knitted hose
> Not ill, and was not dull at needlework;
> And all the country people gave her pence
> For darning stockings past their natural age,
> And patching petticoats from old to new,
> And other light work done for thrifty wives.

When Marian, after running away from her pandering mother, recovers from her illness in the London hospital, her new patron Romney places her in "a famous sempstress-house / Far off in London, there to work and hope." Again, in Book VII, we learn that after Marian's rape, wandering, and brief unhappy work as servant to an adulteress, finds a place with "a mistress-sempstress who was kind /And let me sew in peace among her girls," thus earning enough to support herself and her son.

Sewing promises not just material but moral sustenance. When Romney provides for Marian to enter the seamstress's house, he does so not only for her livelihood but "to snatch her soul from atheism, / And keep it stainless from her mother's face." Similarly, Marian's return to sewing after her rape saves her from the repugnant alternatives that always threaten penniless, ruined women in Victorian stories, prostitution and loveless marriage. Most significantly of all, it is while Marian sews, not while she walks, that she recollects the poetry passed on to her by Wordsworthian peddlers:

> [Marian] told me she was fortunate and calm
> On such and such a season, sat and sewed,
> With no one to break up her crystal thoughts:
> While rhymes from lovely poems span around
> Their ringing circles of ecstatic tune

Although Aurora here emphasizes her difference from Marian, noting her shame at Marian's superior cheerfulness, they share the experience of sewing as the labor enabling poetry. After she has realized her vocation, hiding the "quickening inner life" fostered by walking and reading, Aurora bends to her sewing:

> Then I sat and teased
> The patient needle till it split the thread,
> Which oozed off from it in meandering lace
> From hour to hour. I was not, therefore, sad;
> My soul was singing at a work apart

For Aurora, as for Marian, poetry sings in the silence of her sewing; the book-leaves gleaned from peripatetic wanderings are revoiced in her stitching.

Barrett Browning's reconstruction of sewing as georgic labor, worked through peripatetic, seems complete. In Marian's story, sewing replaces walking as a superior agent of cultivation. But once this reconstruction is accomplished in the middle of Book IV, sewing gradually disappears from *Aurora Leigh*. Despite the reiteration in Marian's second narrative of the pattern of a wanderer redeemed by sewing, sewing never again appears as a present activity in the plot. Imagine, if you will, an *Excursion* in which the walking tour ends with Book I, or perhaps with the single reiteration of a journey to the Solitary's hut in Book III, and in which walking is rarely alluded to again. Imagine, more to the point, an *Excursion* which ends without the promise extracted from the Solitary "That he would share the pleasures and pursuits / Of yet another summer's day, not loth / To wander with us through the fertile vales, / And o'er the mountain-wastes." Despite the endless discourse on other matters in Wordsworth's poem, walking remains the fount of the discourse, the structuring principle of the plot, the foundation of that last appeal to Wordsworthian community. Not so with sewing in *Aurora Leigh*. The possibility of reading sewing as true cultivation, of rewriting women's work as a possible source and vehicle of poetry, gradually fades from the poem.

One might feel, although I do not, that there are problems with a "sewing plot" not presented by a "walking plot." But even if Barrett Browning chose not to write the final books as, for instance, confabulations in a seamstress's shop, or conversations conducted as Aurora and Marian weave or hem, sewing imagery might carry the weight of reconstructed genre. Here again, however, the poem does not bear out its early suggestions. Of about 125 instances of sewing imagery in *Aurora Leigh* as a whole, roughly two-thirds—about 85—of those instances occur in the first four books; in the last two books, there are only twelve instances of sewing imagery, none of them illustrating the famous exchange of love and work Romney proposes in Book IX.

Certainly I am not suggesting that Barrett Browning "should" have written *Aurora Leigh* differently, in accordance with late twentieth-century notions of gender and gendered labor. But imagining the alternatives helps reveal the implications of her choices, as we strive to understand the poem's ideas about women, work and poetry. The elaborate set-up for the generic exchange effected by Marian's story, and the compelling construction of the story itself, suggest Barrett Browning's thorough comprehension of the possibilities opened by that exchange. Nearly everything that follows, on the other hand, refuses those possibilities—almost immediately, in fact. The famous opening of Book V, the defense of domestic epic, has long been lauded as one of the finest parts of the poem, and so it is. But this same section also revises the wheel of Virgil, the progress of genres, in a telling way: Aurora moves from pastoral directly to epic, omitting the "middle way" of georgic. Swept along by the fiery beauty of Aurora's manifesto, we scarcely notice that this omission retroactively excludes the moral lesson of Marian's story, in which sewing relies upon its relation to peripatetic and georgic for the valorization of labor and natural religion.

It is easier to find this dislocation at the end of the poem. In books 8 and 9, Barrett Browning almost completely drops her references to the laborious material agencies of walking and sewing in favor of an abstract discourse on love, which now is made to transcend labor. The final quotation of Revelation underscores the interpretative difficulty. The lines directly foreshadowing that quotation are spoken by Marian at the beginning of her second narrative, as she chides Aurora for righteous ignorance:

> You're great and pure; but were you purer still,—
> As if you had walked, we'll say, no otherwhere

> Than up and down the New Jerusalem,
> And held your trailing lutestring up yourself
> From brushing the twelve stones, for fear of some
> Small speck as little as a needle-prick,
> White stitched on white,—the child would keep to *me*

In this formulation, Aurora walks in the New Jerusalem, carrying an instrument of poetry analogous to the threads of sewing, her purity signified by the invisibility of pricked, stitched "faults." As usual, the connotations are complexly mixed. But the juxtaposition of walking, poetry, and sewing is entirely consistent with Marian's reiterated reliance on sewing as saving labor. In the poem's final lines, on the other hand, only the stones and the Biblical text remain.

Satisfying though the poem's last books may be in other ways, their appeal to divine and transcendent human love simply passes over the questions of gendered labor set out in its beginning, leaving us with what I have come to regard as unresolvable textual ambivalence. I want to privilege what I believe are the hard boundaries of cultural usage, to claim that rhetorical and generic definitions of women's work ultimately prove intractable, holding Barrett Browning to her own version of the old laws: if women walk, they must not walk alone; and men don't sew at all. But I cannot honestly say that the readings I have done here permit such comfort. Rather than settling into any of our proposed positions, feminist or patriarchal, *Aurora Leigh*'s representations of the relations among women, work and writing refuse complete resolution. In this irresolution, then, combined with our own preoccupations, lies one part of our current fascination with Barrett Browning's poem.

FREDERICK WEGENER

Elizabeth Barrett Browning, Italian Independence, and the "Critical Reaction" of Henry James

Few writers as prominent in their own lifetimes fell afterwards into neglect more completely, or have had to wait longer for renewed intelligent attention, than Elizabeth Barrett Browning. A critical climate more and more impatient with inherited social and sexual antinomies has proved unusually favorable to a poet whose work appears to exemplify the fusion of private with public concerns. As one might have guessed, the ongoing restoration of Barrett Browning has focused much of its energies on the political content of her verse, explaining her devotion to the Italian Risorgimento as an enactment, in part, of her own struggle for psychological and artistic wholeness and coherence. What might be called an effort to find the political in the personal aspects of Barrett Browning's career, and the personal in the political, has looked to *Aurora Leigh*, no less than to the more overtly political verse of *Casa Guidi Windows*, *Poems before Congress*, and *Last Poems*, for illustrations of such an underlying interrelationship. In this new, or at least recent, revisionist critical narrative, Henry James is frequently recruited as Barrett Browning's most influential antagonist, largely on the strength of one lengthy passage from an obscure later work in which he discusses her political engagement and speculates about its artistic implications or consequences, as he sees them, in the poet's work. Even the most persuasive attempts to discredit James's skepticism have hardly done justice, however, to the nuances of this rich and vexing passage. Reconsidered

From *Studies in English Literature, 1500–1900* 37, no. 4, (1997) © 1997 Studies in English Literature, 1500–1900.

in its entirety, and in the context of his other statements both on her work and on the Risorgimento, James's response—a surprising encounter between a novelist never very comfortable talking about poetry and a poet who might not have been expected to interest him at all—offers an instructive episode in the clash of critical ideologies, and a salutary reminder of the hazards of negotiating the relations between poetics and politics.

James's assessment of Barrett Browning occurs at a pivotal and dramatic moment in one of the neglected curiosities of his later period, *William Wetmore Story and His Friends* (1903), a biography of the undistinguished American sculptor who became the Brownings' closest friend in Italy. Early in its second volume, James observes, with reference to the tumultuous events of 1859–60, "These, it is needless to say, were months of deep anxiety and suspense for lovers of Italy," a time when "the 'cause' and its issues hung, as never before, in the balance." Conceding the profound effect of these uncertainties on a sensibility like Barrett Browning's, James concludes nonetheless that "it is impossible not to feel, as we read, that to 'care,' in the common phrase, as she is caring is to entertain one's convictions as a malady and a doom. Her state of mind on the public question, as her letters present it almost from the first of her residence in Italy, is an interesting, an almost unique *case*, which forces upon us more than one question; so that we wonder why so much disinterested passion . . . should not leave us in a less disturbed degree the benefit of all the moral beauty." What makes Barrett Browning's devotion to the Italian cause so dubious, in James's eyes, is its disabling and somewhat repellent fanaticism. Combining suggestions of the organic ("a malady") and the oracular ("a doom"), and reimagined from a distance of more than forty years as a characteristically Jamesian "case," her situation in Italy becomes material almost for a turn-of-the-century Viennese study in hysteria:

> We wonder at the anomaly, wonder why we are even perhaps slightly irritated, and end by asking ourselves if it be not because her admirable mind, otherwise splendidly exhibited, has inclined us to look in her for that saving and sacred sense of proportion, of the free and blessed *general*, that great poets, that genius and the high range of genius, give us the impression of even in emotion and passion, even in pleading a cause and calling on the gods. Mrs. Browning's sense of the general had all run, where the loosening of the Italian knot, the character of Napoleon III, the magnanimity of France and the abjection of England were involved, to the strained and the strenuous—a possession, by the subject, riding her to death, that almost prompts us at times to ask wherein it so greatly concerned her.

More than merely a set of political beliefs, Barrett Browning's adherence to the Risorgimento—ironically reminiscent, in this passage, of her other famous "possession," spiritualism—is presented by James as almost a demonic, lethally destructive force that might better have been exorcised for its victim's sake. Treating it as an inflammable (and more than faintly embarrassing) neurotic condition, James's remarks might be said to have inaugurated the critical tendency, only lately challenged, to look at her partisanship not on its own terms but as the symptom of a psychological disturbance originating elsewhere, a displacement onto external matters of certain inner torments, and a response so unbalancing that it hastened the poet's sad decline.

James, in fact, could have derived relatively little evidence of this condition from the papers at his disposal, referring himself at one point to "the few [letters] of Mrs. Browning's that I have before me" and to "my scant handful of brief notes from the latter source." Presumably he would have had in mind the recent 1897 Frederick Kenyon edition of Barrett Browning's correspondence, which substantially publicized her own testimony along these lines for the first time. An extensive earlier selection (her letters to R. H. Horne), reviewed by James in 1877, covered the years immediately preceding her flight to Italy and thus left him with nothing to say about the matters that would concern him at the time he composed his life of Story. Even so, he retrieves in the later work a revealing distinction formulated in his review of her letters to Horne, which exhibit "a very fine moral sensibility" and in which James finds that "Miss Barrett's tone . . . has often a touch of graceful gayety which the reader of her poetry, usually so anti-jocose, would not have expected," much as he will later claim, in assembling his material in the Story biography, "there is scarce a scrap of a letter of Mrs. Browning's in which a nameless intellectual, if it be not rather a moral, grace—a vibration never suggesting 'manner,' as often in her verse—does not make itself felt." Such an effect as this "vibration" seems a good deal milder than the shortcomings that James had cited, rather harshly, elsewhere in his early criticism of her poetry, when he declares that "she is without tact and without taste" and that "her faults of detail are unceasing," adduces "the singularly intimate union of her merits and defects," excoriates "her laxity and impurity of style," and concludes that, while "Mrs. Browning possessed the real poetic heat in a high degree . . . her sense of the poetic form was an absolute muddle." Although focusing on the literary, rather than strictly political, aspects of her career, these remarks from the 1860s and 1870s may be said to culminate in his final statement on Barrett Browning the poet and celebrity, and to underlie his diagnosis of "[h]er state of mind on the public question" in preunification Italy, which accentuated for James the

discrepancy between the "poetic heat" of her work and its muddled "sense of
the poetic form." Despite "their perfect amenity," even her letters, otherwise
favorably contrasted to her verse, suffer in the same way from her
capitulation to the pressures of the Risorgimento, "with the sense, and the
alternations, of all of which Mrs. Browning's correspondence flushes and
turns pale," as ailing and infirm as its overwrought author. Although "[h]er
letters, of this and the previous time . . . reflect her passion, her feverish
obsession, with extraordinary vivacity and eloquence," it is on such a basis
that James proceeds to articulate reservations embracing her poetry as well.
For him, these qualities of Barrett Browning's writing—whether expressed in
her correspondence or in her verse—are firmly rooted in its willingness to
accommodate the sort of political urgencies that obviously disturb James;
and what he sees as the connection between the two is perhaps best
illuminated by the larger themes of the Story biography, and by James's own
understanding and experience of the world that he evokes in writing his life
of the sculptor.

It was in 1848, only a year after their own arrival, that the Brownings
first met the newly disembarked Story and his wife in Florence, their
friendship thus coinciding almost entirely with the poets' married life
abroad. Much of the time, accordingly, James's profile of the sculptor serves
also as a vivid, historically informed chronicle of the years that the two
couples shared in Italy, and of the various political and military developments
unfolding throughout that phase of their lives. In one example, "The flight
of Pius IX. to Gaeta and the establishment of the Roman Republic,"
following the Storys' first visit to Rome, "had marked the year of
revolutions," he observes, "for though these events belong to February 1849,
it was the high political temperature of the previous months that had made
them possible," while the Storys return to witness the French intervention,
and Giuseppe Garibaldi's defense of Rome, in what James describes as "that
most incoherent birth of the time, the advance of French troops for the
restoration of the Pope, the battle waged against the short-lived 'popular
government' of Rome by the scarce longer-lived popular government of
Paris." By April, encountering "great agitation in the streets," the Storys "see
the Lombard reinforcements enter—Milan having had, before this, its own
short, smothered outbreak . . . The approach of the French, to reinstate the
Pope, becomes a reality; on the 30th General Oudinot and his army [of the
French Alps] were hourly expected" in Rome. From the journals of both
Story and his wife, James reproduces a sequence of excerpts that constitute
an almost continuous record of the deteriorating events of April through
June 1849 (as well as a visit to Giuseppe Mazzini); likewise, the next Italian
war of independence is followed, from May through August 1859, via several

letters in which Story's celebrated friend Charles Sumner repeatedly expresses his support, assuring the sculptor at one point. "I sympathise with you completely in all your aspirations for dear Italy and grieve with you in her discomfitures."

As at least one historian has noted, James's use of such documents succeeds in generating considerable immediacy and drama throughout these portions of the Story biography. Yet his own position on the vicissitudes of Italian history during the Brownings' Italian exile is left characteristically nebulous. Although he acknowledges, for example, Sumner's "good fortune to be in Italy at the time of great events, into which no visitor could have entered with a larger sympathy," the attitude that James himself manages to convey sounds not altogether sympathetic: "That Future in which he had so general a faith—on the whole so easy a confidence—was all in the air and tremendously in the balance" early in 1859. His reference to "the lamentable events of 1849" appears to signal an endorsement of the nationalist forces variously beset and besieged following the Austrian victory at Novara, as does James's observation that the Storys, also early in 1849, attend "a concert 'for the benefit of the Venetians.' Which of us, in Florence, at that time, wouldn't have done anything, with passion, for the benefit of the Venetians?" Acknowledging that "the Papacy was then not, as at present, ostensibly patient, but frankly militant," he characterizes the siege of Rome as "an episode followed by a reaction only too markedly in the sense of colour" both ecclesiastical and military. Later regretting Pius IX's flight from Rome, however, James mentions "the paternal, the patriarchal potentate expelled by too rash a population," while he alludes disapprovingly to the aftereffects of another anti-authoritarian initiative undertaken in the spring of 1849: "Florence had by that time put down her foot on the question of a Constitution. She has her constitution now to her heart's content." By reacquainting him with certain recent phases of Italian history, the task of writing Story's life thus appears to have stimulated in James a residual ambivalence about the Risorgimento, an ambivalence expressed now and then in his early travel essays and letters from Italy, sharpened and magnified by more recent visits, and clearly informing his later remarks on Barrett Browning's "feverish obsession."

Ultimately, therefore, it will take more to make sense of those remarks than merely to argue, with one critic, that "James' judgment was hopelessly biased by his antipathy toward progressivist Italian politics." For one thing, his attitude toward the Risorgimento around the time of his earlier critical statements on Barrett Browning's work is more complex, and far less unambiguously hostile, than his insinuations in the Story biography would lead one to assume. In a travel essay of the late 1870s, for example,

James refers to "the fine fresh Italian rule of today," considers it "from the historic point of view . . . a foolish inconsistency to make one's self unhappy over the entrance of the Italians" in formerly papal Rome, and appears to join those who welcome "the intellectual satisfaction of seeing Rome in Italian hands—the postponement of this event acting upon the mind, to their sense, as a good-sized pebble in one's shoe acts upon the physical consciousness. " Such an irritant had been even more active a few years earlier, when James described the Duc de Luynes as "an uncompromising enemy of Italian unity" who "voted in the French Assembly . . . for the scandalous interference of the Republic in Roman affairs," and who "subscribed largely to equip the Papal army at the time of the resistance to Garibaldi in 1867," while expressing categorically, if rather circuitously, his own convictions on this score: "Nothing is more difficult for the Anglo-Saxon mind, in general, than to find tolerance for the French intolerance of the desire of Italy to regulate her home-conduct as she chooses." In 1876, James concludes a review of one of Augustus J. C. Hare's popular travel books on Italy by taking issue with its author's obstreperous illiberal views:

> We differ . . . from Mr. Hare in the estimation in which we hold Italian unity, and the triumph of what he never alludes to but as the "Sardinian Government." He deplores the departure of the little ducal courts, thinks Italy had no need to be united, and never mentions the new order of things without a sneer. His tone strikes us as very childish. . . It is certainly something that Italy has been made a nation, with a voice in the affairs of Europe (to say nothing of her own, for the first time), and able to offer her admirable people (if they will choose to take it) an opportunity to practice some of those responsible civic virtues which it can do no harm even to the gifted Italians to know something about. But on this subject Mr. Hare is really rabid; in a writer who loves Italy as much as he does, his state of mind is an incongruity.

At least as of the 1870s, it appears, there would have been nothing incongruous, as far as he is concerned, in accepting Italian unification, or inconsistent with any genuine love of Italy—making it rather difficult to maintain, with one critic, "that the Italy of the Unity, the Italy still living and creating its *Risorgimento*, does not really exist for James." Recalling their time together in Italy, Mrs. Humphry Ward listed not only "Roman history and antiquities, Italian Art, Renaissance sculpture," but also "the personalities and events of the Risorgimento" among the "solid *connaissances*" that "were to be recognized perpetually as rich elements in the general wealth of Mr.

James's mind," and that revealed to her "perhaps more fully than ever before the extraordinary range of his knowledge and sympathies." At least one cultural historian finds in much of James's travel writing "exceptionally acute social and cultural commentary on post-*Risorgimento* developments," indicating a far livelier interest in the country's political fortunes than one would gather from the expansive scholarship on the Italianate elements of the novelist's work.

His most substantial expression of this knowledge and awareness occurs in James's rarely cited review, in 1877, of Charles de Mazade's biography of Cavour, whom he applauds as "the liberator of Italy," in the course of synopsizing in some detail "the history of an extraordinarily interesting career" that "was . . . one of the most remarkable and most active in the annals of statesmanship." It might seem revealing that, of all the figures of the Risorgimento, James writes at length only of the one who was "the model of the moderate and conservative liberal," whose "liberalism was untinged by the radical leaven," and who "often said . . . that no republic can give as much liberty, and as real liberty, as a constitutional monarchy that operates regularly." At the same time, however, James suggests that a balanced view of the Risorgimento would have acknowledged the equally important role of its more extreme proponents. For example, he observes critically that de Mazade, "keeping in view his hero's conservative side . . . relates in considerable detail the story of the liberation of Italy, with no allusion to Mazzini beyond speaking of him two or three times as a vulgar and truculent conspirator, and with a regrettable tendency to stint the mixture of praise to the erratic but certainly, during a most important period, efficient Garibaldi." He notes, moreover, Cavour's resourcefulness in being "confronted with the constant necessity of presenting an unflinching front to Austria," along with "the necessity, equally imperious, of checking reactionary excesses in Parma and Modena, Bologna and Tuscany," and "of remaining free, especially, from the reproach of meddling with the papacy— an enterprise for which the occasion was not ripe." A riper occasion, he implies, would soon arise, as James goes on to praise not only the results of Cavour's "mingled ardor and tact . . . his tension of purpose, and yet his self-restraint, his inveterate skill in turning events to his advantage," but also "the element of discretion, the art of sailing with the current of events, that enabled him to effect a great revolution by means that were, after all, in relation to the end in view, not violent—by measures that were never reckless, high-handed or of a character to force from circumstances more than they could naturally yield." Finally, and most striking in the light of his later comments in the life of Story, it is "Cavour's relations with Napoleon III," that James considers "the best example of his disposition to use the best instruments and opportunities that offered themselves, and not quarrel with them because they were not ideally perfect." He notes derisively that "the Italian 'patriots' of the mere romantic type could never forgive" the fact "that Italy should appeal for liberation to the oppressor of France," before concluding that "[t]he emperor's sympathy with Italian independence is certainly the most interesting and honorable feature in his career."

At a point in time so much closer to the triumph of the Risorgimento than the Story biography, James's sentiments thus seem, if temperate by comparison, not all that far, ultimately, from those of Barrett Browning: her own view of Napoleon III, however excessive and idolatrous, would have made her, in the novelist's terms, a patriot of more than "the mere romantic type." Even so, his review of de Mazade's biography already establishes the basis on which she will later be distinguished in the novelist's eyes from a figure like Cavour. Compared to Mazzini and Garibaldi, the statesman demonstrates for James "something very striking in such religious devotion to an idea when it is unaccompanied with fanaticism or narrowness of view, and tempered with good sense and wit and the art of taking things easily"; and it is precisely this nuance that survives in his life of Story as James discusses the aftermath, in 1848–49, of the preceding Italian war of independence. "Mrs. Browning thirsted for great events," he observes, "but the Storys were less strenuous and took things as they came," while it is on such questions as "the character of Napoleon III" and "the magnanimity of France"—questions on which the clearer-eyed Cavour took presumably a surer and more accurate view—that "Mrs. Browning's sense of the general had all run . . . to the strained and the strenuous," in "a possession . . . riding her to death." If an inability to take things easily, or 'as they came," is regarded as the mark of a futile immoderate radicalism, few champions of Italian unification would appear to have taken things harder than Barrett Browning, whose advocacy in itself is not so much the problem, according to James, as its misplaced, crippling obsessiveness and, most of all, its grievous effects on her imaginative life. Claiming to be "uneasy" about his own account of Barrett Browning's political involvements "till we have recognised the ground of our critical reaction" to her "case," James goes on to disclose its foundation, declaring that it is "this ground, exactly, that makes the case an example," a cautionary object lesson of which other poets would do well to take heed. "Monstrous as the observation may sound in its crudity," he does not scruple to suggest, "we absolutely feel the beautiful mind and the high gift discredited by their engrossment" in the agitations of the Risorgimento, given over as they were, in his eyes, to a cause that had become both a psychologically and an aesthetically damaging *idée fixe*. For James, "this is what becomes of distinguished spirits when they fail to keep above"—that is, to maintain, under the pressure of accelerating tensions and events, an appropriately Jamesian aloofness from the chaos of historical circumstance, and the messiness of quotidian social or political contingencies. Under an assumption that had become quite dear to James by the time of the increasingly hermetic, involuted fictions of the major phase, the political and the poetic remain incompatible or mutually exclusive, standing, one might say, in an inverse relation to each other: "The cause of Italy was, obviously, for Mrs. Browning, as high aloft as any object of interest could be; but that was only because she had let down, as it were, her inspiration and her poetic pitch." In James's critical vocabulary, the ascendancy of one is practically facilitated by the slackening or relaxation of the other, with the result that Barrett Browning's "inspiration" and "poetic pitch . . . suffered for it sadly—the permission of which, conscious or unconscious, is on the part of the poet, on the part of the beautiful mind, ever to be judged (by any critic with any sense of the real) as the unpardonable sin."

What is revealing here, of course, is James's reformulation of a moral or religious concept into the cornerstone of an aesthetic ideology according to which Barrett Browning falls short as a programmatically and avowedly political poet. The qualities exhibited by "great poets" of "genius"—what James calls "that saving and sacred sense of proportion, of the free and blessed *general*," implicitly connected to a "sense of the real"— are missing in Barrett Browning, whose *vers engagé* exposes a poetic gift disproportionately "engrossed" in a "cause," profanely and irreclaimably self-confined to the local and particular, and artistically compromised as a result. If only Barrett Browning had followed, he seems to imply, the very different "example" that Story and his wife are made to represent throughout James's life of the sculptor. Remarking that they "were afterwards, doubtless . . . to love their old Rome better, or at least know her better, for having seen her at one of the characteristically acute moments of her long-troubled life," James nonetheless indicates the sort of stance one should assume toward, say, the calamities that greeted the Storys on their return to Rome in 1849: "The flight of the Pontiff, the tocsin and the cannon, the invading army, the wounded and dying, the wild rumours, the flaring nights, the battered walls, were all so much grist to the mill of an artistic, a poetic nature, curious of character, history, aspects." A perspective marked by curiosity rather than passionate involvement is thus defined by James as an intrinsically poetic attribute. And this politically noncommittal, not to say indifferent, posture— although obviously at odds with their own testimony—finds an even more nourishing occasion as the Storys "go to watch the barricade-making at Porta San Giovanni, where they 'vote the workmen too lazy to live.' " But this is doubtless all the better for Story, who, studious of movement and attitude, sits and sketches the scene from a pile of timber 'destined to be used in the defence.' The "defence" here, of course, is that of Rome, which becomes in the Story biography, along with more or less everything else about the Risorgimento, a *scene*, something James's visually alert and sensitive predecessors in Italy watch or gaze upon, with his approval.

It is on this basis that the Storys are tacitly differentiated from the more viscerally affected Barrett Browning; and James's habit of endowing the Storys with some of his own most recognizable inclinations becomes a leading pattern of the biography implicating its protagonists in a pervasive theatricalization of their Italian milieu. "The French siege of 1849," as James initially describes it, "was the first public event at which our special friends were to assist," although the nature of their participation is clarified by the time he next refers to the French advance against the recently created Italian republic: "It was at this battle that foreign visitors 'assisted,' as in an opera-box, from anxious Pincian windows." Returning to Rome in 1849, the Storys arrive "in time to place themselves well, as it were, for the drama, to get seated and settled before it begins," at a moment in Italian history when "the drama filled the stage instead of going on, as we see it, behind the scenes." Later, just before he begins to analyze Barrett Browning's "state of mind on the public question," what James calls the "months of deep anxiety and suspense for lovers of Italy" in 1858–59 are similarly characterized in his remark that "public events had hurried over the stage like the contending armies of Elizabethan plays." Nowhere, however, does his life of the sculptor act upon such an impulse more audaciously than when James pauses in narrating the Storys' flight from Rome:

> This chronicler, at all events desiring to miss no impression, since, evidently, to a sharpened appetite for figures and scenes, there was matter for impression—this chronicler trudges by the old travelling-carriage as it climbs the Umbrian hills, hangs about the inn doors, with the ear-ringed *vetturino*, at Narni and Spoleto, at Incisa and Perugia, and wouldn't, frankly, for such sense as we may get from it to-day, have had a single Austrian officer absent or heard a scabbard the less trail along a stone-paved passage. I even retrace our steps, without scruple, to pick up any loose flower of this blood-spattered Roman spring that may be to our purpose.

A sensibility that would retain, on pictorial grounds, the military presence of a brutal, foreign occupying power in a country other than one's own is bound to seem extraordinarily disengaged, if not rather cold-blooded, alongside the earnestness with which the Storys and Barrett Browning, in James's own account, obviously responded to the same events. Like the manner in which his narrative interweaves the larger events of the day with the mundane social and touristic movements of his protagonists in Florence and Rome, and like its many recreational images of revolution and political crisis (or James's tendency to depict the Risorgimento as a distracting inconvenience from which one turns away in favor of a more hospitable Italy), this compulsion to aestheticize throughout the Story biography runs the risk of placing at a trivializing distance the upheavals that so exercised the imagination of Barrett Browning and her contemporaries.

His disposition to take such a view of their surroundings is consistent, of course, with the cultural significance long attached to the Italian milieu not only by the Storys but also by the many other "precursors," as the earlier generation of American expatriates in Rome and Florence are fondly designated throughout James's life of the sculptor. Even as he documents the attentiveness of the Storys and the Brownings to the political and military events around them, it seems no accident that James should establish certain illuminating parallels and continuities between his own later experience of Italy and theirs. More than once, he interrupts his account of the Storys' arrival in Italy to recall, by way of contrast, his own, which occurred on the eve of yet a more decisive stage of the Risorgimento: "Their felicity in this was greater than the comparatively small one with which, in years to come, after alighting, for the first time, at the same threshold, the writer of these lines, though gratefully enough indeed, had to content himself." Deriving what he calls "matter for retrospective envy from the indications of Story's second Florentine autumn," James admits to "making . . . a positive fetish of the fancy out of the image of that precious little city as it might have been lived in and loved before its modern misfortunes," which result, in his eyes, from the political reforms associated with the Risorgimento. Such an impact on everyday Italian life helps explain the wistfulness with which James, following the daily rounds of the Storys and the Brownings, declares that "the terms on which the Italy of the old order was so amply enjoyable . . . make us feel to-day shut out from a paradise." In his recollections, "the old Rome of the old order" withstood the forces of change and modernity just long enough to have presented the young novelist, in 1869, with "a perpetual many-coloured picture—the vast, rich canvas in which Italian unity was, as we may say, to punch a hole that has never been repaired." Turning a movement for sovereignty and political self-determination into a form of vandalism, James feels more than prepared to add that "[t]he hole to-day in Rome is bigger than almost anything else we see, and the main good fortune of our predecessors in general was just in their unconsciousness of any blank space. The canvas then was crowded, the old-world presence intact."

It is one of the implicit ironies of the Story biography that Barrett Browning, by supporting the forces of independence and republicanism, should have insensibly squandered such a rare opportunity and contributed to the punching of that hole in the canvas of the Rome of "the old order" (what he later calls "the sweeter, softer, easier, idler Rome") for which James nostalgically longs. Although he acknowledges that the cause of Italian nationalism "concerned her of course as it concerned all near witnesses and lovers of justice," perhaps only someone far removed in time and temperament from the events in which Barrett Browning and Italy were engulfed could have the complacency to add, as James does, that "the effect of her insistent voice and fixed eye is to make us somehow feel that justice is, after all, of human things, has something of the convenient looseness of humanity about it." The unyielding stance of someone like Barrett Browning, her tenacious responsiveness to the crises around her, are what offends an imagination like James's, as he explains the basis of "our complaint" about the obstructing and obscuring effects of her zealotry: "the clear stream runs thick; the real superiority pays; we are less edified than we ought to be." Edified, that is, by the insistence and intensity of her commitments, as if we are to find superior and more edifying the loftiness of a consciousness evidently prone to transforming landscapes of bloodshed and misery into sources of continual aesthetic gratification.

Here and there in his own early travel essays on Italy, James is certainly more than aware of the perils, and indeed the impertinence, of any purely aesthetic apprehension of that beleaguered country. And, at the same time, it is perhaps understandable that preunification Italy, after four intervening decades of change and chaos, had come to seem idyllic by the time he completed the Story biography, at the age of sixty and with eleven of his twelve visits to Italy behind him. Yet the complexity of James's response to Barrett Browning, and particularly to her political allegiances (or to their residue in her writing), is perhaps best clarified by a glance at his more substantial and admiring remarks on her husband's poetry. While it is Story's verse that serves in the biography as his chief reference point along these line, James might just as easily be talking of Barrett Browning's when he suggests that in his Italianate poems the sculptor "has conceivably not the proper detachment for full appreciation." Alongside Story's diffuse, unfocused experience of Italy, James places "the history of Robert Browning and his inspiration, suggestive as they both are of a quite opposed moral. Italy, obviously, was never too much for the author of 'Men and Women.' "

By contrast to Story's verse, and implicitly to that of his own wife, Browning's work is presented, here and elsewhere in James's criticism, as a model of how to write poetry of or about Italy, a uniquely authoritative example of how to put one's Italian experience to fruitful imaginative use. "This straight saturation of our author's, this prime assimilation of the elements for which the name of Italy stands," James declares in his Browning centenary lecture on *The Ring and the Book*, "is a single splendid case. . . The Rome and Tuscany of the early 'fifties had become for him so at once a medium, a bath of the senses and perceptions, into which he could sink, in which he could unlimitedly soak, that wherever he might be touched afterwards he gave out some effect of that immersion." Rather than a populated region arduously recovering from the events of 1848–49, "the Rome and Tuscany of the early 'fifties" become, in this elaborately unappetizing image, almost a sensorium from which an absorbent imagination derives nourishment—while Browning, in his Italian period, is refigured as a disinterested Jamesian consciousness neutrally registering impressions, presumably aided by "that saving and sacred sense of proportion" absent from his wife's verse, and embodying in his detachment a virtue that she would have done well to emulate.

What James had called "the Italy we felt and cherished in him" is clearly not the Italy of Barrett Browning, the politically convulsive Italy of the Risorgimento, and it is Browning's verse, far more than hers, that the novelist consistently cites in his criticism, letters, and travel essays to describe his own experiences of the land that meant so much to all of them. Indeed, the novelist who once referred to her husband as "a writer of verse of which the nature or the fortune has been . . . to be treated rarely as quotable" never quotes, in the Story biography or in his critical prose, so much as a single line from Barrett Browning's. It is in leaving its material suitably unpoliticized that Browning's poetry of Italy remains for James artistically superior, preferable to verse immersed not in "a bath of the senses and perceptions" but rather in the aesthetically harmful maelstrom of social and political forces with which Barrett Browning so ardently associated herself. Insofar as such a movement fostered political unity and helped democratize the Italian peninsula, James's "critical reaction" in his life of Story—depicting as lamentable the putatively splintering or disintegrating effects of the Risorgimento not only on the work of a poet like Barrett Browning but on Italy itself—would seem to imply reaction in another, less innocuous sense as well. In any event, one of the phenomena that have traditionally defined the critical orthodoxy on the Brownings—the opposition between the politically animated but naive, or rather naively political, poet-wife and the restrained, prudent, sensible poet-husband—might almost be said to have originated in

James's remarks, which introduce a qualifying contrast even in his reference
to the "extraordinary vivacity and eloquence" of the "letters" that "reflect her
passion, her feverish obsession" with the Risorgimento, *while the pulses of her
companion's much more clearly throb*" (my emphasis). More important, perhaps,
James's assessment authorizes also the equally traditional evaluative
distinction between the works of each poet and allows us to uncover the
ideological basis of that distinction, resting as it does on an elevation of the
apolitically Olympian and on a corresponding rebuke of the conspicuously
political. And the sexualized value obliquely but unmistakably assigned to
each is apparent, finally, in the tone and demeanor of his remarks on Barrett
Browning's "insistent voice and fixed eye"—on an "engrossment" evidently
unbecoming in a poet of her sex, and far less palatable than the spirit that
James had discerned, many years earlier, in her pre-Risorgimento letters to
Horne.

          One need not overstress the presence of the political in the poetic,
or ideologize officially critical remarks like his, to be disturbed by James's
caricature of Barrett Browning the partisan. An attempt to demystify by
psychologizing the role of politics in her experience, his appraisal itself
requires demystification by having restored to it the very element that James
finds so deleterious in Barrett Browning's work. Even in his fastidious hands,
however, the political distinction between the Brownings is ultimately far
from absolute; almost as if offering a corrective to his own skepticism on this
score, James allows a counterimage of the two poets to emerge, in fact, from
the very documents incorporated so generously throughout the Story
biography. One notes with gratitude, for example, his use of "a long and very
interesting letter," as James calls it ("so full that I give it without
curtailment"), in which Story reports Barrett Browning's death to Charles
Eliot Norton and quotes her husband's reactions: "'The cycle is complete,'
as Browning said, looking around the room; 'here we came fifteen years ago;
here Pen was born; here Ba Wrote her poems for Italy . . . We saw from these
windows the return of the Austrians; they wheeled around this corner and
came down this street with all their cannon, just as she describes it in "Casa
Guidi' " After his biographer's rather casual speculations about "[h]er state of
mind on the public question," one is struck by the unpatronizing language in
which Story proceeds to eulogize Browning's wife:

> "There stood the table with her letters and books as usual, and
> her little chair beside it, and in her portfolio a half-finished letter
> to Mme. Mario, full of noble words about Italy. Yes, it was for
> Italy that her last words were written; for her dear Italy were her
> last aspirations . . . She is a great loss to literature, to Italy and to

the world—the greatest poet among women. What energy and fire there was in that little frame; what burning words were winged by her pen; with what glorious courage she attacked error, however strongly entrenched in custom; how bravely she stood by her principles!"

To be sure, as Story himself surmises, it was her "agitation" upon "[t]he death of Cavour," which "had greatly affected her" and over which Barrett Browning "had wept many tears . . . and been a real mourner," that "undoubtedly weakened her and perhaps was the last feather that broke her down," thus corroborating James's sense of the physical effects of her political enthusiasms. Yet it is to his credit that James quotes, at such moving length, a passage that so eloquently diminishes the force and authority of his own earlier "critical reaction" to the "case" represented by Barrett Browning. Little more than a decade after querulously wondering about the roots of "so much disinterested passion, so inflamed a desire . . . (and for a people not her own, a people only befriended and admired)," James himself would turn out, after all, to be no less capable of a consuming patriotic fervor on behalf of an adoptive country. And, as he was surely aware, Barrett Browning's hosts themselves—who "so deeply appreciated" what one literary historian calls "her sympathy" and her "support for their political cause . . . that her death . . . was regarded as a national loss," and whose affection "was won by her pre-occupation with the ambitions and fortunes of Italian nationalism"— seem to have felt no urge to wonder "wherein it so greatly concerned her." It is tempting to ponder how different the Brownings' critical legacy might have been had a voice as commanding as James's attempted to take the political Barrett Browning as seriously and eloquently as Story did. "'Oh Italy, thou woman-land!' breaks out Browning, more than once, straight at *that* mark," James would declare shortly afterwards, alluding to another favorite image of the poet's in recording his impressions upon his return to New England in 1904. It is perhaps the strangest of the many ironies surrounding his "critical reaction" in the Story biography that James should ascribe to her husband the very trope with which Barrett Browning articulated her creatively and psychologically liberating self-identification with the Risorgimento, and through which her own work, exploring as it does the twin tyrannies of Austrian/papal rule and domestic patriarchy, has become lately and so powerfully available again.

Chronology

1806	Born on March 6 at Coxhoe Hall, the first child of Edward Moulton-Barrett and his wife, Mary Graham-Clarke. Edward was heir to vast plantation estate in Jamaica and Mary was the daughter of a wealthy merchant.
1807	Elizabeth Barrett Browning's brother Edward, nicknamed "Bro," was born on June 26.
1809	Edward Moulton-Barrett purchases Hope End, a large estate in Herefordshire, complete with Queen Anne house which is converted into stables and offices. Moulton-Barrett would also construct a luxurious mansion in the Turkish manner. Henrietta is born on March 4, 1809, and another daughter, Mary, is born in 1810, but does not survive childhood.
1814	EBB writes "On the Cruelty of Forcement to Man."
1815	EBB and her parents travel to Paris on October and return in November. Battle of Waterloo on June 18.
1817	EBB successfully petitions to join Bro and his student, Daniel McSwiney, in Greek and Latin lessons. EBB also studies French with Madame Gordin who has been engaged to teach her siblings.
1820	On March 6, EBB's first book, *The Battle of Marathon*, an epic in twelve books, is privately published, only five copies of which are extant. George III dies and George IV succeeds.

1821   In April, EBB and her sisters become ill. While her sisters recover, EBB worsens and in June is sent to the Spa Hotel Gloucester for medical treatment. Contemporary diagnostic skills cannot definitively discover her illness. While tuberculosis may have been its source, lack of exercise, anorexia, and her treatments may have exacerbated her condition. In May, EBB's "Stanzas, Excited by Some Reflections on the Present State of Greece" are published in *The New Monthly Magazine* 2nd ser. 2, 59. In July, "Thoughts Awakened by Contemplating a Piece of the Palm Which Grows on the Summit of the Acropolis in Athens is published in *The New Monthly Magazine* 2nd ser. 2, 59. EBB has also been reading Mary Wollstonecraft's *Vindication of the Rights of Woman*.

1822   EBB returns to Hope End around May.

1824   EBB's "Stanzas on the Death of Lord Byron" are published on June 30 in the London *Globe and Traveller.*

1826   EBB's *An Essay on Mind and Other Poems* is published on March 25 by James Duncan in London. In October, EBB begins her acquaintance with Uvedale Price, the scholar and writer on the picturesque.

1827   EBB begins a correspondence with Hugh Stuart Boyd, a blind Greek scholar living nearby at Malvern.

1828   EBB begins to study Greek and Hebrew with Hugh Stuart Boyd. EBB's mother dies on October 7 at Cheltenham, where she had gone to take the waters.

1830   EBB's paternal grandmother, Elizabeth Moulton, dies, leaving £4000 to EBB. George IV dies and William IV becomes King.

1832   Reform Bill passed in June. In February, EBB translates Aeschylus's *Prometheus Bound*. Hope End Estate is sold sometime around June, the Moulton-Barretts having lost a lawsuit over the Jamaican estates and Edward Moulton-Barrett's debts being called in. In August, EBB and most family members settle in Sidmouth. Hugh Stuart Boyd later moves to Sidmouth.

1833   EBB's translation of *Prometheus Bound* published by Valpy. In August, Parliament votes to abolish slavery.

1835   In September, EBB's "Stanzas Addressed to Miss Landon and Suggested by Her 'Stanzas on the Death of Mrs. Hermans'" published in *The New Monthly Magazine*. In December, EBB and family move to 74 Gloucester Place, London.

1836   On May 27, John Kenyon (EBB's cousin and increasingly close friend) introduces EBB to Mary Russell Mitford. EBB's "The Romaunt of Margret," "The Seaside Walk," and "The Poet's Vow" are published in various magazines.

1837   William IV dies and Victoria succeeds. In July, EBB publishes two poems on Victoria in *The Athenaeum*. In December, EBB's uncle Sam dies in Jamaica, leaving her shares in a merchant ship called the "David Lyon" and several thousand pounds.

1838   EBB publishes "A Romance of the Ganges" in *Finden's Tableaux*. On June 6, EBB's *The Seraphim* and *Other Poems* is published by Saunders and Otley.

1840   EBB's brother Sam dies in February in Jamaica. In July, EBB's brother Bro dies in a sailing accident in Tor Bay, and EBB suffers guilt and an ensuing severe illness because Bro had stayed in Torquay against their father's wishes.

1841   In September, EBB returns to Wimpole Street.

1842   EBB's essay, "Some Account of the Greek Christian Poets" is published as a series of four articles in *The Athenaeum*. Her review and essay "The Book of the Poets" is also published in *The Athenaeum*.

1843   EBB writing and publishing numerous poems in magazines. In October, Richard Hengist Horne tells EBB his plans for *A New Spirit of the Age*, to which she agrees to contribute.

1844   *A New Spirit of the Age* is published in March. Contributions by Robert Browning (RB) also appear. On August 13, *Poems by Elizabeth Barrett Browning* published by Edward Moxon, which includes "Lady Geraldine's Courtship." In a letter to Mary Russell Mitford in December, EBB writes that she hoped to write a longer poem similar to "Lady Geraldine's Courtship."

1845   RB's sends his first letter to EBB on January 10. She replies the next day and, soon afterward, discusses her initial idea for what will later be entitled *Aurora Leigh*. She also begins writing in a notebook (now at Wellesley College). On May 20, RB makes his first visit to Wimpole Street.

1846   On September 12, EBB marries RB secretly. A week later they leave for Italy by way of France. During their week in Paris, the Brownings stay mostly in the hotel to allow EBB to recuperate from the journey, but also visit the Louvre and dine at the restaurants. A wedding announcement, without a date, is printed in *The Times*. Her father breaks off all communications, although EBB makes many attempts at a reconciliation. EBB takes her manuscript notebooks with her. On December 24, the couple attends midnight mass in Pisa Cathedral, where EBB is shocked at the irreverence of the congregation and the lack of religious instruction and conviction in the service.

1847   In March, EBB has her first miscarriage, after five months of pregnancy In April, EBB and RB move from Pisa to Florence. In October, the Brownings have recently met the American sculptor Hiram Powers, whose 1843 'Greek Slave' is the subject of a sonnet by EBB in 1850. In July they travel to Pelago and the monastery of Vallombrosa, whose abbot, despite a letter of dispensation from the Archbishop of Florence, refuses to allow entry to a woman. In response, EBB stamps her foot just inside the monastery door.

1848   In February, Grand Duke Leopoldo grants a constitution to the people of Tuscany. RB and EBB watch his arrival at the Pitti Palace from the opera. A Republic is declared in France. In March, EBB, two months pregnant, miscarries again. In May, EBB and RB settle at Casa Guidi in Florence. In June, the killing of five thousand rebel workers in Paris increases EBB's disillusionment with the new Republic. In December, Louis Napoleon Bonaparte is elected President of the French Republic. EBB will later vigorously support Louis Napoleon.

1849   On March 9, Robert Wiedemann Barrett Browning ("Pen") is born. During the summer, EBB shows RB the poems which will become *Sonnets from the Portuguese*. In September, EBB witnesses the entry of the occupying Austrian army into Florence.

1850   In July, EBB experiences her fourth and most serious miscarriage and is ill for some time. Publication of *Poems* in November, which includes "Sonnets from the Portuguese," written during 1845-46. EBB first showed these poems to RB in 1849.

1851   *Casa Guidi Windows* is published in May. From July to September, EBB, RB and Pen are in London. During this time, EBB and RB write to Mr. Barrett seeking reconciliation, but receive a "violent" response from him along with unopened letters which EBB sent him from Italy. In December, the Brownings witness Louis Napoleon's coup d'etat.

1852   In February, RB and EBB are received by George Sand; EBB is far more taken with Sand and her "intense burning soul" than is RB. The Brownings visit London again and, in October, RB attends the christening of Hallam Tennyson. Shortly thereafter, the Brownings leave for Florence, the return south being necessitated by EBB's failing health. The Brownings return to Casa Guidi in November where EBB's health improves.

1853   In March, EBB begins work on *Aurora Leigh* while living in Rome, Bagni di Lucca, and Casa Guidi in Florence. RB works on *Men and Women*.

1854   RB tries to arrange for American publication of both their books.

1855   EBB is ill in January. She has now written 4,500 lines of *Aurora Leigh* in the first draft copy. In June, the Brownings set out for England, and EBB does not work on her poem until December, after they settle in Paris. RB makes an agreement with the American publisher C.S. Francis for *Aurora Leigh*. RB's *Men and Women* published.

1856   In February, RB reads *Aurora Leigh* for the first time and annotates the fair copy transcript (now at Harvard) with his reading dates. By March, EBB has transcribed six books into fair copy and begins writing the last three books. In April, EBB corrects *Casa Guidi Windows* for new edition of *Poems*. In June, the Brownings travel to London and EBB completes the transcribing into fair copy in July. On October 17, EBB writes the dedication to John Kenyon and on October 21, EBB grants exclusive American rights to C.S. Francis. On October 30, the Brownings are back in Casa Guidi and on November 15, *Aurora Leigh* is published simultaneously in London and New York. Reviews begin to appear in November and December. John Kenyon dies on December 4, leaving EBB and RB financially stable.

1857   Second edition of *Aurora Leigh*, a reprint without corrections, is
            published in January. Third edition, a reprint, is published in
            March. Edward Moulton-Barrett dies unreconciled on April 17,
            having disinherited EBB, Henrietta and Alfred, and leaving EBB
            with a feeling of "sudden desolation." In October, RB identifies a
            manuscript shown him by Clotilda Sisted, a well-known social
            figure in the expatriate community of Bagni di Lucca, as that of
            Shelley's "Indian Serenade," found on Shelley's body. Back in
            Florence, EBB continues her close friendship with Sophie
            Eckley. In the Fall, EBB and RB read Flaubert's *Madame Bovary*,
            which Pen later describes as "Papa's favourite book."

1858   In June, Nathaniel and Sophia Hawthorne, the Eckleys, Fanny
            Haworth and the American poet, William Cullen Bryant, spend
            the evening at Casa Guidi and discuss spiritualism. The
            Brownings set out for Le Havre in July, where EBB's photograph
            is taken by and engraved for inclusion in a new edition. In
            September, the Brownings rent an apartment in Paris, their
            visitors including Thackeray and his daughters. In October, EBB
            begins revising *Aurora Leigh*. They return to Florence and then
            winter in Rome with the Eckleys.

1859   The revised, fourth edition of *Aurora Leigh*, with photograph
            frontispiece, is published on June 11. EBB is ill again and spends
            winter in Rome. While RB is distracted with numerous social
            engagements, EBB is home reading, among others, the works of
            Swedenborg. In April, Austria attacks Sardinia/Piedman and
            France declares war on Austria on May 3. In June, the French
            and Piedmontese defeat the Austrians. In July, RB takes charge of
            the irascible Walter Savage Landor, who has been expelled by his
            wife from their house in Fiesole, and France makes peace with
            Austria, which causes EBB distress and a consequent collapse in
            health. August marks the beginning of the end of EBB's close
            friendship with Sophie Eckley.

1860   About mid-January, RB and EBB see a display of swords designed
            by the jeweller Castellani for presentation to Napoleon II and
            Victor Emanuel. *Poems before Congress* is published by Chapman
            and Hall, EBB having sent them a preface which makes a bold
            attack on British attitudes ("non-intervention in the affairs of
            neighbouring states is a high political virtue; but non-
            intervention does not mean, passing by on the other side when
            your neighbour falls among thieves"). Most of the reviews are

hostile, having been offended by the unpatriotic sentiments or believing that women should not meddle in politics. A fifth edition of *Aurora Leigh* is published. In June, the Brownings return to Florence from Rome and, by mid-month, EBB has read George Eliot's *The Mill on the Floss*, which she prefers to *Adam Bede*. EBB continues to follow Italian politics closely despite the news that her sister, Henrietta, has untreatable cancer. In December, the Brownings learn of Henrietta's death. EBB grieves deeply and receives comfort in a letter from Harriet Beecher Stowe.

1861   Winter in Rome. EBB weak and often unable to go out. In June, the Brownings return to Florence. On June 6, Italian revolutionary statesman Cavour dies. EBB is distressed by the loss of the Italian statesman whom she admires and trusts. EBB begins her final decline on June 20 and is diagnosed as having congestion of the right lung. On June 29, EBB dies and on July 1, EBB is buried in the Protestant cemetery in Florence, her coffin of laurel and white flowers borne through the streets. Shops near Casa Guidi are closed and, at the graveside, RB reads from EBB's "The Sleep." A tomb by Frederic Leighton is later erected over her grave. On August 1, RB and Pen leave Florence and return to England.

1862   EBB's *Last Poems* published in March by Chapman and Hall. Most reviews avoid the more political poems and, instead, declare her the greatest of women poets.

Bibliography

Alaya, Flavia. "The Ring, the Rescue, & the Risorgimento: Reunifying the Brownings' Italy." *Browning Institute Studies* 6 (1978): 1-41.

Anderson, Amanda. *Tainted Souls and Painted Faces: The Rhetoric of Fallenness in Victorian Culture*. Ithaca: Cornell University Press, 1993.

Armonstrong, Isobel. *Victorian Poetry: Poetry, Poetics and Politics*. London: Routledge, 1993.

_____ and Virginia Blain, eds. *Women's Poetry, Late Romantic to Late Victorian*. New York: St. Martin's Press, Inc. and London: MacMillan Press Ltd., 1999

Auerbach, Nina. Woman and the Demon: *The Life of a Victorian Myth*. Cambridge: Harvard University Press, 1982.

Blake, Kathleen. *Love and the Woman Question in Victorian Literature: The Art of Self-Postponement*. Brighton, England: Harvester Press; Toyota, N.J.: Barnes & Noble Books, 1983.

Brady, Ann P. Pompilia: *A Feminist Reading of Robert Browning's "The Ring and the Book."* Athens: Ohio State University Press, 1988.

Christ, Carol. *The Finer Optic*. New Haven and London: Yale University Press, 1975.

Cooper, Helen. *Elizabeth Barrett Browning, Woman and Artist*. Chapel Hill: University of North Carolina Press, 1988.

_____. "Working into Light: Elizabeth Barrett Browning." In *Shakespeare's Sisters: Feminist Essays on Women Poets*, edited and introduced by Sandra M. Gilbert and Susan Gubar, pp. 65-81. Bloomington: Indiana University Press, 1979.

Dally, Peter. *Elizabeth Barrett Browning: a Psychological Portrait.* London: MacMillan, 1989.

David, Deirdre. "The Social Wound and the Poetics of Healing" from *Intellectual Women and Victorian Patriarch: Harriet Martineau, Elizabeth Barrett Browning, George Eliot.* Ithaca: Cornell University Press, 1987.

————. "'Art's a Service': Social Wound, Sexual Politics, and *Aurora Leigh.*" *Browning Institute Studies* 13 (1985): 113-36.

Davis, Lloyd, ed. *Virginal Sexuality and Textuality in Victorian Literature.* Albany: State University of New York Press, 1993.

Diehl, Joanne Feit. *Dickinson and the Romantic Imagination.* Princeton: Princeton University Press, 1981.

Donaldson, Sandra M. "Motherhood's Advent in Power: Elizabeth Barrett Browning's Poems about Motherhood." *Victorian Poetry* 18, no. I (Spring 1980): 51-60.

Dowell, Susan. "A Jealous God? Towards a Feminist Model of Monogamy." *In Sex and God: Some Varieties of Women's Religious Experience.* Ed. Linda Hurcombe. New York: Routledge and Kegan Paul, 1987.

Forster, Margaret. *Elizabeth Barrett Browning: The Life and Loves of a Poet.* New York: St. Martin's Press, 1988.

Friedman, Susan Stanford. "Gender and Genre Anxiety: Elizabeth Barrett Browning And H.D. as Epic Poets." *Tulsa Studies in Women's Literature* 5, no. 2 (Fall 1986): 203-28.

Friewald, Bina. "The Praise Which Men Give Women: Elizabeth Barrett Browning's *Aurora Leigh* and *The Critics.*" *Dalhousie Review* 66 (1986): 311-36.

Garrett, Martin. *A Browning Chronology: Elizabeth Barrett and Robert Browning.* London: MacMillan Press Ltd. and New York: St. Martin's Press, Inc., 2000.

Gilbert, Sandra M., and Susan Gubar. *The Madwoman in the Attic: The Woman Writer and the Nineteenth-Century Literary Imagination.* New Haven: Yale University Press, 1979.

Gridley, Roy. *The Brownings and France: A Chronicle and Commentary.* London and New Jersey: Athlone Press, Distributor: Humanities Press, 1982.

Hardwick, Elizabeth. *Seduction and Betrayal: Women and Literature.* New York: Random House, 1970.

Hayter, Alethea. *Mrs. Browning: A Poet's Work and Its Setting.* London: Faber & Faber, 1962.

Herrera, Andrewa O'Reilly, Elizabeth Mahn Nollen, Sheila Reitzel Foor. *Family Matters in the British and American Novel.* Ohio: Bowling Green State University Popular Press, 1997.

Hickok, Kathleen. *Representations of Women: Nineteenth-Century British Women's Poetry.* Westport, Conn.: Greenwood, 1984.

Holloway, John. *The Victorian Sage: Studies in Argument*. New York: W.W. Norton, 1965.

Homans, Margaret. *Women Writers and Poetic Identity: Dorothy Wordsworth, Emily Brontë, And Emily Dickinson*. Princeton, New Jersey: Princeton University Press, 1980.

Houghton, Walter E. *The Victorian Frame of Mind, 1830-1870*. New Haven and London: Yale University Press, 1957.

Karlin, Daniel. *The Courtship of Robert Browning and Elizabeth Barrett*. Oxford: Clarendon Press, 1985.

————. "The Discourse of Power in Elizabeth Barrett Browning's Criticism." *Studies in Browning and His Circle*, 20 (1993): 30-38.

King, Ursula. *Women and Spirituality: Voices of Protest and Promise*. Houndmills, Basingstoke, England: Macmillan, 1989.

Leighton, Angela. *Elizabeth Barrett Browning*. Bloomington: Indiana University Press, 1986.

————. *Victorian Women Poets: Writing Against the Heart*. Charlottesville: University Press of Virginia, 1992.

Lewis, Linda M. "The Artist's Quest in Elizabeth Barrett Browning's *Aurora Leigh*." In *Images of the Self as Female: The Achievement of Women Artists in Re-Envisioning Feminine Identity*, ed. Kathryn N. Benzel and Lauren Pringle de la Vars, eds. Lewiston: Edwin Mellen Press, 1992.

————. *Elizabeth Barrett Browning's Spiritual Progress: Face to Face With God*. Columbia: University of Missouri Press, 1998.

Marks, Jeanette. *The Family of the Barrett: A Colonial Romance*. New York: Macmillan Co., 1938. Reprint. Westport, Conn.: Greenwood Press, 1973.

Markus, Julia. Dared and Done: *The Marriage of Elizabeth Barrett and Robert Browning*. New York: Knopf, 1995.

Mermin, Dorothy. *Elizabeth Barrett Browning: The Origins of a New Poetry*. Chicago: University of Chicago Press, 1989.

————. "The Damsel, the Kinght, and the Victorian Woman Poet." *Critical Inquiry* 13 (Autumn 1986): 64-80.

————. "Elizabeth Barrett Browning Through 1844: Becoming a Woman Poet." *Studies in English Literature*, 1500-1900 26 (1986): 713-36.

Moi, Toril. *Sexual/Textual Politics: Feminist Literary Theory*. London and New York: Methuen, 1985.

Montefiore, Jan. *Feminism and Poetry: Language, Experience, and Identity in Women's Writing*. London and New York: Pandora, 1987.

Rosenblum, Dolores. "Casa Guidi Windows and Aurora Leigh: The Genesis of Elizabeth Barrett Browning's Visionary Aesthetic." *Tulsa Studies in Women's Literature* 4, no. 1 (Spring 1985): 61-68.

Showalter, Elaine. *A Literature of Their Own*. Princeton: Princeton University Press, 1977.

Stephenson, Glennis. *Elizabeth Barrett Browning and the Poetry of Love*. Ann Arbor,
     Michigan: University of Michigan Research Press, 1989.
_____, and Shirley Neuman, eds. ReImagining Women: *Representations of
     Women in Culture*. Toronto and Buffalo: University of Toronto Press, 1993.
Thompson, Patricia. *George Sand and the Victorians*. New York: Columbia University
     Press, 1977.
Taplin, Gardner Blake. *The Life of Elizabeth Barrett Browning*. New Haven: Yale
     University Press, 1957.

Contributors

HAROLD BLOOM is Sterling Professor of the Humanities at Yale University and Henry W. and Albert A. Berg Professor of English at the New York University Graduate School. He is the author of over 20 books, including *Shelly's Mythmaking* (1959), *The Visionary Company* (1961), *Blake's Apocalypse* (1963), *Yeats* (1970), *A Map of Misreading* (1975), *Kabbalah and Criticism* (1975), *Agon: Toward a Theory of Revisionism* (1982), *The American Religion* (1992), *The Western Canon* (1994), and *Omens of Millennium: The Gnosis of Angels, Dreams, and Resurrection* (1996). *The Anxiety of Influence* (1973) sets forth Professor Bloom's provocative theory of the literary relationships between the great writers and their predecessors. His most recent books include *Shakespeare: The Invention of the Human*, a 1998 National Book Award finalist, and *How to Read and Why*, which was published in 2000. In 1999, Professor Bloom received the prestigious American Academy of Arts and Letters Gold Medal for Criticism.

SARAH ANNES BROWN is a British Academy postdoctoral research fellow at Newnham College, Cambridge. She is the author of *The Metamorphosis of Ovid: From Chaucer to Ted Hughes* (1999).

HELEN COOPER is Professor of English Language and Literature, University College, Cambridge. Her most recent work includes "The Strange History of Valentine and Orson" (1999), "Jacobean Chaucer: The Two Noble Kinsmen and Other Chaucerian Plays" (1998) and "Averting Chaucer's Prophecies: Miswriting, Mismetering and Misunderstanding" (1998).

293

DEIRDRE DAVID teaches in the English Department at Temple University. She is the author of *Rule Britannia: Women, Empire and Victoria Writing* (1995) and *Intellectual Women and Victorian Patriarchy: Harriet Martineau, Elizabeth Barrett Browning and George Eliot* (1987).

SUSANNA EGAN teaches in the English Department of the University of British Columbia in Vancouver. She is the author of *Mirror Talk: Genres of Crisis in Contemporary Autobiography* (1999) and *Patterns of Experience in Autobiography* (1984).

TRICIA LOOTENS is Associate Professor of English at the University of Georgia. She is the author of *Lost Saints: Silence, Gender and Victorian Literary Canonization* (1996).

JEROME MAZZARO teaches in the Modern Languages Department at SUNY Buffalo. He is the author of "The Divina Commedia and the Rhetoric of Memory" (1999) and "Alfieri's Saul as Enlightenment Tragedy" (1999).

DOROTHY MERMIN is Professor of English at Cornell University. She is the author of *Godiva's Ride: Women of Letters in England, 1839-1880* (1993) and *Elizabeth Barrett Browning: the Origins of a New Poetry* (1989).

LINDA H. PETERSON is Professor of English at Yale University. She is the author of *Victorian Autobiography: The Tradition of Self-Interpretation* (1986) and co-author of *A Struggle for Fame: Victorian Artists and Authors* (1994, with Susan Casteras).

MARGARET REYNOLDS is Lecturer in English at the University of Birmingham. She is the editor of the *Norton Critical Edition* of *Aurora Leigh: Authoritative Text, Backgrounds and Contexts, Criticism* (1996) and co-editor (with Angela Leighton) of *Victorian Women Poets: An Anthology* (1995).

GLENNIS STEPHENSON lectures in English Studies at the University of Stirling. She is the author of *Letitia Landon: The Woman Behind L.E.L.* (1995) and *ReImagining Women: Representations of Women in Culture* (1993).

MARJORIE STONE teaches in the English Department at Dalhousie University in Johnson City, Tennessee. She is the author of *Elizabeth Barrett Browning* (1995); "The Poet as Whole-Body Camera: Maxine Tynes and the Pluralities of Otherness" (1997) and "Monna Innominata and *Sonnets from the Portuguese*: Sonnet Traditions and Spiritual Trajectories" in *The Culture of Christina Rossetti: Female Poetics and Victorian Contexts* (1999).

MAUREEN THUM teaches English and Honors at the University of Michigan, Flint. She is the author of "Frame and Fictive Voice in Chaucer's 'The Pardoner's Tale" and Kipling's 'The King's Ankus'" (1992).

ANNE D. WALLACE teaches in the English Department at The University of Southern Mississippi. She is the author of *Walking, Literature and English Culture: The Origins and Uses of Peripatetic in the Nineteenth Century* (1993).

FREDERICK WEGENER teaches English at California State University in Long Beach. He is the editor of *Edith Wharton: The Uncollected Critical Writings* (1995).

Acknowledgments

"*Paradise Lost* and *Aurora Leigh*" by Sarah Annes Brown from *Studies in English Literature* 1500-1900 vol. 37, no. 4 (Autumn 1997). Reprinted by permission of The John Hopkins University Press.

"Rebellion: Eve's Songs of Innocence" by Helen Cooper from *Elizabeth Barrett Browning, Woman and Artist*. Chapel Hill: University of North Carolina Press, 1988. Reprinted by permission.

"The Social Wound and the Poetics of Healing" by Deirdre David from *Intellectual Women and Victorian Patriarch: Harriet Martineau, Elizabeth Barrett Browning, George Eliot*, Ithaca: Cornell University Press (1987). Reprinted by permission.

"Glad Rags for Lady Godiva: Woman's Story as Womanstance in Elizabeth Barrett Browning's *Aurora Leigh*" by Susanna Egan from *ESC: English Studies in Canada*, vol. 20, no. 3 (September 1994). Reprinted by permission.

"Canonization through Dispossession: Elizabeth Barrett Browning and the 'Pythian Shriek'" by Tricia Lootens from *Lost Saints: Silence, Gender, and Victorian Literary Canonization*. Charlottesville and London: University Press of Virginia (1996). Reprinted by permission.

"Mapping Sublimity: Elizabeth Barrett Browning's *Sonnets from the Portuguese*" by Jerome Mazzaro in *Essays in Literature* vol. XVIII, no. 2 (Fall 1991). Reprinted by permission.

"The Female Poet and the Embarrassed Reader: Elizabeth Barrett Browning's *Sonnets from the Portuguese*" by Dorothy Mermin from *ELH*, vol. 48, no. 2 (Summer 1981). Reprinted by permission of The John Hopkins University Press.

"Rewriting *A History of the Lyre*: Letitia Landon, Elizabeth Barrett Browning and the (Re)Construction of the Nineteenth-Century Woman Poet" by Linda H. Peterson from *Women's Poetry, Late Romantic to Late Victorian: Gender and Genre, 1830-1900*. Hampshire and London: Macmillan Press Ltd. (1999) and New York: St. Martin's Press, Inc. (1999). Reprinted by permission.

"Love's Measurement in Elizabeth Barrett Browning's *Sonnets from the Portuguese*" by Margaret Reynolds from *Studies in Browning and His Circle*, vol. 21 (1993-1997). Reprinted by permission.

"The Vision Speaks: Love in Elizabeth Barrett Browning's 'Lady Geraldine's Courtship' " by Glennis Stephenson from *Victorian Poetry*, vol. 27, no. 1 (Spring 1989). Reprinted by permission.

"A Cinderella Among the Muses: Barrett Browning and the Ballad Tradition" by Marjorie Stone from *Victorian Literature and Culture*, 21 (1993). Reprinted by permission.

"Challenging Traditionalist Gender Roles: The Exotic woman as Critical Observer in Elizabeth Barrett Browning's *Aurora Leigh*" by Maureen Thum from *The Foreign Woman in British Literature: Exotics, Aliens, and Outsiders*. Westport, Connecticut: Greenwood Press (1999). Reprinted by permission.

"'Nor in Fading Silks Compose': Sewing, Walking, and Poetic Labor in *Aurora Leigh*" by Anne D. Wallace from *ELH*, vol. 64, no.1 (Spring 1997). Reprinted by permission of The John Hopkins University Press.

"Elizabeth Barrett Browning, Italian Independence, and the "Critical Reaction" of Henry James" by Frederick Wegener from *Studies in English Literature 1500-1900*, vol. 37, no. 4 (Autumn 1997). Reprinted by permission of The John Hopkins University Press.

Index